ISRAEL AT THE POLLS
1996

Cass Studies in
Israeli History, Politics and Society
ISSN 1368-4795

General Editor: Efraim Karsh

Peace in the Middle East: The Challenge for Israel
edited by Efraim Karsh

The Shaping of Israeli Identity: Myth, Memory and Trauma
edited by Robert Wistrich and David Ohana

Between War and Peace: Dilemmas of Israeli Security
edited by Efraim Karsh

U.S.–Israeli Relations at the Crossroads
edited by Gabriel Sheffer

From Rabin to Netanyahu: Israel's Troubled Agenda
edited by Efraim Karsh

ISRAEL
AT THE POLLS
1996

Edited by

DANIEL J. ELAZAR
and
SHMUEL SANDLER

FRANK CASS
LONDON • PORTLAND, OR

First published in 1998 in Great Britain by
FRANK CASS PUBLISHERS
Newbury House, 900 Eastern Avenue, London IG2 7HH

and in the United States of America by
FRANK CASS PUBLISHERS
c/o ISBS, 5804 N.E. Hassalo Street
Portland, Oregon 97213-3644

Website http://www.frankcass.com

British Library Cataloguing in Publication Data

Israel at the polls, 1996
  1. Israel. Knesset – Elections, 1996
  I. Elazar, Daniel J. (Daniel Judah) II. Sandler, Shmuel
324.9'5694'054

ISBN 0 7146 4864 7 X (cloth)
ISBN 0 7146 4421 8 (paper)
ISSN 1368-4795

Library of Congress Cataloging-in-Publication Data:

Israel at the polls, 1996 / editors, Daniel J. Elazar, Shmuel Sandler
  p. cm. – (Cass studies in Israeli history, politics, and
society, ISSN 1368-4795)
  Includes bibliographical references and index.
  ISBN 0-7146-4864-7. – ISBN 0-7146-4421-8
  1. Israel. Knesset – Elections, 1996. 2. Elections – Israel.
3. Political parties – Israel. I. Elazar, Daniel Judah
II. Sandler, Shmuel. III. Israel affairs. Special issue.
IV. Series: Israel history, politics, and society.
JQ1830.A9518 1997
324.95694'054 – dc21   97-42872
                                                      CIP

This group of studies first appeared in a Special Issue, Israel Affairs
Vol. 4, No. 1 (Autumn 1997), Published by Frank Cass & Co. Ltd.

ISSN 1353-7121

Printed in Great Britain by Antony Rowe Ltd., Chippenham, Wiltshire

To our esteemed colleagues and good friends

Irving Louis Horowitz
and
Robert W. Tucker

Acknowledgement

The editors would like to thank The Milken Family Foundation for supporting the preparation of this volume for publication as part of the Milken Library of Jewish Public Affairs of the Jerusalem Center of Public Affairs

Contents

Introduction:
The Battle over Jewishness and Zionism in the Post-Modern Era

DANIEL J. ELAZAR and SHMUEL SANDLER

On the 11th of Sivan, 5756 – May 29, 1996 – Israelis went to the polls for the fourteenth Knesset elections since 1949 and the first direct election of the head of government. Under the new system the voters cast two ballots, one slip indicating their choice of party for the Knesset and one slip indicating their choice of person for prime minister. By the next day it was clear that Labor had been defeated in both votes.

The Likud candidate, Binyamin Netanyahu, won the prime ministership and the Labor-Meretz camp lost almost a quarter of its delegation in the Knesset (13 seats). All in all, the Left, together with the Arab parties, declined by 15 percent. While the vote for prime minister was much closer, it was even more insulting, especially to Shimon Peres. As Dan Margalit, one of Israel's most respected columnists, expounded: "Shimon Peres fell at the polls while guarding his political legacy. The giant of Oslo was defeated because he lacked thirty thousand votes, but he failed because he should have gained an advantage of half a million ballots."[1] Indeed, the victory of a relative novice in Israeli politics, at the unprecedented young age of 47, over a political master and the most experienced leader in Israeli politics, in a system that has always given its support to veteran politicians for prime minister, raises the most interesting question of the 1996 Israeli elections.

In our introduction to *Israel at the Polls, 1992*, we questioned the common wisdom expressed at the time, especially by the media, which interpreted the Yitzhak Rabin victory as a "turn-about" (*mahapach*) in Israeli politics. We suggested that "What the 1992 election confirmed was that this process of normalized change of power, that is relatively new to Israel and [has] important implications for the constitutional

Daniel J. Elazar is N.M. Paterson Professor of Intergovernmental Relations, Bar-Ilan University. Shmuel Sandler is Incumbent of the Sara and Simha Lainer Chair in Democracy and Civility, Bar-Ilan University.

health of the Israeli body politic, has now become an integral part of Israeli democracy."[2] The defeat of Labor in 1996, while continuing this pattern, deserves a more probing analysis, which should be undertaken especially by the Labor elite.

The assassination of Yitzhak Rabin caused almost the whole country to rally around the Labor camp. The initiation and advancement of the Oslo peace process had broad support in the polls. The economy appeared to be booming. Therefore, Labor's defeat under these conditions reflects a deeper dissatisfaction than most electoral transfers of power.

When he entered the prime minister's office half a year prior to the elections, Shimon Peres enjoyed an unprecedented level of public support. On the eve of the elections, an impressive convergence of forces supported him including almost the entire Israeli written and electronic media, the lion's share of the Israeli business community, and President of the United States Bill Clinton. President Clinton, perceived as one of the best friends Israel has ever had in the White House, came out with what could be considered an almost open endorsement of Peres three days before the elections. (On the impact of external forces on the elections, see Barry Rubin's chapter.) Neither the timing alone, nor factors like HAMAS terror bombings explain the results. The bombings had stopped by the end of February 1996 after a tough crackdown by the Peres government and pressure on Arafat that seemed to work.

True, the elections took place half a year ahead of their scheduled time, which was to be November 1996, but the date was chosen by Peres himself in consultation with his advisers, at a time when he had a decisive lead.

Nor could anybody blame incitement as a factor that worked in favor of the right. The 1996 campaign and elections were among the quietest in Israel's electoral history. Half a year after the assassination of a prime minister, every party was afraid of being accused of arousing political violence and consequently of being punished at the polls. So how do we explain both the defeat of Shimon Peres and the fall of the Labor-Meretz camp from almost half of the Knesset in 1992 to just above a third, four years later? Were the 1996 elections a vote against the peace process, an expression of disapproval of Peres the man, or were the results related to deeper factors?

In answering these questions we must recognize two opposing trends that have been noticeable over the last several elections. On the one hand, the Israeli polity has been moving closer to post-modern Western politics and thus has been abandoning some of the unique features it had developed during the Yishuv era, such as the emphasis on ideology reflected in a consociational political regime.[3] At the same time, the Israeli polity has retained some of those characteristics, above all its dedication to maintaining the Jewish character of the state. By demonstrating a desire for prosperity and innovation while attempting to preserve identity and tradition, Israel is not unique among Western democracies. Those parties and candidates that apparently did not understand these realities were on the losing side of the 1996 elections.[4]

THE PRIMARIES AND THE CONTINUED "AMERICANIZATION" OF ISRAELI ELECTIONS

Israel continued its shift from European to American-style politics in 1996 with the introduction of direct election of the prime minister. For the first time, Israelis voted directly for the head of government. In addition, all the major parties adopted and implemented some system of primary elections to select their candidates for the Knesset. Americanization was expressed by the universal adoption of the American term "primaries," although there is a Hebrew term, *"bichirot mukdamot."* The leaders of the two main parties, Shimon Peres and Binyamin Netanyahu, had been chosen beforehand. Netanyahu was elected in March 1993 following the defeat of the Likud in the summer of 1992, while Peres was elected to carry the party's banner following the assassination of Yitzhak Rabin.

Since the primaries are a private matter for each party choosing to hold them and are not required by law, each party may schedule its primaries as it pleases. The primaries of 1996 were concentrated in a single week, between March 24 and 28. The Labor and Likud primaries were held back-to-back on March 25 and 26, with Meretz holding its vote the day before. Thus, while the format of each party's primaries was different, the mass media built it up into an American-style show with two successive days of action and hoopla.

The parties, of course, realizing that the media wanted a show, did their utmost to attract media attention to fully exploit the event. There was coverage of pre-primary meetings, 12,000 balloons let loose (by the Likud), grand entrances by party heads at exactly the right moment for prime-time television coverage (both parties), and exit polls to give the viewing audience a preview of the results (which failed miserably, principally because of the deals between interest groups and candidates). The results should have reminded professionals of the 1948 polling debacle at the time of the Truman election, and served as a prelude to the pollsters' prediction of a Peres victory in the May 1996 elections.

Even though there is no state law requiring primaries and the fact and form of the primaries is a matter for each party to decide on its own, once one major party went in that direction, the other could hardly avoid doing the same in a populist age. In 1992, Labor had also chosen its candidates through primaries, while the Likud used a complicated arrangement involving the Likud Central Committee. That arrangement, which in itself was not unfair, created a lot of bad feeling within the party when the Shamir majority faction pushed David Levy's faction out of the first rank, and led to aggressive media and public attacks on its "undemocratic" character. The Likud took the hint and in 1996 tried to produce an even more up-to-date primary system than Labor, using computers rather than hand ballots for the actual voting, recording, and counting of the vote.

In the past, the parties had earmarked safe seats for special constituencies: in Labor – for kibbutzim, moshavim, the Histadrut, Arabs and Druze, and more recently women; in the Likud – for the various components of the party (e.g., Herut, Liberals, La'am), for the factions within it (e.g., the Levy bloc, the Sharon bloc), and for a Druze.

The idea behind the primaries was, in part, to end this allocation of safe seats to special interests, but in practice it has not worked that way. After eliminating the old special interests, both parties had ended up introducing the reservation of seats for new groups or sometimes the old ones in new guise. For example, Arabs and Druze lost their preferential treatment (although Labor actually nominated four, including a dynamic Christian Arab woman from Jaffa), but safe seats were reserved for women in both parties. Labor no longer "reserves" seats for kibbutzim, but the party formed a separate "district" for Labor kibbutzim similar to the territorial districts it used throughout the country.

Where matters did not work out as planned, the party leadership intervened after the vote. Thus, while Labor hoped to have an immigrant from the former Soviet Union on the ticket, the person elected for the immigrant seat was the leader of the Ethiopian political community. While happy to accept the Ethiopian nominee, Labor realized that this ignored the interests of the 600,000 new immigrants from the FSU. At an emergency meeting of a special committee of the most senior party leaders appointed for the occasion, it was decided to hold a special primary election at the Labor party convention in which the 17,000 party members who were new immigrants from the FSU would be allowed to choose a nominee for a place on the list one position ahead of the Ethiopian candidate.

The Likud faced an even more difficult problem. Advised by his former rival, Ariel Sharon, one of the sharpest strategic minds in Israel, Netanyahu understood that the national camp had no chance of winning without forming a "coalition of minorities" (see below) into a united front for the prime ministerial elections. The rules of the new direct election system and the realities of Israeli politics obliged him to make far-reaching concessions to two smaller parties: Tsomet, headed by former chief-of-staff Rafael Eitan, and Gesher, a new breakaway party headed by former Likud minister David Levy.

Levy, embarrassed and angered by his experience in the previous elections when Shamir's people froze his people out of the leading positions on the list, established Gesher, presumably to advance social issues, but actually to ensure that, one way or another, he and his leading colleagues would be in the next government.

In the 1992 elections Tsomet had attracted the votes of the yuppie right wing; that is to say, those successful young Israelis who are analogous to suburbanites in other countries, interested in the environment, personal achievement, private enterprise, and fiscal conservatism on the part of government. They were similar to the left-wing Meretz party in that respect, but rejected Meretz's peace platform and supported the security platform of the national camp. Tsomet had been successful in 1992 beyond all expectations, but during the subsequent four years Tsomet broke into pieces because of Eitan's dictatorial style and the fact that he had picked people who had more personal political ambition than commitment to his "movement."

This time Binyamin Netanyahu brought Tsomet into the Likud for the elections, reserving it seven realistic seats. Naturally, Levy demanded the same for Gesher, which Netanyahu was compelled to concede. Thus, out of the first 42 places on their Knesset list deemed safe for the Likud, one-third had to be given away before the polls even opened on primary day. This meant that at the end of the day a substantial number of veteran Likud politicians were left out of the "safe" seats, including such veterans as former Speaker of the Knesset Dov Shilansky and Geula Cohen (trying for a comeback after leaving the party at the time of the peace treaty with Egypt). Also losing were the designated nominees for the new immigrants – Yuli Koshorovsky, and the Druze community – veteran Knesset member Assad Assad, provoking considerable bitterness in both communities and requiring serious damage control measures. (On the Likud's decline and Netanyahu's victory, see Efraim Inbar's essay. The big losers in the primaries were women; see Yael Yishai's article.)

THE CAMPAIGN

Election day was calm, as Israelis – Jews, Arabs, Druze; religious, traditional, secular; left, right, or center –demonstrated their maturity and the maturity of their democracy in the way the elections were conducted. There were even fewer complaints of violations of election rules in 1996 than in previous years, and such complaints as there were, were almost all related to minor technical matters. It was reported that Prime Minister Shimon Peres had received threats from Jews warning of violence against him, and on election morning he was reported to be under heavy guard. Peres himself accused the Habad Hasidic movement of being the only ones who had broken the general calm of the election campaign. Otherwise, the country quietly went to the polls in astounding numbers.

The behavior at the polls, however, did not reveal the tension that many felt as they entered the last day of four very troublesome years in Israeli history, to set the stage for at least the next four years and, in all likelihood, for the longer term future. Among the religious and Haredi communities, many experienced a comparable feeling to that of the Day of Atonement. Some rabbis even called for fasting. The collective decision to be made would determine public life for the next four years and, to the more Zionist among the Orthodox community, the fate of what they regarded as the Third Jewish Commonwealth.

The most distinct indication of the tension felt at least among some sectors of Israeli society was the rise in voter participation in comparison with the previous election. The June 1992 election had also been very quiet. Participation in the 1992 polls declined to 77 percent from the usual rate of 79–80 percent in the 1980s.[5] In light of the 1992 results, we concluded in our previous book that most of those who abstained from voting were Likud supporters who, while they despaired of the incumbent party, could not bring themselves to cross the line. In 1996, the overall voter turnout was 79.3 percent, with turnout in the Jewish sector exceeding 80 percent. Undoubtedly, the greater turnout worked in favor of the religious and national camps.

There may be no country in the world without compulsory voting where a higher percentage of the voters go to the polls than in Israel. Considering that Israel's automatic registration system continues to include hundreds of thousands of people who have left the country and who, with the exception of diplomats and sailors abroad, have to be in Israel in order to vote, or those who are too old or infirm to get to the polls, there was an over 90 percent turnout of those who physically could vote. Even though the percentages are not excessively disparate among the different groups in the country, a closer look would reveal that certain sectors mobilized their voters almost to their utmost capability.

Nor had the electoral campaign indicated the hidden tension. The vote came after a campaign that was also relatively gentlemanly. Even Shimon Peres admitted as he entered his polling booth that the 1996 election campaign was one of the mildest he had ever encountered. There was little "below the belt" campaigning by anyone. Perhaps the worst examples were the accusations by the Likud that Peres would divide Jerusalem and the Labor counterattack that Bibi (Netanyahu) was not fit for the job. (For an elaborate analysis of the campaign, see the essay by Sam Lehman-Wilzig.)

The exception to this was Meretz. Trailing in the public polls which indicated a likely decline of almost 50 percent in its strength, Meretz under Yossi Sarid, who had displaced Shulamit Aloni, opened an anti-religious campaign that sometimes seemed almost anti-Semitic in its messages. The Meretz campaign seemed to be beneficial to that party and raised their Knesset delegation from an expected six seats, according to the polls, to nine in the elections, still a decline of three seats from 1992. However, the Meretz campaign also seems to have led to an immense backlash that hurt Shimon Peres, probably more than any other single factor.

There was also the not-so-subtle anti-Arab campaign waged by certain elements of the right led by Habad, which took the lead in distributing stickers saying that Netanyahu was good for the Jews. There was a certain symbolic irony in this scheme promoted by Habad, a non-Zionist religious movement, yet very hawkish in its foreign policy positions and traditionally very active in such issues as Soviet Jewry, as well as preserving Jewry worldwide.

The issue of the Jewishness of the state was probably the most salient issue in Israeli public life throughout the last administration, pushed forward by the Oslo agreements and their results. The question of whether a state could be democratic and Jewish was very prominent in the discussions of Israeli intellectuals, highly salient in the constitutional decisions of the Supreme Court and the Knesset, and the most debated issue on the country's political agenda. The mere fact that the Jewishness of the state was even questioned sent chills down the backs not only of religious people but many other Israeli Jews as well. Statements by Minister of Communications, Science and Culture Shulamit Aloni and others of Meretz and Labor's left wing supporting the transformation of Israel into a civic rather than a Jewish state were frightening to many. Statements of the opposite character by Labor's mainstream leaders were not reassuring. Everybody remembered how Labor leaders like Yitzhak Rabin and Shimon Peres had committed themselves never to negotiate with Yasser Arafat and the Palestine Liberation Organization (PLO), or to withdraw from the Golan Heights. While the more extreme elements on the right still hoped to reverse the decision to relinquish parts of the Land of Israel, the more moderate elements and much of the center felt that the struggle was now over the essence of the Jewish state. This was part of the atmosphere on the eve of the elections to the Fourteenth Knesset.

Apparently, to many, the fear of the downfall of the Jewish state was stronger than the disgust over the assassination of a Jewish prime minister by a Jew. Hence, this factor overwhelmed the request of Shimon Peres, Israel's veteran and most experienced statesman, to be reelected for a full term as prime minister. To a majority of Jewish Israelis, the choice at stake was not the integrity of the Land of Israel, but rather a contest over the essence of the Zionist revolution, their own identity, and the establishment of a Jewish state in the Land of Israel. Why did this question come about in 1996?

ZIONISM, POST-ZIONISM, AND THE JEWISH STATE

The end of the twentieth century has witnessed the collapse of one of the most influential ideologies of the modern era – international Communism. The death of the ideology was expressed through the collapse of the Bolshevik regime which, against all expectations, began to unravel in 1989, bringing down with it the Soviet Union in 1993. Both the Communist revolution and its subsequent demise touched almost every corner of the globe. The Zionist response to this collapse was that Zionism, one of the great historic enemies of Bolshevism, had outlasted its seemingly more powerful rival. Following that sense of triumph, there was room for concern that what had happened to Communism as an ideology and to the states that ideology informed might also happen to Zionism and Israel. The fact that the Soviet collapse came from within, through internal decay rather than external military defeat, only added to the apprehension. Is there a basis for this anxiety?

Signs of the metamorphosis of Zionism could be detected in domains traditionally considered the heart and pride of the Zionist enterprise – Israeli academia, the military, and the settlement institutions. In recent years, a group of "new" historians and radical sociologists have adopted a critical revisionist historical view of Israel's birth. Essentially their argument can be condensed into one major idea: the State of Israel was born in sin but that fact was kept unknown because Israeli academia had been mobilized to defend the distorted Zionist narrative.[6]

Their writing varied from "corrected" research which pointed out the often neglected mistakes that accompanied the Zionist enterprise like any other, to outright fabrications about the intentions of the Zionist founders. In the military, while the level of volunteering for the elite fighting units stayed high, declining motivation to serve in the ground fighting units was observed. A slow but steady shift in the traditional sources of leadership was also taking place, from the kibbutzim to the national-religious elements, particularly in connection with the officer cadres.[7] At the same time, the senior leadership of the army for the first time consisted of professionals who had chosen army careers, rather than the first-generation civilians who had remained in uniform because they recognized the necessities of Israel's situation, despite their basically non-military orientation. These career officers were transforming the army into what they hoped would be a more professionalized instrumentality, no longer relying on equal responsibility to serve on the part of all, but concentrating responsibilities on those with combat roles and easing them in connection with those serving behind the lines. These new inequalities, which are possible in a volunteer force, had the opposite effect in a conscript army which had prided itself on the relative equity of the distribution of responsibilities in the past, thereby encouraging those people who found themselves with what they considered to be an undue relative burden to seek to escape it, at least in part.[8]

At the same time, the kibbutzim were undergoing both a financial and social crisis, and in order to rehabilitate themselves entered the capitalist marketplace more fully than before, especially by trying to capitalize on government and JNF-owned land that they rented and cultivated. Within the kibbutzim the collectivist elements were in decline. The introduction of private telephones, television sets, and kitchen facilities reduced communal dining to a minimum. People were being paid for their work in scrip which they could then use to purchase goods from the kibbutz stores, and in many kibbutzim people were even able to take on second jobs within the kibbutz for pay. While the previous Likud governments had directed Israel's urban population desiring to dwell in suburbia to the territories, the Labor government steered them to areas within the "green line." With the decline of agriculture in the technologically expanding Israeli economy, it became increasingly attractive for the kibbutzim and moshavim to sell their land. By doing so they vulgarized one of Israel's sacred symbols traditionally identified with Labor.

The decline of the old symbols was also felt in the traditional institutions. A principal target of the Labor government was the old institutions that to a large extent had brought Labor to power during the early years of the Yishuv. Part of the secret of the Labor camp's ascendance to power was that it was the most successful in institution-building in pre-state Palestine. Those institutions included the kibbutzim and moshavim, the Jewish Agency, and the Histadrut.

Over the years these institutions, especially the Histadrut, lost their attractiveness for many Israelis, inter alia, because they developed manifestations of bureaucracy and corruption. The investigations and trials of officials from the latter two institutions on corruption charges in the early 1990s added to the shaken image of the establishment and its symbols. Even though the young leaders of Labor such as Yossi Beilin and Haim Ramon called for reform of both organizations, their success was more in the realm of demolishing what existed rather than renovation.

Interestingly, the young leadership of Labor did not shy away from competing for the leadership of these institutions. Haim Ramon became Secretary-General of the Histadrut and Avraham Burg, another member of the young Turks of Labor or the "gang of eight" as they were dubbed, competed for and won the chairmanship of the Jewish Agency.

Labor leaders uttered several remarks that shocked the whole country, and essentially hurt them as the heirs to the symbol system promoted by their predecessors upon which the Zionist enterprise rests. Among these statements were Yitzhak Rabin's comment that the Bible was not our "Kushan" (land title) to the Land of Israel, or that the Golan Heights was a land of tanks and not a land of settlement. For a movement that boasted that it was the true settlement movement while its opposition, Herut (the predecessor of Likud), was a movement of rhetoric, such statements undermined Labor's previous advantage.[9]

Similarly destructive was the decline of Labor's image as the party of security. By projecting readiness to yield the Golan Heights to the Syrians, which was seen as a strategic threat to Israel, accompanied by rumors that the Jordan Valley, the virtually unanimously accepted "security border with Jordan" since the Six-Day War, was not included in the lands to be retained by Israel in the Beilin-sponsored secret negotiations with the Palestinians (the so-called Beilin/Abu Mazen negotiations), Labor was abandoning its image as the party of security. A plan formulated by Minister Yossi Beilin and Abu Mazen regarding the division of Jerusalem robbed Labor of another image that had accompanied it since 1967 as the party that would not allow the repartition of Jerusalem.

In short, Labor was relinquishing a whole set of positions and symbols that had been traditionally identified with its policy. The automatic beneficiary was the Likud, the heir of Herut that had once been perceived as a party that was too committed to its abstract ideology of "greater Israel" but now acquired a new image as motivated by security concerns.

While the impact on the electorate of the decline in Labor's commitment to accepted national symbols is difficult to evaluate, the image of Meretz and Labor as left-wing, pursuing the dejudaization of the state, was a factor that can be measured more easily, evident in the gap between the two candidates in the final vote. A careful look at the voting figures in the Jewish and Arab sectors shows this much more starkly than the gross totals. While overall Netanyahu won over Peres with only 50.4 percent of the total vote as against 49.5 percent, taking the Jewish vote alone, Netanyahu won by 11 full percentage points (55.5 to 44.4 percent), a landslide rejection of Peres by the Jewish voters. That was only offset by the landslide vote of the Arab voters for Peres (94.7 to 5.2 percent), with only 17,000 Arabs voting for Netanyahu.[10] Aside from the peace process itself, the Jewishness of the state, an issue raised to prominence by the peace process, was the most visible on the agenda of the Labor government. Rabin, who deep down sensed the importance of this issue, tried to overcome the identity problem in traditional ways. Therefore, in 1992, despite a parliamentary majority based on the support of Meretz and parties with predominantly Arab constituencies, Labor chose to strengthen its coalition with the inclusion of SHAS, reaffirming the point that no Israeli government was considered to be fully legitimate without including one or more religious parties. It was Rabin who in 1992 expressed the need of the government to rely on a Jewish majority in the Knesset.[11] In order to maintain the arrangement, Rabin and Labor went so far as to amend two of Israel's Basic Laws: "Basic Law: Human Dignity and Liberty" and "Basic Law: Freedom of Occupation" – the latter of which had been found by the Supreme Court to invalidate the Knesset-enacted prohibition on importing non-kosher meat. A paragraph was added to both stating that its purpose was "to anchor in the Basic Law the values of the State of Israel as a Jewish and democratic state."[12] Henceforth, this combination became the major issue on Israel's constitutional agenda, with the left wing of Labor and Meretz challenging the compatibility of democracy and Judaism.[13] Not surprisingly, once such views became legitimate within a major Zionist party, similar voices were also heard in Israel's Arab parties.

Undoubtedly, the alliance between Labor and Meretz in the previous government contributed greatly to Labor's defeat in 1996. Although Meretz was filled with self-congratulations the morning after, when it received nine seats as compared to the earliest polls which showed it receiving as few as three, it was still down from the 12 it had won in 1992. Moreover, the disappearance of Tzomet, which in 1992 also ran on a platform with anti-religious overtones but in 1996 was integrated into the Likud, also indicated that the claim of Meretz and some of its allies to represent a secular Israeli majority was overblown. In fact, such a majority does not exit. Most Israeli Jews remain traditional, with ideological secularists and ideological religious more or less equally balanced (see Table 1 below).

Meretz nevertheless represents a hard core secular sector that should not be underestimated.[14] Meretz voters returned to the Meretz fold for the same polarizing reasons that so many religious voters voted for religious parties in 1996. That is to say, they are the hardline ideological secularists or advocates of making Israel neutral in matters relating to Jewish religion and culture. Many of them see Jewish culture as well as Jewish religion as incidental to a much more important (to them) universal or European cultural heritage rather than as central to Israeli life. Others advocate the replacement of Jewish tradition and civilization with a new Hebraic culture that was generated a century ago with the Zionist awakening in Europe.[15]

The continued strength of Meretz is another sign of polarization within the country. Many of the people who were attracted to it were probably attracted by hard-core, anti-traditional Judaism feelings or by even stronger sentiments than other Jewish voters for the continuation of the Peres peace process, but in the end this was not quite enough. All in all, the combined vote for Labor, Meretz and the Arab parties declined from 48.2 to 41.3 percent, with Labor and Meretz declining from 44 to 34 percent.[16]

There is no way of knowing conclusively how much Labor lost because of voter repudiation of its left-wing or anti-religious stances. Leading members of the party such as Shimon Peres and his close advisor Yossi Beilin, as well as the main contenders for the party leadership including Haim Ramon, Ehud Barak and Ephraim Sneh, all made overtures to the religious parties. The first three were identified with Peres's visionary dovish line in foreign policy, the latter two with more security-oriented policies. At the same time, several highly visible Labor MKs, such as Dalia Itzik and Yael Dayan, were identified with anti-religious and anti-national stances.

While by no means the majority, there were visible, dedicated, secularist or left-wing Knesset members high enough on the party list to be reelected, even with the party's great loss. Ironically, since they are among the younger leadership, they will probably inherit the party.

At the same time, one should not confuse issues of religion and the Jewishness of the state. Jewishness is the value system, to use Edward Shils' metaphor, that is reflected in the institutional network that forms the central zone of a polity.[17] It was the capture of this zone and its assortment of symbols that brought the Labor movement into power in the early 1930s even prior to the establishment of the state. Similarly, it was the alliance with the religious parties, especially with the NRP (Mizrachi at the time) and parties from the civil camp that brought them into power in 1935. It was the decoupling between Labor and this assortment of Jewish values and symbols that contributed to their fall in 1977 and again in 1996.

In short, one major error of the Labor-Meretz elite was that they thought they had received a mandate not only to try new and risky avenues in Israeli foreign policy, but at the same time to transform the normative essence of the state.[18] The reality was that they miscalculated the strength of those who would not stand for such a transformation even as they favored the peace process.

THE PEACE PROCESS AND THE "NEW MIDDLE EAST"

The defeat of Labor and Peres should not be interpreted as a rejection of the peace process by the rank and file voters. Here we must distinguish between the peace process and the myth of a "New Middle East." Except for Moledet, a party that emerged two elections ago to advocate "transfer" of the Arab population from west of the Jordan River to other Arab states, and which lost one seat even though it kept the same 2.3 percent of the total vote that it had received in 1992, no other successful Israeli party or personage campaigned on an anti-peace process platform. Sensing public support for the peace process, Netanyahu essentially had accepted the Oslo Accords publicly by April 1996.

Nor was this just the usual pious endorsement of the desirability of peace. All of the parties accepted the reality and binding character of the Oslo Accords. The division was over the details of their implementation and the desirable next steps, with the Likud-led national camp and a majority of the religious camp attacking the Rabin-Peres government for moving ahead without due regard for Israel's security and allowing the Palestinian Authority to get away with actions that were contrary to the agreements made, most especially in the matter of the revocation of the PLO Covenant calling for the destruction of Israel.

At the same time, during the last months of the campaign, Binyamin Netanyahu repeatedly and consistently indicated that a government led by him would accept the accords as binding and move on from there in a more cautious manner that would give the Palestinians full autonomy without sovereign statehood. In the aftermath of the elections, Foreign Minister David Levy first met Chairman Arafat in Gaza, followed by Netanyahu on September 4 and Defense Minister Yitzhak Mordechai on September 13, to discuss the redeployment of the IDF in Hebron.

To a large extent, both Israeli opinion-molders and public opinion were becoming more moderate. Some of the contributors to earlier volumes in the *Israel at the Polls* series identified the development of a dovish trend since the Lebanon War, in contrast to the common wisdom.[19] Although the Likud was pressed toward the right in the 1992 campaign and in the following four years while it was in opposition, that was an aberration. In seeking victory in 1996, Netanyahu had to move the party back toward the center and to form a center-right coalition, which he did. Subsequently he has had to strengthen the centrist elements in the Likud in order to govern effectively. In our book on the 1992 elections, Efraim Inbar argued on the basis of polling data that for all practical purposes the Likud was becoming a centrist party while Labor had moved to the left.[20] Even during the Knesset vote on Oslo, Likud MKs such as Meir Shitrit and Tel Aviv Mayor Roni Milo of the Likud, a former minister in Yitzhak Shamir's government, indicated their support for the Oslo Accords.

Within the new Likud-led coalition, parties such as the Third Way (4 MKs), Gesher (5 MKs), Yisrael Ba'Aliya (7 MKs), and even a sizable share of the Likud and half of the NRP could be considered as supporting in principle the peace process with the Palestinians. A close look at the delegations to the Knesset would show that nearly two-thirds of the Knesset seats went to individuals actively supporting the present peace process in some meaningful way. At the same time, if looked at from another angle, almost as many of the Knesset seats went to parties that supported a more cautious process.

In contrast, there was much less support for Shimon Peres's "New Middle East," a vision that went a few steps too far and produced a reaction against the man and the government that represented it. The term was actually uttered for the first time during the Gulf Crisis and "Desert Storm." At that time, the meaning was more of a future vision of what some Israel leaders hoped would develop in the aftermath of Saddam Hussein's fall. But the war had produced hardly any change in leadership in the Middle East.

The only country in which a change in leadership occurred was Israel. Iraq's mass destruction capability was only curtailed but not totally destroyed, and a new threat was developing in Iran and Syria. Terror, instead of declining, was on the increase and even spreading to other parts of the globe. In addition to Jordan with whom Israel had friendly relations even prior to the peace process, there were some Arab states which were opening up ties with Israel, but these were the moderate and distant states that did not present a threat to Israel. Syria, by contrast, was not ready for full normalization unless Israel would withdraw to the pre-1967 borders, namely, sharing with them the water reservoir of the Kinneret. Islamic fundamentalism was terrorizing not only Israel but also such Arab states as Egypt and Algeria.

It seems that Rabin himself was unsure about his foreign minister's assessment. Had Peres and his supporters taken a more cautious approach and convinced the voters that they were sincere about their caution, they probably would have won. But they pursued a policy of extremism in the pursuit of their vision of peace, most especially with regard to Syria, a palpably reluctant partner, or Arafat, who at best could explain that HAMAS terror was due to Palestinian Authority inefficiency. They maintained an attitude of arrogance as the only pursuers of peace and let victory slip away from them. A declaration by Peres following the March 3, 1996 bombing in Jerusalem that "We are in full war with the terrorist organizations" was not reassuring for the New Middle East.[21] Nor was the onslaught of Operation *Grapes of Wrath* a month later. The Likud's slogan "a secure peace" seemed to many as more realistic than the "New Middle East" that seemed to exist only in the minds of the Israeli government leadership. (For further elaboration on the impact of the peace process on the elections, see Gerald Steinberg's essay.)

THE ASCENDANCE OF THE RELIGIOUS PARTIES

Besides Netanyahu, the biggest victors in May 1996 were the religious parties. All told, the religious camp received 23 seats, more than ever before. SHAS and the National Religious Party received 19 seats, 7 more than in the previous election, while the United Torah Front, the Ashkenazi ultra-Orthodox party, held on to its 4 seats. In addition, Yisrael Ba'Aliya (Israel on the rise or in immigration), the Russian immigrants' party, representing probably the most secular constituency in the country, sent two Orthodox members and two traditionalists to the Knesset, thus reflecting most accurately the situation in the state. The surge of the religious parties, while influenced by a perceived attack on the "Jewishness of the Jewish state," also had additional dimensions.

HOW RELIGIOUS ARE ISRAELI JEWS?

For years, the narrative from Israel and the consensus of the academicians who analyze Israeli socio-political life was that Israel's Jews were sharply divided into two groups: the overwhelming majority who were secular and a small minority who were religious. While figures, even percentages, were not always stated, the general estimate was that 80 percent of Israelis fell into the secular camp and were being religiously coerced in one way or another by the Orthodox 20 percent. More than that, all religious Jews in Israel were assumed to be either dressed in black, demonstrating against the desecration of the Sabbath, or with knitted *kipot* (skull caps) performing religious acts presumed to have connotations of nationalist fanaticism, i.e., Jewish settlers in the territories.

On the surface, the 23 seats won by the religious parties in the new Knesset, just under 20 percent of the total, seemed to reflect the strength of the religious sector in Israeli society. But such an interpretation is misleading, as we know that non-Orthodox and even secular Jews voted for religious parties (especially NRP and SHAS) and religious people voted for other parties including the two major parties, Labor and Likud. Indeed, the addition of religious Knesset members from other parties brings the total religious representation closer to 25 percent. Ignoring the religious vote would thus be a blunder, especially as the religious voters provided the critical votes for the election of Binyamin Netanyahu as prime minister.

TABLE 1

ISRAELI JEWISH RELIGIOUS PRACTICE (%)

Religious Practice	Always	Sometimes	Never
Light Shabbat candles	56	22	20
Recite *Kiddush* (Friday night)	46	21	32
Attend Synagogue (Saturday morning)	23	22	56
Don't work (in public) on Sabbath	42	19	39
Participate in Passover *Seder*	78	17	5
Light Hanukkah candles	71	20	9
Fast on Yom Kippur	70	11	19
Bless *Lulav* (Sukkot)	26	15	59
Observe *Kashrut* at home	69	18	14
No pork, shellfish, etc.	63	16	21
Brit Milah	92		
Bar Mitzvah	83		
Wedding	87		
Burial/*Shiva*/*Kaddish*	88–91		
Mezuzah on front door	98		
Contribute to charity	74		

Source: Shlomit Levy, Hanna Levinson, and Elihu Katz, *Beliefs, Observations and Social Interaction Among Israeli Jews* (Jerusalem: Louis Guttman Israel Institute of Applied Social Research, 1993), Appendix A.

TABLE 2

ISRAELI JEWISH RELIGIOUS BELIEF

"To what extent do you believe or not believe in each of the following?"	Believe Completely (%)	Not Sure (%)	Do Not Believe (%)
There is a God	63	24	13
There is a supreme power guiding the world	57	29	14
The Torah was given to Moses on Mount Sinai	55	31	14
Good deeds are rewarded	52	33	14
The Jewish people were chosen among peoples	50	29	20
A watch from above is kept over everyone	49	32	19
The Torah and *mitzvot* are God's commands	47	29	24
Prayer can help one get out of a bad situation	45	35	20
Bad deeds are punished	44	38	18
The coming of the Messiah	39	29	32
There is a next world	35	35	30
Those who don't adhere to *mitzvot* are punished	27	36	37
Non-observing Jews endanger the Jewish people	21	29	50

Source: Levy, Levinson, and Katz, *Beliefs, Observations and Social Interaction Among Israeli Jews*, ch. 14, p. 101, Table 38.

But the main blunder was the confusion of strict Orthodox observance and religious practices with a more casual observance of traditional Jewish practices. A survey of Israeli Jews' beliefs and practices published in 1993 by the prestigious Guttman Institute of Applied Social Research, tells the true story (Tables 1 and 2).[22]

Taking into consideration the entire Jewish population, Jewish religious practice is high according to most of the usual measures. While the maintenance of those Jewish observances could be explained as residual among Israeli Jews still close to their traditional roots, the claims of the same public with regard to Jewish belief, often a problem of some embarrassment to those who wish to seem modern, is especially impressive.

What we learn from this and other studies is that Israel's Jews are not divided into two groups but into four: in Israeli terms, ultra-Orthodox (*haredim*), religious Zionists (*datiim*), traditional Jews (*masortiim*), and secular (*hilonim*). The ultra-Orthodox, those strangely (to Western eyes) garbed, black-hatted Jews who are featured in all the pictures, represent only 8 percent of Israel's Jewish population. Another 17 percent are religious Zionists who are normally lost to view in many of the studies and statistics because they are generally lumped with everyone else. The religious Zionists are similar to the modern or centrist Orthodox Jews in the diaspora, partaking of most or all aspects of modern civilization while they maintain Orthodox observance of Jewish religious law and tradition.

The third group consists of the majority of Israeli Jews, some 55 percent, who define themselves as "traditional." These Jews are from many backgrounds, but most are Sephardim from the Mediterranean or Islamic worlds. They are people who value traditional Jewish life, but who are prepared to modify *halakhically*-required Jewish practices in those cases where they believe it to be personally necessary or attractive to do so. They cover the whole range of belief and observance from people of fundamentalist belief and looser practice to people who have interpreted Judaism in the most modern manner but retain many of its customs and ceremonies, particularly those connected with home and family.

Many of these "traditional" Jews differ from the Orthodox only in that they will drive their cars on the Sabbath, use electricity, watch television, or go to a soccer game or to the beach, frequently after attending religious services in the morning and the evening before. Many of the men don *tefillin* every morning. What is critical is that all are committed to a major religious component in the definition of their Jewishness and the Jewishness of the Jewish state.

The fourth group consists of those who define themselves as secular, at most some 20 percent of the Jewish population. These are people whose beliefs are secular. The practices of a significant percentage of them, on the other hand, may be quite similar to those of many traditionalists, only they claim to maintain those practices for family and national reasons rather than for religious ones. The fact that Jewish religious observance has such a strong national component makes it a major component of most Jews' national identity even if they no longer see themselves as believers in the Jewish religion.

The Guttman study shows that an astounding three-quarters of the "secular" 20 percent follow the most common traditional religious practices. Only a quarter, or 5 percent of the total Jewish population, say they observe no religious practices whatsoever, a figure which is belied by data showing that 98 percent of Israeli Jews have *mezuzot* on the doorposts of their houses and 92 percent circumcise their male children, to mention only two of a number of observances that are so deeply entrenched in the culture that hardly anyone thinks of them as religious observances.[23]

Moreover, nearly two-thirds of all Israelis believe that there is a God and another quarter believe that it is possible that there is ("not sure"). In a poll conducted by the secular *Ha-aretz* newspaper, out of 120 Members of the Knesset, 91 MKs answered that they believe in God, 20 refused to respond, and only 9 answered in the negative.[24] Even more impressive is that 55 percent of the populace believe in the literal revelation of the Torah by God to the Jewish people at Mt. Sinai, while those who believe that it is possible that this occurred ("not sure") raise the total to 86 percent. So, too, with other measures of belief. At the same time, as in other Western countries, only 27 percent believe that God will punish them for not observing His commandments, even though twice as many believe that the commandments are of Divine origin.

Why, then, have Israelis not sought to eliminate the formal dominance of the Orthodox establishment? Since a majority of Israeli Jews are Sephardim and the Sephardi world never had a reformation like the Ashkenazi world, where religious Jews divided themselves into three or more "denominations," even those who do not pretend to be Orthodox believe that Jewish tradition itself should stand relatively unchanged and should not be fragmented. They reserve for themselves the informal right to pick and choose, but they want the formal religion to remain as is, as in the rest of the Mediterranean world. Identifying with the Jewishness of the state serves as roughly equivalent to the role of the Reform or Conservative synagogue in the diaspora. Indeed, in the whole history of the Zionist enterprise there has been no indigenous movement to reform Judaism or Jewish religion, this on the part of a people who are prepared to have reform movements for everything.

The 1993 survey simply replicates earlier surveys going back some thirty years, despite the Russian aliya which was almost entirely secular. True, the amount of observance has dropped over the years but not appreciably. What is also true is that almost all the elites in Israeli society – cultural, intellectual, political, and economic – are found within the secular 20 percent, so that they frame the public domain of Israel. Moreover, that 20 percent is overwhelmingly Ashkenazi, either Jews from Eastern and Central Europe or descended from them, the ones who are most likely to know English and to be contacted by journalists coming to the country, thus allowing this skewed picture to emerge. At the same time, Israel does not have a secular conservative intellectual elite. The Israeli right wing is identified as such either because of its Jewish-religious or ethno-nationalist stance on foreign affairs, two tenets not very relished in the West.

In the early stages of the election campaign, the polls showed SHAS dropping from 6 to 3 seats and the other religious parties holding their own. SHAS's rise to 10 seats was a concrete indication of the inaccuracy noted above in defining the Israeli population as "religious" or "secular."

Many Sephardim have been drawn to the Haredi-oriented SHAS (Sephardic Torah Guardians) movement, that has grown from a small handful of Jerusalemites dissatisfied with the then Ashkenazi-dominated religious parties to become the third largest party in the country. SHAS has brought to many Sephardim a revival of the religious traditions they knew, presenting them in a way their communities demanded, through the warm-hearted activities of SHAS-appointed rabbis, educators, and preachers. In a way SHAS was countering the efforts at cultural secularization directed by the secular Labor elite at many of the Sephardi immigrants in the 1950s and early 1960s.

Despite this secularization process, there are very few truly secular Sephardim. These people were extremely upset by the hardline secularism of Meretz and the left wing of the Labor party since, as one of them put it, "our Jewishness is in our souls," and they reject all assaults upon the Jewishness of the Jewish state.

SHAS has been successful all along by appealing to that population and their needs. For example, both the State Religious schools, long dominated by the Ashkenazi-led National Religious Party, and the Ashkenazi-dominated Haredi "independent" schools demanded a change in the parent's religious code of behavior prior to accepting the children of Sephardi parents who do not live fully according to the canons of Ashkenazi Orthodoxy. SHAS, which saw itself as an alternative to both Agudat Israel and the NRP, established their own educational movement – El Ha-Maayan – to provide after-school supplementary classes and training for those children in Judaism, of course as SHAS understands it, thus providing a needed, valuable, and much appreciated service to tens of thousands of Israeli families. By providing this service, they provided an educational framework as well as extra-curricular activities for children who otherwise would have found themselves on the street. This was particularly appreciated by large families residing in small apartments in the cities, and those in development towns who suffered from being situated on the country's periphery.

Moreover, since the religious patterns of ultra-Orthodox Sephardim allow more room for interaction with people of different degrees of belief and observance, the ultra-Orthodox SHAS leadership could easily reach out to the traditional SHAS voters and gain their support reciprocally. One need only contrast Ashkenazi and Sephardi synagogues in Israel to see this reality in action. It is not that the Ashkenazim are not "pluralistic." There are appropriate Ashkenazi congregations for every nuance of Ashkenazi religious belief and observance, but each congregation is homogeneous in relation to its particular nuance. Just the opposite occurs in Sephardi congregations, where every congregation is a mixture of worshippers ranging from ultra-Orthodox to minimally traditional who come together to celebrate the same liturgy and religious calendar.

The NRP attracted the equivalent voters, especially from among the Ashkenazim, including those who defined themselves as religious but who had never before voted for a religious party and those who defined themselves as secular but who were concerned about the preservation of Jewish tradition in the Jewish state. The increasingly prominent role of young national religious men in the IDF and the work of young national religious women who volunteer to do national service in development towns and welfare institutions instead of the army, was also appreciated by voters.

But above all, the resounding victory of the religious parties was a direct reaction to the intensely anti-religious atmosphere that seemed to pervade the Rabin-Peres government, although neither Rabin nor Peres intentionally fostered that atmosphere and Peres, unlike Rabin, even made serious efforts to counter it. The fact that Meretz was Labor's principal coalition partner and was given control of the Ministries of Education and Culture and Communications, where Amnon Rubinstein and Shulamit Aloni either pressed for or presided over major steps to both publicly and quietly eliminate signs of Israel as a Jewish state, was seen as an enormous threat not only to those who were themselves religiously Orthodox, but to many Jews who, whatever their own beliefs and practices, felt that Israel's whole *raison d'etre* was in peril. It was estimated that about 50,000 secular Israelis voted for the NRP in 1996, accepting their slogan of "Zionism with a soul."

This alienation was intensified by Labor's Minister of Religious Affairs, Shimon Shitrit, who in a rather oafish way took steps to recognize and foster non-Orthodox forms of Judaism and to bring them within the institutions of the state's religious establishment, steps that the vast majority of Israelis, whether Orthodox or not, do not understand or accept. Even secular Israelis, unless they have ideological reasons for wanting to hit out at the Orthodox establishment, are not interested in non-Orthodox forms of Judaism. In the words of Israel's esteemed professor of political philosophy Shlomo Avineri, "the synagogues to which we do not go are Orthodox."

The coup de grace was the Meretz election campaign which

emphasized what that party saw as the need to further reduce the role of Judaism in the formal functioning of the state. The result was a backlash. Many Sephardim who were religiously traditional and had shifted to the Likud after 1977, moved to support SHAS, and many Ashkenazim who were sympathetic to Jewish religious tradition voted NRP. Even more important, many religiously Orthodox, who in the past had voted for one or the other of the two major parties, apparently voted this time for a religious party out of concern, even fear, for the direction that Israeli society was taking under the Labor government, thus increasing the polarization and sectoral voting. Their ability to vote for the prime minister on one ballot and thus express their national priorities, and with the second to vote for a religious party, also contributed to the strength of the two religious parties. In the past, the religious parties were never able to obtain more than half of the potential religious vote in the country. This time, they seemed to have won a major share of it.

All this no doubt seems strange to voters in many Western, particularly English-speaking, countries where religion and politics, when mixed, are mixed in different ways, mostly because of the differences between Christianity and Judaism (or Christianity and Islam, for that matter) and the tradition of Western liberal democracy that has grown up out of that difference over the past 300 years. The vote for the religious parties was certainly not a vote to turn Israel into a theocracy or even a *halachic* state, despite the attempt by the extreme left to portray the victory of the religious parties as such.

The religious party leaders have reiterated that they had no intention of moving any government that they would join in that direction. They reiterated that they only have two interests: (1) to strengthen the Jewish character of the state, which in concrete terms means to insure that what Americans have come to call "the public square" will remain infused with Jewish symbols and some actions, as it has been since the beginning of the Zionist enterprise, and to have the educational system serving Israel's Jewish population teach the Jewish heritage in appropriate ways; and (2) to see to it that the material and educational interests of the religious population are taken care of; that is to say, that adequate housing and benefits available to all citizens also be made available to those in the ultra-Orthodox community, and that state support be available for the various forms of general and Jewish education that the Orthodox and ultra-Orthodox desire, in the same way that such support is made available to other segments of Israel's educational system. In both respects, the religious parties should be seen as representing the legitimate interests of a large segment of Israel's population, just like any other segment with legitimate interests.

The novelty of the pro-religious vote was that it was depicted as a vote for Judaism and Zionism. We must recall that a large share of the ultra-Orthodox community did not embrace the Zionist idea of building a Jewish state. Both Haredi parties campaigned under the banner of the

Jewishness of the State of Israel. Undoubtedly, the leaders of these parties have always perceived themselves as the "real" Zionists. We need not accept this interpretation as they do. It would be more accurate to define them as neo-Zionists.

In more strictly political matters, there is no monolithic religious view. Indeed, well over half of the religious vote, perhaps over two-thirds, is centrist with regard to the peace process, very much committed to its continuation, albeit with greater caution on Israel's part. That is why, even before the elections, Israeli pundits saw the religious bloc as able to go with either prime ministerial candidate when it came to the formation of a new government. On the peace issue, we may include most of the religious bloc among the centrist parties. (For an elaboration on the religious parties, see Eliezer Don-Yehiya's essay.)

THE CENTRIST PARTIES

As usual, the non-religious centrist parties had difficulties in the election, although, as we have argued throughout our series, the centrist vote constitutes the largest share in the Israeli population. Except in the 1977 elections, and especially following the collapse of the Democratic Movement for Change, centrist parties have had difficulty in gaining a large share of the electorate. The two parties that were considered centrist were the Third Way, a breakaway from the Labor camp over the issue of whether or not Israel should retain the Golan in any peace settlement, and Yisrael Ba'Aliya, the party of immigrants from the former Soviet Union led by Natan Sharansky, which appealed principally to those who were new voters. The Third Way won four seats and Yisrael Ba'Aliya, seven.

The Third Way's four seats were predicted, but, considering the way the movement started and the potential strength of the centrist vote, this has to be considered as a somewhat disappointing finish. This must be related to the fact that many of the initial leaders of the Third Way, in the end, could not bring themselves to leave their "home" in the Labor party and withdrew when the issue came to a head, moving into the party leadership Avigdor Kahalani, a war hero relatively new to politics but a Labor Knesset member and its candidate in Tel Aviv's 1993 mayoral race. The first three candidates on the list were ex-Labor members, while the fourth was Prof. Alex Lubotzky, a religious resident of Efrat, slotted to attract the centrist religious vote.

They waged a fight to convince Israeli voters to support the center, but the fight they waged seemed to most voters as too non-committal; that is to say, they did not make the centrist position forceful enough to attract Israeli voters who seem to have a penchant for sharper stands even when the voters' overall tendency is to the center. This somewhat ambivalent situation has consistently weakened the power of centrist parties to attract voters throughout the history of the state. Yet, the Third

Way did better than all the earlier centrist parties in the last decade and a half, including those headed by charismatic figures such as Moshe Dayan or Ezer Weizman. The mixture of a "war hero," a settler from the Golan Heights, and a settler from Gush Etzion offered forceful credentials for people looking for peace but not at the cost of abandoning vision and security. What was outstanding about this party was that, aside from the Golan Heights where it received 17.7 percent, Third Way support throughout the country hovered evenly around 3 percent.

Yisrael Ba'Aliya did surprisingly well. It is unclear at this point whether these were basically dissatisfied immigrants or whether Sharansky served as a major drawing card. There is no question that Sharansky is an imposing figure. In fact, had he campaigned more broadly as a candidate for general Israeli, not only immigrant, voters, he might have done even better since he rightly gives the impression of having as much leadership stature as Peres and, at the same time, shows the kind of solidity that helped Netanyahu to defeat Peres's "visions." If his Hebrew improves, Sharansky could turn out to be an important contender for even higher office in the future. Most impressive about him is that he is perceived as a genuine believer in the Jewish people and the Zionist idea, a vision that seems lost among the traditional leadership of the state. His victory as well as that of his colleagues was comparable to that of the religious parties, both falling within the category of neo-Zionism. (On Yisrael Ba'Aliya, see Etta Bick's article.)

THE ISRAELI ARABS

The Israeli Arabs both won and lost. Obviously, they feel that they lost with Peres's loss. On the other hand, they clearly established themselves as an important voting bloc in Israeli politics that must be considered as such in political campaigns from now on. Their vote continues to be divided between predominantly Arab parties and mainstream ones, and it is clear that their vote counted for both Meretz and the Labor party. Having established themselves as coalition partners during the Rabin-Peres years, they also gained from the electoral system which elevated their importance in the election of the prime minister. Considering their demographic growth and the electoral system, one could assume that even right-wing candidates will be unable to ignore their weight. But in order to become a true balancing faction, they cannot align themselves with one camp. Should they accept the opportunities that are open to them via the political game, they will be able to continue to increase their political power.

Peres and Labor lost votes among Israeli Arabs because of their anger at the civilian casualties in Lebanon caused by Israel's Operation *Grapes of Wrath* during the election campaign. The military operation was undoubtedly launched in part to demonstrate that Peres would stand firm on matters of Israel's security in the face of the widespread feeling in the Jewish sector that he was "soft" on security issues. This may be an example of the uncomfortable situation in which the Israeli Arabs may find themselves when confronted by contradictions between their political and ethno-national interests.[25] (On the Arab parties and politics, see Hillel Frisch's article.)

THE COALITION OF MINORITIES

In the last analysis, Peres and his coalition lost to an opposition that in many ways was not as attractive as they were. There were many comments during the campaign that, on the one hand, the election was the most fateful in Israel's history, but, at the same time, the voters seemed rather withdrawn. Many voters seemed to have perceived great weaknesses, albeit very different ones, in both prime ministerial candidates and in their parties, and were forced to make a choice for the lesser evil. Except for some of the young (below voting age) activists on the streets, there was little real enthusiasm for any of the political parties or camps among the great bulk of voters. They turned out in record numbers but without any feelings of excitement or happiness, rather with feelings of trepidation and hoping for the best.

Since the 1981 elections, one of the authors of this essay has noticed that the persistent victory of the Likud could be explained according to the "coalition of minorities" or electoral alignment and realignment theory. According to this rationale, the winner in an election is the party or candidate that puts together a broader coalition of sub-system groups that together form a majority. The ability to put together such a majority would also result in the dominance of the parties in power over an extended time, although not necessarily winning every election. The winning coalition would control most of the institutions, but ultimately would lose its power once minorities would become disappointed in the ability of the coalition leader to pursue their interests, and hence defect to the contending major party.[26]

The winning coalition that ruled Israel since its inception, and even prior to it in the pre-state Yishuv since 1933, collapsed in 1977 when Labor, under Yitzhak Rabin and Shimon Peres, lost the support of many segments in Israeli society that slowly defected to the Likud coalition. Starting in 1963, Menachem Begin, the leader of Herut, formed a coalition with the Liberal party and doubled the size of its delegation in the Knesset. The Sephardim, who when new immigrants had voted for the party in power, were slowly drifting toward Herut, with approximately 70 percent voting for the Likud (the heir of Herut) in 1977. In 1973, Begin extended the Herut-Liberal coalition to include the La'am faction, which in itself was a coalition of right-wing factions including the hawkish wing of Labor once headed by David Ben-Gurion.

The last camp to be attracted was the religious camp. The NRP, the traditional partner of the Labor camp since 1935, was going through a transformation with its young guard turning hawkish. Nevertheless, the traditional leadership was moderate, especially the Lamifne faction in the NRP. The final breach of confidence occurred when then Prime Minister Rabin, following an incident over a religious issue, fired the NRP ministers and called for early elections. The victory of the Likud as the plurality party resulted in the NRP, followed also by Agudat Israel, joining the Begin government.

This coalition of religious, hawks, nationalists, and Sephardim held together throughout the 1980s. In the course of that period, the religious parties twice bailed out the Likud: in 1984 when they refused to join a Labor government and forced Peres to form a national unity government with the Likud and share the premiership with Yitzhak Shamir, and again in 1990 when Shimon Peres almost formed a government relying on deserters from the Likud. In 1992, Yitzhak Rabin succeeded in splitting the coalition of minorities because of his hawkish reputation and the desertion of Sephardim and the center from the Likud. Yet Rabin's new majority was dismantled by 1996, due to Labor's readiness for a withdrawal from the Golan Heights, his verbal attacks on the settlers, the lack of attention given to development towns and poorer urban neighborhoods, and the courting of the Arab vote on whom the Labor government was dependent in the Knesset.

One person who understood the implications of assembling a coalition of minorities was Ariel Sharon. Realizing the tendency to rally around Labor in the wake Rabin's assassination, Sharon withdrew his candidacy for the premiership and compelled Netanyahu to persuade the other candidates on the right – Rafael Eitan, leader of the hawkish Tzomet, and David Levy, leader of Gesher – to do likewise in return for giving them and their key supporters realistic places on the Likud list. While this was a high price for the Likud to pay, ultimately this strategy paid off and the coalition held through election day.

In these elections the impact of the coalition of minorities was even more critical than in prior elections. While in the previous elections the heads of the largest parties would negotiate the coalition following the elections, in a direct vote for prime minister the winner is determined by the size of the coalition that would vote for him. The broadest coalition would decide at the polls who would be prime minister. Being in this position provides the winner with an advantage when negotiating with the parties in the legislature. In essence, Netanyahu's victory was composed of three coalitions: the coalition within the Likud composed of Gesher and Tzomet, the one that elected him to the prime ministership, and finally the coalition in the Knesset.

The lack of heterogeneity in the Labor coalition was reflected in several dimensions of the previous government. Out of 21 ministers only four (19 percent) were Sephardim, out of which two were of Iraqi origin (one a wealthy lawyer and the other a former general). While no minister was religious, after the resignation of Arye Deri. Rabbi Yehuda Amital was added as minister without portfolio when Shimon Peres became prime minister. Approximately 60 percent of the ministers resided in the Tel Aviv area, most of them in the northern suburbs of that city, the heartland of the Israeli secular upper and middle class. Two members came from kibbutzim and another two resided in Jerusalem. None of the ministers came from development towns or the south of Tel Aviv (considered the poorer section of the city).

In comparison, in the Netanyahu government over 40 percent of the ministers are of Sephardi origin. A similar percentage of the ministers reside in Jerusalem. Five out of the 17 ministers are religious (including Edelstein from the Russian secular party). David Levy and Moshe Katzav consider themselves religiously traditional and both also come from development towns. Eliyahu Suissa had moved to Jerusalem from a development town following the ascendance of SHAS in the mid-1980s. Only one minister resides in Tel Aviv and two ministers reside in the greater Tel Aviv area, but in Bnei Brak and Petach Tikva, both towns having large religious constituencies. Sharon and Eitan, both former generals, reside in agricultural regions, the first on his farm in the Negev and the second on a moshav. (For an elaborate analysis of Labor's failures in this and other regards, see Giora Goldberg's essay.)

NETANYAHU AND THE FORMATION OF THE GOVERNMENT

Thus Netanyahu's "rainbow coalition" was reflected in his cabinet, and determined by traditional coalition politics, which he hoped to mitigate when building a "presidential" system. Confounding veteran Israeli politicians and political pundits alike who were used to the old system of coalition formation, Netanyahu nevertheless attempted to initiate a premiership as close to an American-style presidency as he could. But his main problem was the dissonance between his government and a peace process framework that had been concocted by a previous government that was composed of a totally different social and ideological fabric.

One of his first steps was a conciliatory speech to a nation which was deeply divided. He did so facing a puzzled audience of Likud faithful, which he was able to turn around, and backed by a glum-looking collection of Likud colleagues on the platform behind him. Netanyahu spoke of continuing the peace process, praised Shimon Peres for what he had accomplished, and spoke in terms of moving ahead on the basis of national unity – a most unusual speech for a victorious political candidate in Israel. Nevertheless, as the first year of his rule confirmed, the other side was not ready to forgive him for daring to win the elections.

Netanyahu's speech was far different from that made four years earlier by Yitzhak Rabin who, also influenced by the idea of a strengthened premiership through the selection of the prime minister on a near personal basis, said "I will navigate, I will take charge, I will lead,

I will set policy," or words to that effect, mostly directed against his internal rival, Peres. Netanyahu, on the other hand, appeared statesmanlike and tried to open the door to all Israelis and the world.

In what followed he was less successful. He soon found out that he did not exactly have a free hand in selecting his cabinet and assigning cabinet positions, that there were those in his party and his coalition who also had demands and who were in a position to force him to deliver. The end result was a de facto compromise between Netanyahu's desires and those of his partners and colleagues, between a presidential and a parliamentary system. Indeed, it is easier to change an electoral system than a political culture. The new prime minister, however, intended to hold the reins of government as closely as possible. His personal staff and entourage consisted of new people rather than veteran members of the Likud, and they were his people. This had contradictory implications. On the one hand, it did give him more control; on the other, it also meant that neither he nor his aides came with much experience and all had to undergo on-the-job training together which led them to make a number of mistakes early in the game.

From the first, Netanyahu set out to shift the peace process on to a new basis, away from Peres's vision of a "New Middle East" which was grounded in major concessions to the Palestinians and the Arab states for the sake of Israel's integration into the region. This meant that the first two months of the new government included rhetorical commitments to the peace process while slowing matters down in the field and planning for some renegotiation of the terms of Israeli withdrawal from Hebron. While the Palestinians initially greeted Netanyahu with a wait-and-see attitude, lack of rapid progress in the fulfillment of the Oslo Agreements as they understood them and as the previous government had fulfilled them, led to increasing dissatisfaction on the part of both the Palestinian Authority and the Palestinian street.

Netanyahu avoided meeting Arafat during those months, although he sent Foreign Minister David Levy and Defense Minister Yitzhak Mordechai to do so, and then when he did take the step, the obligatory picture of the two shaking hands showed Netanyahu with a sour face. This meeting led him to a confrontation with his party's right wing, which convinced him to continue his cautious forward motion, further disappointing the Palestinians and many of Israel's allies.

On the domestic front, shortly after the new government took office it was discovered that the rosy picture of a healthy economy that the Labor government had fostered had been built upon false premises, whereby the government had utilized American loan guarantees and other devices to allow a splurge of consumer spending that the country could not afford; in other words, a long period of what in Israel is called an "election economy." The result was that inflation was rising, the government's estimates of revenue in balancing the budget were false, and measures had to be taken immediately to belt-tighten. Economic growth slowed, in part because of those economic uncertainties and in part because of the new doubts as to the future of the peace process under a Likud government. By the end of the 1996 fiscal year, following the tight monetary policy of the Bank of Israel, it seemed that at least the problem of inflation was under control.

Throughout its first nine months, Netanyahu's new government was racked internally by personality-based quarrels and externally by a hostile Israeli and world media that did not seem to want to let the new government govern. Netanyahu did not receive a hundred days of grace or even ten. Still, by autumn 1996, both assaults had been brought under some control, only to be undone by a poorly-executed decision to open the Hasmonean Tunnel adjacent to the Temple Mount and the Western Wall, which provided the spark that ignited the Palestinians, ostensibly on the grounds that the opening of the tunnel was an effort to destroy Muslim religious sites on the Temple Mount.

Arafat seemed perfectly willing to use this pretext to refocus world attention on the Palestinians' plight and the performance of the peace process, and the spark ignited a larger fire than anyone expected. For the first time, Palestinian police, most of whom were former PLO terrorists, fired on Israeli soldiers, leaving 15 dead and scores wounded. After three days, Arafat ordered his people to clamp down and they succeeded in ending all but incidental violence. They also succeeded in bringing the international community back into the picture, forcing Israel to accept an American presidential invitation to a Netanyahu–Arafat summit in Washington attended by other Arab leaders as well.

Netanyahu, under pressure both at home and abroad to move ahead with the peace process, on the one hand, and from the right to build new settlements, on the other hand, tried to formulate a balanced strategy. Bound by the commitments of the previous government and despite strong opposition from his right wing, he nevertheless implemented a pull-back from most of Hebron, leaving a Jewish enclave in the city. In addition, he committed the new government to turning over more parts of the territories to the Palestinian Authority in three stages. At the same time, after a prolonged delay by the previous government, he started the building of a new neighborhood on the southeastern fringes of Jerusalem. The massive condemnations by the Arab states and the international community indicated the confines that "Oslo" put on Israeli foreign policy. As the first year of the Netanyahu prime ministership progressed it became clear that the discord between his coalition and a process conceived by the previous government extended to a critical level. It is at this stage that Binyamin Netanyahu as well as his Arab and other partners in the peace process are asked to exhibit innovative leadership. (On leadership in the emerging new politics, see Michael Keren's essay.)

NOTES

1. Dan Margalit, "Farewell to Shimon Peres," *Ha-aretz*, June 3, 1996, p.B1.
2. Daniel J. Elazar and Shmuel Sandler, "The 1992 Israeli Elections: Mahapach or a Transfer of Power?" in *Israel at the Polls, 1992* (Lanham, Md., 1995), pp.1–24.
3. The best book on the Yishuv era that emphasizes these features is Dan Horowitz and Moshe Lissak, *The Origins of the Israeli Polity* (Tel Aviv, 1977), especially chs. 6 and 9. See also Daniel J. Elazar, *Israel: Building a New Society* (Bloomington, 1986).
4. For a theoretical-philosophical analysis of these dilemmas, see Yael Tamir, *Liberal Nationalism* (Princeton, 1993). See also Ernest Gellner, *Postmodernism, Reason and Religion* (London, 1992).
5. Central Bureau of Statistics, Ministry of the Interior, Malam Systems, Special Series, No.925, *Results of Elections to the Thirteenth Knesset* (Jerusalem, 1992), p.30.
6. The founding father of the group is considered to be Simha Flapan, the editor of *New Outlook*, in *The Birth of Israel: Myths and Reality* (New York, 1987). This school was carried on by Benny Morris, Avi Shlaim and Ilan Pappe. For a critique, see Efraim Karsh, "Rewriting Israel's History," *Middle East Quarterly* (June 1996): 19–29; idem, *Fabricating Israeli History: The "New Historians"* (London: Frank Cass, 1997).
7. For the depth of the problem, see *Ha-aretz*, September 12, 1996, p.B2, and *Yediot Aharonot*, October 22, 1996, Yom Kippur Supplement, pp.20–22.
8. Efraim Inbar, "Contours of Israel's New Strategic Thinking," *Political Science Quarterly*, Vol.111, No.1 (April 1996): 41–64.
9. *Yediot Aharonot*, April 22, 1994, p.3. On another occasion in 1994, Rabin declared that he favored evacuation of settlements from the Golan because of the supremacy of peace over a few settlements, *Ma'ariv*, April 22, 1994.
10. Binyamin Neuberger, "The Knesset Election in the Arab and Druse Sectors," *The Israeli–Arab Politics Programme, The 1996 Elections* (Tel Aviv, May 1996), p.18.
11. See David Landau's column in *Ha-aretz*, June 3, 1996, p.B1.
12. On the debate in the cabinet and legal interpretation of the Basic Law: Freedom of Occupation, see *Ha-aretz*, November 29, 1993, p.4a. See also *Ha-aretz*, October 24, November 12 and 19, 1993. See also comments by Dedi Zucker and Eliezer Schweid on "The State of Israel: A Jewish and Democratic State," *Constitutional Reform in Israel and its Implications* (Jerusalem, 1995), pp.4–14 (Hebrew).
13. For a comprehensive collection on "A Jewish and Democratic State," see a special issue edited by the late Professor Ariel Rozen-Zvi, *Tel Aviv University Law Review*, Vol.19, No.3, (July 1995).
14. For a poll conducted by Mina Zemah on Israeli secular society, see *Yediot Aharonot*, September 22, 1996, second supplement for Yom Kippur, pp.13–20.
15. Amos Oz depicted this culture as Beit Brenner and Beit Bialik in a lecture given at Bar-Ilan University on the dedication of the Sara and Simha Lainer Chair in Democracy and Civility, November 15, 1996.
16. *Appendix to The Results of the Elections to the 14th Knesset* (Jerusalem: Central Elections Committee, n.d.), p.3.
17. Edward Shils, *Center and Periphery: Essays in Macrosociology* (Chicago, 1978), p.8.
18. The best articulated essay on this misconception was by David Landau, *Ha-aretz*, June 3, 1996, p.B1.
19. Efraim Inbar and Giora Goldberg, "Is the Israeli Political Elite Becoming More Hawkish?," *International Journal* 45 (Summer 1990):631–60; Gad Barzilai, Giora Goldberg, and Efraim Inbar, "Israeli Leadership and Public Attitudes Toward Federal Solutions for the Arab–Israeli Conflict Before and After Desert Storm," *Publius* 21 (Summer 1991):191–209.
20 Efraim Inbar, "Labor's Return to Power," Elazar and Sandler, *Israel at the Polls, 1992*, p.28.
21. *Ha-aretz*, March 4, 1996, p.1.
22 In the late 1970s, the religious observant population was estimated at 23 percent, the secular 40 percent, and the remainder traditional. See Y. Ben-Meir and P. Kedem, "An Index of Religiosity for the Jewish Population in Israel," *Megamot* 24:3 (February 1979):353–62. Another index for measuring religiosity is the distribution of students in elementary schools. The percentage of students attending the State Religious and Independent (ultra-Orthodox) systems was 25.8 percent in 1985. See Dan Horowitz

and Moshe Lissak, *Trouble in Utopia: The Overburdened Polity of Israel* (Tel Aviv, 1990), p.93, Table 2 (Hebrew). For another index, see next note.

23. See Shlomit Levy, Hanna Levinson, and Elihu Katz, *Beliefs, Observances and Social Interaction Among Israeli Jews* (Jerusalem, 1993). It should also be noted that almost all Israeli Jews have some form of Passover Seder. Indeed, one of the observed phenomena in Israel is how many Israelis who are planning to travel abroad during Pesach, which means that they are not concerned about keeping strictly kosher for the holiday as Jewish law requires, schedule their departure from the country after the evening of the Seder.

24. *Ha-aretz,* July 26, 1996, Weekend Magazine, p.19.

25. See also Eli Rekhess, Efraim Yaar and Tamar Herman, "The Attitudes of the Arab and Druse Publics in Israel Towards the 1996 Knesset Elections," in *The Israeli–Arab Politics Programme,* Nos.1 and 4 (Tel Aviv, April 1996); and Assad Ganem, "Political Influence – to the Arabs in Israel Too," *Ibid.*, No.4 (July 1996).

26. Shmuel Sandler, "The Religious Parties," in Howard Penniman and Daniel J. Elazar, eds, *Israel at the Polls, 1981* (Bloomington, 1986), pp.124–5. On applying this theory to American politics, see Theodore Lowi and Benjamin Ginsberg, *American Government, Freedom and Power* (New York, 1993), pp.483–9. See also Anthony Downs, *An Economic Theory of Democracy* (New York, 1957).

THE PARTIES

Netanyahu Takes Over

EFRAIM INBAR

On May 29, 1996, Israelis elected their representatives to the Knesset and, for the first time, they also cast ballots to directly choose the prime minister. Binyamin Netanyahu, the 47-year-old Likud leader and prime-ministerial candidate, was elected by a small margin of slightly less than 30,000 votes (he received 55.5 percent of the Jewish vote, however), while the electoral alignment between his party, Rafael Eitan's Tzomet, and David Levy's Gesher received a disappointing 32 Knesset seats (compared to 40 in the previous Knesset). Despite the fact that the race was very close in its final stage, the Netanyahu victory was received as a surprise, particularly abroad. Netanyahu overcame the efforts of a hostile media and thwarted an international orchestra playing Peres victory music. The election results reflected the impact of the new electoral system, which actually strengthened the power of small parties representing specific and defined sectors in Israeli society. The 1996 elections heralded the beginning of a new era in Israeli politics – the emergence of a new political system, a hybrid with unforeseen domestic and foreign policy ramifications, and of uncertain duration.

This essay reviews the remarkable political recovery of the Likud, under Netanyahu, since losing power in 1992,[1] analyzing the election campaign and discussing the process of coalition forming and Netanyahu's first steps. It concludes by offering a few observations on the election results and an evaluation of Netanyahu's nascent policies.

LIKUD'S TESTS

Following the 1992 electoral debacle, the Likud was deeply in trouble. Yitzhak Shamir, the former prime minister, decided to step down as party

Efraim Inbar is Director of the BESA Center for Strategic Studies and Associate Professor of Political Studies, Bar-Ilan University.

leader, while Moshe Arens, the former Defense Minister and presumably number two in the party, resigned from the Knesset. In addition to its leadership crisis, the Likud was demoralized and disoriented. Moreover, it was in huge financial debt and the party apparatus hardly functioned. The contest for the party leadership among Binyamin Begin, David Levy, and Netanyahu was acrimonious, strengthening the personal animosity between the last two.[2] Nevertheless, in March 1993 the Likud held primaries for the first time, and Netanyahu won the leadership position with a comfortable 52.1 percent share of the vote. He also succeeded in creating a party regime which allowed him great personal control over the party and its institutions, and made the possibility of an intra-party challenge of his leadership before the elections only theoretical. Furthermore, he established a well-oiled party machine and, due to his fundraising skills, the large financial debt incurred in the 1992 elections was eliminated. Most of the rank and file of the party united behind him under the assumption that he was electable, though David Levy and his followers, as well as Ariel Sharon, did not accept his leadership. (Both threatened at some time before the 1996 elections to run for prime minister.) Furthermore, the Likud was successful in the November 1993 municipal elections, winning the important races in Jerusalem and Tel Aviv.

Netanyahu represented a new breed of Israeli politician. A relatively young man who did not grow up in the party, he lacked political experience but displayed much talent in dealing with the media, an increasingly important element in Israeli politics. Furthermore, Netanyahu was a pragmatist with much tactical flexibility. He, more than others, represented and suited the Americanization of the Israeli electoral process.

Netanyahu's additional big test was the September 1993 Oslo agreement with the PLO, which he strongly opposed.[3] Yet several moderates in the Likud, for example MKs Meir Shitrit and Roni Milo, were willing to part with Gaza, reflecting the mood of many in the Likud who had centrist views.[4] Furthermore, Netanyahu and the hard-liners had difficulties presenting a reasonable alternative to the government policies. Indeed, Netanyahu failed to elicit widespread participation of Likud supporters in the anti-government demonstrations, which were dominated by the religious and the extreme right-wingers. Eventually, as described below, the Likud leadership accepted the Oslo accords and promised to minimize the damage by insisting on more stringent security arrangements and reciprocity in the implementation of the agreements with the Palestinian Authority (PA).

In the struggle between hawks and doves within the Likud, the latter had the upper hand. This was not out of character for the Likud, which displayed a capability for moderation in the past.[5] The catalyst for the renewed struggle was the Oslo agreements, which were opposed by most Likud MKs. Yet, Shitrit and Milo abstained when the September 1993 accord was brought to the Knesset for approval. As the accord was implemented (after the Cairo agreement of May 1994), a new situation emerged which was rooted in international agreements. This required a Likud response. A demand to restore the status quo ante was not seen as politically feasible. Furthermore, the departure from Gaza, in particular, was quite popular at home.

A first attempt to design a coherent response to the new developments was led by Zalman Shoval, ex-ambassador to the U.S. and a close advisor to Netanyahu. In the summer of 1994 he published a plan to limit the damage of the Oslo agreement without revoking it and accepting it as a fait accompli.[6] He urged a shortening of the interim period in which additional facts were created on the ground, and a prompt beginning of negotiations with the Palestinians on the final status issues. He suggested the establishment of "security zones" which will include most (not all!) of the Jewish settlements and which will be territorially contiguous to Israel. These zones will be under Israeli sovereignty, while the rest of the territory will be under Palestinian sovereignty. According to the Shoval plan, a Likud-led government will negotiate with a Palestinian leadership elected by a majority of the Palestinians in the territories (the plan was published before the Palestinian-held elections in the territories). Furthermore, Shoval recommended unilaterally implementing his plan, in the absence of Palestinian cooperation. Shoval deviated from the Likud's preferred functional approach[7] to tackling the Palestinian question, and basically advocated a repartition of Western Palestine between a Jewish and a Palestinian state. Shoval emphasized that his plan was a practical approach attempting to set up a bridge between the ideological commitment to the Land of Israel and reality. He based his plan upon political realism and security considerations, which he believed the Likud must adopt in order to regain power and to minimize the damage to Israel.

Shoval was much criticized in the Likud, but his views were accepted in a gradual fashion. A member of the party's central committee, Sinai Kehat, even went to visit Arafat in Gaza in May 1995. Then Netanyahu said Kehat did not represent the party, while some hard-liners demanded his dismissal from the party.[8] In contrast, MK Michael Eitan expressed the view that it would be mere stupidity to throw Kehat out of the party because the Likud needed every vote.[9] Kehat was only suspended from party activities for a year, but he represented a widespread attitude within the party.

Yet, Likud also harbored a militant faction that regarded the Oslo accord as a threat to Israel's survival. Sharon said in June 1995 that a Likud government will not respect the Oslo agreements.[10] Others advocated a harsh response to the emerging Oslo 2 agreement. For example, in July 1995, at a Likud Knesset faction meeting, MK Ron Nachman called for "paralyzing the country" and for not hesitating to break the law in the course of opposing the government. MK Eliyahu

Ben-Elissar justified taking unusual measures because at stake was the very existence of the State of Israel. MKs Yehoshua Matza and Uzi Landau also supported a militant path. In contrast, MKs Eitan, Shitrit, and Ovadia Eli warned against using unlawful methods in opposing the government. Netanyahu refused to accept the extreme suggestions and emphasized his commitment to the rules of the democratic game.[11] The issue was raised again within the executive bureau of the party (Lishka) and many in the Likud found it necessary to distance themselves from Nachman's views.[12] In August 1995, MK Dan Meridor, a leading Likud figure, told a Labor audience that the Oslo agreements were binding on any Israeli government though he did not recommend their implementation without the other side keeping its side of the bargain. He specified that the Palestinian Covenant had not yet been abrogated, and Arafat's calls for *Jihad* continued.[13] Even Sharon said that territorial compromise was better than the autonomy plan of the Labor government and recommended slowing down the negotiations.[14] He also called for speedily starting the negotiations on the final status issues, following an attempt to create a large consensus in the country.[15] In December 1995, Shitrit believed that a majority of the Likud MKs shared his views that the Oslo agreements could not be violated and a Likud government would negotiate with Arafat.[16]

The Likud's gradual adjustment to the emerging political realities in the West Bank and the adoption of moderate positions improved the party's standing, particularly among the centrist voters. Furthermore, Arafat had failed to convince the Israeli public that he was fulfilling his part of the bargain, particularly in the area of preventing terror. At the same time, the realization was slowly growing among Israeli public opinion that the Rabin-led government was inching its way toward a willingness to also part with the Golan Heights, a move which was far from popular. This improved the Likud's political situation among the voters, leading as well to the establishment of the Third Way party.[17] Vocal and tasteless demonstrations against Rabin by right-wing extremists reflected deeper opposition to government policies. Rabin's political discourse and offensive personal style estranged many in the electorate, particularly among those of the center of the Israeli political map. By the summer of 1995, Israelis generally endorsed the peace process, but were lending less support to the specific policies pursued by the Rabin government. The understandings reached with the PLO drew only about 30 percent support, with about 40 percent in opposition and the rest of the public undecided. Despite a slight erosion over time, close to two-thirds opposed any concessions on the Golan Heights even in exchange for a peace treaty, and opposition grew regarding the manner in which the government conducted the negotiations.[18] Indeed, by early 1995 Netanyahu started leading in the polls against Rabin.

Yet, Rabin's assassination on 4 November 1995 put the Likud at great disadvantage as Labor accused the Likud of contributing actively to a strident political atmosphere conducive to political assassination. Laborites blamed the assassination on the Likud and some, Leah Rabin, for example, singled out Netanyahu as responsible for the tragic events.[19] It seemed that right of center political positions on foreign policy and defense issues were discredited. Laborites attempted to capitalize on the situation and proposed early elections.

Yet, once again, under Netanyahu's leadership the Likud recuperated. The first good news was on 27 December 1995 with the decision by popular Maj. Gen. (res.) Yitzhak Mordechai, who had left the Israel Defense Forces (IDF) just a few months earlier, to join the Likud and run for a seat on its Knesset list in the upcoming Likud primaries. He was considered to be a good electoral asset. A similar step a day later by Gideon Ezra, former second in command in the General Security Services (GSS) and senior advisor to the Minister of Internal Security, also served the Likud in its campaign to rehabilitate its image as a respectable middle-of-the-road party. At the same time, an important member of Levy's new party, Prosper Azran, Mayor of Kiryat Shmona, returned to the Likud, following a public welcome back by Netanyahu.[20] Parallel attempts by concerned party activists (including Milo) to put Meridor at the helm of the party, when Netanyahu declined in the polls, did not really take off.[21]

Netanyahu also did his best to minimize the traditional fragmentation within the right-wing camp, which had been politically costly in the past.[22] With Peres convincingly leading the pack of prime ministerial candidates (Netanyahu, Levy, and Rafael Eitan of Tzomet) by getting close to 45 percent support, according to various polls, there was a chance for Peres to win in the first round of voting. Therefore, Netanyahu decided to maximize his chances to be elected premier by removing from the race two candidates who could deny him crucial votes in the first round: Eitan and Levy. Sharon, who wanted to secure his position as one of the Likud's leaders, succeeded in delivering Eitan by mid-February. Eitan's party, Tzomet, seemed not to excel electorally at that time and capitalized on its nuisance value versus Netanyahu to join the Likud list to the Knesset and to secure seven "safe" seats for its own Knesset candidates. The same rationale applied also for Levy and his newly founded Gesher party ¾ basically an ethnic (Sephardi) splinter of the Likud. Sharon was again the mediator and played the role of "unifier" of the "national camp." On 12 March 1996, the agreement between the Likud, Gesher, and Tzomet was finally signed, and all declared that they put the national interest above their narrow interests.[23] The agreement was useful to Netanyahu, but less so to Likud Knesset aspirants who saw 14 "safe" seats on the Likud list handed to Tzomet and Gesher. Likud MK Shitrit criticized the exorbitant price paid to the two partners. He pointed out that it greatly reduced the chances of some devoted Likud MKs, as well as representatives of the "young guard" and the Druse community to be in the Knesset.[24] The displeasure with the agreement among the Likud rank and file was widespread but contained. All realized that under the new electoral system winning the premiership was crucial for the prospects of dividing the spoils after the elections. Indeed, the party's central committee approved the deal on 19 March, with Begin opposing it in splendid isolation. The Likud, which from its beginning has been a "composite party,"[25] had, in the past, several times ceded a part of its parliamentary representation in the course of making inter-party alliances.[26] The close margin of Netanyahu's victory obviously vindicated his decision to pay a high price to bring Eitan and Levy under his fold.

After the murder of Yitzhak Rabin, there was an even greater necessity to distance the Likud and its leadership from the far right. Yet the electoral alliance with Tzomet somewhat undermined the efforts of the Likud to portray itself as a centrist party. Roni Milo, the Likud Mayor of Tel Aviv, reminded his colleagues of the political necessity to be situated in the center of the political continuum and suggested giving greater prominence to centrists such as Meridor and Shitrit.[27] Netanyahu ultimately embraced the positions of the moderate wing in his party.

By February 1996, Netanyahu felt confident enough to launch a counter-attack. The first opportunity was the statement made by Labor's General Secretary about the need to change the party's platform to allow the possibility of ceding part of the Jordan Rift Valley and the settlements in that area – a clear indication of the continuous leftward move of Labor,[28] but also a political blunder, for which he was criticized by his colleagues. Netanyahu, accompanied by Eitan of Tzomet, went on a tour of the settlements in that area and committed his party to table a motion on extending Israeli sovereignty to those settlements. On the same occasion, Netanyahu also declared that under certain conditions (the annulment of the Palestinian Covenant and the cessation of terrorism) he would be ready to negotiate with the Palestinian Authority over the pending final status issues.[29] He projected a pragmatist image as one willing to accept the facts created by the peace process.

A harsher attack on Labor was launched in mid-February: all over the country posters read "Peres will divide Jerusalem." The Likud was smart in emphasizing the Jerusalem issue, a topic very dear to Israeli hearts. By stressing Jerusalem, the Likud associated itself with a political symbol almost all Israelis closely identified with, strengthening the centrist image of the party and its candidate, and at the same time depriving Labor of an important political symbol. Labor initially ignored the challenge, hoping it would not stick, but eventually it was forced into a defensive posture of protesting the "baseless" accusations.

Netanyahu also clarified his analysis of the situation. In a programmatic speech to the Israeli Council for Foreign Affairs on 21 April, he criticized the Oslo agreements but added: "We cannot ignore the facts. We will not return to the six cities that were turned over to the Palestinians. A Likud government will recognize the facts that were created by the Oslo agreements, but will try to minimize the inherent dangers."[30] He pledged to continue to maintain close contacts with the Palestinian Authority on routine matters. Progress on negotiating the final status issues would be dependent, however, upon greater efforts to prevent terror, incitement to terror, and anti-Israeli propaganda, as well as to amend the Palestinian Covenant. Furthermore, he pledged to close Orient House, which had become the seat of Palestinian government in Jerusalem. Netanyahu was also tough with the Syrians. In his opinion, it was not moral to return to Syria a piece of territory – a great military asset – which it lost in an act of aggression. Furthermore, Syria was not yet ripe for an agreement with Israel.[31]

Despite lagging 16 percent in the polls, the Likud, as the main opposition party, agreed in February 1996 to Labor's suggestion to hold elections in May 1996 instead of November.[32] The party held primaries on 26 March 1996 and completed its preparations for the election campaign. The primaries catapulted Yitzhak Mordechai to prominence in the party when he captured first place after Netanyahu (who did not have to run again), followed by Sharon and Katzav. Meridor, the tacit competitor of Netanyahu, was pushed to the sixth slot (with rumors about Netanyahu's people working against Meridor), while the two other party "princes," Begin and Ehud Olmert, preceded him. Few new faces won safe seats, with Gideon Ezra the most prominent (number 12).

THE ELECTORAL CAMPAIGN

It was crucial for the Likud to situate itself at the center of the political spectrum in order to win the elections. Contrary to Likud and Labor propaganda, the country is not divided into the "national camp" and the "peace camp." The correct formula to describe the Israeli public is 30-40-30. A large segment of the adult population is centrist, with only 30 percent leaning to the right or the left.[33] Under such political circumstances, a centrist strategy is the rational choice, particularly in a two-candidate race.[34] This was well understood in the past by the Likud leadership[35] and was used again in 1996. By March, the race between the two largest parties had become much closer, for a number of reasons: the effect of the Rabin assassination on the Israeli public had already become weakened by January and most Israelis had returned by then to their pre-murder positions;[36] the Likud was successful in embarrassing Labor on the issues of the Jordan Valley and Jerusalem; a wave of terrorist attacks at the end of February and the beginning of March, which left scores of Israeli dead and wounded, underscored the internal security problems associated with the Oslo process – issues the Likud had been consistently focusing upon; the dignified reaction of Netanyahu and the Likud to the terrorist attacks (they refrained from protest demonstrations and from attacking the government); completion of the unification of the so-called "national camp"; and moderate signals on the peace process, particularly statements indicating a coming to terms with the Oslo agreements.

The terrorist attacks of February and March were indeed a turning point in the campaign and well served the Likud centrist strategy. On the one hand, the events underscored the security risks of the partnership with Arafat, while they allowed Netanyahu to appear statesman-like. In contrast to his reaction to previous incidents, Netanyahu did not appear at the site where the bombs exploded and refrained from criticizing the government. Following the first suicide bomb attack in Jerusalem, he stressed that on such a tragic day political polemics were inappropriate, and he called for national unity. He also ordered Likud activists not to demonstrate against the government.[37] Olmert, the mayor of Jerusalem, also called for maximum restraint and to refrain from making political use of the terrorist attacks.[38] This line of restraint was maintained even after two subsequent additional suicide bombings, though hard-liners such as Landau, Nachman, and Mena criticized Netanyahu for not calling on Peres to resign.[39] The terrorist acts at the end of February and the negotiations to bring Levy back to the Likud put an end to Peres's large lead in the polls.[40]

An important step in the centrist strategy was the 25 April 1996 decision to accept the Oslo agreements. After many deliberations, a Likud-Tzomet-Gesher high-level special committee officially adopted a new party platform that committed a future Likud-led government to respect international agreements.[41] The document also accepted "the facts created by the various agreements" (it did not mention the Oslo agreements by name) and expressed a willingness to negotiate with the Palestinian Authority on a permanent agreement. The document demanded that the Palestinian Authority fully implement its commitments, in particular to amend the clauses in the Palestinian Covenant calling for the destruction of Israel and to take steps to prevent terrorism against Israel. The document also restated Israel's sovereignty in the Golan Heights. Meridor, Olmert, Katzav, Levy, Mordechai, and Arens supported the new language used. Begin was the only committee member who strongly opposed the new document, while Sharon demanded the stipulation of additional conditions for negotiating with the Palestinians.[42]

This document was an additional indication of the moderation that had taken place in the Likud. It was clearly less ideological, and its commitment to the tenets of Greater Israel were gradually eroded. A security-based discourse to a large extent replaced ideological hawkishness.[43] The desire to return to power was an additional impetus for projecting a moderate image.

The Likud's slogan for the election campaign, disclosed on 7 April 1996, was "Netanyahu – We Make a Safe Peace," which underscored the Likud commitment to peace and undermined Labor's claim for exclusivity in peace-making. At the same time, it stressed an insistence on securing peace without compromising Israel's security, which was in contrast to the agreements reached by Labor with the Palestinians, and the one negotiated with Syria, which entailed a full withdrawal from the Golan Heights.[44] The slogan appealed to Israeli voters because it catered for their thirst for peace, as well as their traditional penchant for security. It was particularly suitable for the undecided voters at the center of the Israeli political map who wanted the peace process to continue but were apprehensive about the security implications of the concessions made by the Labor-led government. Another slogan, adopted after the katyusha attacks on northern Israel, declared: "There is no security. There is no peace. There is no reason for voting Peres." The Likud hammered its message that Labor's apparent political achievements in the peace process were at the expense of security. Peres's defense policy was portrayed as a total failure.

The situation in Lebanon provided good political ammunition for the Likud. There, the Hizbullah conducted a war of attrition against the Israeli military presence in the security zone in Southern Lebanon and that of its Lebanese ally, and occasionally fired katyusha rockets at Israeli urban and rural centers along the northern border. The Labor-led government preferred to limit its military response in order to prevent a costly escalation and so as not to spoil the chances for reaching an agreement with Syria. The opposition criticized this policy of restraint. MK Ben-Elissar claimed that the hesitant policy of Peres was counterproductive, while MK Landau called upon Peres to regard Syria as an enemy and as the culprit for the attacks in Lebanon.[45] The Peres government, under pressure from public opinion to act following Hizbullah's firing of katyushas on the north, went along half-heartedly with IDF recommendations for a military response in mid-April. The modus operandi of Operation *Grapes of Wrath* included several spectacular precision air attacks on targets in and near Beirut and the 100,000 civilians leave their homes. The Peres government believed that pressure on the Lebanese government from refugees and the economic price extracted by Israeli bombing would engender greater Syrian constraints on Hizbullah's freedom of action. Yet, this was hardly the stuff to move the person in control of Lebanon – Syria's Hafez Assad. Operation *Grapes of Wrath* ended with understandings that were hardly better than the previous ones, that again left Assad the final arbiter of what Hizbullah may or may not do in Lebanon.

The failure of Operation *Grapes of Wrath* was evident not only to strategic analysts. Most Israelis did not see the government's military response in Lebanon as a success: only 31 percent of the public were pleased with the results, 36 percent were displeased, while 25 percent had mixed feelings.[46] Peres' slip of the tongue that the understandings would hold until the elections further harmed Labor. Indeed, the Likud capitalized on the fiasco to score points against Peres and his government, underscoring their ineptitude in defense matters. Netanyahu expressed his disappointment with the failure of the government to reach its goals, despite the support it received from the opposition. The fact that the understandings with the Hizballah did not forbid attacks on IDF soldiers was pointed out as particularly disturbing.[47] Sharon even regarded the outcome of the operation as a surrender agreement.[48] Subsequently, adds in the press read: "Peres failed also in Lebanon; after two weeks of fighting, 700 katyushas and the paralysis of the North, nothing changed. Peres relies again on Assad to restrain the terrorists, the North is again hostage of the Hizbullah, and the hands of the IDF are tied by the 'understandings,' as if 66 Israeli soldiers have not been killed since the 'understandings' of Operation *Accountability* (1993)!"

Netanyahu campaigners placed extreme importance on the TV campaign. Their job was to sell to the public a young candidate with a rather short political resume, only 9 years in politics, and to convince them that he was to be entrusted with the future of the country. In the televised messages, Netanyahu appeared in an "oval office" setting to enhance his image as a statesman. This was supposed to counter the anticipated Labor message that "Bibi is not fit."

At the same time, the Likud decided to repeat again and again a few short messages on the dangers of Labor staying in power: Jerusalem will be divided, a Palestinian state will be established, and there will be a withdrawal from the Golan Heights. All three scenarios were opposed by more than two-thirds of Israelis. Arthur Finkelstein, an American campaign strategy consultant hired by Netanyahu, devised an approach based upon clear, short, and repetitive messages.[49] Some within the Likud objected, claiming that political persuasion is different from selling a product in the market. Motti Morell, an Israeli professional advertiser for the Likud's campaign, felt very much at ease with this strategy: "It is not a matter of having nothing else, but we have limited time until election day. We need to get a message across and we could not do it if we tried to produce a new message every day."[50] Likud research also showed, according to Morell, that consistency is very important and that the repetitions were particularly effective with the floating vote.[51] Moreover, in his opinion, the Likud list, which included several popular figures among the undecided, such as Meridor, and candidates with a solid security background, made his job easier.[52] MK Limor Livnat, one of the leaders of the election campaign, also felt that the campaign was focused and there was no reason for making any changes in its middle.[53] Yet, the centrist line of the Likud campaign antagonized many hard-line Likudniks. For example, Gil Samsonov, former spokesman for the party, resigned from campaign headquarters because he felt the campaign lacked clarity and "does not reflect the traditional Likud positions."[54] He also complained that attacks on Peres should have been more aggressive, and that figures such as Sharon and Rafael Eitan should have been given more publicity.[55] Likud hard-liners complained that the advertisement campaign ignored the old-time supporters.[56] MK Dov Shilansky, a member of the Betar old guard, suggested: "We have to call home all the Betar graduates and bring back the ideology to the Likud."[57] Paradoxically, Likud emphasized its commitment to peace, while Labor stressed its security credentials. This was part of the centrist strategy of both parties.

A most important part of the televised campaign was the Netanyahu–Peres debate, which was viewed by as many as 70 percent of the voters according to some estimates. Netanyahu was in his element and did better than his opponent. According to a Labor-commissioned study inquiring into the electoral loss, Labor lost 60,000 votes that evening. Netanyahu succeeded in matching Peres on three dimensions: the better candidate for premiership, credibility, and providing hope.[58] Peres admitted that he was "not at his best," blaming also the lighting and the lack of appropriate make-up.[59]

Immediately after the debate, Yossi Sarid, the newly appointed leader of Meretz, pointed out that what Peres was unwilling to say in the debate – the establishment of a Palestinian state, a full withdrawal from the Golan, and an arrangement to satisfy the Palestinians in Jerusalem – were the positions of his own party, which would eventually be adopted by Labor. Sarid's statement underscored the ideological closeness of Labor to Meretz, hampering Labor's effort to capture the center and further undermining Peres's credibility, an issue which has haunted him for the past two decades.

Meridor, the most credible Likud leader, had stated, "If we want to know what Labor will really do in the future, we have only to listen to what Meretz is saying today – this is what happened in 1992."[60] At the end of the TV ad campaign, the Likud brought out its archives of anti-Peres quotations. The ads featured negative comments on Peres by all of Israel's prime ministers, with the exception of Rabin in order not to invite a backlash.

Unexpected support for the Likud came from two famous generals, never identified before with the party. Former IDF Chief of Staff Lt. Gen. (res.) Dan Shomron, who had left the Third Way in disappointment, stated publicly that he would vote for Netanyahu because the positions adopted by Labor were too dovish and might bring about a full Israeli withdrawal to the 1967 border in the West Bank and the Golan Heights. Shomron expressed his preference for Netanyahu's team to conduct the negotiations with the Arabs.[61] Maj. Gen. (res.) Avraham (Abrasha) Tamir, a moderate, similarly came out in favor of Netanyahu because of Labor's extravagant concessions to the Palestinians.

Meretz supporter Motti Ashkenazi, leader of the protest movement against the Golda Meir government in 1974, expressed his intention to vote for the Likud leader.[62] Similarly, Professor Yehoshua Porat, a distinguished scholar of the Palestinians, and also a Meretz activist, publicly switched to supporting Netanyahu. He claimed that the Palestinian National Council (PNC) convened by Arafat did not cancel the clauses in the Palestinian Covenant calling for the destruction of the Jewish state, as it claimed, causing a political as well as an academic scandal. In his opinion, the PNC just decided to make unspecified amendments in the future. Furthermore, Porat accused Peres of deceit because the language of the Palestinian National Council resolution was coordinated with the Labor-led government. According to a Labor study, Porat's appeal was very large and over half the voters tended to accept his version of what happened at the PNC.[63] This seriously undermined the government's claims that Arafat was making good on his promises.

Netanyahu also had to prove that he was not anathema in the Arab world as Labor tried to portray him. He stated in the beginning of April that the Likud was engaged in a dialogue with several Arab countries, even some without diplomatic relations with Israel.[64] Jordan refused to join in the international production to reelect Peres because of Labor's pro-Palestinian orientation (deleting the article against a Palestinian state from the party platform and allowing the PLO to be active in Jerusalem). King Hussein refused to accept a visit by Peres to Amman. At the same time, the Jordanian ambassador to Israel, Omar Rifai, met with Netanyahu two weeks before the elections and stated that his country would cooperate with any elected government in Israel.[65]

An important sector of the Israeli population which was wooed by both Labor and the Likud, was the ultra-Orthodox (about 8 percent of the electorate), a well-disciplined group with a high voter turnout.[66] Netanyahu and Sharon, in particular, made considerable efforts to convince leading haredi rabbis to endorse the Likud candidate for prime minister. Both emphasized their commitment to the Jewish tradition and the need to strengthen Jewish education in the state's educational system. Netanyahu hired special advisors to make inroads into the haredi community, and special advertising was devised for this sector.[67]

Generally, the haredim were disposed to vote for Netanyahu, as the new system allowed them to split their votes for the prime minister and for their favored sectorial party. During the four years before the elections the haredim watched as Labor moved closer to Meretz, which regularly displayed its anti-religious reflex. Furthermore, Yael Dayan, Avraham Burg and Dalia Itzik, who were perceived as haredi-bashers, gained stature in the party, while Shimon Shitrit, the Labor Minister for Religious Affairs, who tried to reorganize his ministry, threatened their interests. The recurring sentiment among haredim was that whereas Labor looked at the haredim as primitives slowing the march into the next millennium, the Likud looked upon them as valuable – if at times pesty – bearers of the Jewish torch. The haredi community has gradually become more nationalistic, a subject beyond the scope of this essay, and it was natural for the haredim to support a politician with right-wing credentials like Netanyahu.

The rabbinical and political leadership generally shared these sentiments but acted more carefully. As Labor led the race, they preferred not to burn their bridges. Also, they waited for the two parties to make as many promises as possible during the campaign. Only the week before the elections was a decision made regarding whom to support. The call on May 26, 1996 by Agudat Israel's Council of Torah Sages for its followers to cast a prime-ministerial vote "for the candidate whose party is more likely to work in the spirit of religion and Jewish tradition" may be open to interpretation, but in the haredi street it meant Netanyahu.[68] The political leaders of Agudat Israel, Meir Porush and Moshe Zeev Feldman, indeed admitted in public that this was the intention of their rabbis.[69] The revered Rabbi Eliezer Shach was explicit in his support for Netanyahu, which was published on the first page of the Degel Hatorah newspaper *Yated Neeman*. Another important event in the haredi sector during the same week was connected to the Lubavitch sect. Following a meeting with Netanyahu and Ariel Sharon, the Rabbinical Committee of the large Lubavitch hassidic group decided to instruct its members to enlist in the Netanyahu camp. The rabbis were convinced by the two that the close race could be decided by the Arab vote, and this outcome would endanger the Jewish people and the Land of Israel.[70] The Lubavitchers plastered the country with the slogan "Netanyahu is Good for the Jews" and added tremendous elan and organizational skills to the final stages of Netanyahu's campaign.

In the May 1996 elections, the Likud was also well organized, the contribution of Netanyahu's proteges. Furthermore, Gen. Mordechai was put in charge of organizing the campaign. He emphasized the importance of bringing Likud supporters out to vote. He divided the country into regions and put a Likud MK in charge of each region on election day, with thousands of cars at their disposal.[71] The settlers in the Israeli-ruled territories put at the service of Netanyahu all their logistical infrastructure and thousands of volunteers for this election. For example, in contrast to past elections, the Likud was represented at all polling stations (about 6,700), according to MK Uzi Landau who was in charge of the election day effort.[72] Having representatives in the polling station committees or observers for the actual counting of the ballots could turn out to be much more of a deciding factor than lofty ideas and vital issues, particularly in a very close race. MK Landau said: "We reckon if we lose even one vote in each station because of non-kosher practices, then we are cheated out of thousands of votes which could prove pivotal. Each vote counts, which is why we have to get our people to the polls or we have done nothing in all the weeks of campaigning."[73]

Another example of the Likud's organizational capability was its car fleet. On election day Likud lent 5,000 cars with drivers to Sharansky's party (Yisrael Ba'Aliya). Most of the drivers who took the new immigrants to the polls were settlers from the territories who engaged in last minute campaigning for Netanyahu.[74] The immigrants from the former Soviet Union had a record of casting a protest vote against the incumbent government. This worked against the Likud in 1992 but their continuing frustrations with adjustment to Israeli society assisted the opposition party in 1996 – the Likud.

Parallel to their own organizational efforts, the Likud planned and executed a campaign to deny Labor the organizational assets of the Histadrut and government companies. The Histadrut had already been weakened by the policies of former General Secretary Haim Ramon, who came back to Labor after Rabin's assassination; then Likud-hired lawyers bombarded the Attorney General with requests for clear guidelines during the elections for Histadrut and government-related companies. These efforts helped to limit pro-Labor involvement and to create an atmosphere of caution among Labor supporters in positions of importance within the government-related hierarchy. MK Limor Livnat orchestrated these efforts.[75]

Despite Labor's lead in the polls, the Likud won the elections. It made few mistakes. Palestinian terrorism and Hizballah katyushas made the Peres motto about a "New Middle East" look unreassuring on defense matters – an issue dear to most Israelis. The Likud also ran an efficient advertising campaign and was well organized on election day. The victory by only a very small margin indicates that fortune was on Netanyahu's side.

FORMING A COALITION AND GOVERNING

Netanyahu's victory speech before Likud activists in Jerusalem was a well planned and executed performance. The affair started with the consensual song "Jerusalem of Gold," sung by its original presenter in 1967, Shuli Natan. Netanyahu refrained from mentioning any controversial issues and used formulations that everybody could live with. He also emphasized that he was to become prime minister of all Israeli citizens, Jews and Arabs, secular and religious, old-timers and newcomers. His first tour as prime minister-elect included "red" (pro-Labor) Haifa and the Arab town of Taibe, underscoring his message of reconciliation and again proving his rhetorical and theatrical skills.

Forming a coalition, however, required more than rhetoric. The struggle for spoils required political experience, maneuvering and negotiating skills, and, above all, a strategic plan. It is not clear at all that Netanyahu's negotiating team, headed by the designated director-general of the prime minister's office, Avigdor Lieberman, were up to the test.

The new law for the direct election of the prime minister was perceived as giving the prime minister almost presidential powers. The goal was indeed to make him less dependent upon his coalition partners, so that he would not constantly have to give in to their demands for portfolios, money, and special legislation. Under the new system, the small parties had no other choice but to join a Likud-led government and could not threaten to support another candidate for premiership. In theory, this was the only game in town and their bargaining position was therefore reduced. Furthermore, parties such as NRP, SHAS, Third Way, and Yisrael Ba'Aliya were unlikely to risk their unexpected electoral gains by not cooperating with Netanyahu. Nevertheless, the Likud negotiating team gave away important ministerial portfolios such as Construction, Internal Security, and Welfare. The Likud also allowed its coalition partners to chair important parliamentary committees, such as Finance, Knesset, Education, Internal Affairs, and Law and Constitution. In the influential Finance Committee, the Likud had only one member. The NRP was quite surprised at Netanyahu's generosity, which resulted in initially receiving three and a half portfolios (Education, Transportation, Energy, and rotation in the Ministry of Religious Affairs with SHAS).[76] Lieberman explained that the Likud had a moral duty to reward the NRP because it was a true political ally and the only coalition partner that called upon its voters to support Netanyahu. Furthermore, the strategy was to please the coalition partners in order to develop trust.[77] The self-imposed deadline of 17 June for completing coalition-making was also a mistake because it enhanced the bargaining position of the potential coalition partners. Lieberman's counter argument was that the political and economic situation demanded immediate government attention.[78] Furthermore, the fact that Netanyahu had garnered 11 seats in the government for his own party (out of the 18 permitted by the new system) when it represented less than half of the coalition, showed that the coalition formation was not a total failure. In addition, the three most important portfolios in addition to the premiership – Defense, Finance, and Foreign Affairs – remained in the Likud's possession.

At the same time, the senior figures of the Likud, such as Meridor, Katzav, Sharon, and Begin, were kept in the dark during the coalition negotiations, quite an embarrassing situation from their point of view. When they were finally offered cabinet positions, the choices were ones unacceptable to them. Internal party pressure resulted in Meridor getting the Finance Ministry, which Netanyahu had wanted to give to Bank of Israel Governor Yaakov Frankel, and provoked a frantic effort to find a ministry for Sharon. Though all eventually joined the cabinet, the manner in which they were treated constituted an affront to them and was perceived as a callous attempt by Netanyahu to eliminate all potential contenders for the premiership in the year 2000. Offending competitors, but allowing them to build foci of power by being cabinet members, is not smart politics.

David Levy, who became foreign minister as he desired, did not hesitate to embarrass Netanyahu when he initially refused to join the government without Sharon present inside, and two weeks later threatened to resign from the government if the promise to bring in Sharon was not realized, just before Netanyahu's first trip to the United States (8 July 1996). The emerging non-ideological alliance between Levy and Sharon did not bode well for Netanyahu in the future.

Members of the Likud's parliamentary faction also watched in dismay as their leader generously dispensed the top Knesset positions to coalition partners, leaving his Likud allies in the cold. One Likud MK was reported to have complained: "Netanyahu is in power, but the Likud is in opposition."[79] For example, Likud MK Shaul Amor was at one point promised the Labor and Social Affairs portfolio by Netanyahu. When that was given to SHAS, he hoped for Netanyahu's support as Knesset Speaker instead. Eliyahu Ben-Elissar, who almost quit the Likud with Levy when he defected but opted in the end to stick with Netanyahu, similarly hoped that he would be rewarded for his loyalty with the Speaker's post. But Netanyahu did not even come to the election for Speaker. He had requested a postponement of the Speaker's election until after the introduction of the so-called Norwegian law, which would require ministers to vacate their Knesset seats, thereby opening a place for his protege Ovadia Eli, who was on the Likud list to the Knesset. More seeds of his faction's revolt against Netanyahu were sown as the Likudniks rejected his request to postpone the Speaker's election. Neither Amor nor Ben-Elissar were elected, and Netanyahu's list of "election victims" kept growing. Amor's wife fumed indignantly: "We brought Netanyahu to power and this is the thanks we get for it. Netanyahu stuck a rusty knife in our heart and twisted it. Well, we will see who is prime minister in four years' time."[80]

In another act of defiance, Knesset Foreign Affairs and Defense Committee Chairman Uzi Landau teamed up with Labor's Yossi Beilin to submit a bill to cancel direct elections for prime minister. Netanyahu made it clear to Landau that he would vigorously oppose any such amendment.

Substantively, the new government projected a tough but centrist image on the peace process. Domestically, it advocated a free market approach and a vague commitment to the status quo in religious affairs. The Likud refused to accept the Third Way's demand to incorporate into the new government's platform a commitment to pass a law which would require a special majority in the Knesset to make any changes in the status of Jerusalem and the Golan Heights.[81] It also rejected an NRP demand to extend Israeli law to the settlements in Greater Jerusalem and to include in the government platform a clause on the right of Jews to pray on the Temple Mount.[82] The platform included a clause expressing willingness to negotiate a final settlement with the Palestinian Authority, though it stated its opposition to a Palestinian state and the "right of return" for Palestinians to territories west of the Jordan River. The government welcomed negotiations with Syria with no preconditions, though it stated that the maintenance of Israeli sovereignty in the Golan is an element in any settlement. On religious affairs, the Likud refused to accept the NRP demand to return to the 1992 status quo. Generally, the language used in the government policy guidelines which were brought to the Knesset was not offensive and kept all options open.[83]

In foreign policy, Netanyahu immediately opened up a channel of communication with the Palestinians and other Arab actors. His first trip to the United States as prime minister, in July, was a great success. He capitalized on his intimate knowledge of American ways and his public relations skills to convey the image of a tough but reasonable person. The proximity of the American elections (November 1996) was obviously helpful in granting Netanyahu a respite. Some Arab leaders took their cue from Washington's patient wait-and-see attitude toward the Likud-led government. Indeed, Netanyahu's meeting with President Mubarak also went well, to be followed by an Arafat–Levy meeting that also projected a business-as-usual atmosphere. The fears of an immediate catastrophe in Arab–Israeli relations did not materialize. It was only later on that tensions were generated by delays in implementing the IDF redeployment in Hebron and ill-orchestrated policies toward Palestinians and other Arab actors.

At home, Netanyahu succeeded in convincing his cabinet to approve NIS 4.9 billion in budget cuts. It remains to be seen what form these cuts will take. On that occasion, Netanyahu pledged again that Israel will embark on a sweeping liberalization policy, which will include privatization and deregulation alongside the necessary budget-cutting. The Histadrut labor federation called for a general strike to protest the economic measures of the government, signalling to the Likud-led government that the domestic front would be less understanding than Washington.

CONCLUSION

Academics and other pundits will undoubtedly try to learn the "lessons" of the 1996 elections. The truth is that not too much should be read into the election results. The personal context between two men of widely different ages and divergent world views ended almost in a tie. Netanyahu won a razor-thin victory. Despite the fact that it was the first time the public voted on the peace process of the past few years, and that the Peres vision of a new Middle East was not persuasive, the 1996 election results were not a referendum on Israel's soul and road to the future, but represented more of a pendulum effect in Israeli politics. While most parties expressed varying degrees of support for the peace process, Netanyahu and the Likud received a mandate to continue the process, albeit at a slower pace and with greater caution.

Many regarded Netanyahu as a light-weight player. Obviously, as far as the elections were concerned, he was underestimated. He proved that he had the stamina to win a difficult political battle. He successfully fought the media who were cynical about his past and derisive in portraying his policies. He may have made mistakes on the way to taking power, but he proved his pragmatic mettle, as well as demonstrating a healthy ruthlessness which is vital for survival in the political jungle. He definitely strengthened his image as a "winner." He may well find out down the road that some of his decisions, which alienated many of his colleagues in the party, might eventually become costly. Though Netanyahu seems to assume that the emerging political system resembles the American presidential one, with a great concentration of power and considerable latitude for the president, this may not be the case yet in Israel. If he safely passes the hurdles ahead of him, he will still need a political machine to help him be reelected in the year 2000. It remains to be seen whose loyalties he will cultivate and how helpful that may be in his drive for reelection as prime minister.

NOTES

1. For an analysis of the 1992 failure, see Mordechai Nisan, "The Likud: The Delusion of Power," in Daniel J. Elazar and Shmuel Sandler, eds, *Israel at the Polls, 1992* (Lanham, MD, 1995), pp.45–65. For other works about the Likud, see Giora Goldberg, "The Struggle for Legitimacy – Herut's Road from Opposition to Power," in Stuart A. Cohen and Eliezer Don-Yehiya, eds, *Conflict and Consensus in Jewish Political Life* (Ramat Gan, 1986), pp.146–69; Benjamin Akzin, "Likud," in Howard R. Penniman, ed., *Israel at the Polls, The Knesset Elections of 1977* (Washington, D.C., 1979), pp.91–114; Ilan Peleg, "The Legacy of Begin and Beginism for the Israeli Political System," in Gregory S. Mahler, ed., *Israel after Begin* (Albany, 1990), pp.19–50. For a highly critical view of the Likud, see Colin Schindler, *Israel, Likud and the Zionist Dream* (London, 1995).
2. Netanyahu insinuated in a dramatic appearance on Israeli TV that David Levy tried to blackmail him by publicizing an extra-marital affair of his.
3. For Netanyahu's political views, see his *Makom Tachat Hashemesh* (A Place Under the Sun) (Tel Aviv, 1995).
4. For Likud doves, see Giora Goldberg, Gad Barzilai, and Efraim Inbar, "The Impact of Intercommunal Conflict: The Intifada and Israeli Public Opinion," *Policy Studies*, 43 (Jerusalem: Leonard Davis Institute for International Relations, Hebrew University, 1991).
5. Efraim Inbar and Giora Goldberg, "Is Israel's Elite Becoming More Hawkish?," *International Journal*, Vol.45, No.3 (Summer 1990): 631–60.
6. A revised version of the plan was published as "Security Zones in Judea, Samaria and Gaza – How to Accept Oslo and to Survive," *Nativ*, Vol.8 (July 1995): 30–35.
7. For the differences between the functional approach and the territorial compromise approach, see Efraim Inbar, "War and Peace, Fears and Hopes in the 1988 Elections," in Daniel J. Elazar and Shmuel Sandler, eds, *Who's the Boss in Israel. Israel at the Polls, 1988–90* (Detroit, 1992), pp.193–211.
8. *Ha-aretz*, May 2, 1995, p.A3.
9. Ibid., May 16, 1995, p.B3.
10. Raanan R. Lurie, "Interview with Ariel Sharon," *Middle East Quarterly* (June 1995): p.68.
11. *Ha-aretz*, July 6, 1995, p.A3.
12. Ibid., July 7 1995, p.A4.
13. Ibid., August 15, 1995, p.A4.
14. *Israel TV*, 23 August 1995.
15. *Ha-aretz*, August 24, 1995.
16. Ibid., December 1, 1995, p.B2.
17. See chapter by Etta Bick in this volume.
18. This section relies on data collected for the Project on Public Opinion and National Security of the Begin-Sadat (BESA) Center for Strategic Studies at Bar-Ilan University.
19. For a right-wing view of the Labor campaign against the Likud, see Yoram Hazony, "From Arlosoroff to Rabin – The Incitement and the Lesson," *Nativ* (January 1996): 53–5.
20. This was Azran's precondition for rejoining Likud. He held several discussions with

Netanyahu before returning to the party and running for a Knesset seat in the Likud primaries.

21. For Milo's attempts, see *Ha-aretz*, February 25, 1996, p.A1.
22. For this fragmentation, see Giora Goldberg, "The Right Toward the 1996 Elections," *Nativ* (January 1996): 47–8.
23. *Ha-aretz*, March 13, 1996, p.A2.
24. Ibid.
25. For this term, see Akzin, "Likud," p.91.
26. Goldberg, "The Struggle for Legitimacy," pp.147–8.
27. *Ha-aretz*, March 24, 1996, p.A5. He mentioned also Maj. Gen. (res.) Yossi Peled.
28. For Labor's leftward shift see Efraim Inbar, *War and Peace in Israeli Politics. Labor Party Positions on National Security* (Boulder, 1991).
29. *Ha-aretz*, February 16, 1996, p.A3.
30. Ibid., April 22, 1996, p.A7.
31. Ibid.
32. For Labor's electoral behavior, see Giora Goldberg's contribution in this volume.
33. See Asher Arian, *Security Threatened. Surveying Israeli Opinion on Peace and War* (Cambridge, 1995).
34. Anthony Downs, *An Economic Theory of Democracy* (New York, 1957).
35. Moshe Arens, *Milchama Ve-shalom Ba-mizrach Ha-tichon, 1988–1992* (War and Peace in the Middle East, 1988–1992) (Tel Aviv, 1995), pp.12, 14–15.
36. See the review of the polling results of the Tami Steinmetz Center for Peace Studies at Tel Aviv University in *Ha-aretz*, February 5, 1996, p.B3.
37. Ibid., February 25, 1996, p.A8.
38. Ibid.
39. *Ma'ariv*, Shabbat supplement, March 8, 1996, p.10.
40. For an analysis, see the Gallup Poll analysis, Ibid., Shabbat supplement, March 1, 1996, pp.4–5.
41. For the Hebrew text, see *An Action Plan for the 14th Knesset, Elections 1996*.
42. *Ma'ariv*, April 26, 1996, p.5.
43. See Efraim Ben-Zadok and Giora Goldberg, "Gush Emunim and the West Bank," *Middle Eastern Studies* 22 (January 1986): 52–73; and Inbar and Goldberg, "Is Israel's Elite Becoming More Hawkish?"
44. For the Labor-led government's negotiations with Syria, see Efraim Inbar, "Israeli Negotiations with Syria," *Israel Affairs*, Vol.1, No.4 (Summer 1995): 89–100.
45. *Ha-aretz*, March 22, 1996, p.A3.
46. Gallup and Maariv Poll, *Ma'ariv*, May 3, 1996, p.1.
47. *Ha-aretz*, April 28, 1996, p.A7.
48. Ibid.
49. Bina Barzel, "Mysterious Arthur," *Yediot Aharonot*, Shabbat supplement, May 17, 1996, p.9.
50. *Jerusalem Post*, May 17, 1996, p.10.
51. *Ma'ariv*, May 14, 1996, p.10.
52. *Ha-aretz*, 28 March 1996, p.B3.
53. Ibid., May 12, 1996, p.A3.
54. *Ha-aretz*, April 11, 1996, p.A6.
55. Ibid.
56. *Ma'ariv*, May 14, 1996, p.10.
57. Ibid., Shabbat supplement, May 31, 1996, p.2.
58. *Ha-aretz*, August 2, 1996, pp.A1, A6.
59. *Ma'ariv*, Shabbat supplement, July 5, 1996, p.10.
60. *Ha-aretz*, April 8, 1996, p.A4.
61. *Ma'ariv*, May 21, 1996, p.8.
62. Ibid.
63. *Ha-aretz*, May 21, 1996, p.A4.
64. Ibid., April 9, 1996, p.A5.
65. *Ha-aretz*, May 19, 1996, p.A4.
66. For the electoral behavior of the Ultra-Orthodox camp, see Eliezer Don-Yehiya's contribution in this volume.
67. *Yediot Aharonot*, Shabbat supplement, February 8, 1996, pp.6–7.

68. The exceptions were the Belzer, Erloy, and Sanz Rabbis who instructed their followers to cast a blank ballot.
69. *Ha-aretz*, May 28, 1996, p.A2.
70. Ibid., May 20, 1996, p.A1.
71. *Jerusalem Post*, May 28, 1996, p.2.
72. Ibid., May 23, 1996, p.8.
73. Ibid. Electoral fraud was limited, but there were persistent rumors of irregularities in polling stations where the voting district is homogeneous in character, such as in the Arab, ultra-Orthodox, and kibbutz sectors.
74. Interview with MK Zvi Weinberg of the Israel B'Aliya party.
75. *Ma'ariv*, Shabbat supplement, June 7, 1996, p.3.
76. It parted with the Energy Ministry later on in order to allow the formation of a large Infrastructure Ministry for Ariel Sharon.
77. Shalom Yerushalmi, "Interview with Yvette Lieberman," *Ma'ariv*, Shabbat supplement, June 28, 1996, p.16.
78. Ibid.
79. *Jerusalem Post*, June 28, 1996, p.8.
80. Ibid.
81. *Ha-aretz*, June 14, 1996, p.A1.
82. *Ha-aretz*, June 14, 1996, p.A3.
83. For the text, see Ibid., June 17, 1996, p.A4.

The Electoral Fall of
the Israeli Left

GIORA GOLDBERG

During the last 20 years the Israeli political system has become one of the most unstable in the democratic world. This instability has been expressed in four main foci: drastic changes in the electoral laws; the practice of holding elections earlier than stated in the constitutional law; the assassination of a prime minister by an ideological adversary; and changes in voting behavior which produce transformations in the identity of the ruling political party. In 1996 instability was extremely high as, for the first time, all four elements simultaneously contributed to the political upheaval.

While only one political assassination, that of Prime Minister Yitzhak Rabin in November 1995, and only one drastic change in the electoral laws, that of direct election of the prime minister, occurred in the last two decades, indeed during Israel's 49 years of existence, the frequency of the other two kinds of political change was much higher. Five out of six national elections held since 1977 took place earlier than stated in the law (the only "normal" case being that of 1988). On five different occasions, the elections produced a change in the ruling party. In 1977 the Likud won the national elections for the first time. The 1981 elections were the only time in the last two decades in which the incumbent party won, thus ensuring political stability. In 1984 there was an electoral tie between the two political blocs, expressed in the creation of a national unity government. In 1988 the Likud won and again in 1992 the Labor Party, led for the first time by Yitzhak Rabin, came to power. Finally, in 1996 the pendulum swung to the right yet again, and the Likud returned to power under the leadership of Binyamin Netanyahu.

This "pendulum effect" reflects both the political tie between the left and the right which has prevailed since the 1970s, and the dynamic and

Giora Goldberg is Associate Professor of Political Studies at Bar-Ilan University.

dissenting character of a portion of the Israeli electorate. Moreover, during an election campaign, the opposition will naturally make a greater effort to win than the ruling party. Within the opposition, it is more likely that personal interests will be subordinated to organizational interests, and there is greater readiness to make internal reforms, such as the establishment of primaries. Party unity is stronger with a concurrent tendency to comply and adjust to the constraints of reality. Consequently, the relationship between the Labor and Meretz parties was less congenial in 1996 than prior to the 1992 elections when both parties supported each other in order to get into power. In addition, internal non-ideological disputes as well as factionalism within the leftist parties were deeper in 1996. There was the rivalry between Labor ministers Ehud Barak and Haim Ramon, as each regarded himself as Peres' rightful successor, and Meretz had just replaced Shulamit Aloni with Yossi Sarid as the party leader.

That fact that between 1977 and 1992, in four out of five national elections, there were electoral upheavals, full or partial, puts the 1996 electoral results in perspective as they stand in contrast to the "conventional wisdom" that Netanyahu's victory was an extraordinary and unexpected political event. An additional indicator of normality in the 1996 elections was the fifth consecutive failure of Shimon Peres to be elected as prime minister. He won none of the five races in which he led Labor. He failed under both electoral methods – four times under the old proportional representation system and once under the new direct election system. Peres was defeated by all three Likud leaders – by Menachem Begin in 1977 and 1981, by Yitzhak Shamir in 1988, and by Netanyahu in 1996. The only time Peres was not clearly defeated was in the stalemated elections of 1984, and the only time that Labor defeated the Likud in the last 20 years was in 1992 when Rabin, and not Peres, led Labor. Hence, if Peres had won the 1996 elections, his triumph would have been considered as a turning point in his virtually tragic electoral performance, which portrayed him as the eternal loser of Israeli politics. When the political experience of both candidates is compared, Peres had a clear advantage, as Netanyahu had never served as a minister and his parliamentary career only began in 1988. Peres, on the other hand, entered the parliamentary arena in 1959, and before that initiated the Israeli nuclear project as well as the aeronautics industry. He is the sole Israeli politician who served in all four top positions – Prime Minister (1984–86 and 1995-96), Defense Minister (1974–77 and 1995-96), Foreign Affairs Minister (1986–88 and 1992–95), and Finance Minister (1988–90). In the years 1969–74 he served in several ministries – Absorption, Transportation, Communication, and Information.

In 1996 not only did Peres lose to Netanyahu, but the left bloc in the Knesset decreased from a 61-seat majority to a 52-seat minority. Out of the 11 seats that the new center parties achieved – seven by the Yisrael Ba'Aliya party (composed mainly of Russian-speaking immigrants) and four by the Third Way party – nine were captured from the left and two from the right. Moreover, the remarkable increase in the power of both Arab lists emphasizes even more the failure of their partners in the left bloc – Labor and Meretz. That is, both lost a quarter of their parliamentary representation.

If Peres was a permanent loser and if political upheaval following national elections is the norm in Israel, then why was almost everyone in Israel and abroad, including pollsters, journalists, political commentators and analysts, and even political scientists, convinced that this time Peres would be the winner? The main reason was the assassination of Prime Minister Rabin by a right-wing zealot. The assassination triggered internal strife and the worst domestic crisis in the history of modern Israel. The immediate influence of this on the chances of the Likud in the upcoming elections was striking. All polls indicated a terrible defeat for the Likud and a landslide victory for Labor. The focus of this essay will be to explain and understand why the Israeli left, headed by Shimon Peres, was defeated in 1996 in spite of these promising predictions.

THE MAIN CAUSES FOR FAILURE

There are ten main causes for the electoral loss of the left, that is of Labor and Meretz, in the 1996 elections. The first and second causes are related to the assassination of Rabin; the third and fourth deal with the ideological aspects of the 1996 elections; the fifth and sixth take into account developments in the election campaign; the seventh and eighth reasons are related to difficulties in adjusting to the new electoral system in which the prime minister was chosen directly; and the ninth and tenth causes are derived from changes in some of the basic traits of the Israeli political system. Since the margin of victory between Netanyahu and Peres was so small – less than one percent – any one of these ten factors could have been crucial in influencing the final results.

THE ASSASSINATION OF YITZHAK RABIN

(1) The desire of the left to make use of the assassination in order to defeat the right at the polls was understandable and even legitimate. However, the extent of the accusations against all of the right, including the national religious sub-culture and its values and educational system, was enormous. Leftist criticism of the right was, in some cases, extremely offensive. Spiritual leaders, such as rabbis, were investigated by the authorities and political leaders, including Netanyahu, were accused of being responsible, directly or indirectly, for the creation of the social and political atmosphere which had legitimized the use of political violence against the legal power, including the prime minister.

There were a few political leaders on the left, including Prime Minister Peres and Minister Yossi Beilin, as well as some leftist writers, who tried to balance their reaction, especially toward the religious right, but the overall picture was grim for right-wing supporters. Most felt that they were being discriminated against as the left pursued a policy of allegations against all of the right, including the religious. The use of Rabin's assassination by the left backfired in the end because some religious, who believed in Labor's policies, were so angered by left-wing tactics that they chose to vote according to their historical and natural disposition, and not according to their ideological inclinations or affinity to the leading candidates. The pressures exerted on the right by the left pushed many citizens from individual voting, in which the left had a slight advantage over the right, into group voting, in which the right had a clear advantage. In the final stages of the campaign the designers of Labor's strategy, headed by Haim Ramon, became aware of this crucial point and tried to de-emphasize the assassination. However, the damage had already been done and could not be reversed.

(2) The decision of Labor leaders to hold the elections in May was against the best interests of the party. Right-wing feelings of anger toward the overreaction of the left after Rabin's assassination were not immediately formed. If elections had been called for December 1995 or January 1996, the chances of Labor winning were high, although to some extent it could have aroused the old negative image of Peres as an opportunist and a scheming politician. At that time many right-wing supporters were still in shock and were unable to protest against the ruling party, but, for unknown reasons, Peres did not agree with a full exploitation of the assassination by calling for national elections at the earliest possible date.

His second mistake, regarding the timing of the elections, was that after deciding not to call immediate elections, Peres did not wait for the original election day in November 1996, when the political atmosphere, so heated up after Rabin's death, would have cooled down. Instead elections were called for May, when religious and right-wing reaction to the left's harsh attack on them was at its apex. Since it is believed that right-wing supporters tend to be more emotional than left-wing supporters,[1] Labor should have avoided any emotional manipulation of the assassination, for in 1992 it was found that voters who switched from Likud to Labor were characterized by a strong tendency toward rational electoral behavior.[2]

IDEOLOGY AND ELECTION ISSUES

(3) During its four-year term, the Labor Government adopted a dovish policy and initiated the Oslo agreements with the Palestinians. The main component of these agreements was granting autonomy to most Palestinians who dwell in Judea, Samaria and Gaza and withdrawal of the IDF forces from these territories. One of the implications of this

dovish turn was the split in Labor in which some of the hawks, led by Knesset members Avigdor Kahalani and Emanuel Zissman, left the party and founded a new center party – the Third Way. The damage that the new party caused to Peres was marginal, since a clear majority of its supporters preferred Peres over Netanyahu.[3] Labor election strategy was logical as it was clearly based on a turn to the center. This was expressed in Labor's footdragging in fulfilling the agreement with the Palestinians as to the withdrawal from Hebron, and the military initiative against the Islamic terrorists in Southern Lebanon. The sole significant change in the party platform was the deletion of the clause which expressed objection to the idea of a Palestinian State. However, following Labor's sharp turn to the left after the 1992 elections, the chances of a centrist strategy working again were slim.

Following the eruption of the Palestinian uprising (intifada) large sectors of the Israeli public adopted dovish positions.[4] This process was accelerated after the adoption of softer policies by the Labor government. These developments should have been helpful to Labor performance at the polls. However, the Labor party failed to separate the strategic elements of the Oslo agreements from the historical-religious elements. The support given to the agreements by centrist circles in the Israeli public was based on strategic and not on historical-religious grounds. Leftist forces within Labor, together with Meretz, interpreted the peace process as part of an overall transformation of Israeli society from a Jewish-Zionist nation-state, based on the unique destiny and values of Judaism, into a liberal Western democracy. This interpretation was unacceptable to those Israelis who favored the agreements, but opposed any erosion in the Jewish nature of Israel. Thus, Labor lost potential voters from the right, mainly to the Likud, a party which emphasized its commitment both to the agreements and to the Jewish-Zionist nature of the state. Hence, the main election issue of the Likud was the future of Jerusalem, which had not been decided upon in the Oslo agreements. The unity of Jerusalem is not considered as a strategic-territorial question, but as a broad question representing the basic nature of Judaism and Zionism. The most popular slogan of Likud's propaganda was "Peres will divide Jerusalem." Labor denied any intention to divide Jerusalem, but the Likud succeeded in achieving possession of this and other national symbols.

In the past, the three main ideological dimensions of the Israeli political system were defense and foreign policy, religion and state policy, and economic and social policy. In the 1996 election campaign two of them – defense and religion – virtually merged into one new dimension, or continuum, which might be labeled as "Jewishness," that is, viewing defense issues and policies through a Jewish perspective. For Labor this development was harmful, since it lost its clear-cut advantage over the Likud in the dimension of defense and foreign policy. The "Jewishness" issue became the most powerful explanatory variable of the results in the election of the prime minister, but not of the results in the Knesset election in which ethnicity still played a major role.

There were five categories of "Jewishness," according to the self-definition of the voter – ultra-Orthodox, religious, traditional, secular and non-Jewish. The more "Jewish" the voters, according to their own self-perception, the greater the likelihood that they would vote for Netanyahu. It is estimated that Netanyahu gained only five percent among non-Jewish voters, about one-third among secular Jews, about two-thirds among traditional Jews, about 90 percent among religious Jews, and 95 percent among ultra-Orthodox Jews.

Interestingly, support for Netanyahu was greater among voters from the ultra-Orthodox Ashkenazi parties than among the voters of his own party – the Likud. In other words, split-ticket voting was smaller among the ultra-Orthodox Ashkenazi voters than among Likud voters. It is noteworthy that only six years earlier, in 1990, the ultra-Orthodox parties cooperated with Labor in bringing down the National Unity government, and one of them, Agudat Israel, signed a coalition agreement with Labor.[5] The sequence of events from the Oslo agreements through to Rabin's assassination and on to the reactions to this act created a feeling among religious and traditional citizens that, contrary to the past, when crucial decisions about the identity of the state were not made – as a kind of consociational arrangement in order to keep social stability – the Labor government broke with the national consensus. In other words, the Oslo agreements were perceived as part of a process leading to the weakening of the Jewish basis of the State.

(4) The Labor government was too closely identified with the extreme left, mainly with Meretz, and, to a lesser extent, with the Arab lists. The joint stay in coalition with Meretz created the impression that the larger party was influenced by the smaller one. When the Likud was in power it suffered from the same problem of being identified with extreme elements – i.e., the ultra-Orthodox parties.

The prominence of Meretz circles in designing the new Israeli secular culture was evident, especially in the mass media, including both television channels. The influence of Meretz on policies was less than its reflection in the media, but the impression that Meretz was the leading force in the government had a negative impact on the government as a whole. The attitudes of Meretz in regard to religious issues are totally leftist and secular. When Rabin was forming his cabinet after his victory in 1992 he was unaware of the implications of granting the Education and Culture Ministry to Meretz, and especially to Shulamit Aloni. She was perceived, in religious circles, as an ideological enemy. At a later stage Rabin had to transfer Aloni to another position in his cabinet, but the damage had already been done. In spite of the limited influence of Meretz with regard to religious policies, the image of the former as anti-religious caused serious harm to Labor, since not only religious Jews give special importance to religious issues, but also traditional Jews as well. Also the purely secular positions and involvement in anti-religious activities by some Labor Knesset members did not help Labor's image (i.e., Yael Dayan, known as a blatant supporter of the gay community in Israel, an intolerable position to most religious people).

The alienation of the Labor government from the religious communities, although no explicit anti-religious policies were adopted, caused a strengthening of the alliance between the Likud and the religious population. The perceived threat to the religious was so great as to discourage them from supporting Labor in the elections. The relationship toward Judaism of former Labor leaders, such as Ben-Gurion, was vastly different from that of recent leaders like Yitzhak Rabin. While Ben-Gurion had bitter conflicts with the religious circles, at the same time he himself composed a Jewish interpretation of Zionism. Meretz as well as Labor leaders did not speak in Jewish terms and virtually made a separation between Judaism and Zionism. Consequently, Labor electoral gains among religious and traditional voters in 1996 were the lowest ever. The antagonism of religious people toward Labor was so sharp that Labor failed in its bid to use Netanyahu's extra-marital affair and turn the religious population against him.

THE ELECTION CAMPAIGN

(5) The turning point in public opinion occurred during February and March 1996, with the series of five murderous terror attacks in Jerusalem, Tel Aviv and Ashkelon, implemented by Islamic organizations opposed to the peace process. These attacks came after a period of relative quiet. It was at this point that many right-wing supporters ceased to feel guilty about the Rabin assassination and started to report to the pollsters their true voting intentions. The campaign itself was under constant threat of additional terrorist attacks, but the fact that there were no terrorist attacks just before the elections worked in Peres' favor. Peres' attempt to convince the public that the terrorists wanted the Likud to win was not convincing. Meanwhile the Islamic terrorists became more active in Southern Lebanon, but Israel's military initiative, labelled *Grapes of Wrath*, against those terrorists and intended to endow the Peres government with a hawkish image, failed to produce the desired results. In addition, the accidental killing of many Lebanese civilians by the IDF created much international and domestic criticism, mainly by Arab voters whose support of Peres was essential for him to win. In the end, the government decided to call a ceasefire without any gains for Israel, which did not help the Peres campaign.

(6) One of the natural phenomena of election campaigns is that the side leading in the polls usually tries to keep the campaign low key, while their opponent attempts to stir up the campaign in order to change its

inferior position.[6] Surprisingly, the 1996 campaign was the calmest one in Israel's electoral history because both Labor and the Likud were interested in keeping things quiet. Both parties were convinced that they were going to win. The Likud judged correctly by not demonstrating high self-confidence, while its rival unwisely tried to make use of the bandwagon effect, which basically meant joining the winner.

Following the bus bombings in Israel's urban centers in the spring of 1996, the Likud was leading the race, in spite of the better performance of Labor in the polls. Labor strategists made mistakes mainly because of the illusionary polls, and to a lesser extent because ruling parties tend to be victims of that illusion more than opposition parties. Moreover, Labor had the support of the various elites, including the mass media, as well as the frank help of President Clinton, which intensified its over-confidence. At the beginning of the campaign Labor tried to manage a news campaign through its military actions in Lebanon, but after the failure of this operation a few weeks before the elections, Labor stayed inactive, relying on the polls which indicated a clear-cut victory for Peres over Netanyahu. Labor did not even try to control the public agenda by creating election issues. The extremely vulnerable personality of Netanyahu, for example, was not sufficiently criticized, nor was he properly attacked. Labor did not give enough weight to the dimension in which it may have had an advantage – the personal dimension.

In spite of the promising polls, Labor leaders should have been worried by the motives behind the decision of the Likud strategists not to stir up the campaign. The Likud's strategy did not include the typical oppositional accusations of the ruling party being corrupt. Only near the end of the campaign, a few days before the elections, when Labor was unable to respond, did the Likud slightly agitate the campaign by exposing its ethnocentric slogan "Netanyahu is good for the Jews." This last-minute change was done to awaken the activists for election day, as it was clear that Labor would not respond. At the same time, Peres was overshadowed by Netanyahu on the televised confrontation between the two candidates. Peres' lackluster performance came from an exaggerated self-confidence and the deterministic approach of Peres and Labor stemming from favorable polls.

The failure of the polls might be explained by five main points:

• The floating vote traditionally tends to be dominated by the right.

• The supporters of the right were under-represented in the polls due to their living in peripheral locations, as well as their unwillingness to cooperate with the pollsters and with the main initiators of the polls, the mass media, considered to have a left-wing bias by many right-wingers.

• The new election method was unclear to many respondents, whose answers were consequently confused.

• Some right-wing supporters were unwilling to give sincere answers regarding their voting intentions because of fear of retribution by the ruling party.

- Other right-wing supporters were ashamed to express their true position in favor of the parties and the candidate which were being blamed, by some, for Rabin's death.

THE NEW ELECTORAL SYSTEM

(7) Because of the new direct election of the prime minister in 1996, the relationship between Labor and Meretz was complex and undefined. With the old method, Meretz knew how to maneuver between its alliance with Labor and its own independence and uniqueness. In 1992 when Ratz, Mapam and Shinui formed a joint electoral list called Meretz, this new front played an essential role in the victory of the left. Its energy was fully turned against the Likud government and not against Labor. Meretz helped Labor by pushing it toward the center.[7] The direct election of the prime minister necessitated basic changes in electoral strategy which Meretz failed to accomplish. It decided to support Peres clearly and emphasized this step in order to prove to hesitating left-wing voters its total loyalty toward Labor. At first glance that strategy sounded correct, but it created a magnified identity with Peres, who was making enormous efforts to capture the center. Meretz, with its extreme leftist image, was harmful to Peres among those voters in the center hesitating between the two candidates.

Furthermore, after fully supporting Peres, Meretz felt uncommitted to Labor, and perhaps as a compensation, attacked Labor instead of concentrating its attacks on the Likud. Meretz blamed Labor for not telling the voters "all the truth" as to its future policies. Meretz reconfirmed one of the main arguments of the Likud, that Labor's turn to the center was nothing more than an electoral gimmick, and that if Peres won the elections, he would fulfill Meretz policies. Sarid, the new leader of Meretz after Shulamit Aloni's retirement, announced, just after the Peres–Netanyahu televised debate, that Peres was not telling the voters that after the elections Peres would follow the leftist orientation of Meretz. This was the right approach to the floating vote inside the left, but a big mistake with regard to the election of the prime minister. What was right for winning the small inner fight between Labor and Meretz in the Knesset elections, became a terrible mistake for the larger battle between Peres and Netanyahu.[8] At this stage, Labor should have gotten rid of Meretz by declaring that a Labor–Meretz coalition following the elections was only one of a few possibilities.

Another difficulty which Meretz encountered was in preserving its image as a fresh, young, radical and virtually anti-politics entity. In 1992 it was easier for Meretz to sharply criticize the political establishment than in 1996 when it was perceived as a part of that establishment, having participated in the government for the last four years.

(8) While, to some extent, Meretz damaged Peres' chances of winning, the Arab lists, which included the Democratic Front (mainly based on the Israeli Communist Party), and the Islamic list, fought Labor intensively in the Knesset elections. In contrast to Meretz, the Arab lists were much less committed to Peres, and the unintentional killing of Lebanese civilians by the IDF during the Israeli military initiative in Southern Lebanon in April 1996 intensified the anti-Peres trend among Arab voters. The Arab lists declared their support for Peres only shortly before the elections. The deal between the Labor party and the Arab lists was based on the commitment of the Arab lists to mobilize the Arab masses in support of Peres in exchange for an informal relinquishment of the Arab votes by Labor. To some extent that deal was similar to the deal made between the Likud and the ultra-Orthodox parties. However, while the ultra-Orthodox parties achieved a high voter turnout rate, the Arab parties were much less efficient. This difference can be explained by the fact that the deal with the Arabs was a straight political compromise, while the deal with the ultra-Orthodox parties reflected the natural joining of the right with the ultra-Orthodox sector. The alliance between Peres and the Arabs was very worthwhile for Peres, although it deterred some Jewish voters from supporting Peres and Labor.

Since the Arab sector is one of the poorest and most dependent sectors in Israeli society, ruling parties tend to do well at the polls. Nevertheless, in 1996, after four years in power, Labor lost almost one-fifth of its Arab voters and totally failed to attract those Arab voters who, in 1992, voted for right-wing parties. Most Arabs who voted in 1992 for right-wing parties abandoned those parties in 1996, but not in favor of Labor. This failure on the part of Labor to attract Arab votes was related to the new election method and not a mistake in election strategy.

BASIC TRAITS OF THE POLITICAL SYSTEM

(9) For several generations the Israeli left had an organizational advantage over the Israeli right. The right-wing parties, especially Herut and the Liberals (forerunners of the Likud), were parties lacking massive organizational resources, as compared to the left-wing parties which had accumulated organizational wealth by building a network of political and economic institutions. These parties, especially MAPAI (the major component of the Labor party) provided important social services to their members and followers – mainly health and education. The most efficient organization controlled by MAPAI was the Histadrut (General Federation of Labor Unions). Although not as poor as the right-wing parties, the religious parties were not as organizationally developed as the left-wing parties. The left's control of major economic institutions, such as the Histadrut, gave them an electoral advantage over the right.

From the 1970s the economic power base of the left began to decline and the weight of the organizational factor in voting behavior began to diminish. This change was one of the reasons that facilitated the first electoral upheaval of 1977. The main bureaucratic base of Labor, the Histadrut, which included the kibbutzim and moshavim, suffered heavily from the new Likud government and in the late 1980s faced financial collapse.

The transformation of the Histadrut into a trade union was completed after the enactment of the National Health Security Law in 1994 which made it impossible for the Histadrut to keep on supplying health services. An additional factor that propelled the transformation process was the 1994 Histadrut elections in which Labor was defeated by a coalition consisting of a reform faction in Labor led by Haim Ramon, together with the Meretz and SHAS parties. Ramon became the new General Secretary of the Histadrut and completed the process of building a new organization – smaller in size and membership, and narrower in its functions and activities. Thus, Labor lost its historical stronghold and power base. Ramon's return to Labor after Rabin's assassination could not solve the problem the party was facing on the eve of the elections.

On the other hand, the religious parties improved their organizational capabilities, a process facilitated by the growth in their bargaining power since the 1970s. The case of SHAS is the most prominent as organizational power is considered. The increase in the organizational power of the religious parties – mainly the ultra-Orthodox parties – and the decrease of that power by left-wing parties might also be explained by the differences in social solidarity and in communal life between the two sectors. While the left became less cohesive, there was no change in the degree of solidarity in religious circles. As of 1996 the religious parties have taken the lead in organizational power, while the social and organizational networks of the left have weakened. The alliance of the religious parties with the Likud gave the right, for the first time, an organizational advantage over the left that was fully used throughout the campaign and on election day. The right succeeded in mobilizing more personnel and additional resources than the left. This was also reflected in higher voter turnout rates in religious and traditional communities. The Likud was vastly assisted by the organizational networks of the religious parties. The organizational cooperation between the Likud and the religious parties was based on ensuring the support of religious voters for Netanyahu in exchange for a concession by the Likud in the struggle for the religious vote in the Knesset elections. That was one of the reasons for the success of Netanyahu and the religious parties as compared to the poor electoral performance of the Likud.

(10) For many years the left had an additional advantage over the right in that the rate of party identification of its supporters was higher than

that of the right supporters, with the highest rate of party identification
in the religious parties. Arian's findings from the late 1960s showed that
party identification of Ashkenazi voters tended to be higher than that of
Oriental voters.[9] In 1992 it was found, for the first time, that this trend
was reversed – right-wing supporters had higher rates of party
identification than those of left-wing supporters.[10] Party identification
rates remained highest among supporters of the religious parties. These
patterns, as well as the new patterns of party organization, might be
partially explained by social solidarity and communal life as enhancing
the drive to both party identification and organizational resources. The
tendency that was revealed in 1992 has intensified since then, and the
right benefited from it in the 1996 elections. Modern voters, usually
with higher socio-economic status – tend to be less identified with their
parties than traditional and less modernized voters. In the last two
decades the weight of party identification as one of the major factors
which influence voting behavior has decreased, to some extent, in Israel
as well as in other Western democracies. That decrease occurred mainly
among left-wing supporters, while the rate of party identification among
Likud supporters slightly declined and that of the religious parties'
supporters remained stable. Here again, as with party organization, the
alliance between the Likud and the religious parties was very beneficial
to the Likud.

Immigrants do not necessarily follow that pattern. In spite of the fact
that most of them suffer from lower socio-economic status, their short
time in a new country and their political socialization patterns make it
impossible for them to develop solid party identification. But as time goes
by, immigrants whose socio-economic status remains low may develop a
strong identification with one of the political parties. The immigrants from
Arab countries of the 1950s and the 1960s went through that political
socialization process. Nevertheless, most immigrants of the late 1980s and
1990s originated in the former Soviet Union and lack any party
identification and are thus able to change their voting patterns drastically
from election to election. In the case of immigrants from a non-democratic
country there is an additional tendency to volatile voting patterns because
being socialized in a totalitarian political culture causes a very low amount
of trust in the political system and the politicians which can translate into
a protest vote against the ruling party.[11] Voters from the former Soviet
Union followed this pattern twice – in 1992 they expressed nonconfidence
in the Likud government and four years later did the same to help oust the
Labor party from power.

To sum up, the party identification factor among three different
groups damaged the chances of Labor in the 1996 elections. These
included immigrants, who supported the left in 1992 but were not
sufficiently identified with one of its parties, left-wing supporters, whose
party identification had been weakened, and right-wing supporters,
whose party identification had not been weakened since 1992.

THE RESULTS

The results of the 1996 elections will be analyzed along three axes – voting patterns in the elections for prime minister, voting in the Knesset elections, and split-ticket voting.[12]

Elections for the Prime Minister

Since the 1996 elections were the first in which voters could directly choose their prime minister, there is no possibility of comparing the results to any previous elections. Nevertheless, a few observations can lead to some generalizations. The sector in which Peres did best was the Arab one – almost 95 percent of the Arab vote went to Peres; among the Druse, a minority closer to Zionism when compared to Israeli Arabs, he gained only 78.6 percent; among the Bedouin 93.1 percent; and more than 95 percent among Christian and Moslem Arabs. In some cases Peres lost the support of protest voters who supported Netanyahu because of local conflicts. In Taibeh, for example, an internal feud between two large families led the weaker one to support Netanyahu. Consequently, Peres received only 90.8 percent there and Netanyahu achieved more than nine percent.

In spite of the fact that Peres defeated Netanyahu in the Arab sector, a majority of the Jewish vote went to Netanyahu – 55.5 percent for Netanyahu versus 44.5 percent for Peres. An analysis of the voting trends in the Jewish urban sector – 88 cities and towns – reveals five factors which harmed Peres, the strongest being the Jewish element, as mentioned above. The four additional factors were ethnic origin (although the impact of this factor decreased in the 1996 elections for prime minister), social class, centrality and size of city or town. Peres did better among Ashkenazim, among middle and upper class voters, among voters residing in the vicinity of the main metropolitan areas, especially that of Tel Aviv, and among voters residing in large cities. It is estimated that social control is stronger in small communities than in larger ones. Since Netanyahu benefited from highly developed social networks – especially the religious networks – Peres was harmed in the small communities in which these networks were active and prominent. All of these five factors are intercorrelated – Orientals tend to be more religious than Ashkenazim, most of them belong to the lower class, and they tend to reside in smaller towns, away from the metropolitan area of Tel Aviv.

For analysis purposes, the 88 Jewish cities and towns were divided into six categories. Peres did poorly, that is, less than 20 percent of the vote, in five religious, but not necessarily Oriental communities – Kfar Chabad, Netivot, Beit Dagan, Rechasim, and Bnei Brak.

The next group consisted of 13 small and poor development towns with a large religious, mainly Oriental, population in which Peres achieved less than 30 percent – Ofakim, Or Yehuda, Or Akiva, Beit

Shean, Beit Shemesh, Hatzor, Tiberias, Tirat Hakarmel, Yerucham, Safed, Kiryat Malachi, Kiryat Ekron, and Shlomi.

The third group, in which Peres received less than 40 percent of the vote, consisted of 26 cities and towns, not necessarily small towns as in the former group, but with a large Oriental population. Jerusalem is the most important in this group and, to a lesser extent, large towns such as Beer Sheva, Ashdod, Ashkelon, Netanya, Hadera and Lod. The other towns in this group are Beer Ya'akov, Gedera, Gan Yavne, Dimona, Yavne, Yokneam Ilit, Kfar Yona, Migdal Ha'emek, Afula, Atlit, Pardes Chana, Kadima, Kiryat Ata, Kiryat Gat, Kiryat Shmonah, Rosh Ha'ayin, Ramle, Sderot, and Tel Mond.

The fourth group, giving less than 50 percent to Peres, consisted of 19 towns. Unlike the two former groups, most of the towns in this group are from metropolitan areas, such as Petakh Tikva, Bat Yam, Holon, Acre, Mevaseret Zion, Azor, Givat Shmuel, Nesher, Kiryat Yam, Yahud, Nes Ziona, Rechovot, and Ganei Tikva. The other towns in this group are Eilat, Binyamina, Ma'alot, Mitzpe Ramon, Nahariya, and Natzrat Ilit.

The fifth group is the first in which Peres defeated Netanyahu – that is, Peres received more than 50, but less than 60 percent of the vote. It consisted of 18 cities and towns which are much wealthier and less religious than those belonging to the previous groups. The most prominent cities in this group are Tel Aviv and Haifa. Nine additional towns near Tel Aviv belong to this group – Ramat Gan, Ra'anana, Hertzlia, Kfar Saba, Hod Hasharon, Ramat Efal, Kiryat Ono, Rishon Letzion, and Kochav Yair. The remaining towns in this group are – Even Yehuda, Zichron Ya'akov, Karmiel, Arad, Mazkeret Batya, Kiryat Bialik, and Kiryat Motzkin.

In the final group, Peres achieved more than 60 percent of the vote. It consisted of seven very wealthy and non-religious communities, most of them in metropolitan areas – Kfar Shmaryahu, Givatayim, Savyon, Ramat Hasharon, Neve Efraim, Kiryat Tivon, and Omer. In sum, out of the 88 cities and towns in Israel, Peres won in only 25.

The first group is best represented by Netivot, a religious, Oriental, lower class, peripheral and small town in which Peres received only 11.2 percent of the vote. Yerucham (28 percent voted for Peres) represents the second group. It is an Oriental, lower class, peripheral and small town, but much less religious than Netivot. The third group is represented by Gedera (32.3 percent for Peres) which is Oriental, small and peripheral, but not religious and not a lower class town. Binyamina (43 percent for Peres) represents the fourth group – small and peripheral but not religious, non-Oriental and not a lower class community. The fifth group is represented by Kochav Yair (here 53.2 percent of the vote went to Peres), a small suburb in the Tel Aviv metropolitan area. This middle class community is neither religious nor Oriental. Givatayim, representing the sixth category, is a prosperous city in the Tel Aviv metropolitan area, and is neither religious nor Oriental. Peres achieved 63.1 percent of the vote in Givatayim.

Comparing the election results in four upper class neighborhoods in North Tel Aviv (Ramat Aviv, Neve Avivim, Ramat Aviv Gimmel, and Tel Baruch) to those in four lower class neighborhoods in South Tel Aviv (Ezra, Hatikva, Shapira and Kiryat Shalom) reveals clear-cut trends. The average support for Peres in the poor communities was 19 percent, while the average support for him in the affluent communities was 73 percent.

The Knesset Elections

Labor lost 18.2 percent (down from 20.3 percent in 1992 to 16.6 percent in 1996) of its share of the vote among Arabs and 23.7 percent (from 36.3 percent to 27.7 percent) among Jews. Meretz succeeded in retaining its gain in the Arab sector – 10 percent – but lost 23.9 percent (from 9.2 percent to 7 percent) in the Jewish sector. Both Labor and Meretz strengthened their positions among the Druse – Labor increased from 29.3 percent to 40.3 percent and Meretz from 8.2 percent to 12.1 percent of the vote. Both were weakened among the Bedouin – Labor decreased from 17.4 percent to 14.9 percent and Meretz from 11.6 percent to 5.1 percent. Most of the Arab voters who left Labor switched to one of the Arab parties. In the Jewish sector, Labor lost in three sectors – ex-Soviet Union immigrants who supported their new political party, Yisrael Ba'Aliya, middle class voters, mainly Ashkenazim, who switched to the Third Way, and religious and traditional voters who preferred one of the religious parties. An analysis of voting patterns in the Jewish sector reveals that Labor retained its power in its traditional strongholds, but drastically decreased in the segments where the right, especially the religious parties, had dominated for a long time. In 1996 Labor's losses were greater in those sectors in which they were historically weaker. It has already been mentioned that Labor's decline among Arab voters was less than in the Jewish sector. In the kibbutzim, the strongest Labor base, its power increased (from 53.3 percent in 1992 to 55 percent in 1996). Labor lost 2.9 percent to the Third Way, but received more votes from Meretz deserters (Meretz dropped from 36.9 percent to 31 percent). The same trends appeared in the wealthiest suburbs of Israel. In Savyon, for example, Labor rose from 40.7 percent to 44.6 percent, the Third Way achieved 4.7 percent, and Meretz dropped from 19.8 percent to 14.5 percent of the vote. In Kfar Shmaryahu, Labor went up from 48.1 percent to 53.7 percent, the Third Way received 4.1 percent, and Meretz went down from 25.8 percent to 18.3 percent. The reasonable performance of Labor in the kibbutzim and in the wealthiest communities was possible because it was not challenged in those communities by three out of the four threats to Labor (Arabs, new immigrants, and religious voters). Votes lost to the Third Way party were balanced by gains from Meretz.

When the above division into six categories is applied to the elections to the Knesset, it is evident that Labor's main losses were in the cities and towns where the right had an historical advantage over the left. In the first group, that consisting of religious communities and represented by Netivot, Labor declined from an average of 9.8 percent in 1992 to 5.8 percent in 1996, losing 40.8 percent of its support. In the second group (mainly small and poor development towns represented by Yerucham) Labor lost 41.6 percent of its support – down from 22.6 percent to 13.2 percent. In the next two categories Labor lost approximately a quarter of its support – 26.3 percent in the third group, represented by Gedera (from 29.3 percent to 21.6 percent) and 26.6 percent in the fourth group represented by Binyamina (from 38.3 percent to 28.1 percent). In the fifth group, in which Peres defeated Netanyahu and which is represented by Kochav Yair, Labor lost just 14.8 percent of its support (from 43.2 percent to 36.8 percent). In the sixth group, represented by Givatayim, Labor's loss was slight – only 1.6 percent (from 48.9 percent to 48.1 percent).

The differences between these various groups can be partially explained by the different influences of the three forces that threatened the Labor party – the religious parties, the new immigrants' party (Yisrael Ba'Aliya), and the Third Way party. Where only the Third Way was the main threat, especially in the affluent cities and towns, Labor lost more votes to the Third Way than in the other groups, but was compensated by a wave of Meretz deserters. The largest losses to Labor were in mixed development towns where masses of new immigrants settled in Oriental-dominated communities. In Or Akiva, for example, Labor dropped from 20.2 percent to 9.3 percent (a decrease of 54 percent), while Yisrael Be'aliya achieved 18.7 percent, and SHAS rose from 11.1 percent to 21 percent. In Ashdod, SHAS increased from 10.3 percent to 16.4 percent of the vote, Yisrael Be'aliya received 18.5 percent, and Labor's share diminished by 49.9 percent (from 32.7 percent to 16.4 percent). In Ashkelon, SHAS rose from 6.2 percent to 11.2 percent, Yisrael Be'aliya gained 17.1 percent and Labor lost 43.4 percent of its power (down from 29.5 percent to 16.7 percent). Although the main victim of SHAS' boom was the Likud, it is estimated that a minority of new SHAS voters were Labor deserters. Furthermore, some of the new voters for the NRP (National Religious Party) were former Labor voters as well.

Labor's losses in communities in which only one of the threats was realized gives direct proof to the impact of the new immigrants' party and of the religious parties. In Natzrat Ilit, for example, the religious parties rose from 3.3 percent to 5.8 percent, while the Likud's power decreased approximately to the same extent – 31.5 percent to 28.4 percent. Thus, Labor's decline from 49.7 percent to 28.4 percent cannot be explained by the rise of the religious parties, but rather by the success of the Yisrael Be'aliya party – 17.8 percent and, to a lesser extent, by the fact that the Third Way received 2.7 percent. In Arad, Labor declined from 41.9 percent to 29.9 percent while the new immigrants' party achieved 14.6 percent. The religious parties increased their power by 2.4 percent (from 9.3 percent to 11.7 percent), while the Likud lost 5.9 percent. In Karmiel, the religious parties went up from 5.6 percent to 10.4 percent, the Likud dropped from 28.8 percent to 24.6 percent, the new immigrants' party achieved 15.9 percent, and Labor lost 15.8 percent.

If the last three cases exposed the enormous damage to Labor inflicted by the Yisrael Be'aliya party, the next case proves that the religious parties harmed Labor, too. In Kiryat Ekron, the religious parties went up from 15.8 percent to 26.2 percent although the Likud went up too, from 42.1 percent to 44.7 percent. The new immigrants' party received only 2.6 percent while Labor declined from 22 percent to 13.3 percent. Kiryat Ekron is representative of the Yemenite population which, this time, was anti-Labor more than other Oriental groups.[13]

Nevertheless, the greatest threat to Labor was that initiated by the Yisrael Ba'Aliya party. The least dangerous threat came from the Arab parties since their loyalty toward any government led by Labor was never in doubt. The threat of the Third Way party was slightly greater than that of the religious parties. Meretz, on the other hand, was challenged by Labor from the right and by Hadash from the left. A few thousand Jewish voters, many of them young post-materialists residing in the center of Tel Aviv, switched from Meretz to Hadash. For these voters, Meretz had lost its fresh, young and anti-establishment appeal, following four years in the government. Nevertheless, Meretz lost many more votes to Labor than to Hadash. Those Meretz voters who switched to Labor did so because they felt that Meretz was pulling the Labor-led government too rapidly toward ideological and policy changes that could be harmful to the chances of the left being reelected. The further Labor leaned toward the left, the more former Meretz voters turned to Labor. This wave was reversed a few months before the elections as Labor started its move back to the center. Contrary to Labor, which lost different rates of voters in different segments of society, the rate of voters leaving Meretz was the same in all segments of society.

Split-Ticket Voting

The new electoral method made possible, for the first time, split-ticket voting – that is, favoring a party different from that of the candidate for prime minister. Not only were there Peres supporters voting for Likud, and Netanyahu supporters preferring Labor, there were many who did not vote for either of the two major parties. For example, there were combinations like Peres-Meretz and Netanyahu-NRP as these two parties formally adopted one of the two candidates in advance. The Arab parties and United Torah Judaism chose a candidate a few days before the elections, while SHAS did it at the last minute by letting the popular Rabbi Kadourie bless Netanyahu. The Third Way and the Yisrael Ba'Aliya parties stayed neutral on this issue.

When the split-ticket phenomenon is measured by the percentage sum of the results of all the parties, except Labor and Likud, it is revealed that the national rate is 48.6 percent (44.9 among Jews and 81.2 among Arabs). However, in the first category of urban centers, wherein most are religious, an average of 72 percent split their vote. Mainly this index measures the split-ticket voting inside the blocs – such as between Peres and the Arab parties, or between Netanyahu and the religious parties. Much more interesting is the split-ticket voting between the two blocs. In order to measure this phenomenon a new index was developed. This was done by taking the sum (in percentages) of Labor, Meretz, the Arab parties and half of all other parties (except the Likud, Moledet and the religious parties) subtracted from Peres' rate (in percentages). If Peres received more than the left parties and half of the center parties together, the result was positive. A negative result meant that Peres was less successful than those parties. The range of the index was between 100 and -100, where 0 meant no split-ticket voting.[14]

The decision to divide the sum of the center parties equally between Peres and Netanyahu was based on the assumptions that, first of all, Peres was much more popular among Third Way supporters than Netanyahu, while Netanyahu was more popular among the new immigrants' party supporters. At least two-thirds of the new immigrants' party supporters voted for Netanyahu, while more than three-quarters of the Third Way voted for Peres. This difference was balanced by the different sizes of these two parties – 5.8 percent for Yisrael Ba'aliya and only 3 percent for the Third Way. It is assumed that voters for parties which did not cross the electoral threshold (1.5 percent) were divided equally between the two candidates.

The national rate was 2.85, which means that Peres did better than the left parties. About three percent of voters preferred Peres and one of the right-wing or religious parties, while nearly six percent of supporters of one of the rightist or religious parties voted for Peres. If Peres had achieved one more percent of this electorate – seven percent instead of six – he might have won the elections.

Among Jews, the split-ticket voting index stands at 2.9, while among Arabs it is 1.65. In six out of the 88 urban Jewish settlements the scores were negative, but in 82 the scores were positive, which means that Peres did better than the left parties. The average of the five religious communities is a slight 0.5, while that of the seven wealthiest communities is 3.8. The stronger Peres was, the higher the split-ticket voting – 0.5 in the group in which he received less than 20 percent, 2.8 in the less than 30 percent group, 2.9 in the less than 40 percent group, 3.0 in the less than 50 percent group, an exceptional 2.7 average in the less than 60 group and 3.8 in Peres' most supportive group, the seven affluent communities.

It is estimated that supporters of United Torah Judaism and of Moledet were more loyal toward Netanyahu than were Likud, SHAS and

NRP supporters. The aggregate findings shed light on one of the segments which tended to split-ticket voting – Ashkenazi, dovish and religious voters. Some of them voted for Labor in 1992 and Meimad (a dovish religious party) in 1988.[15] This segment, contrary to most religious voters, could easily separate religious issues from security issues and was represented by members of religious kibbutzim. Five religious kibbutzim – Lavie, Sde Eliahu, Tirat Tzvi, Kvutzat Yavne and Be'erot Yitzhak – can be analyzed as a sample of this group. In 1992 Labor received an average of 15.8 percent from this group and dropped to 9 percent in 1996. Peres achieved an average of 25.8 percent, with the average rate of split-ticket voting at 12.4, most of them Peres-NRP supporters. It is estimated that more than 15 percent of NRP supporters among religious kibbutzim voted in such a fashion. This voting pattern was facilitated by the strategic step taken by the leadership of the NRP during the campaign emphasizing that the party would join any winning coalition, led by either Netanyahu or Peres.

CONCLUSION

The electoral loss of the Israeli left in the 1996 elections shed light on the revolutionary potential of the democratic regime. The "poor masses" made a "velvet revolution" against the various elites and the establishment. This is a unique case because Peres and the left were favored not only by the various elites, especially by the mass media, but also by international forces such as President Clinton, the political leaders of most European countries and the leadership of the Arab countries, including the Palestinian Authority. Some people who could not explain the election results in a logical way argued that it was a miracle. This essay has given a detailed explanation of the results from the perspective of political science.

As to the future, it is too soon after the 1996 elections to make a prediction. The pendulum effect in Israeli politics could indicate trouble for the right in the next elections. The unexpected victory of Netanyahu could give rise to Netanyahu-like candidates in both parties. However, the electoral decision in the elections for prime minister was basically ideological, while the personal factor remained marginal. In the Knesset elections, the two most prominent factors were party identification and ethnic origin. After the elections the new electoral method was generally blessed by those who were satisfied with the results and blamed by those who were disappointed. The new method of the direct election of the prime minister will only be ready for a professional evaluation on the eve of the next elections.

NOTES

1. Giora Goldberg, *The Israeli Voter 1992* (Jerusalem, 1994), pp.196–7 (Hebrew).
2. Ibid., p.196.
3. It is estimated that about 80 percent of those who voted for the Third Way party supported Peres.
4. Giora Goldberg, Gad Barzilai and Efraim Inbar, "The Impact of Intercommunal Conflict: The Intifada and Israeli Public Opinion," *Policy Studies*, 43 (Jerusalem, 1991).
5. That agreement was not implemented since Peres failed to mobilize enough support for building a winning coalition. Two Agudat Yisrael Knesset members, Avraham Verdiger and Eliezer Mizrachi, refused to vote for the approval of the Peres government.
6. Goldberg, *The Israeli Voter 1992*, p.108.
7. Ibid., pp.115–17.
8. It is noteworthy that at the opposite end of the political spectrum a similar mistake was not made. The ultra-Orthodox parties were identified with Netanyahu only in the last days before the elections. This identification by both Ashkenazi ultra-Orthodox parties, Agudat Yisrael and Degel HaTorah, was weaker than that of Meretz and was not publicly confessed, but hinted at. SHAS did not make any formal commitment to Netanyahu, although Rabbi Kadourie, one of the most popular spiritual leaders of the religious Oriental community, expressed his support for Netanyahu by blessing him a few days before the elections.
9. Asher Arian, *The Choosing People* (Ramat Gan, 1973), p.88 (Hebrew).
10. Goldberg, pp.195–6.
11. Ibid., *The Israeli Voter*, pp.199–205.
12. Since the Central Bureau of Statistics did not publish detailed results until after this article's deadline, the analysis was based on results published in Israeli newspapers, such as *Ma'ariv*, June 2, 1996, *Yediot Aharonot*, May 31, 1996, and *Zman Tel Aviv*, June 7, 1996.
13. This might be explained by the same reasons – the Yemenites tend to be more religious than other ethnic groups; the special impact that Rabin's assassin was of Yemenite origin; in recent years the issue of the "kidnapping of Yemenite children" was on the top of the political agenda as a group of extremists violently protested against the Labor government over this issue; the two prominent leaders of Labor of Yemenite origin were out of the campaign this time. Yisrael Kesar left the political arena and Avigdor Kahalani left Labor and founded the Third Way party which attracted more Yemenite voters than other Oriental groups.
14. On the methodological difficulties in measuring split-ticket voting see, Giora Goldberg, "Analyzing the Trends of Split-Ticket Voting in Israel," *Journal of Political Science*, Vol.11, No.2 (Spring 1984):83–94.
15. Goldberg, *The Israeli Voter 1992*, pp.178–9.

Religion, Ethnicity and Electoral Reform: The Religious Parties and the 1996 Elections

ELIEZER DON-YEHIYA

The 1996 elections to the 14th Knesset brought the religious parties in Israel their greatest electoral achievement in the political history of the Jewish State. This essay examines the accomplishments of the religious parties in the perspective of their electoral history and seeks to account for their impressive electoral success in the 1996 elections. It will investigate the electoral strategies of the religious parties, their sources of support, and the developments and changes in Israeli society and polity which had a significant impact on the religious parties and the behavior of their potential electorate.

Three religious parties, SHAS, the National Religious Party (NRP) and United Torah Jewry (UTJ) crossed the electoral threshold of 1.5 percent needed to win a seat in the Knesset, gaining together 23 seats, a combined share of 19.5 percent of the votes. The aggregate parliamentary representation of the religious parties had never before risen above 18 mandates. Two other religious lists competed – Telem Emuna, which had split from SHAS and headed by Rabbi Yosef Azran, received 0.4 percent and Yemin Israel, a list headed by Miriam Lapid, formerly of Moledet, which gained less that 0.1 percent of the vote. The overall electoral gain of the religious lists was 20 percent of the total vote.

The electoral achievement of the religious parties is even more impressive since it came after a decline in the aggregate electoral power in the 1992 elections when they declined from 18 to 16 mandates. Thus, in 1996, the religious parties succeeded in increasing their combined parliamentary power by 50 percent, from 16 to 23 Knesset seats.[1]

Eliezer Don-Yehiya is Professor of Political Studies at Bar-Ilan University.

THE ELECTORAL GAINS OF THE RELIGIOUS PARTIES

The electoral gains in 1996 were by no means equally divided. These gains were shared by only two of the three parties as the UTJ only managed to retain its four Knesset seats. The biggest winner was SHAS which raised its parliamentary representation from 6 to 10 seats. Thus, SHAS increased its electoral basis from 4.9 to 8.5 percent. The NRP, the second largest religious party, also increased its parliamentary and electoral power, although not to the same extent as SHAS. The number of its Knesset seats grew from 6 to 9 and its electoral support from 5.0 to 7.8 percent.

There is, however, another and more significant difference between the electoral gains of SHAS and the NRP. SHAS' electoral achievement was by far the greatest in its history. Never before had SHAS succeeded in gaining more than 6 Knesset seats. Moreover, these elections clearly demonstrated that despite being a relative newcomer to Israeli politics, SHAS has had a growing base of support. It should be mentioned here that SHAS first appeared in the 1984 elections when it gained 4 seats. In 1988, SHAS increased its mandates to 6, and this was repeated in the 1992 elections. Therefore, the 10 seats gained by SHAS in 1996 can be seen as the culminating point in the process of electoral expansion and consolidation of a new party.

In contrast to many other new parties that sought to gain entry to the Israeli and West European political arenas, SHAS proved itself to be more than just a "flash party."[2] All the former ethnic lists either failed in their first electoral attempt or proved to be a temporary phenomenon as in the case of SHAS' predecessor, Tami. That party gained 3 seats in its first election campaign in 1981, but lost two of them in 1984 and withdrew from the political arena.

The NRP, on the other hand, is a veteran party formally established in 1956. Its origins go back to the pre-state period, created as it was out of the fusion of the two Zionist religious parties – Mizrachi, founded in 1902 and Ha-poel Ha-mizrachi, founded in 1922.[3] In 1996, the NRP increased its electoral power compared with 1992 and in comparison to all elections since 1981. However, in contrast to SHAS, its achievement was far from being the highest electoral accomplishment in its political history. From its establishment in 1956 and until the 1981 elections, the NRP held always more than the 9 seats won in 1996. Nevertheless, taken from another perspective, the NRP's achievement in the recent elections is all the more impressive given the fact that it increased its parliamentary representation by 50 percent from 6 to 9 mandates, after a protracted period of electoral decline or stagnation.

This period began with the NRP's defeat in the 1981 elections, in which it lost half of its electoral power and declined from 12 to 6 seats. The 1981 defeat was followed by further decline in the 1984 and 1988 elections in which the NRP garnered only 4 and 5 seats respectively. The

NRP gained an additional Knesset seat in the 1992 elections, but it was only in 1996 that it raised its electoral and parliamentary power beyond the 1981 achievement of 6 mandates.

TWO PERIODS IN THE HISTORY OF THE RELIGIOUS PARTIES

The fluctuations in the electoral performance of the NRP in the elections held since 1981 stand in sharp contrast to the pattern of electoral stability that was a distinguishing mark of the religious parties up to 1981.[4] There are two distinct periods in the history of the religious parties in Israel. The first, from the establishment of the state in 1948 until 1981, was characterized by basic electoral stability, while the second, from 1981 to the present, was marked by change and fluctuation in the electoral power of these parties.

In this regard the difference between the two periods is demonstrated by the fact that in the first 9 elections, from 1949 to 1977, the gap between the lowest and the highest parliamentary representation of the religious parties did not exceed 3 seats. The lowest representation – 15 – was in the elections of 1951 and the highest – 18 – in the years 1959, 1961 and 1969. In six out of the nine elections during this period the maximal gap was only one seat as the religious parties gained either 17 or 18 mandates. By contrast, in the years 1981 to 1996, the maximal gap was ten seats. The lowest rate of representation – 13 – came in the wake of the 1981 and 1984 elections and the highest – 23 –in the present Knesset.

The distinction between the two periods in the electoral history of the religious parties applies not only to these parties as an aggregate unit, but also to each one of them. Thus, in contrast to the second period beginning with the NRP's defeat in 1981, the first period was characterized by a high degree of electoral stability. In all the elections held before 1981, the NRP received between 10 and 12 mandates.

The same pattern of electoral stability in the first period and electoral volatility in the second was also evident in the Haredi (ultra-Orthodox) parties – Agudat Israel and Poalei Agudat Israel, although the turning point for these parties was not the 1981 elections. For Agudat Israel the change came in the 1984 elections. In all the previous elections it gained between 3 and 4 seats. In 1984, it lost half of its electoral power, declining from 4 to 2 seats for the first time in its history. In 1988, Agudat Israel raised its parliamentary representation to 5, which was its highest electoral achievement. This was all the more impressive because Degel Ha-torah, having broken from Agudat Israel, gained 2 seats. In 1992, these two parties reunited to become the United Torah Judaism (UTJ) party, but only managed to gain 4 seats, losing 3 out of the 7 seats that they had won as separate lists in the previous election. UTJ retained its parliamentary representation after the 1996 elections, although it witnessed a slight decline of 0.2 percent in its electoral support.

The decline of Poalei Agudat Israel preceded that of the other religious parties. Before 1977 that party won 2 or 3 seats, but in 1977, for the first time in its history, Poalei Agudat Israel won only 1 seat, and in 1981 did not gain a single seat. In 1984, Poalei Agudat Israel joined a nationalist religious list, Matzad, which had split from the NRP, to become Morasha and won 2 mandates. In 1988, it again won 1 seat by joining in an electoral alliance with Agudat Israel. Since then Poalei Agudat Israel has had no representation in the Knesset.

The differences between the two periods in the electoral history of the religious parties is reflected in the balance of power within the political religious camp. The electoral stability that was a mark of the religious parties in the first period resulted in a stable balance of power between the parties. By contrast, the changes and fluctuations of the second period were reflected in marked changes in this balance of power. From its establishment in 1956 and until the 1981 elections, the NRP won approximately two-thirds of the combined vote for the religious parties (the "religious" vote or electorate). However, after 1981, the NRP did not get even half of the religious vote and in 2 of the 5 elections held since then, in 1984 and 1988, the NRP did not win a third of the religious electorate.

This decline in NRP fortunes did not result in a parallel increase in the relative electoral share of the two veteran Haredi parties, Agudat Israel and Poalei Agudat Israel. These parties gained approximately one-third of the religious vote before the 1981 elections. Only in 1988 did they gain more and in 3 out of 5 elections held in the second period, the Aguda parties received less than one-quarter of the combined religious votes.

STABILITY AND CHANGE AT THE ORGANIZATIONAL LEVEL

From 1981, there was a decline in the share of the veteran parties of the total vote for religious parties. This trend was the result of splits in the ranks of these parties and the arrival of new religious parties which competed successfully for the votes of the religious electorate. Here it should be noted that the changes witnessed by the religious parties in the 1996 elections were limited mainly to the electoral level, and were not manifested on the organizational level. That is, the religious parties which won Knesset seats in 1996 were the same 3 parties which won seats in 1992. In this respect the recent elections were different from other elections held since 1981. In the elections between 1981 and 1992, the tendency for change and instability that characterized the religious parties during that period was also felt on the organizational level. Since 1956, when Mizrachi and Ha-poel Ha-mizrachi united to form the National Religious Party, and until 1981, there was no real change in the number and identity of the religious parties. In the elections of 1977, the religious community was still represented by the same 3 parties – the NRP and the two veteran Haredi paries – Agudat Israel and Poalei Agudat Israel.

By contrast, from 1981 until 1992 there was not a single election without considerable changes in the identity of religious parties competing for and gaining seats in the Knesset. Thus, the 1981 elections were the first in which a new religious party, Tami, having seceded from the NRP, gained representation in the Knesset. In 1984, two new religious parties won seats – SHAS with 4 mandates and Morasha with 2. Morasha had been formed by the coalition of Matzad, which had broken off from the NRP and Poalei Agudat Israel. For the 1988 elections, Matzad reunited with the NRP while Poalei Agudat Israel reunited with Agudat Israel. At the same time a division occurred within the ranks of Agudat Israel as the disciples of Rabbi Shach seceded from the party and established their own party, Degel Ha-torah, which gained 2 seats. In 1992, the two Ashkenazi Haredi parties reunited to form a common list called Yahadut Ha-torah Ha-meuchedet – United Torah Judaism. The number of religious parties which held seats in the 13th Knesset fell to three as new religious lists, participating in the 1992 elections, failed to cross the electoral threshold. In contrast to all the elections since 1981, none of the religious parties represented in the 13th Knesset witnessed a split or a reunion in the elections to the 14th Knesset. Again the religious camp is represented by the same three religious parties that gained seats in the 13th Knesset as new religious lists did not succeed in winning even one mandate.

It is too early to know whether the recent elections indicate a trend toward organizational consolidation and stabilization within the ranks of the religious camp. However, it does seem that both the 1992 and 1996 elections point to a reversal of the trend towards fragmentation and fluctuation that characterized that camp since 1981. To a certain extent this can be accounted for by the law enacted before the 1992 elections which increased the threshold for representation in the Knesset from 1 to 1.5 percent of the electoral vote.

This could be a particularly relevant factor in the case of United Torah Judaism, composed of two factions – Agudat Israel and Degel Ha-torah. These factions, having parted ways before the 1988 elections, reunited for the 1992 elections and stayed united for the 1996 elections despite conflicting interests and threats of a renewed split. It seems that the efforts made to reestablish and maintain the alliance were enhanced by the fear that if they competed on different lists, one or both might not cross the electoral threshold. A contributing factor here was the experience of electoral lists which failed to gain a seat in 1992, i.e. Tehiya and religious lists headed by Rabbi Peretz and Rabbi Levinger. This failure was instrumental in deterring religious groups from splitting their parties or forming new ones. It was a central argument in persuading leaders of new religious lists not to participate in the 1996 elections. These pressures resulted in Rabbi Yosef Ba-Gad's decision to withdraw his electoral list, Moreshet Avot.[5] The negative experience of religious lists in 1992 also affected religious voters unwilling to vote for parties with little chance of gaining representation. To a certain extent this consideration may have been a factor in the failure of the two new religious lists, Telem Emuna and Yemin Israel, to gain seats, in a kind of self-fulfilling prophecy.

Other factors also account for the halt and even reversal in the trend of fragmentation and organizational instability of recent elections. It seems that the 1996 elections reflect a growing sense of the need for unity and cooperation within the religious community in Israel. There are several indications for this quest for greater unity within the ranks of the religious community. One of them was the effort made before the elections to form an electoral alliance of all the religious parties. This attempt failed because of strong opposition by Degel Ha-torah which threatened to split once again from UTJ if it joined such an alliance.

However, it is significant that the idea of a religious front gained wide support in various segments of the religious public and a campaign on its behalf was initiated by several activists who established a pressure group by the name of Supporters of the United Religious Front.[6] That group commissioned a public opinion poll which predicted that the formation of an electoral bloc would result in an increase of 2 to 3 Knesset seats for the religious parties.[7] Members of the group lobbied the leaders of the three religious parties who publicly endorsed its aim, albeit with varying degrees of enthusiasm. These leaders held discussions to negotiate the terms for the proposed electoral alliance but backed out mainly because of the resistance of Degel Ha-torah.[8]

Failure to establish an electoral bloc did not preclude negotiations for coordination and cooperation before and after the elections. It was in this spirit that the NRP leader, Zevulun Hammer, suggested that the torah sages of all religious parties call their adherents to only vote for religious parties. This idea was not accepted, as the Haredi spiritual leaders were not willing to give public legitimization to voting for a non-Haredi Zionist party. However, his suggestion to form a united religious bloc for conducting coalition negotiations after the elections was accepted.

THE ELECTION CAMPAIGN – INTERNAL RELATIONS AND "HUNTING FIELDS"

It should be noted that the spirit of accommodation within the religious community was not manifested so much in formal agreements between the religious parties as in the style and content of their election campaigns. The significant fact here is that the religious parties did not attack or compete with each other. Instead these parties focused their efforts on mobilizing voters from their own potential electorate or from those who were outside the religious community. The chairman of UTJ election headquarters, Rabbi Avraham Ravitz, was cited as saying, "We will not attack any religious party. We are not willing to incite ethnic strife. We will not issue one word attacking SHAS." In response SHAS leader Arye Deri said, "We took a similar decision. We are not willing to incite a controversy within the religious public. During the negotiations regarding a united religious front we agreed that the religious parties would not attack each other."[9]

This pattern of relationship stands in striking contrast to past electoral behavior, particularly in the 1988 elections and especially by the Haredi parties. This change in the internal relations within the religious and Haredi camps was noticed by observers of the 1996 campaign. One reporter claimed that "the decision of the three Haredi parties – UTJ, SHAS and Telem Emuna – to refrain from attacking each other prevented much violence and slander, but killed the campaign... Even denigrating pamphlets, the basic weapons in every Haredi controversy, were hardly distributed."[10] A similar pattern was observed in the relations between the Haredi and religious Zionist parties, which were also careful not to attack each other during the 1996 campaign.

There were several factors which accounted for this lack of rivalry between the various religious parties. First, there was the ideological factor, manifested in the growing affinity between the positions of the various religious parties and their adherents on religious and political issues. Two trends were at work here – the religious radicalization of religious Zionist groups and the political radicalization of Haredi groups. While both these trends were not shared by all segments of the two communities they were significant enough to form a basis for a kind of ideological rapprochement between them.

A related development was the growing involvement of the Haredim in the Israeli political system after Haredi parties joined the Likud coalition government after the 1977 elections. This process was enhanced in 1996 as many Haredim actively cooperated in Binyamin Netanyahu's campaign for the premiership. As Netanyahu was firmly supported by the NRP, it also served as a common political ground between adherents of Haredi and religious Zionist parties. The existence of common political ground between the various segments of the religious electorate was further demonstrated by the results of the direct elections for the prime minister in which about 90 percent of religious voters voted for Netanyahu.

Another relevant development was the growing penetration of SHAS into non-Haredi and even non-Orthodox circles. To a considerable extent this had the effect of blurring the political barriers between Haredi and non-Haredi segments of the religious community.

To a certain extent the marked change within the Haredi political camp can be attributed to the special circumstances of the electoral campaigns. The 1995 decision by SHAS to leave the Labor-dominated

coalition and join the other religious parties in the opposition helped to
calm the controversy with the religious camp that had focused on the
SHAS' original decision to join the coalition after the 1992 elections.

One of the distinguishing marks of the 1988 campaign was the sharp
controversy between Rabbi Shach, founder and spiritual leader of Degel
Ha-torah, and Rabbi Menachem Mendel Shneerson, the late Lubavitzer
Rebbe and leader of the Habbad Hasidic sect. That controversy was one
of the main factors behind the decision of Rabbi Shach to break away
from Agudat Israel.[11] It prompted the active involvement of Habbad in
the 1988 campaign of Agudat Israel. This Habbad activity, which greatly
contributed to the electoral success of Agudat Israel in 1988, was also a
major factor in the intensification of the rivalry between that party and
Degel Ha-torah. The reunification of Agudat Israel and Degel Ha-torah
in 1992 brought about the withdrawal of Habbad from internal Haredi
politics and marked the depolitization of the controversy between
Habbad and the followers of Rabbi Shach, thus contributing to the
restoration of relative peace within the Ashkenazi Haredi world.

There was, however, another important aspect to Habbad's
involvement in the 1988 campaign which has wider implications for the
general issue of relationship between the religious parties and the
changes that have occurred in this area. The involvement of Habbad in
that campaign was instrumental in mobilizing wide segments of the
electorate from outside the haredi community to the Aguda camp. Most
of them were traditional Sephardi Jews influenced by Habbad. These
were the same voters whom SHAS considered to be its natural potential
electorate. Thus, during the 1988 campaign, SHAS and Agudat Israel
were competing in the same "hunting field," which caused the strife
between these parties. The term "hunting field" has been used by Angelo
Panebianco[12] to denote specified segments of the population which are
regarded by a certain political party as its potential electorate and the
main focus of its campaign efforts. In 1992, leaders of UTJ once again
attempted to attract Sephardi voters by placing former SHAS member,
Rabbi Yitzhak Peretz, in a top position on their list of candidates for the
Knesset. In spite of this, the Sephardi voters turned their backs on UTJ
and supported SHAS. This caused a sharp decline in the electoral share
of UTJ forcing Peretz to give up his seat in the Knesset in favor of an
Ashkenazi candidate from Degel Ha-torah.

Thus, the 1992 elections demonstrated that traditional Sephardi
Jews, particularly those from North African segment, were the almost
exclusive domain of SHAS. Not all were willing to come to terms with
this political reality as seen by the unsuccessful attempt of Rabbi Yosef
Azran, who had left SHAS, to compete for the Sephardi vote in 1996.
The Ashkenazi leaders of UTJ realized before Azran's defeat that the
Sephardi sector was not their "hunting field" and concentrated their
efforts on their own Ashkenazi community.

However, not all Sephardi voters in the religious camp went to SHAS.

The NRP won the support of quite a significant number of Sephardi voters and the results of the elections indicate that it even widened its electoral share in Sephardi population centers. However, the NRP was never a real threat to SHAS for the bulk of religiously traditional Sephardi voters. After the 1981 elections the NRP derived most of its electoral support from the religious Ashkenazi sector and this did not change significantly in the 1996 elections. The great decline of the NRP in 1981, when it lost half of its electoral support, was due, to a large extent, to the desertion of many Sephardi voters who preferred to cast their votes for Tami (an ethnic Sephardi party which split off from the NRP), or for the Likud. Although Tami failed to retain its voters, most did not return to the NRP. Many returned to the Likud, but a large number lent their support to the newly established SHAS party. The NRP, after a series of failed attempts, eventually realized that it could not win back most of its former voters from SHAS.

That is not to say that the NRP has become an Ashkenazi party. While losing many of its Sephardi voters, the NRP has kept many others within its ranks and has induced young voters of Sephardi origin to join. Nevertheless, the NRP, like UTJ, was not competing in the same "hunting field" as SHAS during the 1996 elections. Still a minority in the NRP, most Sephardi voters for that party differ from most SHAS voters. First, while all traditional Sephardi Jews are targeted by SHAS those of North African origin are its most ardent supporters. The NRP, on the other hand, has more electoral appeal with other Sephardi groups such as the Yemenites or the Tripolitanians. Secondly, as is also indicated by the results of the 1996 elections, SHAS was most successful in residential areas with heavy concentrations of Sephardim, many of whom are located in development towns. The NRP electorate is more evenly spread out and many, if not most of its Sephardi voters, live in ethnically mixed neighborhoods.

The third and most important point is that many of the Sephardim who have voted for the NRP since 1981 have undergone a process of acculturation to the Ashkenazi religious Zionist culture, and most of them have internalized the religious nationalist worldview which had become common among religious Zionists since the Six-Day War. Many of these Sephardim are graduates of yeshivot affiliated with the religious Zionist camp.

By contrast, the bulk of SHAS voters are traditional Jews who were educated in state religious schools but who did not really integrate into the religious Zionist sub-culture. They did not study in Zionist yeshivot and were not members of the religious Zionist youth movement, Bnei Akiva. Graduates of Ashkenazi yeshivot played a central role in the establishment of SHAS and were its first high ranking leaders. The yeshivot from which SHAS founders graduated were in the Haredi Ashkenazi world where they had felt ethnically discriminated against and which gave them the incentive to found a Sephardi party. In contrast to its leaders, most SHAS voters are not Haredim (ultra-Orthodox) and many of them are not even Orthodox. In this respect, too, the typical Sephardi supporter of the NRP is different from that of SHAS.

This does not mean that there was no competition between SHAS and the NRP. However, the 1996 elections attest to the fact that the leaders of both SHAS and NRP chose to concentrate their efforts on those segments of the population considered to be their most natural potential supporters. The results of the recent elections confirm these considerations. To a certain degree the results can also be interpreted as a kind of self-fulfilling prophecy influenced by the mobilization efforts of the parties. However, the relevant point here is that both NRP and SHAS did not compete for voters. This is even more so for UTJ as it has accepted the fact that it has become an almost exclusive Ashkenazi Haredi party. Thus we can say that one of the major reasons for the relatively internal peace within the religious camp in the 1996 electoral campaign was the fact that the various religious parties realized that each one of them had its own distinct hunting field. UTJ concentrated on Ashkenazi Haredim while SHAS directed its campaign at traditional Jews of Sephardi descent, and the NRP concentrated its efforts within the ranks of the religious Zionist camp with an additional effort to reach secular Zionists worried about the Jewishness of the State of Israel.

It should be noted that there was a marked difference between UTJ, on the one hand, and the NRP and SHAS, on the other. UTJ did not make a serious attempt to reach voters beyond its Haredi sub-culture and it surely did not try to appeal to non-religious voters. By contrast, both the NRP and SHAS did make efforts to reach voters beyond the borders of the religious community. These efforts proved to be much most successful in the case of SHAS, but it is significant that both these religious parties were not content to limit their electoral appeal to religious voters.

There are still distinct differences between the kind of potential voter from outside the religious community approached by the NRP and SHAS. SHAS concentrated its efforts on traditional Jews from the Sephardi sector and began to mobilize well before 1996, but its impact of SHAS on the Sephardi sector has grown in recent years. This is evident by both the campaign strategies and the electoral achievements of SHAS within this sector. SHAS inroads into non-Orthodox but traditional Sephardi circles played a major role in its impressive electoral success in the last elections. This will be elaborated upon in our discussion of the electoral strategies of the religious parties.

In its efforts to expand its electoral appeal beyond the religious camp, the NRP turned to a very different source of potential voters than did SHAS. These were secular Zionists, most of whom were Ashkenazim with right-wing inclinations. Thus, SHAS and the NRP were expanding their "hunting fields" in different direction and thus avoided confrontation.

The NRP and SHAS employed different electoral strategies to expand their pool of potential voters. SHAS used traditional or religious symbols and slogans to appeal to a wide audience of Sephardi Jews. The NRP addressed its non-religious audience with symbols and slogans taken from classical Zionist repertoire such as the need to renew values of pioneering and love of the Land of Israel and the Jewish people.

This motif of defending the Jewishness of the Jewish state was common to all religious parties who used it among religious and non-religious voters alike. It was linked, explicitly or implicitly, to the charge that under the Labor-led government there was a tendency to devalue the Jewish character of Israel. Although the Meretz party was blamed as the chief culprit for initiating this trend, the Labor party was also held responsible for Meretz's anti-religious and post-Zionist cultural activities.

A common enemy or threat can serve as a powerful uniting factor and therefore the "Meretz factor" within the Labor government is relevant to this discussion of relations within the religious camp during the 1996 campaign. The spirit of unity and cooperation within the religious camp was enhanced by the formation of a coalition government after the 1992 elections in which Meretz replaced the religious parties as a pivotal party. A common enemy or threat can also be used as a powerful weapon and tool of mobilization by a political party. This will be elaborated upon below in our discussion of the electoral strategies of the religious parties in the 1996 campaign.

THE ELECTORAL STRATEGIES OF THE RELIGIOUS PARTIES

The "Meretz factor" played a considerable role in the 1996 election campaigns of all the religious parties. The Labor-led coalition, with Meretz in charge of educational and cultural affairs, was presented as striving to weaken and even eradicate Jewish tradition and values and to replace them with a totally secular, hedonistic and permissive way of life, imported from the West. In order to reverse the dangerous trend of moral and religious decline in Israeli society and to retain and enhance its Jewish character, the religious parties concluded that they had to replace Meretz as the influential factor in the shaping of Israeli society and culture. Thus, in their campaign the religious parties pointed to attitudes and policies of the outgoing government and its ministers which were instrumental in encouraging both permissive behavior among Israeli youth and their lack of knowledge of Jewish values and tradition. A special emphasis was placed on the decision of Meretz Minister of Education Amnon Rubinstein to select subjects for Matriculation exams by lottery resulting in the dropping of the Bible as a subject in the 1996 exams. In reaction to this, UTJ prepared an education broadcast in which a teenager with long hair and an earring was shown saying, "It does not disturb me that they decided to remove the Bible from the Matriculation. If that is what the people in high office decided, they surely know why."[13] While he spoke a hand pushed aside a closed Bible as a journal called *Technologies* was drawn closer.

The religious parties also made use of a Supreme Court ruling which, in their opinion, reflected the trend toward the secularization and westernization of Israeli society. A ruling by Aharon Barak, president of the Supreme Court, was interpreted as putting into question the legitimacy of aspiration for the application of Jewish Law to the judicial system. In response to Barak's ruling, the United Torah Judaism party published a poster which declared, "The cat is out of the Bag! Constitution + the Supreme Court = anti-religious coercion. We will ward off the war against Judaism. We must save Israel from their hands!"[14] A similar line of response was adopted by SHAS, whose leader, Arye Deri announced to a SHAS party assembly, "I am saying to Judge Barak that SHAS perceives the laws of Torah as the true laws of Israel and it will strive with all its strength to apply them in the State of Israel."[15]

While all the religious parties targeted Meretz as a serious threat to the Jewishness of Israel, it was the NRP which placed a special emphasis on this factor in its electoral strategy. An election poster distributed by the NRP was headlined, "Let the NRP deal with Meretz."[16] Meretz responded with the warning, "If Peres is tied to the NRP, the peace process will be halted."[17] These attacks were used by both parties as a mobilizing tool to win more votes. Nachum Langental, chairman of the NRP campaign claimed that a senior member of Meretz suggested that they should continue to slander each other because this was good for their common interest – taking votes from the large parties.[18] Langental responded, "We are happy to be attacked by Meretz."

Meretz was used as a negative symbol of secular society and culture, portrayed as morally deficient and a serious threat to Jewish values by the religious parties. During an assembly opening the NRP electoral campaign, party leader, Zevulun Hammer, presented secular society as tainted by permissiveness, drug addiction, drunkenness and the breaking of family ties.[19]

The NRP was, nevertheless, careful not to attack secular Jews as such. Instead it placed the blame on avowedly secular, individualistic and universalistic trends in Israeli society and their militant adherents in the political and cultural establishment. In contrast to its previous campaigns, the NRP did not emphasize political issues such as the Oslo Accords or even the planned withdrawal from Hebron.[20] Instead it focused on the need to preserve and promote Jewish and Zionist values and in this spirit the NRP's main slogan was, "The NRP – Zionism with a soul," which a non-religious journalist predicted would be regarded as "the most effective electoral slogan in the history of the State."[21] In line with that slogan, the NRP invested efforts to attract non-religious voters by stressing its devotion to Jewish and Zionist values.

Campaign strategies are shaped by considerations with regard to the nature of the main target groups and the efficient means to approach them and to gain their trust and support. The notion of a target group is related to, but distinct from, the notion referred to above as a "hunting field." By definition a target group is inside the borders of a party's "hunting field," and is a group to which the party pays special attention in its election campaign. In 1996, the NRP added to its traditional target group (the religious Zionist community) two other groups – non-religious voters with right-wing inclinations and a strong attachment to Jewish and Zionist values, and religious Zionists who did not vote for the NRP in previous elections.

In order to attract non-religious voters the NRP gave prominence to non-religious people who had declared their support for that party. In its first election broadcast, the NRP presented a non-religious man who said that he decided to wear a knitted kipa because of "the persecution of the religious public in the wake of the Rabin murder." In its second broadcast, another non-religious person said, "he envied the parents of those boys and girls who preferred struggling for the integrity of the Land over wallowing in the smoke and alcohol of discotheques."[22] The NRP also presented the actor Yehuda Barkan explaining that "as a Jew I was looking for a party which would promote Jewishness and Israeliness and therefore I decided to go with the NRP, as it embodies Zionism with a soul."[23]

While attempting to reach voters outside of the religious Zionist community, the NRP also tried to win back voters who had left them or who had never supported the NRP despite their strong links to the religious Zionist sub-culture. These people did not vote for the NRP before for many reasons. Most of them were right-wing voters who did not trust the NRP to stand firmly for preserving the integrity of the Land of Israel and for promoting the cause of the settlements in the administered territories. In particular they were worried that the NRP might join a coalition government led by Labor. Thus, they preferred to cast their vote for the Likud or for parties such as Moledet or Tehiya. On the other hand, there were religious Zionists who felt that the NRP had gone too far to the right. In 1988, these people split from the NRP and established the Meimad movement which failed to gain a Knesset seat and has not run in an election since then.

The common denominator among religious Zionists who did not vote for the NRP in the past was that they did not feel that religious values and interests were under serious threat and therefore they could give priority to political and other considerations. The strong emphasis of the NRP on the negative attitude of the former Labor-led coalition toward Jewish tradition was designed, to a large extent, to persuade these people to return to the fold in order to take part in the crucial battle for the defense of Judaism against the threats of non-Jewish and post-Zionist secularism.

In contrast to the NRP, SHAS and UTJ did not use the "religion is in danger" motif to persuade voters who had left them to "return home."

The United Torah Judaism party emphasized the threat to Torah values and way of life to entice Haredi voters to participate in the elections and to prevent them from casting their votes for right-wing parties such as Likud or Moledet. SHAS, on the other hand, strove to retain and broaden its electoral support base in the Sephardi community by pointing to the harm inflicted on that community and its traditional way of life by modern Israeli society and its secular culture.

In contrast to the NRP, there was not much innovation in SHAS' election campaign. Its non-involvement policy in the contest between Netanyahu and Peres was in line with its strategy in previous campaigns when SHAS was not willing to identify itself with any of the two major parties. Although SHAS political leader, Arieh Deri, had declared before the 1992 elections that his party preferred a coalition with the Likud, he did not commit to joining only a Likud-led government and in contrast to the other religious parties, SHAS joined the Labor-led coalition that was formed after the 1992 elections.

In the 1996 campaign, SHAS basically elaborated on the motifs and tactics from its previous campaigns and directed its efforts towards the same target group – traditional Sephardi Jews. Thus, SHAS again used slogan "to restore the crown to its [glorious] past," which was designed to identify SHAS with a promise of renewal for Sephardi Jewry and its traditional culture.

As in previous election campaigns, Rabbi Ovadia Yosef played a central role in the 1996 SHAS campaign. His authority and popularity within the Sephardi community had been further enhanced after his successful efforts to gain independent stature vis-a-vis Ashkenazi Torah giants such as Rabbi Shach. Also his televised Torah lectures which were broadcast on video screens in many centers around the country increased Rabbi Yosef's influence. His undisputed authority among most Sephardim was strengthened by the political fate of former SHAS leaders, Rabbis Peretz and Azran, who questioned Rabbi Yosef's authority and found themselves outside SHAS with no power base.

The charismatic personality of Rabbi Yosef and his enormous influence on Sephardim of various backgrounds and degrees of religiosity was used by SHAS to broaden its electoral appeal. In 1996, as in previous elections, he was flown by helicopter from one mass rally to another, and greeted everywhere with great enthusiasm.

During last year's campaign, Rabbi Yosef was joined by another charismatic figure, Rabbi Yitzhak Kedouri. Rabbi Kedouri, known as the "eldest mystic," stood at Rabbi Yosef's side at SHAS election rallies and urged his listeners to vote for SHAS. However, it was his blessings and good luck charms (*kameiot*) which caused the most publicity and controversy. Using these blessings and charms to encourage people to vote for SHAS was a technique used before, in the 1992 elections.[24] Yet, in 1996, SHAS made a more elaborate and extensive use of the mystical qualities of Rabbi Kedouri and especially of his *kameiot*. This was linked to the growing popularity of Rabbi Kedouri in certain circles of society and their enhanced interest in various forms of mysticism.

The distribution of *kameiot* aroused the anger of many both within the religious camp and outside of it. Rabbi Mordechai Eliyahu, adopted by the NRP as their spiritual mentor, even issued an halachic ruling against the use of these good luck charms, which angered the leaders and supporters of SHAS. The matter of the *kameiot* was one of the few controversial issues within the ranks of the religious camp during the 1996 elections. However, the main opposition to these "charms" came from Meretz activists who persuaded the chairman of the Elections Committee, Judge Theodor Or, to forbid their further distribution, ruling that this practice was a violation of the elections laws. Nevertheless, SHAS succeeded in distributing most of the *kameiot* before Or's ruling took effect. Instead of hurting SHAS' campaign, the controversy contributed to its success by enabling SHAS to present itself as a party feared and persecuted by political rivals from inside and outside the religious community.

Although it is difficult to assess the actual impact of these "charms" on the electoral success of SHAS, it is important to note that these and other practices such as the giving of blessings to SHAS voters have an impact only because they are identified with a venerated spiritual leader. Another point of interest is that many of the admirers of Rabbis Yosef and Kedouri are traditional, but not Orthodox Sephardi Jews. The importance that SHAS attached to this group was clearly demonstrated by a television broadcast in which soccer players were presented seeking and receiving the blessing of Rabbi Ovadia Yosef.

The United Torah Judaism party also made use of the identification of its target groups with spiritual leaders and their willingness to follow their lead and to obey their directions. What is common to both parties and distinguishes them from the NRP is this attitude of reverence and obedience toward the Torah Sages, which goes beyond the halachic-religious arena and has an effect on political matters. In contrast to SHAS, UTJ did not distribute *kameiot* but rather used public calls by famous rabbis and heads of yeshivot to support UTJ. It also notified potential voters of blessings given by these spiritual leaders to those who responded to their call. The NRP, on the other hand, did not make use of blessings, but it sought the public support of spiritual leaders such as the former Chief Rabbis, Avraham Shapira and Mordechai Eliyahu.

A common campaign tactic was the emphasis by religious parties on their achievements in establishing institutions which advance the ideals of their adherents and serve their spiritual and economic needs. In particular, all the religious parties stressed their achievements in the educational sphere. The NRP emphasized the system of state religious schools, yeshiva high schools and the Hesder yeshivot (a combination of religious studies and army service). SHAS stressed the importance of its education system, El Ha-mayan, while UTJ indicated its role in defending and promoting the traditional Haredi yeshivot. All the religious parties stressed their educational (and other) institutions' dependence on government aid which in turn depends on the degree of political power of these parties.

During the 1996 campaign, the religious parties deemphasized controversial issues such as foreign and defense policies. This was particularly true of SHAS and UTJ, which avoided issues such as the status of the administered territories and the peace process. The NRP, as noted above, stressed the importance of the Jewish character of Israel rather than emphasizing the integrity of the Land of Israel. In this way it could draw support from all sides of the political spectrum, including non-religious Zionists. For that purpose, the NRP claimed that its list of candidates was politically balanced even though among its first six candidates were four with strong right-wing views. Attempting to bring back former NRP voters, that party publicized endorsements from people such as former Tehiya leaders,[25] on the one hand as well as from political moderates such as Rabbi Aharon Liechtenstein, head of the Hesder yeshiva, Har Etzion who has been identified with Meimad. In his public endorsement of the NRP, Rabbi Liechtenstein expressed the view that issues of foreign and defense policy should be dominant in the elections for the prime minister, while in Knesset elections, the voters should focus on social matters and the Jewish character of the State.[26]

It seems that this line of thought played a considerable role in the decision of the NRP not to emphasize foreign and defense issues. NRP leaders realized that these could be left to the campaign for the premiership, which would allow them to concentrate on issues that could serve to highlight the special message of their party, such as the struggle for preserving and enhancing the Jewish character of Israel. This strategy was in line with the NRP's endorsement of Binyamin Netanyahu as its preferred candidate for prime minister. The NRP was telling its potential voters, most of whom were religious with right-wing leanings, that they could strengthen their political position by voting for Netanyahu while taking care of their religious or Jewish concerns by voting for the NRP.

SHAS, on the other hand, endorsed neither Netanyahu nor Peres for prime minister. Instead it called on its voters to back SHAS in the Knesset and to decide for themselves which candidate to choose for prime minister. The common denominator was that SHAS, the NRP and UTJ were all telling their potential voters that the new electoral system enabled them to split their vote – one vote for prime minister and one for the party which stands for their religious concerns.

Not only did the new system influence the campaign strategy of the religious parties, but it had a significant impact on the electoral achievements and political position of those parties. Due to their electoral gains, they became a pivotal force in the government coalition formed by Netanyahu. As a result of these gains, the religious parties regained the political power lost after Labor formed the government in 1992. This increased power is manifested in the number of cabinet portfolios and other political resources allocated to them, resulting in their having an impact on decision-making.

THE IMPACT OF THE NEW ELECTORAL SYSTEM

The electoral and political achievements of the religious parties stand in a striking contradiction to predictions that were made before the elections. It was predicted that a further decline in the power of the religious parties would be brought about by the new law for the direct election of the prime minister. As a matter of fact, the change in the elections laws was motivated, to a large extent, by the desire to reduce the power of small parties in general and religious parties in particular. The expectation that the religious parties would lose power was based on the assumption that the political impact of these parties was dependent on their position as the balance of power in the process of forming a coalition. It was therefore predicted that the religious parties would lose that position in the dual-ballot system because they would no longer decide who would form the government or who would be the prime minister.

It was also assumed that the electoral share of the religious parties was likely to decrease because voters would not be willing to split their vote. Thus, it was presumed that a major party whose candidate is running for prime minister has an advantage over a smaller party not fielding a candidate. This assumption was shared by some of the small parties who feared that religious voters might be inclined to vote for the party of their choice for prime minister. Haredi leaders were especially worried as many Haredim were actively involved in Netanyahu's campaign. An editorial published in a Bnei Brak newspaper three days before the elections stated that "the dual-ballot system of voting...might affect many in our camp so that voting for the prime minister will be followed by casting their ballot for his secular party..."[27] The Haredi weekly, "Ha-mahane Ha-haredi," published a feature story entitled, "The Secular Parties are Sweeping Across the Haredi Public." It said that, "the Torah sages had expressed their anxiety over the campaign's overwhelming effect on many Haredi youth who were distributing promotion materials [for Netanyahu's campaign]."[28]

Haredi spokesmen also accused Likud activists of using Netanyahu's popularity in the their community to encourage Haredi voters to support the Likud. Leaders of the Likud's religious sector denied that they intended to take votes from the UTJ party saying that they were only mobilizing religious support for the election of Netanyahu. Nevertheless it was reported in "Ha-mahane Ha-haredi" that Haredi youth working for Netanyahu had claimed that attempts were made to convince them to vote for the Likud, and not for UTJ or SHAS.[29] It is not clear if Likud activists were indeed trying to enhance the electoral appeal of their party among the Haredim. However, it is apparent that the Haredim and other adherents of small parties were worried about the impact of the double voting system on the electoral fortunes of their parties.

There were nevertheless those who predicted that the new system of elections would strengthen the religious parties. In fact the main reason that most of the NRP's Knesset members supported the introduction of direct elections for the prime minister was the assumption that their party would profit because it would enable religious voters to express their political positions in choosing a prime minister, while taking care of their religious interests by voting for a religious party. SHAS shared this point of view and even though it did not endorse the proposed change in the election system some SHAS members did not vote against the proposal thereby enabling its passing by the Knesset.

The assumption that the new system would be beneficial to the religious parties was also expressed during the 1996 election campaign. Avraham Stern, one of the NRP's Knesset candidates, pointed to the new election system as the main factor behind the increase in his party's electoral base of support predicted by the polls. According to Stern, NRP members soon realized "the advantage that it gives to the NRP. Our people want to decide who will be the prime minister. This time they can cast one ballot for prime minister and one for the NRP."[30]

The results of the 1996 elections were widely interpreted as confirming the view that the new system of elections was responsible for the electoral gains of the religious parties and the decline of the major parties. The outgoing prime minister, Shimon Peres, sharply criticized the new system when he argued that "even those members who advocated changing the system did not imagine that the major parties would decline and the small parties would increase their electoral power base."[31] Referring to the electoral achievement of the religious parties, the sociologist, Moshe Shoked, noted that the actual impact of the change "contradicted the expectations of its learned initiators."[32]

Not all political observers agree that the new system was the main cause for the decline of the two major parties. Former Tzomet MK (Member of Knesset), Yoash Tzidon, one of the imitators of the new system, has argued that the results of the Knesset elections were caused by changes in voter attitudes and not by the two-ballot system.[33] Another advocate of the system, Bernard Susser, has admitted that the supporters of the system were proven wrong in "contending that the prime ministerial election would naturally focus the vote on the two large parties."[34] However, Susser argues that the decline of the major parties and the rise of the small parties was affected, to a large extent, by the political strategy of the major parties to invest all their resources in the prime ministerial contest and very little in the Knesset elections. Susser predicts that "this mistake will not be repeated in the next elections." He claims that "the voters themselves, having realized the outcome of ticket splitting may well moderate their own tendencies to abandon Labor and the Likud for the allegedly greener pastures of the smaller parties."[35] This implies that while the rise of the religious and other small parties was helped by the two-ballot system, this outcome was not foreseen or intended by the voters and therefore it cannot be portrayed as a necessary product of that system. Susser's opinion can be countered by suggesting that the achievements of the religious parties were largely related to the deliberate use of the new system by voters seeking to increase the power of the small parties, while at the same time influencing the election of the prime minister.

In analyzing the impact of the new system, it should be noted that it did not increase the electoral power of all small parties. Both Meretz and Moledet lost seats, while the United Torah Judaism party only retained it parliamentary share. From this we can conclude that the impact of the new system depends on the type of parties involved. Meretz and Moledet, being ideological parties with a political agenda, do not claim to represent societal groups or sub-cultures distinguished by their internal solidarity and way of life or ethnic origin. It is unlikely, therefore, that the vote for these parties would be influenced much by the system of elections. UTJ also did not benefit from the new system because it draws it support almost exclusively from a Haredi sub-culture whose members would vote in any case for the party that represents their way of life and shared interests and is endorsed by the Torah giants.

The parties which were most successful in the 1996 elections were SHAS, the NRP, Yisrael Ba'Aliya (a new Russian immigrant party) and the Arab parties. All these parties are either religiously or ethnically based, while their voters, unlike UTJ, were also affected by national policy considerations and leadership. Many of these voters did not vote for religious or ethnic parties in previous elections, even though they identified with their cultural and social message, because they wished to influence national policy making and determine who would be the prime minister by voting for one of the major parties. The two-ballot system enabled these voters to directly influence the election of the prime minister and thus the making of national policy, while at the same time expressing solidarity with their religious or ethnic communities and promoting their interests by voting for parties that represent these communities.

SOURCES OF ELECTORAL SUPPORT

The change in the electoral system was only one of several factors that contributed to the impressive accomplishments of the religious and ethnic parties. Our interest is with those factors that, combined with the new system, accounted for the increased power of two of the religious parties – the NRP and SHAS.

First of all, we have to look at the sources of additional votes cast for these two parties. Due to the large increase in the total number of voters, the religious parties needed a considerable number of additional votes just to retain their electoral share and parliamentary representation. The number of valid votes in the 1996 elections was 3,051,594 as compared to 2,616,841 in 1992 – an increase of 434,753, the largest in the history of Israel.[36] Many, if not most, of the new voters were new immigrants from the former Soviet Union with very little knowledge of Jewish tradition or attachment to it. It is unlikely that the religious parties gained any meaningful electoral support from that source of new voters. Also, both the NRP and SHAS lost almost all of their voters in the Arab sector. Thus, in 1992, these parties gained almost the same percentage of electoral support in the Arab sector as in the Jewish sector. This support dropped drastically in the 1996 elections when SHAS' share declined from 4.8 to 1.3 percent and the NRP dropped from 4.7 to 1.7 percent of the Arab vote.[37] Due to both the immigration and Arab factors, the religious parties needed a considerable increase in their share of votes from the veteran Jewish population in order to maintain their percentage of the total vote and thus their parliamentary representation. The fact that the religious parties not only retained, but greatly increased, their electoral power makes this accomplishment even much more impressive.

Like the new immigrants, the young first-time voters were not a significant source of additional votes for the religious parties. Thus, the soldiers' vote, which constitutes a large portion of first time voters, caused the loss of one seat each for SHAS and the NRP. As the third-largest religious party, UTJ retained its electoral share and even increased the number of its voters but it could not have been a major source of additional votes for the other religious parties. All this means that SHAS and the NRP succeeded in winning over a large number of voters who had previously supported non-religious parties.

One likely source of such electoral support was former Tehiya voters. In 1992, Tehiya failed to gain a seat in the Knesset and in 1996 it did not run. Most former Tehiya voters seemed to have voted for the NRP. The move of voters from Tehiya to the NRP was a process seen already in the 1988 elections.[38] Many people also left Moledet for the NRP, and even though it gained support from former Tzomet adherents and Habbad, Moledet lost one seat, largely due to the desertion of voters for the NRP.[39] However, the votes of former Tehiya and Moledet supporters cannot account for most of the increase in NRP's electoral power, especially in view of the negative impact of the immigrant and Arab vote. In addition, Tehiya and Moledet were not a source of extra votes for SHAS.

It is obvious that the NRP and SHAS attracted voters from the two major parties, the Likud and Labor. Both these parties suffered heavy losses in the 1996 elections. Labor dropped from 42 to 34 seats, while the united electoral bloc of the Likud and Tzomet, who together held 40 seats in the 13th Knesset declined to 32 seats in the present one. Because it gained many votes from former supporters of Meretz, which lost 3 out of its 12 seats, the loss of Labor voters to other parties was even greater than what is suggested by its loss of 8 seats.

The overwhelming majority of former Labor votes went to the new immigrant party, Yisrael Ba'Aliya, which gained 7 seats, and to the Arab parties, which increased their parliamentary representation from 5 to 9 members. An additional winner of former Labor votes was The Third Way, a splinter party from Labor, which gained 4 seats. The religious parties, especially the NRP, did gain a small part of their additional votes from former Labor voters, most of whom are politically moderate religious Zionists. Many of them voted for Meimad in 1988 and for Labor in 1992. They turned to the NRP in 1996 because of its renewed emphasis on religious issues rather than on political ones, and especially because the new system allowed them to vote for Peres for prime minister and for the NRP in the Knesset elections.

It is interesting that the new electoral system encouraged both moderate and hardline religious Zionists to vote for the NRP. The reason being that both groups realized that the crucial issues of foreign and defense policies would be decided in the prime ministerial contest, while religious and cultural matters would be decided in the Knesset elections. In addition, there was a general feeling within the religious community that the Jewish character of the state was at stake. The Labor-Meretz coalition and the attacks on the religious public after the murder of Rabin both contributed to the feeling that religious people were a besieged minority, regardless of one's political leanings.

The new NRP voters were quite varied in terms of party backgrounds, ideological leanings and ethnic origin. They formerly supported right-wing parties such as Tehiya and Moledet, but also the Likud and Labor. While many of the new NRP voters were political hardliners, there was also a significant number of centrists or moderates among them. Most of these voters were religious Zionists who were returning to the fold, and a few secular Zionists concerned about the Jewish nature of the State of Israel. While many of these new voters were Ashkenazy Jews, the NRP also increased its electoral share in the concentration of Sephardi Jews.

In contrast to NRP voters, the overwhelming majority of SHAS' new electorate were traditional Sephardi Jews who, before the 1996 elections, voted for the Likud. They had never before voted for SHAS or for any other religious party and they were not a part of the religious sub-culture. A breakdown of election results according to locality indicates a strong correlation between the electoral losses of the Likud and gains by SHAS. These gains were most remarkable in localities in which there was an especially sharp decline in the electoral power of the Likud. Another finding was that while the electoral gains of SHAS far exceeded those of the NRP in development towns (where there are heavy concentrations of Sephardim), the NRP gained more than SHAS in the "religious cities." Thus, while SHAS increased its share of the electorate in development towns by 6.7 percent and the NRP by 3.1 percent, the Likud lost 10.4 percent. In the "religious cities," on the other hand, SHAS gained only 0.5 percent while the NRP grew by 2.4 percent and the Likud lost 2.4 percent of the electorate.

Like the NRP, SHAS also benefitted from the two-ballot system of elections, as well as from the perceived threat to the Jewish character of the State. However, other significant contributing factors were at work here too. To a large extent, the election results can be perceived as the culmination of a process of change seen in the sources of electoral support for SHAS and in the balance of power between it and other parties, especially the Likud. When SHAS was established in 1984 it drew most of its support from former voters for other religious parties such as Tami, the NRP and Agudat Israel. Accordingly, most of SHAS' voters were observant Sephardim of the Haredi and non-Heredi type.

By 1984 there was a certain portion of former Likud voters among SHAS' electorate but they were a minority of that electorate and many of them were observant Jews. By contrast in subsequent elections since 1988, most of SHAS' new voters were former supporters of the Likud and also traditional but non-orthodox Sephardi Jews.

To a certain extent the achievements of SHAS in the 1996 elections can by accounted for by the same factors that initiated the process of change which brought about its rise to power. In my article on the religious parties in the 1988 elections I indicated several factors that contributed to the rise of SHAS and its continued electoral successes. One was the power of SHAS' spiritual leadership to attract supporters by its promise to renew and revitalize the glorious tradition of Sephardi Jewry and to return its lost dignity. SHAS leaders not only disseminated their message through speeches and slogans, but more importantly they created and developed a nation-wide system of educational and welfare institutions for the Sephardi population and especially for its younger generation. In this way SHAS leaders demonstrated their determination to give concrete meaning and content to their promise to serve the interests of Sephardi Jewry and to work for its spiritual revival.

In addition, SHAS has benefitted by the disappointment of many Sephardim in the Likud, which did not make good on its promises to improve and promote the economic conditions and social status of the Sephardi community. Contributing factors to this were changes in the leadership of the Likud and in its internal balance of power. An especially important factor was the resignation of Menachem Begin, the charismatic Likud leader whose traditional leanings enhanced his popularity among the Sephardim.

Another development which encouraged the estrangement of Sephardim from the Likud was the defeat of David Levy in the struggle for the Likud's leadership, when he was pushed aside by his Ashkenazi rivals. Levy's defeat and the ongoing tension between Levy and Netanyahu exacerbated Sephardi feelings of alienation from the Likud, a party once considered their political home. Although Levy's splinter faction, Gesher, later formed an electoral alliance with the Likud and Tzomet, many of Levi's followers were not willing to vote for that alliance and, like many other Sephardim, voted for SHAS in 1996.

In their move away from the Likud, most Sephardi voters never considered voting for the Labor party because that party is deemed responsible for the wrongs committed during the absorption process of Sephardi immigrants and for what they consider to be their inferior status in Israeli society. In addition, the secular image of Labor was a problem for traditional as well as Orthodox Sephardim. They cared about the Jewish character of Israel which meant, for them, promoting the role of Judaism in the country. The experience of a Labor-led coalition government which included Meretz further contributed to the negative image of Labor among traditional Sephardi Jews. This, too, motivated them to vote for SHAS, a party which stands for defending both the interests of Sephardi Jews and the values of Traditional Judaism. Thus, SHAS has become the only real alternative to the Likud.

In contrast to the other religious parties, SHAS alone joined the coalition government with Labor and Meretz, although it later withdrew from that government. In spite of this, SHAS managed to take electoral advantage of both its prior participation in the coalition and its later withdrawal from it. In its electoral campaign SHAS presented its initial decision as an attempt to do whatever possible to defend the vital interests of religious Jews and particularly those of the traditional Sephardi community from within the coalition. Its justification was that in order to preserve their educational system, El Ha-mayan, which was dependent on government financial aid, SHAS had to join the Labor government. Thus, the argument goes, SHAS had to join Labor and Meretz in order to protect the religious values and vital interests of the traditional Sephardi community. According to SHAS leaders, only when they realized that the government was determined to pursue its secular policies did they decide to withdraw from the coalition. Many of the traditional Sephardim were convinced by these arguments.

While all of the above factors contributed to the impressive electoral success of SHAS, the new electoral system played an especially important role. Both SHAS and the NRP benefitted from the new system in the 1996 elections. For the NRP, the dual-ballot system neutralized the potential impact of national policy considerations in the Knesset elections by allowing voters to express their policy preferences in the prime ministerial contest and their religious preferences in the Knesset elections. For SHAS, the new system enabled traditional Sephardi Jews to express their rejection of Labor by voting for Netanyahu while declaring their traditional-ethnic solidarity by voting for SHAS. Despite their disappointment with the Likud and their reservations about its leader, most Sephardim voted for Netanyahu, not because of his positive qualities, but rather because Shimon Peres was associated with the their negative image of the Labor party.

The results of the prime ministerial contest point to the continuity of the basic division of the Israeli electorate into two almost equal camps consisting of two broad coalitions of voters. One camp lent its support to Netanyahu and voted for right-wing or religious parties. This camp represented a wide coalition of religious and Sephardi Jews (most of whom were from lower income groups) with right-wing voters. The other camp consisted mainly of Ashkenazi, secular Jews with left-wing leanings mainly from high income groups together with Arab voters. While the balance of power between these two camps had remained basically intact since the 1977 elections, there have been considerable changes within each camp and especially within the right-wing camp. This was primarily manifested in the shift of religious and traditional Sephardi voters from the Likud to the religious parties, and especially to SHAS.

SUMMARY AND CONCLUSIONS: THE ROLE OF SOCIETAL CLEAVAGES

The specific factors behind the electoral accomplishments of the religious parties in the 1996 elections can be integrated into a more general model which accounts for the changes and transformations undergone by the religious parties on both the electoral and organizational levels. The basic assumption of this model is that both the initial stability of the religious parties in the period preceding the 1981 elections and the fluctuations since then can be related to the pattern of fragmentation within Israeli society and its religious community. The impact of these divisions was in itself influenced by developments and changes that affected the nature and degree of their political relevance.

This impact was discussed in my previous article on the 1988 elections. This discussion will be summarized here with some modifications of the initial model and its application to the two recent elections. During the Yishuv period and the early years of Israeli statehood, the religious parties were aligned along two main lines of separation. One division manifested itself in differing attitudes toward Zionism and modern Israeli society and culture. The other division was the ideological-class rift between adherents of left and right-wing parties, in the original sense of these concepts, reflecting differing attitudes to social issues and class orientations. This division, which dominated the Yishuv and early Israeli society, also had an impact on the religious community. Cross-cutting through these two lines of division led to the establishment of four religious parties, representing the right and left of each of the Zionist and Haredi wings of the religious community. While these two lines of cleavage separated the various religious parties from each other, they were all separated from the secular parties by their attitudes on problems of religion and state.

The decline in the political relevance of the ideological-class division in Israeli society, which began after the establishment of the State, had an almost immediate impact on the religious political camp. In the 1955 elections, the two religious Zionist parties, Mizrachi and Ha-poel Ha-mizrachi formed an alliance and in 1956 they united into one party – the National Religious Party. The two Haredi parties, Agudat Israel and Poalei Agudat Israel also aligned in 1955, an alliance renewed in 1959 and in most later elections. Although these two Haredi parties never entered into an official merger like their Zionist counterparts, this was due to differing attitudes toward Zionism and the state of Israel and not to class division. Poalei Agudat Israel took a centrist position between the NRP and Agudat Israel.

While the political relevance of class division had been greatly reduced, the political potential of the basic division in attitudes toward the Jewish religion and its role in society had not diminished. During the first years of Israeli independence, there was even an increase in the political relevance of the religious-secular divide because of the intense debate over issues of education and religious legislation. As a result, the political behavior of most members of the religious community reflected the impact of the religious–secular rift as well as their internal division into religious Zionist supporters of the NRP and Haredi supporters of the Aguda parties.

To a large degree, the relative equilibrium of these two lines of cleavage accounted for the basic stability of the religious parties until the 1981 elections. This pattern of electoral and organizational stability was under growing pressure due to developments that affected the structure of societal division and their political role. On the one hand, there was the division between moderates and supporters of hardline positions on issues of foreign and defense policy, particularly the issue of the administered territories. The other rift was the ethnic division between Ashkenazim and Sephardim. The ideological division between political doves and hawks grew in importance and political relevance after the Six-Day War in 1967 and especially after the Yom Kippur War of 1973, and it became the dominant line of cleavage in Israeli society. The political relevance of the ethnic rift grew after the Likud victory in 1977.

As the political impact of ideological and ethnic divisions grew, there was a decline in the political relevance of religious differences. This was due to several factors, including the consolidation of the status quo arrangement in the area of state and religion, the decline of militant ideological secularism and the rise of a new civil religion with a more positive attitude toward Jewish tradition.[40] A significant development was the Likud victory in 1977, under the leadership of Menachem Begin, whose party defended the interests of the religious community and conceded to most of its political claims.

The changes in the political potential and relevance of the various societal divisions had a profound impact on the religious political camp, especially in the 1981 and 1984 elections. These changes initiated and augmented the fragmentation process within the religious parties after the 1981 elections. In addition, the divisions played a significant role in the turning of religious voters to non-religious parties.

The possible impact of the newly politicized divisions on the religious parties could have lead in three different directions. First, it could induce the traditional parties to change their policies and attitudes so as to adjust to the new divisions. Second, it could lead to the formation of new groupings which strive to represent both the old and the new divisions. Third, it could also have the effect of driving people away from their traditional political family to other political groups having more political relevance for them. This effect would be greatly enhanced if there was also a reduction in the political relevance of the older line of division.

The NRP reacted to the growing impact of the territories issue on the religious Zionist public by adapting hard-line policies and stressing the principle of the integrity of the Land of Israel. This could be the reason for the delayed impact of the ideological division on the electoral support for the NRP. However, there were those in the religious Zionist community for whom the political radicalization of the NRP had not gone far enough, and they did not trust NRP leaders to do what was needed to defend the integrity of the Land of Israel. The leaders of this group reacted in one of two ways. Some voted for the Likud or right-wing parties like Tehiya or Moledet. Others preferred to establish a new political party which claimed to represent both the religious and ideological issue. Thus, they formed a new party, Morasha, before the 1984 elections. Later this group reunited with the NRP, after that party's political platform came into line with their way of thinking. Likewise, the political moderates of the NRP established the Meimad party, after the NRP had radicalized its political platform.

The ideological rift was not the main factor behind the defeat of the NRP in 1981, a defeat from which it did not recover until 1996. The electoral decline of the NRP was caused mainly by the growing political impact of the ethnic divide. In contrast to its almost immediate response to the ideological cleavage, the NRP was late in responding to the growing political significant of the ethnic division. Those for whom the ethnic issue was a priority reacted in one of two ways. Some of them withdrew their support from the religious camp, voting for a non-religious party, the Likud, which in their view better represented the Sephardi case. Like those NRP voters who shifted to non-religious parties because of ideological considerations, those who cared about the ethnic issue were also influenced by the declining political relevance of religious issues.

Other voters who attached political significance to the ethnic division preferred to vote for new parties like Tami and SHAS, which claimed to represent both the religious and the Sephardi cause. The growing disappointment of Sephardi voters with the Likud, enhanced their identification with SHAS as the true representative and guardian of the Sephardi community and its traditional culture pushed them to vote for SHAS, a process culminating with the 1996 elections.

The results of those elections reflect a profound change in the nature of the ethnic rift and its political implications. That rift played a central role in the electoral decline of the religious parties in the 1981 and 1984 elections when these parties lost almost one-third of their aggregate electoral share. The impact of the ethnic factor was later halted and reversed, as is evident by the results of the 1996 elections in which the impressive rise to power of the religious parties was primarily due to the electoral gains of SHAS. The ethnic division, which formerly had induced the withdrawal of voters from the religious camp, turned out to be a significant factor in the mobilization of voters to that camp.

There was no such reversal in the role of ideological issues. However, the electoral achievement of the NRP in the 1996 elections indicate that the controversy over the administered territories and relations with the Arabs no longer had a negative impact on the electoral fortunes of the NRP and the religious political camp. The significant development here was the return of religious voters to the NRP having, in previous years, cast their ballots for non-religious parties – either to the right or to the left of the political spectrum.

Both the NRP and SHAS reacted similarly to the emerging political role of the ideological and ethnic divisions. Both strove to halt and reverse the negative impact of these divisions by claiming to stand for values and interests related to the ideological or to the ethnic cleavage in addition to their role as defenders of the religious cause.

SHAS was more successful than the NRP in this regard. SHAS not only restrained the negative impact of the ethnic division, but later turned it into a positive factor for political expansion of the religious political camp by attracting voters to it. Only in 1996 did the NRP manage to restrain the negative impact of the ideological rift on its electoral fortunes. Even in these elections, the NRP did not succeed in reversing the impact and turning it into a significant factor of mobilization and expansion for the NRP and the religious camp. Although it did attract voters from outside the religious Zionist sub-culture, the main factor in the electoral recovery of the NRP was its success in inducing members of the religious Zionist community to "return home." SHAS, on the other hand, owes its impressive electoral success to its ability to attract voters from the traditional, non-religious, Sephardi community.

There are several reasons for the differences between SHAS and the NRP. First of all, when the ideological and ethnic divisions emerged as important factors in the political arena, the NRP was already a veteran party whose power base was squarely in the religious community. It was also an Ashkenazi-led party with a tradition of moderate positions on matters of foreign and defense policies. SHAS, on the other hand, was a relatively new party, which based itself on a combination of religious and ethnic factors. As noted above, the NRP responded slowly to the ethnic rift, but after the Six-Day War took a stand on ideological issues, although it had to invest great effort to win the confidence of ideological hardliners in the religious Zionist camp.

Second, the NRP had to compete with other right-wing parties for nationalist voters. Some of these parties, such as Tehiya and Moledet, deliberately appealed to religious voters in their election campaigns and nominated religious personalities as their high ranking candidates for the Knesset. By contrast, because of its leadership and its ethnic composition as well as its work in the fields of education and welfare services, SHAS presented itself as the most faithful and authentic representative of the Sephardi community with no serious competitor in the traditional sector of that community.

This is related to the third point. The traditional sector of Sephardi Jewry is much larger than its counterpart in the Ashkenazi community which tends to be sharply divided between religious and secular Jews. Therefore, SHAS had far greater potential for expansion into the ranks of non-Orthodox Jews than did the NRP.

Despite the distinctions between the NRP and SHAS, their electoral success in 1996 also reflected what they had in common. Both were helped by the negative experience of the religious and traditional communities with the Labor-Meretz government. This factor played a major role in the reactivation of the political potential of the religious issue. Following 1977, when the Likud rose to power, the religious community felt that the Jewish character of the State and the interests of the religious community were in good hands. Thus, many religious people concluded that they had less need for a religious party to represent and defend their basic values and way of life. However, with the return of Labor in 1992, and its subsequent partnership with the anti-religious Meretz party, the religious community felt threatened.

The decline in the political role of religious issues paved the way for the increased political impact of ideological and ethnic matters on the religious community. In the same way, the repoliticization of religious concerns was a contributing factor in restraining and reversing the negative impact of other issues on the religious parties.

The negative impact of the Labor-led government was one of the reasons for the reactivation of the political potential of religious issues. Not only observant people but also many traditional Jews were antagonized by measures taken such as the appointment of a Meretz member to head the Ministry of Education and Culture, and the attempts to undermine the religious status quo with the help of new basic laws and the Supreme Court. Another factor was the post-Zionist ideology in certain circles of the social elite. These developments, stressed in the electoral campaign of the religious parties, persuaded many religious and traditional Jews that the position of religion in Israel needed the protection of strong religious parties.

The other important factor contributing to the electoral success of the religious parties was the impact of the new electoral system. We have dealt at length with this factor and here it will be summarized in terms of our model of societal cleavages. The parties which benefitted from the new electoral system were either religious or ethnic parties. The two-ballot system neutralized the political effect of ideological divisions. The reason being that ideological concerns and policy preferences can be defended and promoted through the election of a chief executive while religious or ethnic identifications and interests can be expressed in parliamentary elections. In this way the introduction of the two-ballot system in Israel neutralized the negative impact of ideological issues on the religious parties by allowing religious voters to promote their ideological positions and policy preferences through the premiership contest while expressing their identification with religious or traditional causes in the Knesset elections.

NOTES

1. In comparing the achievements of the religious parties in the two recent elections by percentage of the total vote, religious lists which did not pass the electoral threshold in either election must be taken into account. In the 1992 elections these included Geulat Israel, a split-off party from Agudat Israel headed by Eliezer Mizrachi which gained 0.5 percent, and Torah and Eretz Israel which had left the NRP and which gathered 0.1 percent. The combined percentage of votes for religious lists in 1992 was 13.8. In 1996, they increased their share of the electorate by 6.2 percent.
2. This concept is taken from C. Houss and D. Rayside, "The Development of New Parties in Western Democracies Since 1945," in I. Maisel and J. Cooper, eds, *Political Parties* (Beverly Hills, 1978).
3. See Eliezer Don-Yehiya, "The Ideology and Policy of Rabbi Reiness and the Mizrachi Movement Under His Leadership," *Ha-zionut,* Vol.8, 1983.
4. See Eliezer Don-Yehiya, "Religion, Social Cleavages and Political Behavior: The Religious Parties in the Israeli Elections," in D. Elazar and S. Sandler, eds, *Who's the Boss? The Elections in Israel, 1988 and 1989* (Detroit, 1993), pp.83–129.
5. See Menachem Rahat, *Ma'ariv,* May 27, 1996.
6. Ibid., 17 April 1996.
7. Shachar Ilan, *Ha-aretz,* May 25, 1996.
8. See reports by Rahat, *Ma'ariv,* April 1, 1996.
9. Shachar, *Ha-aretz,* May 9, 1996.
10. Idem, "The Haredim Will Vote Netanyahu," *Ha-aretz,* May 23, 1996.
11. Angelo Panebianco, *Political Parties: Organization and Power,* trans. by Marc Silver (Cambridge, 1988).
12. Don-Yehiya, "Religion, Social Cleavages and Political Behavior", pp.83–129.
13. *Ha-aretz,* May 14, 1996.
14. Shachar, ibid., May 10, 1996.
15. Ibid.
16. Rinat Klein, *Ma'ariv,* April 15, 1996.
17. Ibid. April 29, 1996.
18. Ibid.
19. Shachar, *Ha-aretz,* May 2, 1996.
20. Ibid.

21. Shalom Yerushalmi, "The Miracle of the NRP," *Ma'ariv,* May 27, 1996.
22. *Ha-aretz,* May 8, 1996.
23. Liora Ha-cohen, *Ma'ariv,* May 8, 1996.
24. See Aaron P. Willis, "SHAS – The Sephardi Torah Guardians: Religious Movement and Political Power," in Asher Arian and Michal Shamir (eds), *The Elections in Israel, 1992* (Albany, 1995), pp.126–28.
25. *Ha-aretz,* May 13, 1996.
26. Ibid., May 27, 1996.
27. "Thoughts in Front of the Curtain," *Kol Ha-ir,* May 26, 1996 (editorial).
28. "The Secular Parties are Sweeping Across the Religious Public," *Ha-mahane Ha-haredi,* May 16, 1996.
29. bid.
30. Shachar Ilan, "The NRP are expecting that the dual-ballot system will enhance the power of their party," *Ha-aretz,* May 29, 1996.
31. Gideon Alon, "Peres: The Electoral System Divided the People along Ethnic Lines," *Ha-aretz,* June 19, 1996.
32. Moshe Shoked, "Let Bibi Rise," ibid., June 6, 1996.
33. This argument was raised by Tzidon in a symposium on the election results and the new electoral system held by the Jerusalem Center for Public Affairs.
34. Bernard Susser, "The Direct Election of the Prime Minister: A Balance Sheet," in this volume and *Jerusalem Letter/Viewpoints,* No.346, November 15, 1996, p.4.
35. Ibid.
36. Alon, *Ha-aretz,* June 2, 1996; Giora Goldberg, *The Israeli Voter* (Hebrew) (Jerusalem, 1994), pp.177–8.
37. *Ma'ariv,* May 31, 1996.
38. Goldberg, *The Israeli Voter,* p.127.
39. In the 1996 elections, Moledet gained the support of 68.6 percent of the voters in Kefar Habbad. In the 1992 elections, most of Kefar Habbad voters supported Eliezer Mizrahi's Geulat Israel party, which did not win a seat in the Knesset.
40. Charles S. Liebman and Eliezer Don-Yehiya, *Civil Religion in Israel: Traditional Judaism and Political Culture in the Jewish State* (Berkeley and Los Angeles, 1983).

The Arab Vote:
The Radicalization of
Politicization?

HILLEL FRISCH

Three hundred and ten thousand Arabs, just over 10 percent of the total electorate, voted in the 14th general elections. Like the haredim and national religious, they transformed the election for the prime minister into a referendum on the peace process by voting overwhelmingly for one candidate over the other (94.8 percent for Peres, 5.2 percent for Netanyahu; see Table 1).

TABLE 1

THE ARAB VOTE FOR PRIME MINISTER, 1996
(% of all ballots cast)

Of total votes:	Votes	%
Peres	276,370	88.0
Netanyahu	15,072	4.8
Blank Ballots (Disqualified)	19,016	7.2
Of valid votes:		
Peres		94.8
Netanyahu		5.2
Of total Arab electorate:		
Total Arab electorate	407,923	
Arab voters in 1996 election	310,458	
Valid Arab votes	291,442	

The vast majority of each of the two sectors also voted for the "sectoral parties" which claimed to represent them. Thus, the Democratic Front for Peace and Equality–Democratic National Bloc (the DFPE-DNB) – a coalition of the Israeli Communist Party, independents, and radical nationalist groups – and the United Arab List (UAL) – an alliance between the moderate segment of the Islamic Movement and the Arab

Hillel Frisch is Lecturer in Political Science, The Hebrew University of Jerusalem.

Democratic Party (ADP) – captured 62.4 percent of the Arab vote. Together they secured nine seats. One of the seats went to Tamar Gozansky, a long-time Communist party member and a veteran Member of Knesset representing the DFPE.

In neither case did the victory of the two coalitions come at the expense of the veteran party that formed it. The DFPE-DNB coalition secured 37 percent of the Arab vote in 1996 compared to 23.2 percent when the DFPE ran alone in the 1992 elections, increasing its representation in the Knesset from three to four members.[1] Only one of five seats in the coalition was allotted to the DNB coalition partner.

The UAL, a coalition comprising 'Abd al-Wahab Darawsha's Arab Democratic Party, and moderate fundamentalists from the Islamic Movement,[2] secured 25.4 percent compared to 15.2 percent when the ADP ran alone in 1992. The two new members of Knesset from the UAL were both members of the Islamic Association. The Progressive Coalition, another Arab party, headed by Muhammad Zaidan, received 3.2 percent of the vote.[3] Zaidan and his followers had split off from the ADP after the second ADP member of Knesset, Talib Al-Sani', refused to rotate with Zaidan according to an agreement reached before the 1992 elections.

All told, the 14th Knesset includes 11 Arab members of Knesset, compared to 8 in the 13th Knesset (see Table 2). For the first time in the history of the state, the number of Arab and Druze representatives in the Knesset were almost proportionate to their percentage in the actual electorate. Of the 11 members, 8 belonged to the two coalitions; Walid Sadiq of Meretz got in by a hair's breadth as the ninth person on his party's list; and Labor MK Nawaf Masalha, former deputy minister of health, had been allotted in consociational fashion a sufficiently secure place (number 17 on the Labor party list) to win him a seat despite his party's dismal electoral performance. The eleventh was Druze MK Salah Tarif of Labor.

TABLE 2

NUMBER OF ARAB AND DRUZE MEMBERS OF KNESSET BY PARTY

	1992	1996
DEPE-DNB	2+1* seats	4+1* seats
UAL	2	4
Labor	2	2
Meretz	1	1
Likud	1	–
Total Arab Seats	8+1*	11+1*

* Tamar Gozansky (Jewish)

Two other Arab candidates were not so lucky even though they were placed in positions on the Labor list that were considered secure. Former Mayor Hajj Yahya, who had become notorious for condoning wife-beating, and, in utter contrast, Nadia Hilu,[4] the first Arab woman candidate and the first Arab to contest a national slot in the Labor primaries rather than the slot designated for the second Arab Labor candidate in the primaries, failed to make it into the Knesset.

Clearly, then, of the five parties that contested the elections, the victors in the Arab sector were the two major Arab lists – the DFPE-DNB and the UAL. Together they surpassed the combined performance of the three Arab-dominated parties in the 1988 elections, held in the midst of the intifada. Even more impressive, these two parties' share of the Arab vote exceeded the share of the two largest Zionist parties among the Jewish electorate, thus stemming a 20-year trend of increasing fragmentation in the Arab vote.[5]

The fact that nearly two-thirds of Israeli Arabs voted for Arab parties left the center and center-left Zionist parties far behind, and the religious and the right in the doldrums. Labor secured only 16.6 percent of the vote, compared to 20.3 percent in 1992 (see Table 3). For the first time, Labor slid from being the second to the third largest party in the Arab sector behind the two Arab electoral blocs. Meretz succeeded in maintaining its level of support (10.5 percent to 9.7 percent in the previous elections).[6] The right-wing and religious Zionist parties' share of the Arab and Druze vote declined precipitously from 18.1 to 5.2 percent (see Table 3). This is usually the case when the right-wing Zionist parties are in the opposition and thus no longer control key patronage-dispensing ministries such as the Ministries of Interior and Religious Affairs.[9] Obviously, many of these voters were convinced of a Labor victory.[8]

TABLE 3

THE ARAB VOTE FOR THE KNESSET, 1992–96

	1992			1996	
	Votes	%		Votes	%
Non-Zionist Parties					
DFPE	60,073	23.2	DFPE-PNB	113,773	37.0
ADP	39,766	15.2	UAL	78,104	25.4
PLP	23,222	9.2	AFPC (Tibi)	2,087	0.6
			SDAM	1,351	0.4
			The Progressive Coalition	13,983	3.2
Total votes cast for Non-Zionist Parties	123,061	47.6		204,944	66.6
Zionist Parties					
Labor	48,440	20.3		51,045	16.6
Meretz	23,787	9.7		32,287	10.5
Likud-Gesher, Tzomet and Religious Parties	42,450	18.1		15,989	5.2
Others	9,953	4.3		16,297	5.3
Total votes cast for Zionist Parties	124,970	52.4		102,503	33.4
TOTAL VOTES	248,031	100.0		307,497	100.0
Participation Rate		68.3			77.0

Source: Adapted from Ozacky-Lazar and Ghanim, Appendix 2.

Needless to say, it is the Arab voters who are likely to be affected most by the defeat of the Labor government. The right-wing government, indebted to the ultra-Orthodox and Orthodox for their support, must almost surely divert more resources their way – not necessarily at the direct expense of the Arab sector but certainly at the expense of long-term plans to close the considerable gap in government allocations between the two populations and reduce the even more considerable gaps that exist between them in actual social welfare levels.[9] Early into the new administration, leaders in the Arab sector were indeed protesting the government's disregard of the concerns of its Arab citizens.[10]

Their partisanship, which also increasingly characterizes the haredi community, is more costly, however. The Haredim might be increasingly exposed to periods of political boom and bust – a boom when the right-wing government is in power (though the cycle may be smoothed out because of the prime minister's newly created independence); a period of bust when they are not. The Arabs, by contrast, can by no means be assured of the same munificence in the boon years from their "partners", mainly because the relationship of the haredim to the right is less problematic than the relationship between the left and the Arab parties.[11]

One way of analyzing the election results is to ask whether, from the long-term perspective, Labor and the left stand a better chance of reversing the effects of the 1977 "mahapach" and becoming the winning favorite by cementing an alliance with Arab voters or parties, now that the haredim have seemingly allied with the right. To address the issue requires more than just an electoral analysis, but a prognosis as well on the peace process and the ability of Jewish Israeli society to countenance in the near future the active participation of Arabs in *the governance* of Israel, rather than merely tolerating their demonstrative performance of civil duties and the enjoyment of individual civil rights.[12] Addressing this issue would require a separate article. Suffice it to say at this point that so dovish a figure as Uzi Baram, who headed Labor's campaign in the Arab sector, questioned the possibility of forming a government that rested on Arab consent, while Ehud Barak, Peres' successor to lead the Labor party and contest the election for prime minister in the next round, has been even more blunt by describing it as a liability.[13]

But the full answer, and this represents the second issue, also depends on the way Arabs perceive and mobilize on behalf of concepts such as "a state for all its citizens" (as opposed to the reigning concept of Israel as a Jewish state), and press for recognition as a national minority. Generally, the more they challenge the Jewish nature of the state rather than making do with an equal share of state resources, and the broader the functional autonomy they demand as a national minority, the more difficult it will be for Labor to forge an alliance with the Arab parties.[14] Should the participation of groups who formerly refrained from the electoral process be perceived then as one more proof of politicization within the state as the dominant communal group defines it, or are Israeli Palestinians increasingly participating in the political process armed with a radical agenda that might lead to more rather than less polarization and confrontation with the state and the Jewish majority?

The overwhelming victory of the two Arab lists raises a third issue. Before the IDF's *Grapes of Wrath* campaign in Lebanon in the spring of 1996, the crisis of the Arab party was the dominant theme in both the Hebrew and Arabic press. Ian Lustick's prediction after the 1988 elections that Arabs would increasingly vote for Zionist parties advocating integration seemed, two months before the elections, to ring true. Arab parties were castigated for their lack of ideological distinctiveness, especially after the Labor party platform dropped its opposition to a Palestinian state.[15] Even more disturbing to Arab voters was the penchant of Arab politicians to useless fragmentization. In March, three months before the elections, no less than eight Arab lists were officially contesting the elections.[16] In a poll conducted between the third and fifth day of the *Grapes of Wrath* Campaign, but just before the Kafr Kanna incident on April 18 in which over 100 Lebanese were killed by IDF shelling, 40.2 percent of those polled stated that they intended to vote for Labor, more than double the percentage that in fact did. A mere 17.1 percent said they would vote for the DFPE-DNB, after they had already entered into a coalition. Only 13.6 percent said they intended voting for the ADP (the poll took place before the ADP and the moderate Islamists formed one list). In addition, 16.6 percent said they were undecided, and only 6.6 percent said they would not vote at all.[17]

Was the fine performance of the Arab parties contextual, due to the *Grapes of Wrath* offensive in Lebanon which alienated Arab votes,[18] or structural, induced either by the new system that allowed a split vote,[19] or by a secular trend in the Arab sector towards ethnonational parties?[20] Can one generally impute structural trends from electoral behavior that is affected so greatly by context?

The same question may be posed regarding other novelties of the elections, for example, the opportunity for the first time to choose between religious and secular Arab parties. Is the fact that only two members of Knesset belong to the fundamentalist camp so significant? Does the pluralism within the Arab sector suggest that there is a built-in institutional bulwark against a fundamentalist sweep in that sector as so many have feared elsewhere in the Arab world, and does the participation of radical political groups indicate a long-term willingness to work within the system?[21] Many of these questions are related to the larger issue of whether Israeli Arabs are politicizing or radicalizing, which we now turn to. But they are also related to the discussion following this section concerning the importance of structural versus contextual variables in explaining voting behavior.

THE INCORPORATION OF RADICAL GROUPS IN NATIONAL
ELECTORAL POLITICS

Social scientists have a penchant for dichotomies. One of the most
elegant may be found in Smooha's distillation of the debate on Israeli
Arabs since 1977 when the DFPE, the predominantly Arab and
communist-led front, won 50 percent of the Arab vote. Many critics
have claimed that since then Israeli Arabs have been radicalizing or
Palestinizing and therefore drifting out of the Israeli system into the orbit
of the PLO, Israel's former ethnonational enemy. The specter of
widespread confrontation with the state seemed unavoidable, especially
as the strong vote for the DFPE followed the bloody confrontation of
Land Day on March 30, 1976. Smooha, writing in 1980, strongly
disagreed.[22] He claimed that Israeli Arabs were politicizing rather than
radicalizing, working within the system to assure equal civil rights, equal
allocation of the state's resources, and the resolution of the *external*
Palestinian problem on the basis of a two-state solution.[23] The resolution
of the Palestinian problem, in his view, would enable Israel's Arabs or
Palestinians to devote their energies toward the achievement of the other
two goals. Smooha received support from Lustick, another astute
observer of Israeli Arab affairs, who claimed (contrary to what he
thought in the past), that in the elections from 1988 on, Arabs were
increasingly voting in strategic fashion for Zionist left-wing parties
rather than registering either a protest vote by casting their ballots for
Arab or predominantly Arab parties, or voting for instrumental reasons
for right-wing Zionist parties when they were in power.[24]

There is good reason, on the basis of two contradictory
developments, to interpret the 1996 election campaign and voting
patterns among Israeli Arabs in a way that suggests the necessity for a
more subtle and dynamic model. On the one hand, former radical groups
participated in the general elections for the first time, apparently a
validation of the politicization thesis. Substantial segments of two major
Arab ideological groups, situated on opposite extremes of the ideological
spectrum, decided for the first time to contest Israel's national elections.
Exercising the right to vote is typically perceived as a form of recognition
of the state. The radical left-wing *Abna al-Balad* [Sons of the Village][25]
and an offshoot, *Al-Ansar,* both of which had vitriolically denounced
participation in the "Zionist" elections for over 20 years, entered the
DFPE-DNB coalition. On the other end of the spectrum, a major
segment of the Islamic Association, led by the movement's founder,
Shaykh 'Abdullah Nimr Darwish, entered into a coalition with the ADP
to form the UAL. By participating, these groups have helped to
incorporate all major ideological trends in the Arab sector into the wider
political arena, and to incorporate most of Israel's by now politicized
Arab population into fulfilling one of the more important civic duties –
the act of voting. It was little wonder that for the first time in 20 years,

the rate of participation among the Arab population increased
dramatically, from 69.7 percent in 1992 to 77 percent in 1996, the
highest participation rate in nearly 30 years (see Table 3). This may not
have been quite as high as the Jewish participation rate in these elections,
but it did equal the Jewish average in the past three elections. Moreover,
the participation and representation of the Islamists in the Knesset has
introduced an ideological pluralism in a sector which since the
establishment of the state has had to choose between Zionism and non-
or anti-Zionism. In 1996, voters were able to choose between a leftist-
secular, predominantly Arab party, and a traditional religious one. The
former choice reflected a deeply cleavaged society. Political analysts had
merely analyzed its depth from election to election or from polling
survey to polling survey. Now there is room for potential cross-cutting
cleavages that should assist in the further normalization of the
relationship between the minority and the state. The institutionalization
of this difference mirrors the differences between religious and secular
parties in the Jewish electorate.

THE INCORPORATION OF RADICAL GROUPS – POLITICIZATION OR RADICALIZATION?

On the other hand, this incorporation of new groups has changed the
party platforms of the two major winners in the 1996 election campaign
making these two new coalitions committed to changing the identity of
the Jewish state. Coalition-building with more radical groups was bound
to radicalize party platforms. A comparison of the DFPE platform of
1992 with the platform of the DFPE-DNB coalition in 1996 yields far
more differences than such a comparison in the UAL. This may be due
to the intellectual stature of 'Azmi Bishara, one of the leaders of the
major group to enter into the coalition with the DFPE. Bishara, an Israeli
Palestinian, is a professor of philosophy at Bir Zeit University and a
former fellow of the Van Leer Institute in Jerusalem, who has long
championed "a state for all its citizens" and, in lieu of that, recognition
of Israel's Arabs as a national minority. He has also expressed serious
reservations regarding the Oslo agreement. Culturally, he has vowed to
combat, from a secular perspective, the "Israelization" (*Asrala*) of Israel's
Arabs, and formed a movement in 1992 that championed these causes.[26]
These found their way into the joint campaign platform just as Bishara
had meanwhile made his way into the Knesset.[27] According to the
introduction of the coalition's platform:

> The cooperation between "The Front" [the DFPE] and the "Bloc" is
> based on a common political and social program that is epitomized
> by the incessant struggle to realize the just, comprehensive, and
> enduring Israeli–Palestinian and Israel–Arab peace, to make the State
> of Israel democratic and a [state] for all its citizens, to ensure

complete national and civil equality for the citizens of Israel, Jews as well as Arabs...and by the struggle for recognition of the Arabs who are citizens of Israel as a national minority.[28]

Section B of the program entitled "The State of Israel and the Equality of Arab Citizens" is even more explicit about the need to transform the Jewish state into a "state for all its citizens":

In order that Israel become a democratic state and a state for all its citizens, we shall fight for the abolition of discrimination and national suppression on all levels and to ensure complete equality for the Arab citizens in such a way that the laws of the state and its symbols, including the flag and the "national" anthem, will conform to these principles.[29]

These statements are fraught with tension from a political philosophical point of view. The aspiration to make "the State of Israel democratic and a state for all its citizens" is a liberal sentiment which treats individuals as citizens irrespective of their ethnic belonging. At the same time, its authors feel that the search for equality must also take into account the collective identity of the Arab Palestinian minority. This tension between liberalism and collective minority identity is hardly novel; it permeates Israel's Declaration of Independence and the Israeli state ever since. The demand to recognize Israel's Arabs as a national minority might be interpreted as a recognition of Israel's ethnorepublicanism in which all citizens enjoy civil rights but that the state is identified with the national majority.[30] Recognition of Israeli Arabs as a national minority would go some way in "equalizing" the collective status between the two communities, just as citizenship renders individuals equal in their rights and obligations to the state.

The problem with that interpretation lies in the wording. The platform reads "to make Israel a democratic state," implying that Israel is not at present a democratic state.[31] Will Israel only be democratic when it cuts its ethnorepublican knot? Will the only legitimate national identity belong to the minority? Must Israel forfeit its Jewish identity as a state to be democratic?

If changing the basic identity of the state becomes the new thrust of the DFPE-DNB, then the statement that Arabs are politicizing might have to be tempered. While the Arabs might be increasingly incorporating into state structures, they are at the same time increasingly attempting to change the essence of the state. This essentially means that they are both politicizing and radicalizing. Under these circumstances, relations between Israel's Arabs and most of Israel's Jews might become more strained in the foreseeable future because of increasing Arab participation in the state's institutions.

Similar ideas appear in the UAL's platform, though the tone is different in order to emphasize the Islamic identity of most of Israel's Arab citizens.

The Arab masses in Israel are proud that its glorious and powerful cultural and national roots are the very same glorious and powerful roots of the Arab and Islamic nations. Its belonging to the Palestinian people is a feeling of belonging that a brother shares with his brother, the son to his father, and the mother to her son. This is a belonging from one womb....Our citizenship in the State of Israel is the true citizenship which respects the principles of fruitful civilized coexistence and cooperation in building the common house. Any idea or law that tries to consider us as strangers in our house and our sole motherland, of which we have no other, is racist and unjust and has no business remaining in the legal code, no matter how large the majority that stands behind it.

In the same manner that Arab masses in this country realize that they are an Arab minority in the State of Israel, they also realize that the State of Israel is itself a minority in the Arab and Islamic region. Inasmuch as the Jewish minority in the region has the right to live in peace in the State of Israel alongside all the neighboring states and, above all, [alongside] the independent Palestinian state whose capital is Jerusalem, similarly the Arab minority itself has the right to live in Israel in honorable freedom on its land and to enjoy all its rights which Divine enactment and just manmade laws have instituted.[32]

The items on the two parties' agendas are basically the same. Both seek state recognition of Arabs as a national minority. Other mutual concerns include exercising the Palestinians' right to return to the villages "from which they emigrated" in 1948, bringing to an end the expropriation of Arab land, and placing endowment land and income under an independent committee of Muslim Arab citizens, the latter concern being more elaborately laid out in the UAL platform. The DFPE-DNB's program, by contrast, far more elaborately addresses national security and foreign affairs issues than that of the UAL by seeking, in addition to the withdrawal from all occupied Arab territories, the destruction of all nuclear arsenals in the area including, of course, Israel's; the demand that the state sign the Nuclear Disarmament Agreement; and the revocation of all strategic agreements with the United States. The first two are standard demands that the Arab states make on Israel; the last reflects Israeli Communist Party doctrine and former close ties to the Soviet Union.

Another item related to security in the DFPE-DNB program calls for the abolition of compulsory military service for Druze, for which the DFPE has been campaigning for over two decades. All the Arab parties consider Druze to be Arabs and object to classification or differentiation among the Arab citizens in Israel. It is clear then from the campaign platforms of these two political blocs that polarization between the majority of Jews and the majority of Arabs will persist even if the Palestinian state issue is resolved on terms the Arabs regard as acceptable.

Formally or officially, this new assertiveness of "a state for all its citizens" reflects radicalization. Political parties are not legally allowed to question the Jewish nature of the state.[33] But whether this process reflects radicalization in the political sense, however, depends in the long run largely, but not solely, on ideological trends within Labor and Meretz. Will they go along with "a state for all its citizens?" This brings us back to the issue raised earlier of the possibility of cementing an historical alliance between the left and the Arabs. 'Azmi Bishara tends to doubt this possibility – hence, his emphasis on securing the status of a national minority.

There is also a class division that has to be overcome for such an alliance to prosper. Ironically, the flip side of the presumed diminution of Jewish identity and commitment to the collectivity may be a more assertive libertarianism among both Labor and Meretz members. The left then may be less committed to affirmative action regarding Arabs. Yet only pursuit of such a policy can significantly reduce the gaps between the two communities. Thus, the diminution of the left's Jewishness might only exacerbate the ethnic and class divisions between the left and the Arabs in the long run.

THE *GRAPES OF WRATH* CAMPAIGN AND THE ELECTIONS

Arab voters seemed to have been incensed by Shimon Peres's disregard of their sensitivities merely, from their perspective, in order to woo swing voters who presumably voted for Rabin and Labor in the 1992 elections and who were now thinking of voting for Binyamin Netanyahu, the Likud candidate.[34] More cool-headed were the Arab politicians (obviously not including the candidates of the Arab parties) who recognized the rational basis for the *Grapes of Wrath* campaign.[35] As far as they were concerned, Peres was suffering the after-effects of the Likud campaign's focus on the multiple bombings in later February–early March and repeated rumors of deals struck between Deputy Minister of Foreign Affairs Yossi Beilin and Abu Mazen, Arafat's close advisor and architect of the Oslo peace talks, to divide Jerusalem. Peres thus needed to display strength in Lebanon where a high degree of consensus existed among the Jewish electorate for a continued and forceful Israeli presence there. The Higher Follow-up Committee for Arab Affairs duly called off a general strike scheduled for April 14, three days after the beginning of the offensive.[36] After the Kafr Kanna incident, however, the Arab political leaders found it impossible to exercise such restraint, boycotted meetings with Israeli officialdom, and called upon Arabs to cast a blank ballot instead of voting for Peres.[37]

To extricate itself from its predicament, Labor seems to have struck a deal with the Arab parties.[38] The Labor party would reduce its electoral campaign to woo voters in the Arab sector from the Arab parties in return for pledges from leaders of the Arab parties to desist from calling upon Arab voters to cast a blank ballot in the elections for prime minister in retaliation for Peres's Lebanese policy.[39]

FROM FRAGMENTATION TO NEAR UNITY: THE ARAB COALITIONS

There are two other plausible reasons why the Arab parties fared so well while Labor performed so poorly: the Arab parties' willingness to cooperate among themselves, and the possible implications of the split vote that the new election system seems to have offered. For the first time since 1984, when the DFPE's monopoly was broken and more than one predominantly Arab party contested the elections, Arab lists unified rather than fragmented. Before 1984 there had been only one predominantly Arab political force, the DFPE. In 1984, Muhammad Mi'ari, a former founding member of the *Al-Ard* pan-Arab party that was banned in the early 1960s, formed the Progressive List for Peace, a party closely identified with the PLO mainstream.[40] A third party emerged in a moment of intifada enthusiasm when 'Abd al-Wahab Darawsha, a former Labor MK, formed the ADP in April 1988. In the aftermath of the 1989 municipal elections, a fourth possibility emerged as Islamic Movement candidates successfully contested mayoral elections in three major Arab towns. In the 1992 elections, however, the Islamic Brotherhood balked at contesting the elections, only to see their influence and profile wane considerably. This might possibly have been the reason why Darwish spurned the decisions taken at the Islamic Movement's general conference held in March to contest the elections nevertheless.[41]

At no time did the fragmentation seem more pervasive and pernicious than at the outset of the 1996 election campaign. The most serious threat to Arab unity came from Ahmad Tibi, an Israeli Arab physician who serves as advisor to Yasir Arafat and as one of his major spokesmen in the Israeli media. Tibi's decision to contest the elections also reflected badly on the institutionalization of Arab politics.[42] He was the third "personality" to form a one-man party, the Arab Federation for Progress and Change, in the space of 12 years. Even worse, he decided put his name forward for election after Mi'ari's PLP had already accepted defeat and decided not to join the contest and when the ADP seemed to be on its last legs. Tibi's forceful campaigning, it was feared, would destroy the ADP's chances of passing the required minimum threshold of 1.5 percent without any assurance that Tibi's bid would be any more successful. All attempts by prominent intermediaries in the Higher Follow-up Committee for Arab Affairs to bring Tibi together with Darawsha under one roof failed completely.[43] The ADP was also being hurt by the religious right. 'Atif Al-Khatib, a former member of the Islamic Movement who fell out with Kemal Al-Khatib, a leader in the Islamic Movement and a relative, formed the Arab Islamic Bloc in January

1996.[44] Yet without the endorsement of the moderate wing within the Islamic Movement under 'Abdullah Nimr Darwish, which Tibi did not have at the time, all that could be expected was that he would draw votes away from the ADP. The party had enjoyed Darwish's tacit support in the past. The left, as already noted, was even more fragmented. The Sons of the Village, and the Progressive List composed of former members in the PLP, were both officially contesting the elections.[45]

Darwish's decision to contest the elections changed the dynamics on the right dramatically. Darawsha knew from the previous elections that Darwish's support was indispensable. This was all the more the case in the present election campaign when he faced both Tibi, the other bidder for an alliance with Darwish and, to a lesser extent, Khatib.[46] To secure his alliance with Darwish, Darawsha was ready to make an unprecedented move in Arab Palestinian politics – to demote himself from heading the newly formed UAL list to second place.[47] All previous attempts at bringing Darawsha and Mi'ari together in past elections, or Darawsha and Tibi in the present election campaign, had floundered on this point.[48] Now Darawsha yielded to a political novice, 'Abd al-Malik Dahamsha, a member of no great standing in the Islamic Movement, a lawyer and former prisoner convicted for membership in Fatah in 1971 before becoming a returnee to the faith. Talib al-Sani', an incumbent MK, a lawyer and member of a prominent Bedouin tribe in the northern Negev, was third on the list while al-Khatib was placed sixth. Al-Sani' was crucial to Darawsha for his ability to draw votes among the Bedouin.[49] The ADP secured 35.1 percent of the vote in the Bedouin sector in the 1992 elections, over double the percentage of votes the party received within the Arab sector as a whole (see Table 4). In the 1996 elections their share of the Bedouin vote jumped to 64.3 percent, indicating that the alliance with the Islamic Movement also attracted votes. The recent spread of fundamentalist sentiment among Bedouin is not unique to Israel but has been observed in Jordan, Kuwait, and Bahrain as well.

TABLE 4

VOTE FOR THE KNESSET IN THE BEDOUIN SECTOR 1992, 1996:
39 PRECINCTS (%)

	1992	1996
Labor	17.4	14.9
NRP	2.5	0.7
Yahadut HaTorah	0.7	0.4
Third Way	–	0.2
DFPE (DNB)	2.8	2.3
Likud	15.6	1.5
Meretz	11.6	5.1
ADP (UAL)	35.1	64.2
Progressive Coalition	–	7.3
SHAS	8.8	0.5

However, there was also a price to pay for forming an electoral coalition – the rupture it caused within the Islamic Movement, particularly between Darwish and his adherents and Ra'id Salah and Shaykh Kemal Al-Khatib. Salah is the mayor of Umm al-Fahum, the largest wholly Muslim town in Israel, situated on the former green line that separated Israel from the West Bank. The agreement spelled the end for Tibi, who personally withdrew one week before the elections rather than face electoral defeat. He found no comfort even in Arafat, whose neutrality in the elections was calculated this time to promote unity and thus improve Peres's chances of remaining in power. His party continued to campaign nevertheless, securing only 2,000 votes.[50]

No less impressive was the unity achieved by the left. The coalition led by the DFPE included the Sons of the Village and the Al-Ansar, Muhammad Mi'ari and supporters of his defunct party, and the Progressive List headed by 'Azmi Bishara, founded just before the previous elections but which had not contested them. Nevertheless, not all on the left were persuaded to join. Some groups within Abna al-Balad continued to object to participation in elections, and Zaidan's party opted to run on its own. Another very small radical left-wing group of Jews and Arabs, "Support for the Democratic Action Movement," headed by Asaf Adib, Samia Nasr and Kemal al-Ja'fari, also chose to run on their own but won no more than a few hundred votes.[51]

Even more surprising, the two major coalitions – whose constitutive elements (the DFPE, the ADP, and the Islamic Movement) had been bitter foes in past years – subsequently entered into a surplus vote agreement.[52] In the two previous elections, Arab parties forfeited votes which would have accorded them at least one more representative in the Knesset had they achieved such an agreement.[53]

These acts of unity and rational cooperation no doubt increased the popularity of the parties involved. Yet the victory could have been equally induced by the change in the electoral system, where the vote for prime minister was separated from the vote for the party. If previously, Arab voters had to choose between casting a strategic vote for Labor, or an ethnic protest vote in favor of the Arab party of their choice, they were now able to do both. They could vote strategically for the leader most likely to make peace and reduce inequalities, while at the same time voting for an Arab party which expressed their ethnic identity, in addition to being concerned with their particular needs. Arab voters may simply have taken advantage of the new system, much like their Jewish counterparts, by transforming the vote for prime minister into a referendum on the Oslo peace process, and turning the vote for the party into an assertion of their particular identity and interests. The reduction of the dilemma may have also contributed to increasing voter participation. Unfortunately, there is no conceivable way to test the relative importance of these reasons to explain the fine performance of the Arab parties compared to the poor performance of Labor.

THE COHESIVENESS OF THE ARAB SECTOR

No review of the Israeli Arab vote can be complete without an analysis of how social or sub-group differences within the Arab sector correlated with voting patterns. Among the Bedouin, for example, voting patterns differed radically from the distribution of the vote in the Arab sector as a whole. Are other differences, by type of settlement (mixed cities, wholly Arab towns, large villages, small villages), by religion (Islamic, Christian, Druze), and by region, equally salient?

The most sensitive fault line within the Arab community lies between Muslims, who comprise over 80 percent of the non-Jewish population, and Christians who comprise ten percent. The Palestinian Authority, for example, has conformed to Jordanian practice and has created seats specially reserved for Christian candidates in its 89-person legislative assembly, even though the law mandating this was passed only after substantial criticism by many segments of the Palestinian public. In the 1996 elections, the question arose as to what degree the DFPE-DNB rested on Christian support. Since the ballots are obviously blind to religion and the question is still regarded as ideologically taboo and too volatile to be included in polling surveys, analysts must make do with broad geographical comparisons between regions that yield only a partial and often inaccurate picture. A comparison between voting patterns in the triangle, the wholly Muslim area contiguous to the West Bank and eastern Galilee in which Christians comprise at least 15 percent of the population, suggests that religion was not a key factor in voting for either the DFPE-DNB or the UAL. In fact, a higher percentage in the Triangle voted for the DFPE-DNB than in eastern Galilee (53.7 percent compared to 41.7 percent).[54] Religion, therefore, does not seem to have been a salient factor in the elections. It is important to note that 'Azmi Bishara was the only Christian candidate from either party who became a Knesset member. Previously, Christians played prominent roles in the DFPE. This marginalization, however, has little if anything to do with sectarian tensions, but rather with two both qualitative and quantitative dimensions: the modernization of the Islamic majority and the continued high population growth rate of Israeli Muslims compared to Christians. Obversely, this modernization should in no way be construed as implying any weakening in the salience of confessional belonging and social encapsulation within these communities.

An analysis of voting patterns by type of settlement, compared to the 1992 election results, presents a more complicated picture. On the one hand, the gap in support for Labor between the small villages as compared to large villages and towns increased considerably. On the other hand, the differences between large villages and large towns decreased. In the small villages (on the basis, albeit, of 60 polling booths), 25.8 percent voted for Labor compared to 27.7 percent in the previous elections. In the large villages, support for Labor stood at 13.8

percent compared to 20.8 percent in 1992, and in the towns 12.9
percent compared to 16.6 percent (see Tables 6–8). The towns differed
from the large villages in the greater support they gave to DFPE-DNB
compared to the large villages – 47.1 percent compared to 37.3 percent
(see Tables 6 and 8) – but this may be due to an odd coalition of forces
between Islamists in Umm al-Fahum, who voted out of local patriotism
for Hisham Mihamid who headed the DFPE-DNB list and hails from the
town, and left-wing supporters in Nazareth, the largest Arab town,
whose voters have consistently supported the same party.

TABLE 5

VOTE FOR THE KNESSET IN THE DRUZE SECTOR 1992, 1996:
58 PRECINCTS (%)

	1992	1996
Labor	29.2	40.3
NRP	10.9	7.0
Yahadut HaTorah	0.8	0.5
Third Way	–	2.5
DFPE (DNB)	6.9	14.3
Likud	24.9	11.7
Meretz	8.2	12.1
ADP (UAL)	2.5	5.1
Progressive Coalition	–	0.5
SHAS	7.1	4.2

TABLE 6

VOTE FOR THE KNESSET IN LARGE VILLAGES 1992, 1996:
244 PRECINCTS (%)

	1992	1996
Labor	20.7	13.8
NRP	4.9	1.3
DFPE (DNB)	22.1	37.3
Likud	7.7	1.1
Meretz	9.3	11.3
ADP (UAL)	17.8	27.7
Progressive Coalition	–	5.0
SHAS	4.5	1.1

TABLE 7

VOTE FOR THE KNESSET IN SMALL VILLAGES 1992, 1996:
60 PRECINCTS (%)

	1992	1996
Labor	27.7	25.8
NRP	5.9	1.7
DFPE (DNB)	11.0	21.8
Likud	6.9	2.3
Meretz	18.8	16.7
ADP (UAL)	13.1	23.3
Progressive Coalition	–	4.0
SHAS	8.1	2.7

TABLE 8

VOTE FOR THE KNESSET IN TOWNS 1992, 1996: 278 PRECINCTS (%)

	1992	1996
Labor	16.6	12.9
NRP	2.0	1.1
DFPE (DNB)	32.5	47.1
Likud	5.5	1.5
Meretz	9.5	7.4
ADP (UAL)	14.1	24.6
Progressive Coalition	–	2.7
SHAS	3.5	0.6

CONCLUSION

Israeli Arab voting in the 1996 elections reflects a degree of radicalization which is expressed in clearer, more forceful, and more magnified demands for a "state for all its citizens" and for recognition as a national minority, but which is encapsulated in the larger process of politicization. Such politicization was reflected in a far higher participation rate in the elections as well as by the inclusion of radical groups that hitherto abstained from contesting them. We are, moreover, surer of the salience of politicization than we are of gauging the salience of radicalization. This is because much of the salience or magnitude of radicalization may be contextual. The success of the two Arab coalitions may be due to the *Grapes of Wrath* campaign and therefore may reflect an ephemeral situation rather than deeper structural processes. The inability of analysts so far to generate theories of Arab voting behavior with good predictive ability may be due to a major methodological problem: drawing structural conclusions from political events that are highly influenced by contextual factors. This has long been known in the analysis of attitudinal data and may apply to elections as well.

NOTES

1. Sara Ozacky-Lazar and As'ad Ghanim, As'ad, *Ha-hatzb'aa Ha-'aravit Ba-bhirot La-Knesset Ha-14, 29 May 1995* [The Arab Vote for the 14th Knesset, 29 May 1996], Giv'at Haviva, *Skirot' Ha-'aravim BeIsrael,* No. 19, January 1996, p.12.
2. *Ha-aretz,* April 8, 1996.
3. Ozacky-Lazar and Ghanim, *Ha-hatzb'aa Ha-'aravit,* p.12.
4. See interview with Nadya Hilu, *al-Sinnara,* February 16, 1996.
5. An attempt to convince the leaders of the Arab lists to prevent fragmentation in the Arab vote took place at a conference held by the Dayan Center at Tel Aviv University, *Ha'aretz,* May 8, 1996.
6 *Ha-aretz,* April, 14, 1996.
7. Gabi Zohar, "Peilei Ha-avoda Hitgaisu Meuhar Midai," [Labor Party Activists Organized Too Late] *Ha-aretz,* July 2, 1996.
8. Ibid., April 22, 1996.
9. See "Barnamij Hadash [Muqtatafat]," *Majallat al-Dirasat al-Falastiniyya,* Vol.27, No.2 (Summer 1996), pp.93–5.

10. *Ha-aretz,* December 4, 1996. Dan Meridor, the Minister of the Treasury, was even asked, in an interview with *al-Sinnara,* November 28, 1996, whether Netanyahu's inability to meet with Arab leaders and the unwillingness of the government to meet their demands stemmed from a policy to punish Arab voters for their overwhelming support of Peres, to which Meridor replied: "hogwash."
11. See, for example, Dan Margalit, "Memshala Tahat Va'adat Ha-Ma'akav" [Government under Follow-up Committee], *Ha-aretz,* April 18, 1996.
12. See "Barnamij Hadash [Muqtatafat]," pp.95–7.
13. *Ha-aretz,* October 17, 1996.
14. See, for example, ibid., April 18, 1996. See also As'ad Ghanim, "Medina Le-kol Ezraheiha" [A State for all its Citizens], ibid., December 25, 1994. According to Ghanim, a political scientist at Haifa University, "it is unacceptable for a state to identify with one national group alone as it is in Israel."
15. See the demands of the Arab Israeli leaders to call on Arab Israeli citizens to vote for Peres, ibid., April 2, 17, 1996.
16. Ozacky-Lazar and Ghanim, *Ha-hatzb'aa Ha-'aravit,* p.6.
17. *Al-Sinara,* April 19, 1996. The poll was conducted by the Yafa Nazareth Polling Group.
18. See, for example, *Ha-aretz,* April 19, 1996; Shmuel Toledano in Ibid., April 22, 1996.
19. Dani Rabinowitch, "Hatzba'at HaAravim" [The Arab Vote], *Ha-aretz,* May 3, 1996.
20. See, for example, Ibid., June 11, 1996.
21. Ibid., April 8, 1996.
22. Sami Smooha, *The Orientation and Politicization of the Arab Minority in Israel* (Research Report submitted to the Ford Foundation, Israel Foundation Trustees, 1980).
23. Sami Smooha, "Minority Status in an Ethnic Democracy: The Status of the Arab Minority in Israel," *Ethnic and Racial Studies,* Vol.13, No.3 (July 1990), pp.389–417; introductory chapter to his *Arabs and Jews in Israel: Conflicting and Shared Attitudes in a Divided Society* (Boulder, 1989).
24. Ian Lustick, "The Changing Political Role of Israeli Arabs," in *The Elections in Israel,* Asher Arian and Michal Shamir, eds (Boulder, 1990), pp.115–31.
25. On the Abna'a al-Balad, see, 'Aziz Haidar Wataniyya, *al-Haraka al-Wataniyya al-Taqaddumiyya-Abna'a Al-Balad: Dirasa fi al-Qawmiiyya wa al Wataniyya fi al-Fikr al-Siyasi bayna al-Falastiniyyin fi Israel* (Bir Zeit, 1995).
26. See 'Azmi Bishara "al-'Arabi al-Israili: Qira'a fi al-Khitab al-Siyasi al-Mabtur," *Majallat al-Dirasat al-Falastinyya,* Vol.24 (Spring 1995), pp.26–54.
27. See interview with Bishara in *Ha-aretz,* April 23, 1996.
28. "Barnamij Hadash Muqtatafat," p.93.
29. Ibid., p.94.
30. On the concept of ethnorepublicanism, see Yoav Peled, "Strangers in Utopia: Ethno-Republican Citizenship and Israeli Arab Citizens," *American Political Science Review,* Vol.86, No.2 (June 1992), pp.432–43.
31. See "Barnamij al-Qa'imat Al-Tajammu' [Muqtatafat]," p.93.
32. "Barnamij al-Qa'ima al-'Arabiyya al-Muwahada [Muqtatafat]," p.95.
33. H.C. 1/65 *Yiridor vs. Central Election Committee,* 19(3) P.D. (Piskei Din), 365 (in Hebrew) [Judgment Law reports of the Supreme Court, published by the Israel Bar Association]. See also, H.C. 32/84 *Numan et al. vs. Election Committee of the 11th Knesset,* 39(2) P.D. (Piskei Din), 225, and compare with H.C. 1/88 *Numan et al. vs. Election committee of 12th Knesset,* 42 (3–4) P.D. (Piskei Din), 177.
34. Dani Rabinowitch, "Al Hatzba'at Ha-'Aravim" [On the Arab Vote], *Ha-aretz,* June 3, 1996.
35. See, for example, the results of the meeting between Uzi Baram and Ibrahim Nimr Husain, ibid., April 30, 1996.
36. Ibid., April 18, 1996.
37. Ibid., April 19, 1996.
38. Ibid., April 29 and 30, 1996.
39. Ibid., April 22, 1996.
40. Ozacky-Lazar and Ghanim, *Ha-hatzb'aa Ha-'aravit,* p.11.
41. Ibid., p.13.
42. Sami Smooha and As'ad Ghanim, "Roletat Ha-bhirot shel Ahmad Tibi" [Ahmad Tibi's Voting Roulette], *Ha-aretz,* January 21, 1996.

43. Ozacky-Lazar and Ghanim, *Ha-hatzb'aa Ha-'aravit,* p.11.
44. *Sawt al-Kutla,* January 1996.
45. Khalid A'id, "Taswit Falastiniyyi al-48 fi al-Intikhabat al-Israiliyya: Nata'ij wa al-Dalalat," *Majallat al-Dirasat al-Falastiniyya,* Vol.27 (Summer 1996), p.27. See also Ozacky-Lazar and Ghanim, *Ha-hatzb'aa Ha-'aravit,* p.12.
46. Ozacky-Lazar and Ghanim, *Ha-hatzb'aa Ha-'aravit,* p.11.
47. *Al-Sinnara,* April 12, 1996.
48. *Kul al-'Arab,* January 19, 1996. See an interview with Tibi in *Kul al-'Arab,* February 2, 1996.
49. *Al-Sinnara,* April 16, 1996.
50. Ozacky-Lazar and Ghanim, *Ha-hatzb'aa Ha-'aravit,* p.11.
51. Ibid., p.13.
52. *Al-Sinnara,* May 15, 1997.
53. "The Arab Vote in the 1992 Elections: The Triviality of Normality; The Significance of Electoral Power," in Daniel J. Elazar and Shmuel Sandler, eds, *Israel at the Polls, 1992* (Lanham, 1995), p.105.
54. Ozacky-Lazar and Ghanim, *Ha-hatzb'aa Ha-'aravit,* Appendix 5.

Sectarian Party Politics in Israel: The Case of Yisrael Ba'Aliya, the Russian Immigrant Party

ETTA BICK

The success of the Russian immigrant party Yisrael Ba'Aliya (YBA) in the 1996 elections is unprecedented in the history of Israeli political parties. Never in the almost five decades since the state was founded had a group of relatively recent immigrants been catapulted into two ministerial posts in the government and seven Knesset seats. These novice politicians succeeded in uniting a plurality of immigrants from the Confederation of Independent States behind a united leadership, gaining an approximate 38 percent of the immigrant vote. In sharp contrast to the previous election, when the overwhelming majority of immigrant voters gave their vote to the established veteran parties and pointedly snubbed the immigrant parties, in 1996 ethnic solidarity flourished in support of Natan Sharansky and the Yisrael Ba'Aliya party.

The potential electoral strength of the immigrants from the Soviet Union in 1996 was estimated at between 12 and 16 seats, a force which could hold the balance in the stalemate between the two party blocs. Estimates of the number of eligible immigrant voters ranged from 550,000 to 600,000. Arrivals after 1989 numbered 450,000 and the rest were veteran immigrants from the 1970s.[1]

The Soviet immigration of the 1990s was different from earlier waves of immigration to Israel. The Russians were by far the most educated group of immigrants: 61 percent of the recent arrivals had 13 or more years of education and over 42 percent had scientific and academic training, a figure four times the average in Israel. Most had worked in white collar professions in the CIS. The age distribution of the immigrants was older relative to the general Israeli population. Many families arrived with three generations: a grandparent, a son or daughter and spouse and a child. (This was in contrast to earlier waves of immigration from North

Etta Bick is Lecturer in Political Science at the College of Judea and Samaria of Bar–Ilan University.

Africa and Middle East countries, or the recent Ethiopian immigration which were characterized by extended families and a large number of children per family.) The arrival of such a mass of people in a relatively short period of time, almost 700,000 people in seven years, strained the Israeli economy and overloaded absorption facilities.[2]

This essay compares the success of the YBA in the 1996 elections to that of other ethnic lists in the past, while looking at previous ventures by Soviet immigrants to run a separate list for the Knesset. It further analyzes the impact of the structural change of the political system (i.e. the direct election of the prime minister) on the electoral fortunes of the YBA, especially whether it encouraged votes for smaller parties and among them the YBA. Also reviewed are the key issues of the YBA campaign in an attempt to characterize the immigrant vote. For instance, was it a protest vote, indicating the failure of the absorption process and a rejection of Israeli political parties? Did it reflect a desire to separate from the Israeli veteran majority or was it perhaps paradoxically an integrationist party? On the left–right continuum of Israeli politics, where did the YBA place itself? Was it a centrist party as it claimed and if so, on which issues?

Finally, this essay will assess the importance of such operational factors as leadership, funding and campaign organization to the electoral success of the party, in comparison to earlier attempts by Russian immigrants to gain representation in the Knesset. It will also briefly consider the importance of the Russian language press as the primary arena where the contest for the Russian immigrant vote took place.

ETHNIC LISTS IN PAST ELECTIONS

The Sephardic Lists

The achievement of the YBA in the 1996 elections is impressive and singular in Israel's political history. Never before had an immigrant party attained such success at the ballot. The YBA received almost 175,000 votes which gave them seven seats in the Knesset.[3] Attempts by ethnic leaders in the first decades of the state to run ethnic lists with the support of new immigrants had only minimal success. In the first national elections, in 1949, a united Sephardic list gained four seats and a Yemenite list one seat. In 1951, the immigrant vote had already been distributed among the major parties, leaving the Sephardim with only one seat. Subsequent ethnic lists, representing Yemenites and North Africans and a united "Oriental list" failed to come even close to the 1 percent minimum needed to gain representation in the 1960s and 1970s. Hannah Herzog suggests that the parties' ethnic appeal was not translated into particular ethnic demands; ethnic identification was not a "goal" but was rather a means of attracting electoral support. Their platforms were in fact integrationist in content, and included demands for greater social equality and a more fair distribution of values in Israeli society.[4]

Later attempts by Sephardim to set up their own parties, the shortlived Tami party in 1981 and the ultra-Orthodox SHAS party in 1984 were more successful because they were not narrow "ethnic" parties as such (they were not tied to any particular Oriental ethnic group) but were rather broader based social protest parties led by formerly mainstream political leaders. Both Tami and SHAS started as protests by ambitious political leaders against the underrepresentation of Sephardim in the veteran parties, the justification for establishing their own independent lists. Both Tami and SHAS called for greater social and economic equality and integration into Israeli society. In addition, both were religious parties (SHAS being ultra-Orthodox and Tami traditional) which promoted a return to traditional Separdic values, and in the case of SHAS, a strengthening of religious observance.

The leaders of Tami denied being an "ethnic party" as such. Eli Dayan, one of the founders of the list, disclaimed that Tami was an ethnic party: "This is not an ethnic list," he said. "This is a list of authentic leaders, a list which opposes the system, in support of national social ideas, which appeal to all people."[5] Significantly, the leaders of both Tami and SHAS had been key figures in mainstream Israeli public affairs before deciding to form a separate "ethnic" party. For example, Aharon Abuhazeira had been the Minister of Religion in the Likud led government and an MK from the National Religious Party before he left to form Tami. Second on the Tami list was Aharon Ouzan, the former Minister of Agriculture, and an MK from the Labor party. SHAS was founded by Rabbi Ovadia Yosef, who had been the Chief Rabbi of Tel Aviv and had served for ten years as the influential and respected Sephardic Chief Rabbi of Israel. More than half of Israel's population is of Oriental origin, and therefore both parties directed their appeal to a considerably broad spectrum of Israeli society. Party activists and supporters of both parties were born in Israel or long-time residents, and educated in Israel's schools. Neither party in the 1980s could be classified as an "immigrant party" nor as a narrow "ethnic" party as such. Tami rode a wave of social protest and dissatisfaction in 1981 and got three seats. But by 1984 it had disappeared from the party system, its leaders having been absorbed back into the mainstream parties. SHAS took some of their votes in 1984. It received four seats in 1984 and since then has more than doubled its electoral strength, obtaining a record ten seats in 1996. SHAS is today a significant force in Israeli politics, similar to the ultra-Orthodox Agudat Yisrael party among Ashkenazim. It has placed great emphasis on organization, "encapsulating" the voter.[6] It has set up local offices in communities around the country and has established its own schools, youth movements, afternoon programs for children, adult education programs and other services which have strengthened the ethnic identity of their voters and their affiliation with the party.

Russian Immigrant Lists

There were several unsuccessful initiatives in the past to run an immigrant party to represent the interests of immigrants from the Soviet Union. In the 1970s there was a sharp increase in the number of Russian immigrants permitted to leave the Soviet Union under the policy of "reunification of families." Approximately 160,000 immigrants immigrated to Israel. In 1981 immigrants set up their own Knesset list (the List For Russian Immigrants) but it gained less than 1 percent of the vote. The overwhelming majority of the immigrants preferred to distribute their votes among the veteran parties and in general directed their energies toward absorption into the mainstream of Israeli life. This was compatible with their motivation for coming on aliyah: support for Zionism which included integration into Israeli society.[7] Their absorption difficulties were not an issue in the election campaign nor were their votes assiduously courted by the political parties. In sharp contrast, many of the immigrants who came to Israel in the wave of 1989–92 were not Zionists by ideology. Many came for socioeconomic reasons and were therefore more impatient and less forgiving of what they saw to be the inept absorption policies of Israeli governments.

In the 1992 elections, the Soviet immigrant vote was a primary target of many of Israel's parties. The wave of immigration that began in 1989 brought into the electoral system 300,000 new potential voters from the former Soviet Union. It was uncertain how their vote would be distributed and what impact it would have on the array of forces in the party system, but it was anticipated that their votes could shift the balance of Israeli politics. For more than a decade, the Israeli electorate had been divided down the middle on questions of the peace process and the territories. In 1984 and in 1988, National Unity governments were established; the former, because neither the right bloc nor the left could form a coalition on its own; the latter, a move by the Likud to broaden the coalition so as not to be dependent on the support of more right-wing nationalist parties.[8]

All the political parties, with the exception of the Arab parties and SHAS, campaigned vigorously among the Russian immigrants in 1992. Campaign literature was translated into Russian and special advisors were appointed by the parties to plan their strategy among the immigrants. Prime Minister Shamir addressed the immigrants directly in Russian in a television commercial; Labor leader Shimon Peres haltingly conversed in Russian at absorption centers and caravan parks to underscore his efforts to learn the language with a private teacher. The smaller nationalist parties Tsomet, Tehiya and Moledet also sought out the Russian vote whose support they thought would be critical to their crossing the threshold of 1.5 percent. The Likud allotted a safe seat to Georgian politician Ephraim Gur who had moved from Labor to Likud during the coalition crisis of 1990, and Tehiya and Tsomet included Russian immigrants on their lists, although not in "safe" positions.

In addition to the intensive campaign of the major parties for the Russian immigrant vote, three immigrant lists also ran: DA (Democracy and Aliyah) headed by Yuli Koshorovsky, Tali (Israel Renaissance Movement) headed by Robert Golan and Yad B'Yad Gimlaim Ve'Olim (Together, Pensioners and Immigrants) headed by Abba Gefen. The three lists had almost no budget, little if any, organization and were faced with vigorous competition from the well-funded, better organized veteran parties. All three emphasized domestic issues in their campaign: jobs, economic assistance and better absorption. Of the three lists only DA's Yuli Koshorovsky was well known among Russian immigrants; he had been a leader of the Aliyah movement in the Soviet Union and a teacher of Hebrew. In the months prior to the election, former Prisoner of Zion Anatoly Sharansky vacillated whether or not to run at the head of a separate immigrant party. Sharansky was the acknowledged leader among Russian Jews, perhaps the only one who commanded the respect of a majority of immigrants. He was also the symbol of the struggle of Soviet Jews to emigrate to Israel around the world and was admired both in Israel and in the Diaspora as a man of courage and determination. In the end, Sharansky decided not to run in 1992 because he did not have enough time to organize an effective campaign, nor the funds needed to develop a grassroots organization of volunteers and campaign workers. He also had difficulties assembling a unified list.[9] DA's leader Kosharovsky did not have the stature or international reputation of Sharansky; the build-up of anticipation that Sharansky would in fact lead a united Russian party and then the resulting disappointment when he did not, further damaged DA's chances by conveying to the voter that Kosharovsky lacked the leadership needed to effectively represent immigrant interests.

All three immigrant lists failed to inspire voter confidence that if elected they would have the know-how, connections or political clout to improve the conditions of Russian immigrants. Moreover, many Soviet immigrants followed the polls and analysis in the Russian press and were aware that a vote for a marginal, immigrant party was likely to be a wasted vote since none were predicted to cross the threshold. The results were disappointing as predicted: only 5 percent of the Russian immigrants voted for the immigrant parties. Yad B'Yad, received only 0.3 percent of the national vote (even with an appeal to pensioners) and Tali 0.05 percent. DA did better with 11,399 votes or 0.4 percent. The overwhelming majority of immigrant voters had voted for either Labor (47 percent) or Likud (18 percent).[10]

THE YBA: CONTRIBUTING FACTORS TO ITS ELECTORAL SUCCESS

The success of the YBA in the 1996 elections needs to be contrasted to the failure of the immigrant lists in 1992 and understood in light of the performance of both Labor and Likud governments in immigrant absorption. What constellation of factors contributed to totally different results in 1996? Why were 175,000 Soviet immigrants willing to give their support to a Russian-speaking immigrant party in 1996, while in 1992 only a little over 20,000 did so?

Structural Factors: The Direct Election of the Prime Minister

In March 1992 the Knesset amended the Basic Law: the government was to institute direct election of the prime minister concurrent with elections to the Knesset. The law was implemented for the first time in the 1996 elections and had a major impact on the nature of the campaign and on the electoral results. The law provides for the election of the prime minister directly by the voters, the winner requiring an absolute majority of the popular vote to take office. The authors of the law anticipated that there would probably be several candidates competing in a first round with the probable outcome being that no candidate would get a majority. A second round would then follow between the two candidates with the greatest number of votes. But in fact, as the deadline for submission of candidacies for the 1996 race approached, competitors from within the larger parties cut deals in support of one main candidate and nominees from the smaller parties withdrew from the race after promises of compensation. The first round competition therefore narrowed to two candidates, Binyamin Netanyahu from the Likud and Shimon Peres from Labor.

Direct election of the prime minister influenced the electoral strategy of all the parties and the ballot considerations of the voters. Labor and the Likud devoted most of their campaign efforts and airtime in the media to the election of their candidate for prime minister, Binyamin Netanyahu or Shimon Peres. The strategy was quite straightforward. Since the candidate who won the race for prime minister would form the coalition, it was more important to win that critical race than to gain more or less seats in the Knesset election. Given the divisions in the Israeli electorate and its multi-party proportional system, the prime minister-elect would inevitably have to form a coalition with other partners. One of the two main parties, even if it had the largest number of seats in the Knesset, was likely to remain in the opposition if it did not win the prime ministerial race. (Unless the prime minister-elect chose to form a national unity coalition, an option which neither candidate found attractive at the outset.) Therefore the main effort of both large parties in the campaign concentrated on winning the Peres–Netanyahu race. Promotion of their candidate put both the Likud and Labor in a dilemma: if they followed a strategy of appealing to the broadest number of voters in order to elect their candidate for prime minister they would have to tone down their campaign against the smaller parties and special interest parties in order not to alienate their voters in the prime-ministerial race. Potential YBA and Third Way voters were critical swing votes in the race for prime minister. The religious parties were also open to persuasion although less so than the Third Way and the YBA.

The explicit Labor party strategy in 1996 was therefore constraint; not to attack Meretz, the Third Way or the YBA in its political advertising and if attacked by any of them, not to respond in kind. Haim Ramon, head of the Peres campaign revealed Labor's strategy: "It is only important that Peres wins...there is no value...to the outcome that the Labor party will end up with 50 seats and Peres won't be elected prime minister."[11] Therefore special care was taken not to alienate potential Peres voters among the smaller parties.[12] In effect, the institution of the direct election of the prime minister blunted the race for the Knesset and enabled the smaller parties to run without a particularly hostile opposition from either Labor or the Likud.

The second effect of the reform of the direct election of the prime minister was its impact on electoral choice in the Knesset elections. Voters were given two ballots, one for a party in the Knesset and one for the prime minister. The two ballots gave the voter the option of splitting their vote thereby expressing two different preferences or interests; for example, Orthodox voters could vote for one of the religious parties on religion and state issues, and vote for the more moderate Peres or more hawkish Netanyahu on foreign policy and peace process questions. Both the Likud and Labor faced a loss of support in the party vote from voters who may have voted for them in the past predominantly on foreign policy issues. Under the old system domestic issues such as religion and state, Jewish education, and social policy issues were subordinated to the main focal point: issues of war and peace and the future of the territories.

The change in the electoral system clearly facilitated the success of a well organized, appealing immigrant party. In the 1996 elections Soviet immigrant voters could express their concerns on national issues such as war and peace together with all other Israelis, as an act of integration and belonging, but in their second vote they could support their particularist demands as a distinct community. A vote for prime minister was a national mainstream choice; the vote for the YBA was sectarian. It voiced a protest against the glitches in the absorption process and a disappointment with both the Likud and Labor parties.

In a successful campaign pitch, the centrist Third Way party instructed the voter to select either the more right wing Netanyahu or the more left leaning Peres for prime minister and vote for the Third Way party to keep the prime minister in the center. The speaker in the advertisement questioned the wisdom of voting for one of the main parties, Likud or Labor, as well as their candidate for prime minister. He asked, "What did your vote achieve? Putting bread into a pita!" (i.e. a vote for the party and its candidate was a wasted vote, like a bread sandwich with a bread filling). Instead: "Vote for your choice for prime minister and vote for the party which will keep him in line." While the message was directed primarily at potential centrist voters (that a strong Third Way in the coalition would restrain government policy), it was not lost on other voters. Nearly half of the voters in 1996 opted to split their vote and give one vote to the smaller parties. The religious parties, the YBA, Meretz, the Arab parties and the Third Way were the beneficiaries of the electoral reform at the expense of the large parties, Likud and Labor.

The YBA gained an additional benefit from the direct election of the prime minister – the courtship of the party by the candidates for prime minister. At the YBA's first party conference in the Jerusalem Convention Center both candidates for prime minister, Shimon Peres and Binyamin Netanyahu, appeared before the delegates. Both candidates made special efforts to praise the leadership, courage and integrity of party leader Natan Sharansky and refrained from any hint of criticism of him or of the party. The participation of these two national figures at the founding conference added recognition and legitimacy to the fledgling party, giving it "mainstream status," and attention which no "immigrant" list had ever received in the past.[13]

Content Factors: the Issues in the 1996 Campaign

(a) Social and Economic Issues: Disappointment with Both Main Parties

The rejection by Soviet immigrants of the Likud and their overwhelming support for Labor had been an important factor contributing to the electoral defeat of the Likud in 1992. Almost 50 percent of the immigrants voted for Labor and 13 percent for Meretz and only 18 percent is estimated to have gone to the Likud.[14] Post-election analysis concluded that their vote was predominantly based on economic and absorption issues rather than foreign policy or political ideology. Early predictions of political pundits erroneously gave the Likud a guaranteed edge over Labor because it was thought that Soviet immigrants would instinctively reject any hint of socialism which would remind them of the Soviet totalitarian regime. The Labor party took this forecast seriously and eliminated many of the party's socialist symbols, like the red flags, the red membership card, and the party's socialist anthem. Others predicted that immigrants would support the Likud or other right wing parties because they held relatively hardline views on the nature of the peace process and national security. This too proved to be mistaken. In fact, the immigrants in 1992 voted on bread-and-butter issues and domestic policies and not on foreign or defense policy.

The immigrants' vote in 1992 was largely one of protest against the Likud government's incompetence and inefficiency in solving immigrant absorption problems. The key issues at the time were jobs and housing and the Likud government was considered incompetent if not delinquent in its policies. In the months prior to the election, unemployment among the recent arrivals had ranged from 40 to 60 percent and many of the employed were working at menial jobs, in sharp contrast to the white collar jobs they had held in the Soviet Union. Many immigrants in their 40s and 50s had been told that their skills were unnecessary in Israel or insufficient and at the same time that they were too old to retrain in other fields. The prospect of being unemployed was particularly upsetting to the immigrants who had come from a society with "full employment" and which had stigmatized the unemployed as being "parasites" on society. In the months prior to the election the number of immigrants arriving in Israel dropped, partly as result of the discouraging reports emanating from Israel on the prospects of finding appropriate employment.[15]

Housing, an expensive component of most Israelis' budget, was the second major problem after employment. Israel had almost no public rental housing, and in the private market apartments were scarce and expensive. More available housing was located in the periphery of the country, predominantly in development towns where prospects of employment, especially for academics, were worse than in the cities. While no immigrants were left homeless or without minimum support, there was gross dissatisfaction and growing frustration with the solutions that were provided.

In 1992, the immigrants had voted on economic and absorption issues and overwhelmingly gave their vote to Labor, 47 percent to 18 percent. In a post election interview, Sharansky, later to head the YBA list in 1996, explained, "The fact that the Likud did not relate to the olim's problems seriously…caused the immigrants to vote no confidence in the Likud. Labor needs to understand that it was not their election campaign that drew the votes of the immigrants; it was a protest against the current government and an expression of hope for change in the order of priorities of the next government."[16]

The Labor government, during the years 1992–96, concentrated first and foremost on achieving peace with the Arab states, normalization of relations and furthering economic ties with states in the Persian Gulf and with the European Community. Its supposition was that a booming economy would create jobs for all Israelis, the new immigrants as well. However, the immigrants were impatient for immediate remedies to their employment and housing needs, and in 1996 they punished Labor as well. Disillusionment with their experiences with Likud and Labor-led governments nurtured the idea that their own independent immigrant party led by the immigrants themselves would be more effective than any of the veteran Israeli parties.[17] Only 13 percent of the immigrants who voted for Labor in 1992 voted for them again in 1996, and approximately 68 percent of them voted for the YBA.[18]

(b) Injured Community Pride
Sharansky's analysis of the 1992 vote as a protest vote against the Likud was an accurate forecast of the 1996 race as well. The Russian immigrants four years later were neither beholding to Labor nor

committed to it. On the contrary, despite a general rise in the living standards and employment situation of many of the immigrants, they judged the Labor government's record on absorption, employment and housing and education as little better than the Likud's performance four years earlier. These material issues, important as they were, were not the critical issues in the campaign in 1996. Injured pride and disappointment with Israeli society and leadership became the salient issues of the campaign. These emotional issues united Soviet immigrants behind their own leaders, and led them to reject both large parties. While issues such as rental housing and hostels for the elderly and the development of jobs and more research facilities for Soviet scientists were high on the agenda of the YBA, social integration and acceptance, self-esteem and respect were the key rallying points.

One of the central issues of the YBA campaign was the status of and respect for the Russian community within Israel. The immigrants had been offended by frequent references in the Israeli media to alleged criminal activities of immigrants from the former Soviet Union. Articles about the existence of a Russian mafia, prostitution rings and instances of domestic violence and child abuse were regarded as maligning the entire immigrant community. This was particularly painful to the immigrants in view of the absence of positive articles lauding the many talents of the new arrivals. Community leaders decried the policy in the media of identifying suspects by their country of origin, thus giving the mistaken impression that there was a crime wave by Russian immigrants.[19] Disparaging remarks by Labor government ministers about the alleged involvement of immigrants in fraud and prostitution added to the slight.

Ora Namir, the minister of Labor and Welfare, further incensed the immigrants when she stated that "one third of the immigrants are elderly, one-third are single mothers and one-third welfare cases," insinuating that the immigrants were indeed a heavy burden on Israeli society. A petition demanding Namir's dismissal was signed by 40,000 immigrants, but their request remained unanswered. Stories frequently appeared in the press about immigrant children who were harassed by spiteful Israeli classmates.[20]

Yuri Stern, number four on the YBA list, had immigrated to Israel in the first wave of Russian immigration in the 1970s. He voiced the feelings of frustration and pain of many of the recent immigrants: "I myself have never felt so 'Russian' as in the last few years, when every Russian businessman is considered a mafioso and each blonde {female} immigrant is a prostitute. When they beat up a Russian immigrant child, I feel that that boy is me, the boy who was beaten up in Russia."[21]

Many immigrants were stung by the arrogance and insensitivity of veteran Israelis they encountered. They were pained at what they perceived to be slurs on the quality of education they had received in the Soviet Union and a rejection of their scientific elite. Scientists, engineers, and other academics, many of them having stood at the top of their professions in the Soviet Union were working in Israel at low level jobs in their fields or in a totally different fields. It was estimated that 70 percent of Soviet Jewish professionals in Israel were still working in menial jobs in 1995.[22]

Only a lucky few had gained recognition and entry into Israel's academic circles, and grant money and research facilities were limited. While some Soviet scientists had special research grants for immigrants from the Ministry of Absorption, many of these projects were rapidly coming to an end. Teaching possibilities were limited by inadequate language skills. Rejection of their science elite by the Israeli establishment symbolized, for many, the general condescension of veteran Israelis toward the new immigrant. Many Russian immigrants felt unappreciated; their potential untapped.

This sentiment was reflected in a 1996 Dahaf Institute public opinion survey. New immigrants were asked whether they thought that veteran Israelis saw them as contributors to society or a burden. The answers were mixed. Only 15 percent answered that Israelis thought they contributed greatly to the society; 36 percent answered that they were thought to "contribute somewhat" to society; 33 percent answered that Israelis saw the immigrants as a burden on society; and 13 percent answered that they were considered neither contributors nor a burden. When asked to characterize in what way did Israelis "absorb" new immigration, a majority answered that they acted with "animosity" or with indifference. Only 38 percent said that Israelis were open toward new immigrants.[23]

This became the key issue emphasized in the YBA campaign. YBA leaders stressed community pride, respect, and recognition. They expressed it in Zionist phraseology: give the immigrants the opportunity to contribute their talents and skills to the development of the state. The issue of employment for Soviet scientists was more than just economics; it became a symbol of the immigrants' struggle for integration and respect. Party leader Natan Sharansky, former head of the Zionist Forum which had lobbied the government for contracts and academic employment for new immigrants, sharply criticized the Israeli government for wasting valuable human resources which could make a valuable contribution to the country if utilized correctly.[24]

Yuri Stern described the underlying feelings of malcontent which fed the protest vote in 1996: "We're not talking here about a failure of absorption in its simple meaning. Today we are speaking of a rebellion of the immigrants, not only of the new ones, but also of the more veteran ones. People do get by somehow. However, neither they nor the state gain...all the potential benefits. Absorption is minimal and the state reaps [therefore] only the minimum. Consequently, we are not talking about a failure of absorption but rather a missed opportunity in history."[25] Both the Likud and Labor had concentrated on material solutions to immediate absorption problems and had ignored the more painful issues of rejection and stigma which concerned the Russian immigrants. A native Russian party understood these issues and utilized them to appeal to the immigrant vote.

Not only did the major parties, Likud and Labor, fail to address these intangible emotional issues, they tactlessly exacerbated the problem. Despite the immigrants potential electoral power, (four of Labor's seats were attributed to the immigrant vote in 1992) neither party at the outset reserved a safe seat for a new immigrant on their Knesset list. The Likud originally set aside the thirty-first place for an immigrant. It was won by Yuli Koshorovsky, founder and leader of the DA party in the 1992 elections. However, after political agreements between the Likud and Tsomet and with David Levy's Gesher faction, the Likud had to adjust the list to make room for Tsomet and Gesher's representatives. The seat reserved for immigrants was moved down to 45, an unsafe seat. Netanyahu, already under pressure from angry Likud regulars who found themselves placed in unrealistic spots on the Knesset list, was not interested in removing additional "party insiders" for an "immigrant" outsider. Many immigrants regarded the decision as an affront to the Russian immigrant community. It further strengthened the appeal of an independent immigrant party which would reduce the dependency of the immigrants on the "handouts" of the Likud.

The situation was no better in the Labor party. Labor, for the most part, ignored the immigrant vote in the formulation of its list. The order of the seats was determined by primaries in a popular vote by party members. In the district primary in the north, Ronen Plot, a veteran immigrant from the Soviet Union, won the election and was ranked an unrealistic number 43. Preelection predictions did not expect Labor to get more than 30–40 seats at best.

The party decided to set aside a safe seat, number 29, for a new immigrant to be selected in the primaries. To the dismay of Labor leaders and undisguised enjoyment of YBA leaders, the seat was won by Adiso Masala from Ethiopia in a nine-way race. (Masala's main opponents were two immigrants from the Soviet Union, Sofia Landver, who had the strong backing of Prime Minister Shimon Peres, and Sergio Michaeli.) Masala's success can be attributed to a widespread feeling of sympathy for the plight of Ethiopians, generated by revelations that the Blood Bank routinely discarded blood donations from Ethiopian immigrants on suspicion that they may be infected with the AIDS virus. Immediately preceding the Labor primaries, Ethiopian immigrants had organized massive protest demonstrations against government policy which they charged was racist and discriminatory.

Masala's victory stunned party leaders who quickly understood that Labor's chances of gaining a large portion of the Russian immigrant vote had been seriously damaged. Moreover, the immigrants' pique at Labor could have serious repercussions on the Netanyahu–Peres race which was predicted to be close. Articles in the Russian language press assailed the Labor party. For example, a headline in the Russian language daily *Novosti* bluntly wrote "Peres, forget the immigrants!"[26] Worried Labor leaders proposed reserving a "special" safe seat for a Russian immigrant and to hold another special primary election. Party leader Shimon Peres explained that the special election was "to correct a mistake." He continued, "I don't know if choosing an immigrant for the list will cause all the immigrants to vote for the Labor party but I do know that if we don't do it, we will cause a stinging affront (*elbon tsorev*) to one of the most important immigrations in our state."[27] A special session of the Labor party congress was quickly convened in order to approve the special election. Just two hours before the deadline for submitting final lists to the Central Election Committee, the immigrant vote of the "special primary" was counted, and Sofia Landver became number 25 on the Labor list.

The whole episode was a public relations fiasco. It reinforced the feeling among many immigrants that the governing Labor party was indifferent to their needs and its ranks closed to them. Particularly in light of the sensitivity of the community on issues of status and respect, the Labor party had indeed mishandled the issue and strengthened the arguments in favor of an independent immigrant party.[28]

(c) A National Renewal of "Zionist Values"

A central theme of the YBA campaign was the promotion of greater aliya, the strengthening of Zionist values and contributing to the country. The YBA was unabashedly a Zionist party. It advocated the restoration of Zionist values such as the ingathering of the exiles, volunteerism, and strengthening Jewish identity among Israel's youth through more Jewish and Zionist education in Israel's schools. Better integration and employment for immigrants were an integral part of Zionist ideology, since immigration was a benefit to the country.

The party's name Yisrael Ba'Aliya was selected for its dual message: "Israel on the rise" and "Israel in immigration". YBA leader Natan Sharansky presented to the public a vision of a revitalized Zionism at a time when some Israeli intellectuals were describing this period as the post-Zionist era, when integration into the Middle East and into the world of nations was the message. He advocated making immigrant absorption and attracting many more new immigrants the national priorities of the new government. Sharansky advocated bringing to Israel another one million immigrants from the CIS and from western countries, and he opposed any change in the Law of Return which might limit the relatives of Jews who were not themselves Jewish from joining them in Israel.[29] He argued that the state of Israel should not only be a place of refuge but rather attract immigrants by its quality of life and opportunities for self-realization.[30]

(d) Looking Inward: Rebuilding Communal Institutions

Party head Natan Sharansky proclaimed at the founding convention of the YBA that it is "not an ethnic movement, but an all-Israel movement."[31] While the YBA promoted itself in universalist terms as a party which appealed to all supporters of a strengthened aliya and to all immigrants, new and veteran, it was in fact a narrow sectarian party. Its formal and public presentation of a universal message was consistent with immigrant party positions throughout Israel's political history. All immigrant parties in the past had presented their message in the broadest terms possible: in favor of integration into Israeli society, Zionism, equal opportunity for all citizens, etc.[32]

But, in fact, the party directed most of its appeal to Russian immigrants in their language and promoted those issues specific to their needs. Support for the YBA came almost entirely from Russian immigrants, primarily from those who arrived after 1989. Immigrants from Ethiopia, who were also relatively recent arrivals to Israel, did not identify with the party, nor was their vote courted. The candidates in the first seven places on the YBA list were immigrants from the Soviet Union with the exception of Zvi Weinberg, who was a Canadian active in the struggle for the Soviet Jews and fluent in Russian. The campaign commercial on public television was in Russian and almost all the advertisements for the party appeared in Russian in the Russian press. Although the party platform was phrased in more general and universal terms, the party's central program was to find practical solutions to the housing and employment problems of the Russian immigrants.

According to Roman Bronfman, head of the party faction in the Knesset and deputy chairman of the party, YBA leaders intended the party to serve a dual purpose: in addition to its political representation function, it would also fill an organizational void in the Russian immigrant community. Bronfman explained that one of the primary goals of the YBA was to rebuild a feeling of communal identity and pride for Russian Jews in Israel. Jewish community institutions in Russia and the Ukraine had been weakened, if not totally destroyed by 70 years of Communist rule. Soviet Jews were left without a sense of community, without a leadership and without any organizations, religious or secular, with which they could identify. (Among Jews immigrating from the Baltic states, the situation was somewhat better since some of their communal institutions had remained in weakened form since they had been subjected to Soviet rule for a shorter time.) An important part of the restoration process was the strengthening of Russian culture in Israel and the continuation of Russian language studies and special enrichment programs for immigrant children.[33] Another expression of the "Russian" perspective was the special interest expressed by party leaders in improving Israeli foreign relations with the CIS. They criticized current Israeli foreign policy as being "imbalanced," concentrating too much on the United States and Western Europe. Yuli Edelstein, for example, criticized the way the foreign ministry conducted its relations with the former Soviet Republics, implying that it did not give them the proper attention they deserved. He suggested that in the future the immigrants could serve as a bridge between the two countries and did not even discount the possibility that better relations would also mean giving the CIS a greater involvement in the peace process.[34]

Bronfman denied that the development of a Russian communal identity and pride and separate independent institutions at this time would counterbalance and conflict with the integration process. Israeli policymakers have already rejected the concept of "a melting pot" society, or absorption through assimilation and have learned from the mistakes of the first decades of the state. Bronfman contended that Israeli society in the 1990s was being created by the interlacing of communities "shiluv," with each community preserving some of its special character and culture. Since a real combination or interlacing of society can take place only among communities which preserve their particular culture, language and traditions, the YBA saw itself as instrumental in leading the Russian community and strengthening it from within.[35]

(e) Defense and the Peace Process: the YBA as a "Centrist" Party
The YBA defined itself as a centrist party on foreign policy issues. It supported the continuation of the peace process, as did both major parties. However, it did not advocate major territorial concessions as did Labor or a policy of no concessions as presented by the Likud. It opposed the establishment of an independent Palestinian state, as did the Likud and the Third Way as well as many members of the Labor party. The YBA was a centrist party not out of conviction or ideology but rather due to pragmatism, and compromise. Pre-election surveys indicated that Russian immigrants generally leaned more to the right on issues of territories and compromise. For example, in 1992, 46 percent of the immigrants polled said that Israel should not return any of the territories, while 40 percent were willing to return only some of them.[36] In 1996, YBA leaders decided not to identify the party with either the right or the left in order to garner the support of the largest number of Russian immigrants, irrespective of their positions on the peace process. The strategy to position the party in the "center" was a decision by candidates who were themselves not "centrist" at all and paradoxically, neither were most of their potential voters. The seven candidates on the list hold different opinions on the peace process as do the general Soviet immigrant population. Sharansky, for example, was known to be a personal friend and associate of Netanyahu and his wife, Avital, was closely associated with Yeshivat Mercaz Harav and its right-wing views. Although he took care not to endorse either Netanyahu or Peres or the political program of either the left or the right, it was widely assumed that he leans more to the right. Yuli Edelstein, resides in Alon Shvut, Gush Etzion (Judea) and had clearly identified himself in the past with

the right. Marina Solodkin and Roman Bronfman had been active in local Labor politics and were thought to lean toward the Labor position on the peace process.

Unlike the Third Way party, whose leadership and voters identified ideologically with the party's "centrist" position on foreign policy and the peace process, the YBA position in the middle represented the least common denominator acceptable to their voters. In its attempt to gain the widest support from the community, it deemphasized the ideological differences and stressed unity on domestic issues. This pragmatism was evident in the party's decision not to endorse either of the candidates in the prime minister's race. This position was maintained throughout the campaign. YBA candidates also refrained from announcing their own personal preferences for prime minister. Non-endorsement enabled them to gain the widest support from all Russian voters and left options open with both candidates to join the coalition. The YBA correctly assumed that a centrally placed immigrant party would be vital to any coalition. In short, the YBA made a strategic choice to be in the center, not an ideological commitment.[37]

(f) Issues of Religion and State

On issues of religion and state the YBA walked cautiously in the middle. There were several subjects of concern to Soviet immigrants which were promoted by the YBA. The YBA categorically opposed any change in the Law of Return which would limit the eligibility of non–Jewish relatives of Jews from coming to Israel under the provisions of the law. MKs from the ultra-Orthodox parties had proposed amending the Law of Return in order to prevent the aliya of thousands of non-Jews who were the grandchildren of one Jewish parent and their non-Jewish spouses. Israel government sources reported that about 25 percent of the new immigrants from the CIS were in fact non-Jews according to Orthodox Jewish Law.[38] This proposed amendment, were it to be passed by the Knesset, would prevent family members of many immigrants who remained in the CIS from ever immigrating to Israel. It would also in effect cut immigration rates, since many families would choose to remain in the CIS or to emigrate to other countries rather than split up.

A second issue in religion–state relations was support for instituting civil burial arrangements in Israel. A growing problem for Soviet families with a spouse, parent or child who was not Jewish according to the definition of the halacha (Orthodox Jewish Law) was that the burial societies (Chevrot Kadisha) refused to bury a non-Jewish person in a Jewish cemetery. This presented a particular problem for couples where either the husband or the wife was not Jewish and they wished to be buried next to each other. A temporary solution had been provided by several secular kibbutzim who permitted outsiders to be buried on the kibbutz for a fee, irrespective of their religious affiliation. The issue was not controversial in and of itself, since the immigrant leaders did not demand that non-Jews be buried in the Jewish cemetery contrary to Jewish law, but rather that some respectful provision be made somewhere else, and without any additional costs. The YBA promised the immigrants that it would act to find an immediate solution to the problem.

Other issues advocated by the YBA were the creation of special religious courts to expedite conversions, and the appointment of a public committee to find a civil solution to the problems of couples who cannot be married according to Jewish law and have no alternative solution available to them in Israel. On both of these issues the YBA took care not to attack the official Rabbinate head-on. It took a relatively moderate position on these issues, asking for greater flexibility and understanding within the confines of Israel's religious framework. It did not call for instituting civil marriage in Israel for all Israelis nor the introduction of Conservative and Reform conversions, both positions advocated by the left-wing Meretz party.[39]

This choice of a relatively moderate policy was for strategic and ideological reasons. The YBA did not want to be identified with a head-on attack on the religious establishment for several reasons. First, it wanted to encourage the inculcation and strengthening of Jewish identity and values among the immigrants. For example, on the issue of Jewish education the YBA endorsed strengthening Zionist studies and Jewish cultural education in Israel's secular schools. An attack on the rabbinate would achieve the opposite effect. Second, the party did not want to be identified with the Meretz party which strongly advocated the dismantling of the religious establishment in Israel. The immigrants who were dependent on the Rabbinate to help them on issues of conversion, marriage and divorce did not want to embark on a collision course with it. And third, and perhaps most importantly, two of the seven people at the top of the YBA list, Edelstein and Weinberg are themselves Orthodox, and party leader Sharansky is traditional in his lifestyle (his wife is Orthodox). They strongly oppose instituting a general option of civil marriage in Israel or granting equal status to the Reform and Conservative movements. A significant minority of immigrants opposed these changes as well. Therefore the best position electorally was in the "center": to support changes which would remedy some of the acute problems within the community without antagonizing the rabbinical establishment, the religious parties or tradition-oriented party supporters.

ORGANIZATIONAL FACTORS: LEADERSHIP, ORGANIZATION, AND FUNDS

Unlike the 1992 elections which took place during the main wave of Russian immigration, by the time of the 1996 elections immigration had slowed down to an average of 6000 per month. In comparison to 1992, many of the immigrants were relatively settled and had become better acquainted with Israeli politics and politicians. Immigrant leaders had sufficient time to consider whether to run a separate list for the Knesset, to survey public opinion to see if such a party would have enough support among the immigrants to pass the threshold and to assemble a forceful dynamic leadership. The experience of immigrant parties in 1992 indicated that the Russian immigrant voter was wary of "wasting his vote" on a party which would not cross the threshold.

Leadership

One of the key factors which attracted immigrant voters to support the YBA was the man who stood at its head, Natan Sharansky. He was a consensus figure, the only person among the Russian leadership who could unite the Russians behind him. Any other choice would have split the immigrants along right–left lines, or religious–secular lines. He was respected for his personal integrity and courage. A former Prisoner of Zion, imprisoned for nine years in the Gulag, Sharansky was a symbol the world over of the struggle for human rights in the Soviet Union. In the 1980s, the struggle to free Sharansky had caught the imagination and support of human rights advocates in western capitals. Diaspora Jewish leaders had organized their communities to work for his release, and continued to maintain connections with Sharansky afterwards.

In 1986, Sharansky founded the Zionist Forum, an advocacy organization devoted to improving the conditions of Soviet immigration and easing the absorption process. Sharansky became the chairman of the organization and from that position led the fight for more government funds, better housing and better employment opportunities for immigrants from the former Soviet Union. He traveled to the United States and other western countries in order to raise money for the Zionist Forum. His respected stature among American Jews and world leaders increased his standing within the immigrant community at home. Foreign opinion, according to Roman Bronfman of the YBA, carries significant weight among the Russian immigrants in Israel.[40]

The other candidates who were at the top of the YBA list were also well known in the aliya movement and had impressive academic credentials. Number two on the list was Michael Nudelman, a former economics professor, who had immigrated to Israel in 1991 and sat on the city council of Kiryat Shemona, representing a local independent immigrant list. The director of the election campaign and number three on the YBA list was Yuli Edelstein, the deputy chairman of the Zionist Forum and a close associate of Sharansky. Like Sharansky, Edelstein had been a Prisoner of Zion having spent three years in a Soviet prison because of his Zionist activities. He immigrated to Israel in 1987. He had served as the advisor to Binyamin Netanyahu on immigrant affairs. Others on the list were Dr. Yuri Stern, spokesman of the Zionist Forum, Dr. Roman Bronfman, an economist who was a Labor party representative on the Haifa city council and Marina Solodkin, a sociologist by profession who had been active in local immigrant politics in Ashkelon. The YBA list also included an immigrant from Canada, Professor Zvi Weinberg, who it was hoped would broaden the party's appeal among immigrants from western countries. As a group, the candidates heading the YBA list were the most highly educated to sit in the Knesset. In contrast, MK Ephraim Gur's immigrant list "Unity and Aliya" met the fate of previous immigrant lists.[41] Gur, originially from the Georgian republic, was an ethnic candidate, in effect a "shtadlan" who had had eight years in the Knesset (in Labor and the Likud) and was viewed as having had little impact on policy toward immigrants and immigration. His support came mainly from non-Russian immigrants, from the former Soviet republics of Central Asia and from the Caucasus. He had been a relatively unimpressive member of Knesset, achieving notice in the press mostly for the political deals he made with the Likud in 1990. Gur reportedly had been willing to join the YBA in return for a second place position on the ticket. When his terms were refused, Gur decided to run alone. By his own admission, his campaign lacked funds and organization. Primarily, though, it lacked a man of vision and authority at its head. In the tradition of immigrant parties of the past, the Unity and Aliya party failed to cross the threshhold and did not get a seat in the Knesset. The party received 22,736 votes, more than all three immigrant parties had received together in 1992, following the general trend in 1996 toward sectoral voting.

Funds

Sharansky was a seasoned fundraiser with a network of connections in the United States and Western Europe, connections he had established while working for the Jewish Agency and the Zionist Forum. The YBA was founded in June 1995 as a political movement. Already in the summer of 1995, Sharansky went on a fundraising lecture tour of the United States to raise money for the movement. He maintained close ties with several big donors to Jewish philanthropic causes, those who took particular interest in helping to settle immigrants from the former Soviet Union in Israel. While a party spokesman would not disclose details about the movement's supporters abroad and how much they contributed to the campaign, he did admit that the YBA had adequate funds to run the campaign before the government funding was allocated and that most of the funding came from supporters abroad.[42] Since pre-election polls predicted that the YBA would get a minimum of four seats, the party could spend more freely with the expectation that under Israel's campaign finance law the party would be reimbursed per member of Knesset after the election. The party paid thousands of party workers on election day to get the voters to the polling stations and to cast their ballot for the YBA. On election day Sharansky flew by helicopter to seven cities and towns (Ashdod. Ashkelon, Shderot and Ofakim in the south and Carmiel, Upper Nazareth and Haifa in the north) to drum up additional support for the campaign. This was the election style of a "winner," an image successfully cultivated by Sharansky throughout the campaign.[43]

In order to change the image of marginality of immigrant parties, the YBA recognized the importance of gaining positive media coverage to establish the legitimacy of the party in the eyes of the immigrants and among Israelis. The latter were of particular significance since the leaders believed that Russian immigrants would give their support only to a party which they thought had the respect of other Israelis. One of the main difficulties of the immigrant parties in the past and of the Unity and Aliya party of Ephraim Gur in 1996 was the marginal image they projected, as being outside the system (parties and leadership which suffered from the same difficulties as the immigrants themselves). It was this impression that Sharansky and his advisers sought to avoid. They decided to create a major media event surrounding the founding convention of the party. The conference was held at the Jerusalem Conference Center on March 17, 1996. Over 1500 delegates participated in the meeting, as well as many observers. At the convention the party list was chosen by the delegates. Both candidates for prime minister, the then prime minister, Shimon Peres and Likud leader Netanyahu addressed the audience and the media, both electronic and print, gave wide coverage to the conference. The event propelled the YBA into the circle of "legitimate" parties, and strengthened Sharansky's status among the immigrants as the unchallenged leader. The follow-up to the conference was in parlor meetings, organized round table discussions and even Hyde Park style debates in parks and town centers.

The YBA hired a staff of advisers and managers and organized an army of paid campaign workers to work for the party in the weeks prior to the election. Several thousand campaign workers phoned potential voters and canvased neighborhoods where there was a high concentration of Russian immigrants. Many of these workers were age 50 plus, many of whom were unemployed. Work on the campaign gave them temporary employment and income. According to Roman Bronfman, the head of the YBA campaign, these workers were effective in explaining to the new immigrants how the election system worked, where to go to vote and most significantly, the importance of casting their vote for the YBA.[44] A post-election internal study by the Labor party, analyzing the failure of Peres' campaign among the immigrant vote, cited the effective organization of the YBA on election day as a key influence on the voters' choice. It further suggested that YBA campaign workers on election day contributed to a decrease in support for Peres since most of the campaign workers were Netanyahu supporters. Russian neighborhoods were canvased by 17,000 YBA campaign workers with lists of names and addresses of potential voters in hand. They explained to the immigrants where to go and what to vote and when necessary drove them directly to the polls.[45] An inside poll taken by the YBA two days before the election indicated that the decided immigrant voters were split 50–50 between Peres and Netanyahu and 20 percent were still undecided. Post-election day estimates gave Netanyahu 60 percent or more of the immigrant vote.[46]

THE RUSSIAN PRESS

Another important factor contributing to the electoral success of the YBA was the Russian press. There are more than 20 daily newspapers, weekly magazines and monthly journals that are published in Israel in Russian. Most Russian families read a daily paper and sometimes two. The immigrants from the Soviet Union read more newspapers and magazines than any other group in Israel.[47]

The pros and cons of having a separate Russian immigrant party were debated in the press for several months before the election. According to Stas Kapitnick, YBA liaison with the Russian press, the main daily newspapers *Novosti Nideli, Vesti* and *Vremya* did not initially support the establishment of a separate Russian party. They published numerous op-ed articles for and against the party but did not take an editorial stand of their own. At the start of the campaign the editors of both Novosti Nideli and Vesti were skeptical of an immigrant party. They maintained the paper's neutrality until one month before the election when both papers came out in support of the YBA and called on their readers to vote for it on election day. Their endorsement was very important since they had considerable influence on their readers' opinions. Kapitnick suggested that newspapers had particular impact on the opinions of middle age voters and older, who paid close attention to the opinions they read in the press and were very influenced by them. Ephraim Gur placed many advertisements in the Russian press attacking the YBA and Sharansky, but without much impact. The papers were flooded with political advertising of the various parties. The YBA put less emphasis on advertisements and more on articles and letters to the editor. It paid close attention to articles in the Russian press and insisted on its right to respond to any articles criticizing the YBA or its leadership. The Russian press was an important framework within which the competition for the Russian vote took place, and within it the YBA clearly had the upper hand.[48]

CONCLUSION

The YBA was clearly a big winner in the 1996 campaign. It received almost 175,000 votes, which gave it seven Knesset seats and two ministerial posts. The combination of structural change of the political system (the direct election of the prime minister) and disappointment with the two major parties created fertile ground for the growth of an immigrant party. Forceful unifying leadership, competent organization and more than sufficient funds propelled a narrow, sectarian party into a significant force in Israeli politics.

It is uncertain however whether the YBA will continue to be a dominant political actor and popular party among the Russian immigrants in future elections. Their continued popularity depends on several factors, some contingent on the effective performance of the party representatives in the government and in the Knesset and others contingent on the rate of change within the immigrant community itself and its relations with the veteran Israeli society. As the immigrants become more integrated into Israeli society and their initial problems of employment and housing are resolved, will they continue to support a sectarian Russian party? In other words, in the best scenario, will the success of the YBA ultimately be the cause of its disappearance from the political system?

One factor which will influence continuous support for the YBA will be the degree to which it will succeed in finding real solutions to the problems of the immigrants and in impressing its constituents that it is indeed committed toward advancing their interests. Party MKs face a difficult task. The immigrants may have exaggerated expectations of what can be done to improve their conditions, many of which are beyond the scope of influence of the MKs. For example, immigrants have high expectations that YBA MKs will facilitate appropriate employment, housing, loans, research grants and other benefits which were lacking under previous governments. The immigrants, being from a Communist system, may regard their newly elected representatives as they did party "apparatchiki," and expect them to use their positions in order to arrange favors and solve problems.

This is a dilemma for the new MKs. Many of the immigrants' problems have no quick or easy solutions. Some employment problems require long term investment and the development of infrastructure before new jobs can be created. This takes time and planning, often years until results are seen. Jobs for overtrained middle-aged academics will not be found in development towns overnight, if at all. They will still be obliged to work at menial jobs if they cannot find suitable employment. Immigrants who expect immediate solutions are bound to be disappointed.

Other reforms and aid programs require the approval of the government and funds from the Treasury. For example, the educational reforms advocated by the YBA (a longer school day, increased science and math studies) depend on the approval of the Minister of Finance and the entire government. But at the end of 1996, the Netanyahu government announced mandatory budget cuts in all government offices, and denied funds for the implementation of a longer school day in all schools. Ministers and MKs in the coalition were obliged to vote with the government in support of the national budget law, despite their dissatisfaction with this or that provision.

Politics involves conflict over the distribution of limited resources. The YBA in the Knesset and in the government will be competing for resources against representatives of other sectors, many of whom are more seasoned politicians. For example, the original conditions of the YBA for entering the government was attaining two ministerial posts: the Ministry of Housing and another "economic" ministry. However, it had to compete with the Agudat Yisrael party which has a special interest in housing projects for their ultra-Orthodox constituents. In the ensuing bargaining process, Sharansky had to compromise on the Ministry of Industry and Trade and the Ministry of Immigration and Absorption in exchange for Netanyahu's promise to support YBA programs for immigrant scientists and hostels for elderly immigrants and other assignments.

The expectations of the immigrants from their newly elected MKs far exceed the latter's ability to fill them. Five months after the election the "requests" portfolio on the shelf in MK Bronfman's office was overflowing with letters, and a second portfolio was already filling up. There was one portfolio labeled "requests filled" which had a few papers inside and plenty of room for more. YBA representatives in the Knesset are beset daily with requests for intervention on matters involving government offices, banks, employers, housing – subjects which immigrants hope will be expedited more effectively with MK involvement.

As members of the government, YBA ministers will be occupied with a wide range of policy issues, most of which do not deal directly with the immigrants' concerns. The negotiations over the withdrawal from Hebron and the next phases of the Oslo accords, for example, were issues which Edelstein and Sharansky had to study and make decisions about. Discussions over whether to build Jewish housing in the Arab neighborhood Ras el Amud in Jerusalem may take precedence on the government agenda over the establishment of hostels for elderly immigrants (as advocated in the YBA platform).

With an eye on the next election, the YBA ministers need to take heed not to lose touch with the people who sent them to the Knesset, since unlike the MKs they are more removed from the day to day operation of their offices. Their aides need to be open to requests from the public and give the impression, at least, that the minister is "concerned" and working to find solutions to their problems. This is especially relevant in the case of Yuli Edelstein as minister of Immigration and Absorption, to whom many of the complaints and problems of immigration will be sent. The immigrants voted for the YBA in the hope that their own political party will advance their interests better than the existing channels. If they are disappointed, the party will be punished at the polls.

Prior to the elections the YBA recruited voters with the assistance of paid campaign workers. Their employment ended after the election. As of now there are no permanent party offices or staff in cities and towns throughout the country nor has there been any membership drive to get people to belong to the party in the interim between elections. This is an area which needs attention if the party is to maintain its support. A model to learn from is the Sephardic SHAS party, which has doubled its support in the past 12 years. A large part of the continued electoral success of SHAS is its extensive involvement in the community, in schools, afternoon programs, adult education and other projects. Similarly, YBA local offices could serve as channels between the party and the voters, giving them an address where they can direct requests or complaints. They could sponsor cultural programs in Russian, extra-curricular programs for children and ulpanim for immigrants, as well as other services which would assist the immigrants' adjustment to Israel and at the same time strengthen their ties with the party.

NOTES

1. *Yediot Aharonot,* April 23, 1996.
2. See Bernard Reich, Meyrav Wurmser and Noach Dropkin "Playing Politics in Moscow and Jerusalem: Soviet Jewish Immigrants and the 1992 Knesset Elections," in Daniel J. Elazar and Shmuel Sandler, eds, *Israel at the Polls, 1992* (Lanham, 1995), p.129.
3. *Ha-aretz,* May 31, 1996.
4. See Chana Herzog, "Ha-omnam Adatiyut Polilit," *Megamot,* XXVIII, 2–3 (1984), pp.332–5.
5. Ibid., p.342.
6. See E.S. Welhofer, "The Political Incorporation of the Newly Enfranchised Voter: Organizational Encapsulation and Socialist Labor Party Development," *Western Political Quarterly,* Vol.XXXIV, No.3 (September 1981), pp.399–414. It is doubtful whether the success of Tami or SHAS can be attributed to a change of attitude of the general Israel public toward the legitimacy of running a sectarian "ethnic" list. The Russian lists, described below, did not attract media attention or voter support in the 1981 and 1992 elections, while Tami in 1981 and SHAS in 1988 and in 1992 did.
7. Asher Arian, *Politics and Government in Israel* (Hebrew edition) (Tel Aviv, 1990), p.41.
8. After the breakdown of the coalition in 1990, Yitzhak Shamir succeeded in forming a narrow coalition with the religious parties, nationalist parties and a defector from the Labor party, which held until January 1992.
9. Interview with MK Roman Bronfman, Jerusalem, October 23, 1996.
10. Reich, Wurmser and Dropkin, "Playing Politics," pp.140–46.
11. Orit Galili, *Ha-aretz,* May 20, 1996.
12. Ibid. Others in the Labor party disputed this strategy. Yossi Beilin, who headed labor's campaign in the immigrant sector, contended that the worst case scenario should also be taken into account, i.e., if Peres is defeated, wider party representation in the Knesset would enable Labor together with the Arab parties and Meretz to form an obstructive bloc and prevent Netanyahu from forming a coalition. This would bring the country to new elections again. Beilin advocated a more direct active campaign among the immigrants, even if it meant attacking the YBA.
13. Ibid., March 18, 1996.
14. Reich, Wurmser and Dropkin, "Playing Politics," p.146.
15. Although bread-and-butter issues were still important concerns of Soviet immigrants in 1996, the majority were relatively settled, the difficulties of adjusting to a new country notwithstanding. A survey by the Dahaf Institute conducted five weeks before the election among immigrants who arrived in Israel after 1989, indicated that 24 percent were very satisfied they had come on aliya and 55 percent said they were quite satisfied. 20 percent said they regretted the move. When asked whether they ever contemplated migrating from Israel, 74 percent said they never considered it, and 14 percent said they

did think of it occasionally. Only 1 percent said they already had plans to leave, and 5 percent said they thought about it often. (6 percent said they thought of migrating only at moments of crisis.) *Musaf Yediot Aharonot,* April 23, 1996.

16. Reich, Wurmser and Dropkin, "Playing Politics," p.142.
17. The YBA advocated the transformation of Israel's economy into a free, competitive liberal economy. Its program included accelerating the process of dismantling state cartels and more privatization of state-owned industries; increasing free competition in the banking industry; breaking the power of professional unions and the Histadrut; reducing excessive bureaucratic spending and the establishment of free industrial zones. Yisrael Ba'Aliya, *Platform for the Elections to the 14th Knesset,* Executive Summary, May 1996.
18. Poll by Kalman Gair and the Teleseker Institute, published in *Ha-aretz,* August 2, 1996.
19. Perhaps because they were accustomed to government control over the press, they directed their anger at the government for permitting such articles to be printed.
20. *Musaf Yediot Aharonot,* April 23, 1996, p.5.
21. Yuri Stern's interview with Lili Galili, *Ha-aretz,* March 21, 1996.
22. Gary Rosenblatt, "Between the Lines; Still Fighting the Establishment," *Jewish Week,* March 17, 1995.
23. *Musaf Yediot Aharonot,* April 23, 1996.
24. Cynthia Mann, "Israel Failing to Meet the Challenge of Soviet Aliyah, Sharansky Charges," *Jewish Telegraphic Agency,* July 3, 1994.
25. Stern's interview with Galili, *Ha-aretz,* March 21, 1996.
26. Edith Rogovin Frankel, "The 'Russian Vote' in the 1996 Elections," *East European Jewish Affairs,* Vol.26, No.1 (1996), p.15.
27. *Ha-aretz,* April 8, 1996.
28. Edelstein, number three on the YBA list, said that the YBA would stress in their campaign "that... Labor appointed a representative from the CIS only in order to get electoral advantage and not because it was truly concerned for the interests of [these] immigrants." *Haaretz,* April 1, 1996.
29. *Jerusalem Post,* July 3, 1994.
30. See the YBA *Platform for the Elections to the 14th Knesset,* Executive Summary, May 1996.
31. *Jerusalem Post,* September 6, 1995.
32. Herzog, "Ha-omnam Adatiyut Politit," pp.332–42.
33. Interview, MK Roman Bronfman, Jerusalem, October 23, 1996.
34. *Ha-aretz,* June 13, 1996.
35. Interview, Bronfman, October 23, 1996.
36. Reich, Wurmser and Dropkin, "Playing Politics," p.137.
37. Interview, Bronfman, October 23, 1996.
38. *Ha-aretz,* June 9, 1996.
39. *Ma'ariv,* May 31, 1996 and the Executive summary of the YBA Party Platform, May 1996.
40. Interview, Bronfman, October 23, 1996.
41. Gur's "Unity and Aliya" party was the result of a merger agreement between Ephraim Gur's Unity and Aliya party and Ephraim Faynblyum's Aliya party. See Edith Rogovin Frankel, "The Russian Vote".
42. Interview, Bronfman, October 23, 1996.
43. *Ha-aretz,* May 30, 1996.
44. Interview, Bronfman, May 23, 1996.
45. *Ha-aretz,* January 30, 1997.
46. Frankel, "The Russian Vote," p.22.
47. Interview with Stas Kapitnick, Tel Aviv, November 6, 1996.
48. YBA press liaison Stas Kapitnick and MK Bronfman emphasized the importance of the Russian press as a central provider of information and as an important forum for discussion in interviews with them. Frankel, in her article, stressed this point as well.

FACTORS, PROCESSES, AND ISSUES

External Influences on the Israeli Elections

BARRY RUBIN

Israel's elections are often considered to be more affected by external factors than those of any other democratic state. Such potential influences were especially apparent in the 1996 voting. The *New York Times* remarked – with some hyperbole – that it was the most internationally scrutinized election in modern history and claimed that there was widespread intervention by many parties: "President Clinton has virtually campaigned for Prime Minister Shimon Peres, and Israel's peace partners in the Arab world – Yasser Arafat, of the Palestine Liberation Organization, King Hussein of Jordan, and President Mubarak of Egypt – have made no secret of their preference for him."[1]

Several clarifications, however, should be immediately added to the above statement. First, these elements' existence – with the main important exception of terrorism, discussed below – did not have much, if any, affect on the voting. Voters are usually indifferent to such endorsements or may even react against them, out of patriotic motives or if the source is considered to be unfriendly or to have conflicting interest to their own country. Opposition candidates try to reinforce these reactions.

There is no constituency in Israel responsive to such endorsements, with the possible exception of Israeli-Arabs, but they already hold parallel views to foreign Arabs – i.e., favoring the Arab–Israeli peace process and the creation of a Palestinian state.

Similarly, Jewish Israelis may already agree or disagree for their own reasons with the views expressed by foreign leaders or media, but are not going to be swayed by them to change their minds.

Ironically, it is far easier for Israeli factors to have at least some impact on an American election than vice-versa. This is due to the fact that in the United States there exists a constituency which is attuned to

Barry Rubin is Senior Resident Scholar at the BESA Center, Bar-Ilan University, and editor of the *Middle East Review of International Affairs*.

Israel's views and problems. And since members of Congress are elected individually – rather than by party list, as in Israel – the high proportion of Americans friendly to Israel (including non-Jews) may take into consideration a candidate's record on the issue. These considerations do not apply in Israeli elections.

Second, outside forces whose behavior can affect Israel's election indirectly – the United States, the Palestinians, Arab countries, Iran, revolutionary Islamic terrorist groups – were merely pursuing their own interests and carrying out existing policies during 1996, rather than purposefully trying to influence Israel's election. In short, they did not act any differently than they would have acted had there been no Israeli election at the time.

To draw examples from different areas, the Soviet invasions of Czechoslovakia in 1968 or Afghanistan in 1979 could be said to have hurt the incumbent Democratic administration in America and helped the Republicans in upcoming elections. Similarly, China's rapprochement and the USSR's detente with the United States during President Richard Nixon's administration might be assessed as a deliberate effort to help conservative Republicans remain in the White House. Hundreds of other such cases can be elucidated. But internal U.S. electoral considerations had little to do with the aims being pursued by foreign regimes.

THE U.S. FACTOR

The 1992 Israeli elections offer an important example and a necessary case in point for analyzing the 1996 elections.[2] During the months before the 1992 voting, the United States conditioned the provision of $10 billion in loan guarantees over five years on Israel slowing or ceasing the construction of Jewish settlements in the West Bank and Gaza.

It could be argued that this policy was both intended to help and did help the Labor party opposition. In fact, this is precisely the interpretation made by many Likud party leaders, most notably then-Defense Minister Moshe Arens in his book on the era, whose pointed title was *Broken Covenant: How U.S. Foreign Policy Compromised Israel's National Security.* Arens wrote:

> [President George Bush's] administration's repeated attempts to interfere in Israel's internal politics had been without precedent in the history of the relations between the United States and Israel, and probably without precedent in the relationship between any two democratically elected governments. The traditional diplomatic dialogue between the President and the prime minister of Israel…was often replaced or supplemented by backstage consultations and maneuvering between the White House and State Department and the leaders of Israel's Labor party.
>
> …in the months after the Likud defeat [in the 1992 elections]

Bush gave [newly elected Prime Minister Yitzhak] Rabin everything he had withheld from [Prime Minister Yitzhak] Shamir, including the loan guarantees...[3]

Inasmuch as it concerns the 1992 elections, Arens' thesis rests on two ideas:

- That American policies were designed to bring about the Shamir government's defeat and its replacement by the Rabin government.

- And that these U.S. actions did have some impact favoring Rabin in the 1992 elections.

A brief examination of these two points helps illuminate external influences on the balloting four years later. Clearly, the Bush administration did not have good relations with the Shamir government from the moment that Bush took office in 1989. Some of this tension was a result of personal frictions but it was mainly based on differing interests and policies. Tensions between the White House and Likud prime ministers went back at least as far as differences over the 1982 Lebanon war.

Since the 1970s, the U.S. government long favored a land-for-peace deal as the centerpiece of its efforts to end the Arab–Israeli conflict. It viewed the expansion of settlements as a barrier to diplomatic progress. During the 1988–90 era, the United States was trying to encourage a new round of negotiations. After Shamir rejected the American plan, Israel's national unity government collapsed and a new center-right cabinet was formed in early 1991. This new government made rapidly increasing the size and extent of Jewish settlements on the West Bank one of its highest priorities.

There is, therefore, nothing surprising about the conditioning of loan guarantees on a slowdown of settlement activity. The U.S. government did not want to pay for a project totally opposed to its own views and strategy. Other problems in bilateral relations in 1992 also grew out of tactical differences over arranging negotiations. Thus, while there can be no question but that Bush and his advisors preferred a Labor party victory in Israel's elections, there is not the slightest evidence that they did anything to further this goal, or deviated in the slightest from what they would have done had there been no election. Indeed, given the conflicts between U.S. and Israeli policy, American pressure was far less than might have been expected.

Further, there was no speck of proof that Bush's hostility so affected Israeli voters as to hurt Shamir or help Rabin at the polls. Given a general Israeli perception that Bush was hostile to their country, any such U.S. effort might have easily backfired. The Likud tried to use nationalism to gain voters' support against any perceived American interference. As then-Prime Minister Menahem Begin said during another era of U.S.–Israel friction, over Lebanon, Israel was not a "banana republic" to be manipulated or bullied by the United States.

Roughly parallel situations existed for the 1996 Israeli election. This time, however, the relative situations of Israel's government and opposition were reversed. Now, the incumbent, Prime Minister Shimon Peres, enjoyed excellent relations with the United States while cooperating with it in a peace process while his opponents, led by Binjamin Netanyahu, were highly critical of the government's policy.

Thus, it was obvious to everyone that the Clinton administration preferred the Labor party-led government's reelection. As a *Washington Post* article put it, "The Clinton administration...has unabashedly aligned with Peres."[4] But what did this actually mean in practice? Great powers do not distance themselves from allied leaders merely because their country is having an election. The important question is whether the U.S. government did anything differently in order to seek Peres' victory. Were significant special benefits given to Israel's incumbent government to sway voters? Did the United States alter its policies or positions to make a Peres victory easier? The answer on both points is clearly: No.

The U.S. government was merely continuing to follow its own consistent policy agenda. For instance, it never argued for slowing down the peace process in order to help Peres show he was moving more cautiously. Nor did it ease up on encouraging Israel toward the domestically unpopular idea of giving up the Golan Heights as part of a negotiated settlement with Syria. This course was pursued even though the Peres government was showing signs of increasing skepticism about the Syrian track. On the contrary, the Clinton Administration pressed hard for advancing talks with Syria in early 1996. During Secretary of State Warren Christopher's Middle East visit, on January 10, he said that it was vital that negotiations move forward at an "intensified pace."[5]

This strategy was maintained for strategic, personal, and American domestic political reasons. The U.S. government argued that an Israel–Syria peace was a necessary precondition to a wider regional solution. To improve its own image at home and to achieve a foreign policy success before its own November 1996 elections, the Clinton administration wanted a breakthrough with Syria and even rashly predicted that it would happen during 1996. Despite Israeli urgings, Washington had been reluctant to pressure Syria either on the talks or on clamping down against anti-Israel terror in southern Lebanon. U.S. policy did not shift to help Peres in the months before the election.

Similarly, the Clinton administration did not change its position on Israel–Palestinian negotiations, consistent since the 1993 signing of the Oslo accords, or offer any additional benefits to Israel in the context of the ongoing peace process. American policy was totally consistent in urging that progress be made and commitments be fulfilled, while calling on Arafat to act more firmly against Palestinian terrorism. A year before the Israeli elections, for example, in May 1995, Clinton had stated that U.S.–Israel "strategic cooperation is now deeper than ever," citing the holding of the largest-ever joint military exercise with Israel and U.S. Defense Department contracts to buy more than $3 billion of military products from Israeli companies.[6]

A strong U.S. reaction against the bloody terrorist attacks on Israel in February–March 1996 was totally consistent with existing policy and probably would have occurred no matter who was in power there. Following this series of bus-bombings, which seemed to jeopardize the Israel–Palestinian peace process, Clinton called an anti-terrorist meeting of world leaders at Sharm al-Shaykh, Egypt, which expressed support for the peace process and promised international cooperation against terrorism. This effort was in line with long-term U.S. attempts to mobilize European allies against Iran, Libya, and other sponsors of terrorism.

After attending this gathering, Clinton flew to Israel for a brief visit on March 14, addressed the Knesset, and met with both Peres and Netanyahu. As a result of this crisis, the U.S. government provided additional bomb-detection equipment and other counterterrorist assistance to Israel, valued at $100 million, some of which had been in negotiation for over a year.[7]

To suggest that the international counterterrorist conference and Clinton's visit to Israel were designed to assist Peres in a partisan manner does not seem to have any basis. The U.S. counterterrorist efforts and general attempts to promote the peace process were long-term American policies. Clinton also met Netanyahu during his visit. It seems likely that the U.S. actions would have been precisely the same if there had been no Israeli election scheduled.

This analysis is equally true for U.S. policy toward Israel during the next big regional event, its Operation *Grapes of Wrath* in Lebanon. In fact, this was a somewhat bipartisan policy within Israel, since the Likud supported a tough stance against Hizbullah attacks on northern Israel. "We want the katyushas to stop," said a U.S. official, "for a long period, not a week or 10 days." Clinton stated, "Clearly the truce was violated by Hizbullah."[8]

But the administration still refused to put more pressure on Syria to deter that threat, a step that might have helped Peres' popularity at home. Even Christopher's humiliation during his April shuttle, when Syrian President Hafiz Asad snubbed him during a visit to Damascus, did not provoke this kind of tougher position.

Similarly, Peres's April visit to Washington was a routine trip, given the important bilateral issues between the countries, the recent Lebanon crisis, and the escalating U.S. campaign against terrorism. The talks were focused on these issues with no spectacular departures in order to reward Peres or raise his standing at home.[9]

The main claim of actual U.S. interference in Israel's election is made in reference to a remark by Clinton shortly before the balloting, during a general answer to a question on the subject. He remarked that the election was a referendum on whether or not to continue with the peace process but added that no matter what the election's result, the United States would continue to stand alongside Israel: "We believe that, ultimately, it's the only way to bring peace and security. And we want both peace and security. I think that's what they all want. I think that's why the race is so close...If they decide to stay on the path of peace, we will share the risk...Whatever decision they make, we, obviously – all countries – will accept and respect. But if they decide to stay with peace, we will do what we can to make sure they can have security as well."[10]

Clinton's statement mainly noted the obvious – that Israel's election largely hinged on attitudes toward the current peace process – and repeated the same phrases often used by high U.S. officials during the three previous years. It could be interpreted as saying that a victory for the Likud, which opposed the existing process, would damage the prospects for peace and lead to a diminution of U.S. support. But the text shows that this was not Clinton's intention.

After all, Clinton said that whatever decision Israeli voters made, the United States would accept and respect it. He noted that the United States would continue helping Israel seek peace, stating that he believed both candidates sought this goal. The "race is so close," he implied, because the differences between them were not so wide. If the winner chose "to stay on the path of peace" – which Netanyahu said he would do, albeit in his own way – the United States would assist the effort.

The key phrase that might provoke controversy was, "If they decide to stay on the path of peace, we will share the risk." Of course, if Israel did not make compromises – by, for example, giving up territory – then there was no such ventured potential risk for the United States to share as a guarantor of the process.

This was a common U.S. formulation for many years. For example, Vice-President Al Gore had said on a March 1995 visit to Israel, "We understand that peace is not an unmixed achievement for Israel, that every step you take in its direction not only involves risk, but too often precious and innocent blood."[11] Clinton had remarked in May 1995 that if the United States failed to aid "allies who take risks for peace...we will never convince anybody else that we stand behind our commitments." Using almost exactly the same words as in the 1996 statement, he added that Israeli risks for peace would be "minimized" by U.S. help to Israel allowing it to "defend itself by itself."[12]

Clinton was attempting in May 1996 to give a noncommittal answer. His statement's wording may have made it open to a partisan interpretation, implying that one candidate would continue to seek peace and the other would not do so. But the context makes it clear that this was not his intention. And the reaction has more to do with observer's expectations and the intensive scrutiny being given any syllable rather than any U.S. attempt to intervene in Israel's election.

White House spokesperson Mike McCurry repeatedly clarified these points in a May 28 press briefing. Asked whether Clinton, "by implication, is...saying one candidate is for peace and the other is not?" he replied,

> No, I think he made it very clear that's a decision that has to be made by the people of Israel and those issues have been debated in the context of their election...The President reiterated [an often-expressed U.S. theme], that as Israel takes further risks for peace towards the goal of a just and comprehensive lasting peace in the region, the United States will stand with Israel as it takes those further risks...I'm not going to endorse any candidate and neither did the President.

As an example of the need for U.S. assistance in response to Israeli risks, he added that if Israel moved toward an agreement with Syria, "there will be substantial security risks that Israel would need to look at carefully, and we are prepared to be there."[13]

While there can be no doubt that the Clinton administration preferred a Peres victory, this stance remained implicit. There was no significant interference in Israel's election. Nor is there any reason to believe that any Israeli voters were swayed by this U.S. preference. Ironically, however, the issue found its way into the American election. The Republican party's platform stated, "We strongly oppose the Clinton administration's attempts to interfere in Israel's democratic process."[14]

Both the public neutrality and private partiality of this American attitude were clear immediately after Netanyahu's victory. On an official and public level, Clinton noted, "We ought to give the new prime minister a chance to put his government together and develop a policy," while promising to continue support for Israel. At the same time, a U.S. official privately professed himself "absolutely devastated" by the outcome and predicted, "The consequences will be catastrophic."[15]

In short, the United States carried out business as usual during the period leading up to the Israeli elections. Aside from the arguable wording of a single Clinton statement, there was no hint of explicit partisanship or interference. If Washington was following a strategy largely parallel to that of Peres, this was simply a result of a long-standing American policy and perception of its own interests unrelated to the imminence of an Israeli election.

On the Israeli side, Peres' camp could claim that he had built U.S.–Israel relations to an unprecedented closeness and that his reelection would guarantee the continuation of such tight links. Netanyahu's partisans could counter that their man knew America very well and would maintain good ties or – conversely – that U.S. efforts to push Israel into actions that were against its own interests should be resisted.

ARAB STATES AND THE "FRUITS OF PEACE"

By moving toward normalization with Israel, Arab states were in effect helping to make Peres and his policy look better. Improving relations seemed to demonstrate that there was a new Middle East. Continuing the peace process along the lines favored by Peres would, then, seem to be working, reducing the risk of war and giving Israel new foreign investment and trade opportunities. Several Arab states opened offices in Israel; Israeli and Arab officials met increasingly within a number of frameworks and over a range of issues.[16]

As in the case of the United States, it was widely assumed that most Arab rulers favored Peres's reelection and additionally conjectured that they would act to help him. But in practice, moderate Arab states did not make gestures toward Israel along these lines during the campaign.

For example, after conducting interviews in several Arab capitals, a *Washington Post* article stated, "Moderate Arab leaders are quietly pulling for...Peres, albeit with little enthusiasm," because they feared the Likud's victory "could delay or even derail Middle East peace talks" by its opposition to a Palestinian state and support for expanding Jewish settlements. More indifference toward who won, or at least less enthusiasm for Peres, was deepened, however, by anger over Israel's April bombardment of Lebanon and post-March closure of Gaza and the West Bank. Still, a senior Saudi official said: "A Likud government...will definitely not just delay the peace process, it will unravel it," perhaps leading "to the brink of war." Muhammad Sid-Ahmed, a moderate Egyptian intellectual writer, wrote: "Arab leaders would prefer to see Peres as 'the lesser of two evils'."[17]

But to argue that, objectively, a Peres government was more likely to follow a policy closer to what moderate Arab governments preferred does not prove that, subjectively, they saw the situation in this way. Arab leaders, intellectuals, and journalists often contended that there was no real difference between the two candidates.[18]

Such an attitude arose from several factors including long hostility to Israel (believing, in essence, that all Zionists were alike), focussing on continuing conflicts of interest with Israel, distrusting Peres' intentions in fulfilling the agreements, lack of knowledge about Israeli politics, and the concept (especially strong in Egypt) that a Likud government would – as had happened with the Camp David accords – be better able to make a compromise agreement. Some also claimed that a harder-line leader might be better able to make concessions, in the tradition of French President Charles de Gaulle with Algeria, or Nixon's withdrawal from Vietnam or detente with China and the USSR.

Al-hayat, a London-based Arabic newspaper generally backed by Saudi Arabia, published a cartoon showing Peres and Netanyahu both with fists in the air as they deliver the same speech through a single megaphone. A senior Egyptian official said: "Without a doubt there is a difference between Labor and Likud, but I don't think it's the difference people are talking about. I don't think Likud is anti-peace, and I don't think Labor is for peace at any price."[19]

The peace treaty with Jordan was a great gain for Israel and the most dramatic transformation outside of the Israel–PLO breakthrough. After almost a half-century of conflict, the border was opened, friendly exchanges began, and Israelis could travel freely to their eastern neighbor.

Jordan's situation was especially intimately tied to political developments regarding Israel and the peace process. The two countries had a number of common interests. Israel gave Amman a good counterweight against threats from Iraq, Iran, and Syria, while King Hussein's peacemaking dramatically improved U.S.–Jordan relations. Both countries opposed radical groups in the region or the spread of revolutionary Islamic fundamentalism. Moreover, they had a mutual goal of preventing a Palestinian factor that was aligned with radical regimes or dedicated to subverting the Palestinian populations in their own countries.

Jordan was the least enthusiastic of all Arab countries in supporting an independent Palestinian state. Yet at the same time, Amman had to worry about a breakdown in the peace process producing violence, radicalizing Palestinians (including those in Jordan itself) and leading to a large flight of refugees from the West Bank, and a harder-line swing in Arab politics that would isolate Jordan.

King Hussein had a long, close personal relationship with the incumbent prime minister. Jordan's decision to make a full peace treaty with Israel objectively helped Peres by demonstrating a success for his policy. The warm relations created and the ability of Israelis to travel to Jordan after a border closure of almost half a century provided striking evidence of a change in the region and an improvement in Israel's situation.

Thus, Jordan's interests were mixed, making its interlocking security considerations with Israel and the Palestinians required it to safeguard its interests regardless of any successor regime in Israel. "We have a neutral position," Jordan's Minister of Information (and before that, its first ambassador to Israel) Marwan Moasher said during the Israeli election campaign. Jordan's treaty was with Israel, not with any specific government there.[20]

Similar positions were taken by other moderate Arab states whose move toward normalization with Israel provided the Peres government with "fruits of peace" which it could argue showed the success of its policy. Aside from Jordan, these states included Morocco, Tunisia, Oman, Mauritania, and Qatar. Some Muslim, non-Arab states – notably Indonesia – had also warmed in their ties with Israel. But these moves were related to the new regional situation and the peace process's breakthroughs. No special bonuses for Peres seemed timed to coincide with – and thus affect – the election campaign.

Similarly, Egypt and Saudi Arabia did nothing to make Peres's strategy look better in the context of Israeli elections. While Cairo had earlier been moving to some improvement in relations with Israel, despite three years of U.S. urging to be cooperative, the Saudis continued trying to slow Israel's normalization with other Arab states. Cairo, too, while being a leading Arab promoter of the peace process, remained relatively cool toward Israel, especially jealous of its successes in building relations with other Arab states.[21]

For the moderate Arab regimes, to help Peres would require special concessions on their part. For example, President Husni Mubarak might have made his long-promised visit to Israel, or the Saudis could have taken a major step toward recognition of Israel or normalization. Such an act, however, would have conflicted with their own domestic and inter-Arab interests. Consequently, they did nothing in that direction.

Thus, Egypt, Jordan, other moderate Arab regimes, and some non-Arab countries (including Turkey) had made the foreign policy of Israel's Labor party government look successful by improving political and economic relations with Israel after the Oslo agreements. Peres and his supporters could argue that these "fruits of peace" showed that their strategy was worthwhile and was bringing benefits to Israelis. To what extent this assertion affected Israeli voters is uncertain but it is clear that these Middle East and Third World countries made no concerted or conscious effort to affect the election.

Peres's argument was that continuing the peace process along the lines he had been following would produce a full peace with all the Arab states except the most extreme ones. The progress made since 1993 was said to confirm this fact and to be a benefit brought about by the incumbent government's policy.

The Israeli opposition's view was less clear. It fully supported the rapprochement with Jordan, but sometimes suggested that the advances had been exaggerated, while on other occasions attributing them to other factors that would continue to prevail even if Israel took a tougher policy toward the Palestinians and Syria.

THE PALESTINIAN FACTOR

Objectively, the external factor that had the most important effect on Israeli voters' perceptions and decisionmaking was the Palestinians. Since the 1996 election was largely a referendum on attitudes toward the peace process, it was also a poll about the performance of Yasser Arafat and his Palestinian Authority (PA) as peace partner, neighbor, and ruler.

Among the questions Israelis pondered were: Has the situation of deep hostility over so many decades really changed? Are the Palestinians truly ready to make peace? Is Arafat willing and able to live up to his commitments? Could a Palestinian state be a stable and peaceable neighbor, or would Israel's security require continued retention of the West Bank and Gaza? And the foremost issue of all in the elections became the debate over whether a Palestinian regime could reduce anti-Israel terrorism, or wished to do so.

The government side said that Arafat was doing a reasonable – if imperfect – job in trying and succeeding at containing terrorism, while generally living up to his other commitments. The fact that Arafat's supporters had completely ceased involvement in anti-Israel terrorism was highlighted. Continuing the peace process would increase both his ability and willingness to do more, thus enhancing Israel's security.

The opposition challenged Arafat's credibility, calling him either unwilling to constrain HAMAS and other groups involved in terrorism or even secretly helping them. PA violations of its commitments were highlighted – including its semi-clandestine operations in east Jerusalem and failure to extradite wanted terrorists. The Likud's most provocative television commercial showed Peres and Arafat walking hand-in-hand, interposed with pictures of the February–March terrorist attacks. Tying Peres to Arafat was certainly seen as a way to discredit the prime minister.

At least some leading figures in the Israeli government miscalculated Arafat's priority on ensuring its reelection.[22] Certainly, Arafat could be expected to favor Peres's reelection. As with other external factors, however, his willingness to do something to further that outcome was a horse of a different color. In short, Israeli electoral considerations had little to do with Arafat's strategy or tactics, even though one could argue that the outcome was of major importance to his – and the Palestinians – future.

Above all, the PA leader was motivated by his more immediate – in this context one might say shorter-range – self-interest. An air of wishful thinking prevailed within the PA.[23] This meant that he was responsive to making concessions due to Israeli pressures and the opportunities offered by a compromise negotiated solution (i.e., the existing peace process's success). But he also had to balance these factors off by taking into account domestic pressures against making more concessions to Israel, as well as certain differences he had with Peres's offers and positions.

Actions he undertook which did – or should have – helped Peres were undertaken in order to preserve or stimulate parallel Israeli cooperation, like the scheduled Israeli withdrawal from Hebron and an end to the closure of the territories. The most important of these was his post-March crackdown on HAMAS and other groups committing terrorism, involving hundreds of arrests. This step was effective in greatly reducing the level of violence in the last two months of Israel's election campaign, but it was too late to reverse the credibility Arafat had already lost on this issue.

One area where Arafat and the PA might have been expected to help Peres directly was by influencing Israeli-Arab voters to cast their votes for the prime minister. Exactly how much Arafat did behind the scenes in direct contacts with this group of Palestinians is not known. But Israeli-Arab voters were overwhelmingly going to chose Peres over Netanyahu, no matter which party they backed for parliament. During the course of the campaign, the Israeli-Arab parties told their supporters to vote for Peres. They would have done so whether or not Arafat urged such a stance. Dr. Ahmad Tibi, an advisor to Arafat who had formed his own party to contest the race, withdrew when it became clear that he would only split the Arab parliamentary vote and had little chance of winning a seat. It was said that the PA might have pressed him to pull out as his poor showing would prove an embarrassment to them.

Arafat had less influence over the two largest Arab-supported parties: the Communists and the United Arab List, whose coalition included Islamic fundamentalists who did not like Arafat. Discontent with the government's performance, especially the Lebanese Arab casualties during the *Grapes of Wrath* operation, seemed likely to produce a higher rate of Arab abstentions.

While quiet contacts took place between the PA and Israeli-Arab parties, these did not change what would have happened otherwise. At any rate, while Israeli-Arabs gave Peres a huge amount of support, the degree to which they did not vote at all or cast blank ballots for prime minister may well have cost him the election. By discouraging east Jerusalem Arab residents from voting at all in the election (to reject Israel's claim of sovereignty over that part of the city), the PA also cost Peres thousands of votes. Consequently, if Arafat lobbied for Peres, he did not do so very effectively.

The PA's bigger problem was the difficulty in establishing credibility among Israelis for Palestinian groups that had been so long at war with that country, used terrorism against it, and openly called for its destruction. The dramatic events involved in the peace process's breakthrough between 1993 and 1996 had healed many wounds and produced real hope and enthusiasm within Israel. But deep suspicions remained. Continuing problems of terrorism, shortcomings in Arafat's performance and rhetoric, and real differences or fears about the future all exacerbated these problems.

In the end, some Israeli voters found Arafat's performance a reason to vote for continuing the existing peace process by voting for Peres; others took a critical view of Arafat's record and backed Netanyahu. Given that so many Israelis were already committed to a particular view of the situation, and that Netanyahu's margin of victory would be so small, it is hard to estimate precisely how this factor balanced out on May 28, 1996.

RADICAL ANTI-ISRAEL FORCES

There were many radical forces opposing the ongoing Arab–Israeli peace process and seeking to wreck it. Anti-Israel terrorist groups tried to attack the country, its citizens, and its interests by all possible means and at all possible times. Such states included Iran, Iraq, Libya and – to some extent – Syria and Sudan, as well as a range of revolutionary movements using terrorism, most notably the Lebanese Hizbullah and the Palestinian HAMAS.

This situation was not in itself an issue in the Israeli election. It was universally accepted within the country and there was also a basic consensus about what to do concerning this problem: try to isolate and weaken the main state sponsors of terrorism, and decisively defend Israel's security from such threats. The two sides in Israeli politics also had generally similar views on strategic policy and on the military aspects of handling the attacks from Lebanon.

But this factor did affect Israel's election in two particular respects: Through the anti-Israel terrorist campaign of HAMAS and smaller extremist Palestinian groups; and from attacks on Israel's northern border by Hizbullah, with Syria's permission and backing. The main parties and voters held alternative interpretations of the situation.

The Radical Palestinians' Terrorist Campaign

Those Palestinian groups opposed to the existing peace process – HAMAS, Islamic Jihad, the Popular Front for the Liberation of Palestine (PFLP), and the Democratic Front for the Liberation of Palestine (DFLP) – had launched many terrorist attacks since the signing of the Declaration of Principles in 1993 and continuing during the months leading up to the election campaign. Some of these operations took place within Israel itself; others were directed against Israeli civilians, soldiers, or installations in the West Bank and Gaza.

Although a large portion of such plans were foiled – by prior arrests, the terrorists' mistakes, or the action of defensive forces on the scene – enough were successful to inflict several hundred casualties. The attacks were of many types, including individual knifings, drive-by shootings at automobiles or passers-by, kidnappings, and – most significantly – suicide bombings directed against buses or pedestrians.

This phenomenon was a constant presence but reached its peak in a wave of five fatal attacks in Israeli cities during February–March 1996. The most important were three suicide-bombings, two on Jerusalem buses, and a third at a major Tel Aviv intersection. These events had a tremendous effect on the mood in Israel. In fact, they were a turning point – perhaps *the* turning point – in determining the outcome of the election.

The level of terrorism significantly declined between early March and the election, a development attributable to tougher Israeli security measures and a PA crackdown. Still, this issue – and especially the February–March violence – became not only the campaign's central debate, but the most important theme in the opposition's advertising, and perhaps in decisionmaking by hitherto undecided voters.

The incumbent government, its allies, and supporters had two main arguments to explain these events. First, the high level of terrorism was dubbed the desperate acts of those who knew that the peace process was defeating them. The January Palestinian elections, resulting in victories for Arafat and his supporters, coupled with splits in HAMAS showed that events were moving in the right direction. Since the assaults were an effort to destroy this progress, for Israel to change course would be to give the terrorists a victory.

Second, the government insisted that the ongoing peace process would reduce terrorism by strengthening the PA, giving it the willingness and power to repress or constrain these forces and the Palestinian population an incentive to reject them. In short, the terrorism upsurge was said to be a transient phenomenon that would be eliminated most quickly and completely by continuing the policy of negotiation and compromise. Arafat's crackdown on the terrorist groups following the February–March attacks was taken as proof of this assessment's correctness.

During the election campaign, the opposition and its supporters portrayed the upsurge in terrorism as proof that the government's policy had failed. In contrast, they claimed that terrorism was increasing precisely because of the compromises implemented in the peace process. The PA was said to be ignoring or even, at worst, abetting HAMAS's activities. Thus, continuing the existing policy would further intensify the level of anti-Israel violence. There was no real peace, but only intensified violence, while Israelis were said to fear going about their daily activities.

There is little evidence as to the intentions of Palestinian terrorist groups directly vis-a-vis Israel's election. Certainly, they wished to wreck the peace process by undermining support for it within Israel, while "proving" to Palestinians that Israel had no intention of fulfilling its commitments and that they were more effective battlers for Palestinian rights than Arafat.

Generally, they looked on the existing peace process as an Israeli trick and as a betrayal by Arafat of the traditional goal of destroying Israel. The PA's consolidation of power weakened the prospects for Islamic forces to seize hegemony among the Palestinians. At the same time, HAMAS was constrained by fear of Arafat's repression, knowing also that by acting to split the Palestinian people it would become a pariah. Finally, trying to prevent Israeli withdrawals put HAMAS in the ridiculous – and unpopular – position of seeking to preserve the occupation.

There is very little evidence that the HAMAS attacks were connected with the election. According to Muhammad Abu Warda, a HAMAS activist who recruited the suicide bombers, the goal of the February–March terrorist attacks was to bring down the Peres government. Israeli army intelligence officers made similar suggestions, and even Christopher suggested that Iran was dispatching terrorists for such a disruption. It is possible that the PA's police – who had arrested him – urged Abu Warda to say this. During his trial in August, however, Abu Warda's boss, Hasan Salama, said that the attacks had nothing to do with the elections.[24]

Perhaps intimidated by the PA's crackdown, stronger Israeli security measures, and a closure of the territories, the terrorist groups were far less effective during the latter part of the election campaign. Nonetheless, the impact of their attacks on Israeli voters – no matter what the radicals' intentions – was undoubtedly the most powerful external factor influencing the election.

Fighting in Lebanon and Perceptions of Syria

Hizbullah and radical Palestinian groups had been carrying out attacks against Israel since the 1970s. Iran sponsored these attempted cross-border raids, while Syrian forces which occupied much of Lebanon, permitted and facilitated them. Israeli forces operated in a security zone in southern Lebanon, in conjunction with the Israel-backed South Lebanese Army. The level of attacks rose and fell, often increasing at times when Syria had an interest in showing its leverage. Since Lebanon was a virtual Syrian satellite, any Israeli effort to make peace with that country was subject to a Syrian veto.

In contrast, the Syria–Israel front in the Golan Heights had been quiet since 1974. Bilateral negotiations began after the 1990 Madrid conference but made little progress, often being broken off for months. Despite offers by Prime Ministers Rabin and Peres implying that the entire Golan Heights would be returned to Syria in exchange for a full peace, Damascus did not accept this offer and raised new demands.

Israel's government had argued that a peace with Syria was necessary to achieve a comprehensive agreement with almost all the Arab states. Yielding this territory – albeit with early warning stations and troop limits in the zone – was said to enable a true peace that would thus make war unlikely and reduce the military value of Golan for Israel. Finally, an agreement with Syria was the necessary precondition for peace with Lebanon and a new situation that would pacify southern Lebanon. Conversely, the failure to make progress on negotiations would make a war with Syria more likely.

Many Israelis opposed yielding the strategic Golan Heights to Syria. Indeed, a new party – the Third Way – was formed by those splitting from the Labor party largely over this issue. The opposition charged that giving up this high ground would endanger Israel's security. In other words, it asserted that concessions to Syria would be too risky, making a future war with that country more, rather than less, probable. Moreover, it argued that continuing the talks should be conditioned on Syria ceasing to support Hizbullah and other attacks on Israel from southern Lebanon.

How did Syria and Hizbullah relate to Israel's election? Hizbullah clearly subscribed to the "all Zionists are alike" school of thought. As one of its leaders, Sheik Hassan Nasrallah, put it, "The only difference between Peres and Netanyahu is that Peres is a better liar."[25]

The question of Syria's intentions in the negotiations is both complex and unresolvable. Many observers assumed that Damascus wanted a deal

over the Golan and, thus, would prefer Peres to be reelected since he was
offering something much closer to Syrian demands. This was the view
held by Israel's government and by the United States for most of the
1993–96 period, though both of them were increasingly doubtful toward
the end of this time.[26]

An alternative view, however, is that Syria had good reasons in terms
of national and regime interests for avoiding a negotiated settlement. If
Israel's regional situation was normalized, it could act more effectively
against Syria's interests and ambitions while undermining Damascus's
domination over Lebanon. In addition, Syria's leverage within the Arab
world would be greatly reduced, the Palestinian card lost forever, and its
arguments for obtaining Arab aid sharply limited. U.S. power would be
increased as well, to Syria's detriment. According to this approach, Syria
would be equally, or more, pleased to see Peres replaced by a government
which did not present a "threat" of a political solution.

Whether or not Asad had any conscious preference, he made things
harder for Peres. By refusing to be more conciliatory in negotiations, the
Syrian leader undercut the Israeli government's theory that a diplomatic
agreement was probable and that Damascus was flexible. By continuing
to back anti-Israel terror, especially in southern Lebanon which
produced Israeli casualties, Asad raised Israeli voters' perceptions that
external dangers and a need for defense were more salient than regional
opportunities and chances for peace. By helping extremist Palestinians
carry out terrorism within Israel and the territories, while inhibiting
Arafat's flexibility toward compromise, Asad also damaged the process's
success and hence, indirectly, Peres's standing at home.

As the election approached, Hizbullah – with Iranian help and Syrian
compliance – escalated its attacks. During April, Hizbullah fired large
numbers of katyusha rockets into northern Israel, leading to Israeli
retaliation and the large-scale *Grapes of Wrath* operation in April–May.
Although sometimes portrayed abroad as a vote-seeking effort by Peres,
his refusal to react to a major assault on Israeli citizens would have
guaranteed his defeat. Moreover, by angering some Israeli-Arabs – who
may have been moved to abstain from voting at all – this campaign may
have sealed his defeat.

Whatever their intentions – if they had any – toward Israel's election,
Hizbullah, its sponsor, Iran, and also Syria viewed the incumbent Israeli
government as an enemy and sought to injure it. Their actions damaged
Peres' reelection effort.

SUMMARY

Unquestionably, the United States, to a slightly lesser extent Arafat, and
to a somewhat lower degree moderate Arab states, preferred a Peres
victory. These parties, however, did little to affect the election campaign.
In each case, they could easily have done more to help Israel's existing

government. In some of his actions, Arafat might have harmed Peres' standing.

Radical regimes and terrorist groups might have objectively favored an opposition victory as a way of weakening a peace process they opposed. Again, however, there is little evidence that a wish to affect Israel's election shaped their behavior.

Some Israeli voters were likely swayed in the government's direction because they accepted its claim that such a choice would both ensure good U.S.–Israel relations, reward progress in normalizing Israel's links with moderate Arab states, and lead to a stable solution in negotiations with the Palestinians. Such voters would consider the government's combination of flexibility and toughness an effective tool in combatting and defusing the terrorist threat from radical forces. A vote for the opposition would constitute a victory for the terrorists and lead to a greater threat of tension or even war in the future.

By the same token, others voted in a different manner, doubting that an opposition victory would damage U.S.–Israel relations (or considering this a necessary risk since U.S.-supported policies could hurt Israel's security). They thought the current government's policy was disastrous, or at least felt that Israel could get more from the Arab states and the Palestinians while giving up less. They deemed Arafat's performance unsatisfactory, not proving a real change in Palestinian intentions, failing to meet his commitments and thus not meriting concomitant Israeli concessions. Giving up the Golan was considered more of a risk than a way to attain peace; Lebanese and Palestinian terrorist attacks were viewed as more the result of the existing peace process than a last-ditch, doomed effort to block it.

In short, the external factors were perceived through two alternative world views. Israeli voters were divided almost exactly evenly in holding these different concepts. While specific conclusions about the external factors were often after-the-fact rationales to justify an individual's already held convictions, Binyamin Netanyahu's tiny margin of victory might be attributed to such issues, most notably the terror of extremist Palestinian groups, doubts about Arafat's credibility or performance, and concerns over Syrian behavior and intentions.

NOTES

1. *New York Times*, May 28, 1996.
2. Barry Rubin, "U.S.–Israel Relations and Israel's 1992 Elections," in Asher Arian and Michal Shamir, *Elections in Israel* (Albany, 1994).
3. Moshe Arens, *Broken Covenant: How U.S. Foreign Policy Compromised Israel's National Security* (New York, 1995), p.301.
4. John Lancaster, *Washington Post*, May 27, 1996.
5. *Reuters*, January 10, 1996. Ironically, Christopher himself was becoming increasingly doubtful about Syria's willingness to make peace with Israel at the same time. But this resulted in no change in U.S. policy. See *Los Angeles Times*, May 3 and *Washington*

Post, May 22.

6. Clinton's speech to the AIPAC conference, May 7, 1995. Text in *Near East Report*, May 15, 1995, pp.66-7.
7. United Press International, March 6, 1996; *New York Times*, March 14 and 17, 1996.
8. *New York Times*, April 16, 1996.
9. Clinton's speech to AIPAC conference, op. cit.; April 30, 1996 joint statement, *New York Times*, April 29, 1996.
10. *Jerusalem Post*, May 29, 1996.
11. *Mideast Mirror*, March 24, 1995.
12. Speech to AIPAC conference, op. cit., pp.66–7.
13 Text from White House Office of the Press Secretary, May 28, 1996.
14. Text of the Republican party's platform, August 1996.
15. *Jerusalem Report*, June 27, 1996, p.32. A *New York Times* editorial of June 2, 1996, said that Netanyahu's election meant that the Arab–Israeli peace process which the Clinton administration worked so hard on "is effectively dead."26. *Washington Post*, May 22, 1996.
16. On the government's conception, see Efraim Inbar, "Contours of Israel's New Strategic Thinking," *Political Science Quarterly*, Vol. 111, No. 1 (Spring 1996), pp.41–64.
17. Lancaster, *Washington Post*, May 27, 1996.
18. This was repeatedly confirmed in the author's own off-the-record interviews.
19. Lancaster, *Washington Post*.
20. Ibid.
21. For a discussion of these issues, see the author's *Assessing The New Middle East: Opportunities and Risks*, Bar-Ilan University BESA Center, Security and Policy Studies, 1995. On Egypt's attitude, see also the author's article in *The European Wall Street Journal*, June 21, 1996.
22. Author's interviews with Israeli leaders, both before and after the election.
23. Author's interviews with Palestinian leaders both before and after the elections.
24. Muhammad Abu Warda, interview with Israel television, March 6, 1996; *Ha-aretz*, March 7, 1996. Salama interview with Israel Television, August 11, 1996.
25. Interview in the *Financial Times*, cited in *Yediot Aharonot*, August 14, 1996.

The Media Campaign: The Negative Effects of Positive Campaigning

SAM LEHMAN-WILZIG

The title of this essay involves a conundrum while constituting a play on words as well. In addition, it hints at several paradoxes and ironies which lie at the heart of Israel's media campaign in the 1996 elections to the Knesset and for the position of prime minister.

The conundrum can be summed up thus: why is it that the candidate/party which carried out the more negative campaign eventually succeeded in "winning" the election? (The term "winning" is in quotation marks for two reasons: Binyamin Netanyahu won by the slimmest of margins and the Likud garnered less seats than Labor). Under normal electoral circumstances, of course, such a question would not constitute much of a conundrum, as negative advertising has become almost a de rigueur practice in Western democracies, and especially the U.S. (where it has proven to be more effective than a positive campaign),[1] from which Israeli campaign strategists draw sustenance.[2] Given the fact that Netanyahu learned and continues to practice American-style "media politics", there should be even less surprise at the Likud's use of a negative campaign. Why, then, is there a conundrum?

For the simple reason that the entire campaign was run – by all parties – in the shadow of Prime Minister Yitzchak Rabin's assassination. Beyond the fact that the assassination itself was at times a substantive issue in the campaign, indirectly used by both major camps as a weapon as we will see below, more than anything else it served as an extremely powerful background factor repressing the natural urge of all parties to attack the opposing camp. This was doubly the case due to the rancorous debate following the assassination as to which political camp was "at fault", and the succeeding public hand-wringing about Israeli society's becoming too aggressive, too violent – indeed, in danger of descending

---

Sam Lehman-Wilzig is Associate Professor of Political Studies at Bar-Ilan University, and Chairman of Israel's Political Science Association.

into "civil war" (the oblique term generally used was "the end of the Third Temple", connoting the reborn State of Israel). As a result of public revulsion and fear of a real societal cleavage, a general consensus arose among virtually all politicians and electoral pundits that a negative campaign would only boomerang against its users. And indeed, while certainly not an "angelic" campaign, the 1996 elections took a higher road and tone than many if not all which preceded it.

So the conundrum – one of the central questions which this essay will try to answer – stands: how did the Likud get away with it against the tide of public opinion which wanted a clean campaign? Of course, we shall first have to show that the Likud's campaign was indeed more "negative" than Labor's.

As mentioned, the title is also a pun on several levels. On the one hand, it can be taken at face value: the candidate (Peres) whose campaign was mostly positive in tone, suffered the negative consequence of losing the election. A closer investigation of why his campaign emphasized the positive, however, reveals that it was not merely a function of the party's respect for the memory of former Prime Minister Rabin or due to the trauma of his death, but perhaps more important due to the fact that almost everyone involved within the party and outside of it (media and the public itself) were positive that Labor and PM Peres would win the election. Thus, a "don't-rock-the-boat" philosophy prevailed in the Labor camp, involving a strategy of not egging on the other side with under-the-belt mudslinging.[3]

A second pun involves the word "media". While the campaign's overt election propaganda was produced by the parties and then published/broadcast through the mass media, there was another – covert – campaign going on: that of the mass media themselves. Here the paradox was present at its fullest, for while the personal political identification of most Israeli journalists is left of center and there is some evidence that quantitatively the campaign coverage was slightly skewed to the left,[4] the mass media's qualitative coverage of events throughout the period under discussion in fact constituted an (unintentional) campaign strengthening of the Likud's and Netanyahu's message. From much of the media's perspective, then, its behavior – while perhaps positive from a professional perspective – had a decidedly "negative" outcome.

There were other "paradoxes" and "ironies", which will be fleshed out in the course of the essay.

NEGATIVE CAMPAIGNING IN ISRAEL'S PAST

Unlike other "new" democratic countries receiving their independence after World War II (for example, India, Pakistan) which have suffered from the start from a high level of political violence in general and during election campaigns in particular, Israel has stood apart as a young democracy without significant political bloodshed. There is not a single politically-motivated recorded fatality during an Israeli election campaign in its 48 years of existence. In fact, within the dominant Jewish sector only two Jews have been known to die in the course of a political demonstration, while the number of attempted political assassinations from 1948 onwards can be counted on one hand – in marked contradistinction to the situation prior to 1948.[5]

However, perhaps as an alternative outlet for real existing political hostility, the level of verbal violence in Israel has been very high throughout, with terms such as "traitor", "terrorist" (and worse) being bandied about from the early 1950s onwards. This was due in part to the wide ideological gap between the two major camps (Labor and Herut) as well as the deeply existential issues being debated and voted upon: foremost being war and peace, and national territorial boundaries. That gap has been closing since the late 1970s (after all, the Likud gave back all of Sinai and uprooted settlements; both camps have signed peace treaties with former Arab enemies), but as a final settlement moves into view – with its potential high price in territorial concessions and uncertainty regarding ultimate security and the sincerity of the other side – the shrill tone of national debate has not abated. Indeed, one of the paradoxes worth mentioning in this context is that the closer the two camps become in principle, the more strident the tone needed to mask their respective ideological "treasonous" inconsistency as well as the greater the need to distinguish themselves from the opposition through voice and not substance. This last point can be seen especially clearly in the 1996 campaign with the complete blurring of substantive differences in both camps' election slogans: Labor's "A Strong Israel with Peres" and the Likud's "Netanyahu· Making a Secure [Sure] Peace".

In short, bombs do not go off in Israeli election campaigns (at least not set by Israeli citizens), but verbal pyrotechnics are certainly de riguer (as they are during non-campaign periods).

THE NEGATIVE ATMOSPHERE IN 1996

As noted above, the country was in a sour spirit from November 1995 onwards as a result of the assassination of Prime Minister Rabin. The Palestinian terrorist bus bombings of February and March 1996 merely turned the public's mood into something akin to national fear and mourning. And here we arrive at our next paradox: simply put, the formal election campaign of ads and slogans did not need to be negative, as the news environment which enveloped the campaign was highly negative in its own right.

That the media covered the bombings in depth was not at all surprising; nor was the "sensationalist" style of their coverage. Isolated bus bombings over the previous two years had raised the "gore threshold" to new heights (depths) for Israel, although the deadly series in February–March 1996 led to an even higher level of intensive media coverage, what Liebes (in press) calls "Disaster Marathons": full cover-page pictures of the mangled buses and especially television's preempting hours and hours of programming to bring non-stop, live coverage of the deadly events. In short, even before the "formal" campaign commenced (usually considered to be two months before election day), the media – in the wake of the situation in the field – had already set the public agenda which can be summed up in one word: "Security".

This is an extremely important point which bears elaboration. As virtually all research in the field of communications acknowledges, the media are not capable of significantly changing the public's opinion, i.e. what to think, but they are very influential in determining the public's news agenda, i.e. what to think about.[6] The overwhelming (highly frightening) media coverage of the bus bombings determined from the start that the central item on the election agenda would not be the accomplishments and failures of the Labor government or the lack of clearly enunciated alternative policy on the part of the inexperienced Netanyahu, but rather a (non)issue of the highest importance but one which was not completely (or even largely) in the hands of any Israeli government – Arab terrorism which had struck in the past at Labor and Likud-led coalitions alike.

This does not mean that both camps were at an equal disadvantage. The bombings were particularly disadvantageous to Labor, not merely because they occurred under its watch. Rather, it did not enable Peres and his party to play up their strongest points: the successes of the peace process (Oslo Accords, peace treaty with Jordan, a distinct thawing of the Arab world's animosity), in addition to significant accomplishments on the domestic front (improvement of the educational system, national health insurance program, massive highway construction, etc.). In short, when Prime Minister Peres decided on new elections in the beginning of the year, he planned to run on the Rabin/Peres government's successful record – a clear advantage over Netanyahu, who played mostly to the public's inchoate fear. By the time the campaign actually began, however, the public's fear was real and palpable as a result of the media's news coverage (itself, of course, a reflection of reality). Subsequent media election coverage would pall by comparison, in the shadow of the security agenda "monster" which the media played upon incessantly. Indeed, the formal ad campaigns of the parties and candidates would pall as well. By all accounts, the 1996 elections to the Knesset were the "quietest" and "dullest" in a long time – at least until the drama of election night and the final results.

THE ELECTION CAMPAIGN STRATEGY

Overall, the two main parties and candidates for prime minister faced a situation far more complex than usual in approaching the campaign and in devising a general strategy. Not only did they have to take into account as usual the possible campaign of their rival and prepare proper responses, but unlike previous campaigns (except for 1973) they also had to very carefully take into account the "public mood" as a result of the traumas over the previous half year. Moreover, the two-vote campaign complicated matters considerably as it meant that two campaigns had to be waged: for the Knesset list and for the prime minister.

Given that this was Israel's first national campaign in which each citizen had two votes (a similar system existed on the municipal level since 1978, but little could be learned from that vastly different situation in which many independent, non-ideological party lists ran and won), the campaign strategists were groping in the dark. The basic decision made by both camps was not to devise two separate campaigns but to mesh the two, with the campaign for prime minister given priority. This last point was a result of the new constitutional fact that the winning candidate for prime minister would automatically form the government, regardless of whether his party was the top vote-getter on the Knesset list election (as indeed occurred in the end; Likud ended up with two seats less than Labor). It should be noted, however, that while tactically correct, the ultimate result proved this strategy to be a disastrous one for both Labor and Likud. By concentrating most of their advertising on Netanyahu and Peres, the two parties together ended with the lowest combined Knesset seat total since 1965, barely constituting more than half the Knesset (66 of 120 seats). While some ticket-splitting was to be expected, there is little doubt that the fact that the two major parties did not do much (in the way of election propaganda) to minimize the phenomenon, contributed significantly to the steep decline in their Knesset support. The next elections will almost certainly not see a repeat of such a weak party campaign.

The major question for Labor and Likud was whether to run a positive or negative campaign. Between the two, it was Labor which actually had the more difficult choice, given its (and Peres') early lead in the polls. Why, then, a difficult choice? Because the temptation and the wherewithal for Labor to run a negative campaign were many and varied. Indeed, a list of possible Netanyahu/Likud weak points which could have been potentially attacked as a strategic campaign policy shows how potentially vulnerable the Likud was to a massive campaign attack.

First and perhaps foremost was Netanyahu's earlier fanning the flames of political hatred in several Likud demonstrations prior to the assassination – either overtly (using highly charged epithets) or covertly (not denouncing on the spot morphed pictures of Rabin in a Nazi uniform or a doll of Rabin being burned in effigy at demonstrations where Netanyahu appeared and did not immediately leave in protest when these protest paraphernalia appeared on the scene). While it was obvious to most Israelis that the Likud had absolutely no direct involvement in the assassination, the Likud certainly did its share in supporting an environment in which violent opposition to the peace process could be concretely manifested by others. We shall return to this point below in the context of Labor's campaign strategy.

Second, Netanyahu's personal "immorality" as exemplified in the "hot videotape" incident a couple of years earlier when he appeared on television and admitted to having an extra-marital affair (he was already twice-divorced), indirectly but quite obviously accusing his Likud opponent David Levy of political blackmail through the threatened use of a videotape which purportedly filmed Netanyahu "in the act" (the tape was never found, and there are doubts that it even existed). While Israelis are not as puritanical as American society (former Chief of Staff and Foreign Minister Moshe Dayan was widely acknowledged as having many extra-marital affairs), such dirty linen was almost never washed in public. The fact that a politician would himself publicly divulge this was damaging in itself, but more important, it lent the opposition possible legitimacy to bring up the issue as a campaign topic.

Moreover, Netanyahu's extra-marital affairs also constituted a (potentially) significant substantive campaign issue. For the first time in Israel's political history the Haredi (ultra-Orthodox) sector faced the unpalatable situation of having to vote for a non-religious candidate, as a result of the new system of direct prime ministerial elections. While the natural tendency of the vast majority of Haredim was to support Netanyahu for his position on the Territories ("Holy Land"), the choice was not an easy one psychologically because of his confirmed adultery. The temptation for Labor was great to play up Mr. Netanyahu's dalliances (in comparison to Peres' longstanding marriage to Sonya, who preferred to stay out of the eye of the media) in the hope of denying him the Haredi vote – not in the television spots (which the Haredim do not watch) but in billboards and the general press, which a sizable proportion of the Haredi sector do read on occasion. In the end, though, the decision was made not to break the Israeli traditional taboo of campaigning on "bedroom" issues.

Third, as a result of the aforementioned innuendo by Netanyahu that Levy was behind the "blackmail", the latter ultimately left Likud to set up his own party (Gesher). This came after a couple of years in which the two former party colleagues were not on speaking terms, indeed had taken to denouncing one another (Levy more than Netanyahu). Thus, it came as somewhat of a shock when Levy announced at the start of the campaign that he would not run for prime minister, and would coalesce his party into the Likud Knesset list. It was clear to all that Likud now was being led by two politicians who palpably could not stomach each other – an extremely ripe, almost necessary, opportunity for Labor barbs during the campaign, which again did not in fact appear.

Why not? Among other considerations, Peres and the Labor Party strategists were mindful of the possible boomerang effect of focussing on the Netanyahu–Levy animosity, for the same situation held in the earlier relationship between Rabin and Peres himself – an association which was highly acrimonious (serious allegations were leveled by each against the other in their respective "memoirs"). However, they ultimately settled into a very fruitful working relationship under the previous Rabin-led government and such a precedent could have easily suggested to the public that Levy and Netanyahu could also as easily work together.

Nevertheless, the major reason for Labor's avoidance of a heavily negative campaign was strategic: a conscious decision on the part of the campaign staff – especially Haim Ramon at its head – to take the high road, certainly a legitimate approach given Labor's lead at the time in the polls. Indeed, an article appearing two days after the elections spelled out the various campaign television spots and newspaper ads that Labor had produced – almost all of them negative – which were not televised/published. As Avner Barel, the leading advertising strategist of the Labor campaign noted:

> Haim had many temptations which were hard to avoid, but he stood firm... For example, to deal with Bibi [Netanyahu] below the belt. Take the vilification which preceded Rabin's assassination. We have incredible footage of Bibi standing on a platform [during a demonstration] with a gigantic sign on the bottom 'Death to Arafat' [this well after the signing of the Oslo accords]. Bibi is orating and yelling while in front of him, indeed right in front of him, people are using a knife to slice up a picture of Rabin. And Bibi doesn't stop it and doesn't do a thing. We were dying to show this but Haim...prevented it.[7]

Nor was such a decision based on gut feeling alone, as Barel notes. When showing "attack ads" to focus groups comprising the "floating voters", undecided between Peres and Netanyahu, the response was unenthusiastic to say the least because of their aversion to tying the Likud to Rabin's assassination. As Ramon explained in making his strategic decision not to run a negative campaign:

> I would like to remind you to whom we're advertising. To Likud, as well as SHAS [Sephardi Haredim] and NRP [National Religious Party], supporters who are considering splitting their vote [between their own party list and Peres]. They are just waiting for a reason which would enable them to return home, to Bibi, and the only reason that they are still with us is that even in their eyes Bibi is not fit to be Prime Minister... Anything we do which will turn into a conflict between two camps... might well send them back.[8]

This is not to say that Labor's campaign was totally positive. On one issue it did use negative advertising: "Bibi Is Not Fit" (to be prime minister). This was a "legitimate" issue because of Mr. Netanyahu's lack of experience at the highest levels of government (he never even served as a Minister, only as Deputy Minister). The use of the nickname "Bibi", instead of using "Netanyahu" (after all, neither Labor nor Likud used the name "Shimoleh" or even "Shimon" in describing Peres) also added to the attempted portrayal of the candidate as "childish". In a sense, this was ironic and dangerous for Labor for the reason that the country was interested in having new faces in the government, not to mention the fact that Peres had already run (and "lost") as the head of the party in four previous Knesset elections, so that "Not Fit" was a pejorative which the public had already defined the Labor leader in the past. Nevertheless, given the highly sensitive situation of peace negotiations it was clear that most of the public preferred to have the government in experienced hands.

The Likud along with Netanyahu, on the other hand, had a less difficult choice regarding its campaign strategy precisely because it was well behind in the polls through most of the campaign. This does not mean that the strategy was clearcut from the start, but only that its choices were more limited.

The problem facing the Likud could be summed up as follows: in order to close the gap it had to have a forceful, vigorous campaign, which in Israeli terms (as in most Western countries these days) meant some measure of negative-attack campaign advertising. On the other hand, as the political climate for such a campaign was not propitious to say the least – in part because of the Rabin assassination as well as the fact that many former Likud supporters were wavering and would be further turned off by a nasty campaign initiated by Likud – the question of finding the right "balance" was a critical one.

The solution which the campaign strategists hit upon was to have Netanyahu appear "statesmanlike" while concentrating in "neutral" fashion on the one topic which not only was the weakest part of the Labor (otherwise impressive) armor, but which ipso facto was negative in its very essence: National (and Personal) Security.

This worked on two separate but interrelated levels. On the higher national plane, a large segment of the population – while supporting the overall direction of the peace process – was extremely wary of the speed and the price of the Oslo Accords. The problem was less objective than psychological, but as the late Anwar Sadat noted it was precisely the psychological barrier (of mutual mistrust) which constituted the greatest obstacle to peace in the Middle East. By hammering again and again on the security side of the "Peace with Security" slogan, Netanyahu and Likud were playing to the public's deepest fears without appearing overly (and overtly) negative.

A prime example of this was the way in which Likud managed to undermine the Labor government's "accomplishment" in forcing the PLO to declare that it was changing its Charter (calling for Israel's destruction). Instead of a frontal attack against Peres and Arafat on the issue, they brought out Professor Yehoshua Porat – one of Israel's top Arabists, and a supporter of Meretz (!) – who publicly declared that the

Charter was not canceled by the PLO leadership and was probably not going to be rewritten in light of the "promises" made by Arafat to Peres.

Whether this was true or not is irrelevant to the discussion here; what is relevant and highly illustrative is that the Likud managed to attack the trustworthiness of the government, of the PLO and of the entire peace process by getting someone else – an academic expert from the Left of the political spectrum! – to do the dirty work. As Iyengar and Kinder have noted: "according to countless persuasion experiments, the influence exercised by a message does depend significantly on the credibility of its source: expert and trustworthy sources exert more influence than inexpert, untrustworthy sources."[9] And indeed, Labor's highly interesting post-election report authored by Shadmon and Geyer (entitled the "Post-Mortem" which had an obvious internal Labor political bias, but was quite objective in analyzing the Opposition's campaign) concluded that the Likud succeeded in raising serious doubts in the minds of many voters through Professor Porat regarding the PLO Charter controversy. Labor's subsequent publication of campaign ads signed by other academicians who argued the reverse were pale and ineffective by comparison.[10]

Second, as noted above, the Israeli public was feeling decidedly unsure of its security on a personal level as a result of the bus bombings in February–March. Here very little needed to be done during the campaign as the horrific pictures and accompanying public hysteria were emblazoned in the public's mind for the entire period of the campaign.[11] The mere mention of the bombings or anything suggesting Arab terrorism was enough to bring back the recent traumatic memories and further reinforce the "security" message of the Likud. This was not merely done to "hold" the Likud's traditional supporters but to garner new support, given the first-time ballot for prime minister which forced each of the two major parties to address voters who had never voted for the party.[12] As Iyengar and Kinder further note: "Merely feeling anger, sadness, or fear may cause viewers to alter their political judgments."[13]

In a sense, then, we find here a curious symbiosis between the Likud's campaign and the mass media's coverage during this period. Studies issued soon after the election came to the conclusion that the press's quantitative reportage of the campaign was relatively balanced (naturally, the incumbent prime minister Peres and his governing party Labor received somewhat more ink, given that they were still running the country), with coverage between the two candidates and the two leading parties almost equal in the final weeks of the campaign.[14] While empirically this was true, it does not take into account the damage done to the Labor cause (or inversely, the unintended background "friendly" environment laid for the Likud) by the media's bus bombing reportage immediately prior to the official two month campaign. Statistical analysis can be enlightening, but should not be taken as the final word – especially when dealing with such subjective and psychological matters as campaign advertising and the "national election agenda". The same holds true, of course, for the data which will be provided in this essay. It is to be understood as a basis for understanding the election campaign, and not as the objective campaign itself.

METHODOLOGY

Israel's three major Hebrew-language daily newspapers – *Yediot Aharonot*, *Ma'ariv*, and *Ha-aretz* – were analyzed over the two month period prior to Election Day, from the perspective of the parties' paid political advertisements. This study does not include the televised campaign spots of the campaign's last month, in part because of the aforementioned low level of viewership (as compared to newspaper readership which reaches the 85 per cent level among adults). In any case, as both major parties ran a strategic campaign overall, with much the same messages being sent through all the media, it is highly doubtful that the data would in any significant way be different had television ads been included.

All of the paid ads by all the parties were analyzed for the two month period (see Table 1). Among other things, we discovered that a not insignificant number of ads were placed by ideological movements not formally affiliated (if at all) with any of the parties. These are included in Table 1, but not in the tables thereafter. Indeed, in order not to complicate matters unduly, the rest of the tables will focus on five of the six parties which advertised most heavily: Labor (83 ads), Likud (82), Meretz (67), Third Way (39), and the National Religious Party – NRP (21). The sixth, which we shall not analyze in depth, was Moledet which placed 50 ads – an astounding number given that it had only three seats in the outgoing Knesset and won only two seats in the 1996 elections. One other party – far more significant (it garnered 10 seats in these elections) – was the haredi-Sephardi party SHAS, but it only advertised twice (once in Yediot, once in Ma'ariv, on election day!), a result of an "alternative media" campaign strategy (see below).

A sliding scale was established – from 1 to 5 – which enabled us to assess the degree of "negativity" or "positivity" in each print ad. A score of 1 indicated that the ad was all negative, i.e. focussed on attacking one or more opponents or opposing ideological positions (e.g. "Peres Will Divide Jerusalem"; "Bibi Isn't Fit"). A score of 5 indicated that the ad dealt only with promoting the position of the advertising party/candidate. Scores of 2 or 4 indicated that the brunt of the ad was negative or positive with a minor focus on the reverse, while a score of 3 meant that there was an equal amount of negative and positive elements. All neutral party ads such as the official Election Commission overseeing the campaign, were not included in this study.

There was no problem of inter-coder variability as only one person did the scoring, under the guidance and supervision of the author. This is not to say that there were not problems of subjective evaluation and of precise scoring. Regarding the former, the scorer was given explicit instructions to discount her own political tendencies and view the ads through the eyes of a "neutral" observer, although one who understood code words and symbols of Israel's political culture (see below). For what it's worth, she is a right-wing supporter, so that the overall finding that the Likud's campaign was more negative than Labor's cannot be a function of any scoring subjectivity based on ideological bias.

Regarding the second problem – precision of scoring – many times it was hard to determine whether to provide a score of 2 or of 3, or of 4 or 3, given that we did not base our judgment on the quantity of words, but rather the ad's overall "impression". Such an overall impression included the use of pictures which could be "positive" or "negative" in their own way. To be sure, there are two ways of "perceiving" campaign ads. One is to stick to the ad's textual and pictorial denotation, i.e. what the words and pictures "mean" in a purely "objective"/dictionary sense. The other is to score the ad in its connotative sense, i.e. the way the average Israeli – with all his/her "cultural baggage" – understands the words/pictures. While the second approach obviously is more "subjective" and thence more open to interpretation, it is still the preferred one because what we are attempting to measure here is not the campaign in and of itself but rather the interplay between the election propaganda and the public, i.e. the influence of the former over the latter. In any case, it is universally understood that advertising of all sorts (and certainly political advertising) works on several levels, the simple semantic one usually being less important than the "sub-text".

The only element not taken into account in the scoring was the party's/candidate's ongoing campaign slogan. Here the problem was not of interpretation but of conscious ambiguity: at times a slogan could be highly positive and negative at one and the same time, making it extremely difficult and problematic to score it in any meaningful manner. We shall return, though, to the phenomena of ambiguous slogans in our extended discussion a bit later.

FINDINGS

As can be seen from Table 1, the overall tone of the 1996 election campaign tended to the positive side: 3.58. This reinforces and corroborates our introductory point regarding the fact that after the Rabin assassination the general public (and as a consequence, the parties in its wake) was in no mood for attack politics. Indeed, if one removes the Likud's score (2.45), the overall average approaches 4.0 – a very positive campaign indeed!

Moreover, against common sense it turns out that the smaller parties waged a much more positive campaign (averaging 3.78) than the two major parties together (3.25). If one were to believe conventional wisdom that negative campaign advertising is the way to get the public's attention and support, this election totally undercuts this thesis given the election results in which Labor and Likud together were weakened relative to the smaller parties.

TABLE 1

POSITIVE/NEGATIVE SCORERS – ALL PARTIES

Party/movement	Positive/ negative total	Numbers of ads	Overall average score
1 Labor	336	83	4.05
2 Likud	201	82	2.45
3 Meretz	225	67	3.35
4 Moledet	187	50	3.37
5 Third Way	171	39	4.38
6 Dor Shalom/Peace and Security Council	115	28	4.11
7 NRP	89	21	4.24
8 "Pikuach Nefesh" (Against Ceding Territory)	28	12	2.3
9 Security and National Strength Forum	40	8	5.0
10 Future of Israel	7	7	1.0
11 Israel's Right	30	7	4.28
12 Meimad	25	5	5.0
13 Communist Party	10	2	5.0
14 SHAS	10	2	5.0
15 Chabbad	8	2	4.0
16 Golan Settlers	5	1	5.0
17 Fathers' Heritage	5	1	5.0
18 Joint Committee of Organized Struggle	2	1	2.0
19 Gil (Pensioners)	4	1	4.0
TOTAL	1498	419	3.58

Further breakdowns of the data are revealing in other ways. To begin with, the evolution of the campaign shows a relatively clear trend of moving towards negative/positive equilibrium. In other words, in the second and last month of the race, each of the four central parties moved in a direction away from its initial ("month 1") approach and towards the overall campaign "norm" (see Table 2). This meant that the Likud trended toward a somewhat more positive campaign over the course of the race, while Labor, Meretz and the NRP became somewhat more negative.

TABLE 2

CAMPAIGN NEGATIVITY OVER THE COURSE OF THE CAMPAIGN

Political Party	Month 1 (29/3–4/28)	Month 2 (29/4–29/5)	Last Week (23/5–29)
Likud	2.27	2.53	3.8
Labor	4.23	3.75	4.1
Meretz	3.60	3.20	4.00
NRP	4.60	4.16	4.20

Of no less interest in this regard is the last column of Table 2. All four parties took a more positive propaganda stance in the last week of the campaign compared to the rest of the final month (as the election week score is included in the final month tally, the difference is even starker than it seems at first glance). As the final week of the campaign is critical – and in this election that was obviously the case to everyone involved at that time – it becomes obvious that in the crunch, the parties moved in a very positive direction within the format of the paid-for advertisements. The reason for emphasizing this last phrase shall be discussed in the next section.

Another interesting finding relates to the specific newspaper in which the ads appeared. Table 3 clearly shows that the parties' propaganda strategies had a differential element to them. Briefly and succinctly put, with the exception of the NRP which placed but one ad in *Ha-aretz* (thus, the following point is not really relevant in the case of this party), all three major parties ran a far more negative campaign in the two mass circulation dailies Yediot and Ma'ariv than they did in the elite paper Ha-aretz.

TABLE 3

NEGATIVE/POSITIVE PROPAGANDA BY NEWSPAPER

	Labor	Likud	Meretz	NRP
Yediot	3.89	2.34	2.90	4.20
Ma'ariv	3.97	2.35	3.10	4.27
Ha-aretz	4.35	2.88	4.00	4.00

This indicates a couple of things. First, that the parties do not run a scattershot campaign but rather phrase their messages in the language that specific target audiences will most be amenable to. In our case here, it is obvious that all the parties view the less educated public as being more susceptible (or amenable) to attack advertising than their more higher educated compatriots. One could also offer that the latter type of public is less swayed by emotional/negative propaganda and is more open to (or seeks) cognitive/ positive messages and/or information.

DISCUSSION

The data seem to be rather clearcut: the Likud ran a more negative campaign than Labor (and the other middle-sized parties). However, even the scores which the Likud garnered on the negative-positive spectrum were not indicative of an extremely negative campaign. This is especially true when one considers the political science truism that elections are usually lost by the incumbents and not won by the opposition, thus necessitating a campaign by the party out of power to be more critical of the governing party than vice versa, in order to win the election.

However, the matter is not as simple as it seems, for as already suggested earlier, one cannot merely focus exclusively on the advertising campaigns of the parties to determine the degree of constructive/negative messages sent. There exists another player in this game – the journalists themselves and the news "product" which they publish/broadcast.

It had become clear by the 1992 elections to the Knesset – when cable television was already in operation (Channel 2 was still televising "experimentally") – that the general public was becoming jaded with campaign advertising – as could be seen from the very low percentage of viewers who watched the aggregated TV ad segments over the last month of the 1992 campaign. In the final analysis, the viewership in 1996 dropped even further: a mere 21 per cent (vs. 25 per cent in 1992) watched "almost all" the TV campaign spots, while the number who did not view them at all rose from 40 per cent to 46 per cent.[15] As Israeli election law allots to each party free air time (based on the number of seats in the outgoing Knesset), the parties were hardly going to bypass this medium. However, their strategy changed. Instead of a "frontal assault" on the voter, the thrust would be indirect and perhaps all the more effective because the public would not be aware of the "interests" behind it. As Avraham Burg, Labor's chief of liaison with the press, admitted right after the election:

> We made a strategic decision that the campaign would be of "news" and not of explanation through the papers. From the moment we decided that, it was clear that the print and electronic media would play a dominant role in our field. The way we worked was to transfer information on our candidate's activities and pronouncements in a constant flow, while at the same time transferring juicy investigative files (on the opposing candidate...) so that the journalists would use them if they so wished.[16]

The Likud, as well, used the strategy of feeding the press with "news" on numerous occasions but the tactic had another dimension, with the disinformation working on two different levels.[17] On the one hand, strategic "high-level" politics, e.g. the anonymous leak to Ma'ariv that Netanyahu was considering Jerusalem Mayor Ehud Olmert as Defense Minister, while Yediot Aharonot received the "scoop" that it was actually Dan Meridor who was under consideration – all this to reassure the undecided voters that more hawkish senior Likud members such as Ariel Sharon were not going to be in control of defense/foreign policy. On the other hand, the Likud campaign also worked feverishly to feed "low level" news, which demanded an instant decision on the part of the journalists whether to publish or withhold: for example, false reports of Labor supporters attacking Likud campaign workers (probably to "balance out" the true incident of some Labor supporters being attacked by Likud workers).

The two parties' media strategists not only worked overtime on such "news" initiatives, but also ran a very sophisticated "reaction" press campaign whereby every negative news report (from each party's perspective) was met by pressure on the journalist to "balance out" the picture (with, of course, information fed by the party) or outright threats on the journalist as to "closing the news flow" in the future if the critical reporting did not cease (ibid).

One could list at great length the numerous examples of attempted manipulation of the media's campaign reporting, most of it to present the other side in negative light. However, the key point here is that the real electoral battleground for the hearts and minds of the voters took place where the voters could not see it! Indeed, it would not be an exaggeration to argue that the 1996 Israeli election campaign was carried out on two different levels: the overt and the covert, the ads and the news. While the public's nominal attention was turned to the official and formal newspaper ads and radio/television spots, it was more influenced in the final analysis by the "news campaign" working on the national psyche in an indirect – and at times subliminal – fashion.

The 1996 election had three central (and according to many observers, the most critical) campaign initiatives which most probably determined the outcome of the prime minister ballot, and in which we can see several of the points made in this essay: "negative" campaigning in a non-overtly negative fashion; using the news to "trigger" subterranean issues and feelings; the importance of the "news campaign", especially as it tied in with the formal ad campaign. The three examples are: the SHAS "amulet campaign"; the TV debate; and the election slogan "Netanyahu: Good for the Jews".

The SHAS party's campaign to distribute magical amulets blessed by mystic Rabbi Kedouri (as well as his picture, a memorial candle and a series of blessings) was perceived/portrayed by the media as one of the more bizarre election ploys in Israel's history, albeit with very significant effect (this certainly was not the first time that items such as amulets were used in an Israeli election campaign, but it was the first time that they received such widespread media coverage). The effect resulted from two factors. First, being portrayed as bizarre – as well as probably illegal by Israeli election law standards (no physical gifts may be distributed nor can blessings be offered) – the Israeli press had a field day with the whole operation, obviously highly critical. However, for the average potential SHAS supporter the wide media coverage only reinforced the "importance" of the amulet/blessing, thereby providing SHAS with a huge amount of free "positive" publicity. It must be noted that SHAS is unusual in the Israeli context in that it is a "crossover" party, garnering support among Haredi Jews (many of whom do not read the mainstream press and have no television sets in their houses) as well as sizable support from "traditional", albeit non-religious, Jews in the underprivileged neighborhoods and development towns who do consume media as other Israelis. The unexpected increase of SHAS from six to ten Knesset seats, strengthening Netanyahu's hand once the government was formed, can be traced in significant part to the unintended "symbiosis" between the national media and the SHAS campaign – the former portraying the phenomenon in negative terms, the latter's supporters filtering these reports through their own perceptual screen and looking upon the amulet campaign as a meritorious act.

Perhaps even more to the point was the "negative" side of the positive amulet campaign. While distributing amulets is in no way a negative act (except insofar as it may reinforce superstitions at the cost of rational electoral behavior), once again we find here a situation where one thing "triggers" another. In this case, the amulets and blessings were distributed and understood by their recipients as protecting them (as long as they kept their written promise to vote for the party) from evil people and bad events. Indeed, Rabbi Kedouri promised them: "Blessing, Security, and Success". In the Israeli context, the "security" element meant but one thing – terrorism. As the "Post-Mortem" report noted, the SHAS amulet campaign fed off the media's incessant discussion of possible terror activity during the election campaign:

> One of the unintended consequences of the large amount of information in the media regarding the Iranians' desire to influence the Israeli elections through Hamas terror, was the successful marketing of the amulets... The high level of public fear of terror stood in the campaign background and the voters' decision until the last day. The astounding success of the amulet campaign by SHAS-Kaduri was a result of this fear level.[18]

The second example of major consequence was the single TV debate between Peres and Netanyahu. The latter suffered from an image among the public of being inexperienced, especially compared to Peres – Israel's lone ruling elder statesman.

The result of the debate was instructive in the context of our discussion. In the eyes of most "objective" (academic) observers, including this writer, Netanyahu's performance was clearly superior (even Peres' media advisers admitted as much after the campaign). However, the general public did not view it that way, at least initially: telephone polls taken immediately after the conclusion of the debate did not indicate any clear victory for either side.[19] However, the newspaper headlines the next day told a different story: "Netanyahu Wins! [the Debate]", for example, was plastered across the front page of Israel's largest daily *Yediot Aharonot*, and the snowball effect commenced on the undecided voters until the elections three days later (for every voter who changed his/her mind and voted for Peres as a result of the debate, six voters did the reverse). Again, the main point bears repeating: "The debate's influence was not felt the night of broadcast on both TV channels, but rather only over the course of the next day... [as a result of] the newspaper headlines which appeared the following day [after the debate]" (ibid). Thus, just as with the bus bombings, we see here another quite clear case of the media "enlarging" the effect of the subject being reported on, to the extent that the more significant effect is media-induced and not reality-induced – again, unintentionally, but for "professional" (that is, marketing) journalistic reasons.

The third and final campaign initiative proved to be the most controversial of all. Early on in the race, several Likud stickers appeared with a decidedly "negative" (anti-Labor) message: "Bibi or Tibi" (Ahmed Tibi, an Arab–Israeli physician who serves unofficially as Arafat's adviser) and "A Strong Palestine with Peres" (removed quite quickly). However, the most important and effective sticker ironically (but not coincidentally) was phrased in very "positive" language: "Netanyahu – Good for the Jews". Indeed, the term "Good for the Jews" is part and parcel of Jewish culture (whenever something happens around the world, unrelated to the Jewish people, the standard Jewish line has been: "Yes, but is it good for the Jews?").

What could be offensive or negative about that? In a country such as Israel, with a sizable Arab minority which is considered by many Jewish Israelis to be a potential fifth column (there is virtually no evidence to support such a contention), the use of "Jews" instead of "Israelis" was a clear code that only with Netanyahu in power could the country's most basic "national" (in both senses of the word) interests be safeguarded. Moreover, for some time the extreme right wing had been arguing that a referendum on ceding the Golan to Syria must receive a majority of the Jewish vote, and throughout the campaign it was also noted that Peres might win with only a minority of the Jewish vote.

It must be pointed out that the campaign sticker (and ad campaign) was initiated and paid for by the haredi Lubavitcher HABAD movement, and that there is no evidence that the Likud was behind this initiative, which after all did very indirectly suggest some form of racism. On the other hand, the Likud did not disavow the slogan. But more to the point within the general thesis of this essay is the fact that once again it was media coverage of the slogan and the ensuing public debate which lent it a high level of campaign resonance and possibly its decisive influence on the outcome of the prime minister race.

This is not in any way to suggest that the media were wrong in reporting on the debate regarding the slogan (and, indeed, most press commentators criticized it strongly), but rather that once again the media's behavior led to the opposite effect of what it (perhaps) intended. The more coverage provided of the controversy, the more stickers appeared, and the more stickers that appeared, the greater the impact (unconscious or otherwise) on precisely those undecided voters, most of whom were former Likud supporters who were probably seeking (certainly subconsciously) a trigger to enable them to "go home" despite their misgivings as to Netanyahu's candidacy.

One final ironic aspect of the campaign must be noted, fitting in well

with the general paradoxical environment of the 1996 election campaign
– the Meretz election propaganda and its effect. Early indications were
that Meretz was in danger of losing several Knesset seats, with only
about five seats predicted for it in the polls. This was probably due to the
fact that Labor's peace process was continuing apace, thereby
preempting Meretz's chief campaign issue. As a result, Meretz turned to
its second line of assault: bashing the religious camp, in order to bring
back its traditionally secular (and in part strongly anti-religious)
supporters. This is not the place to delve into the complex issue of
religion and state in Israel (discussed elsewhere in this volume), but the
closer Election Day loomed, the more strident and blatant Meretz's
campaign.

Did it succeed? Tactically yes, strategically no. Meretz did indeed
return to its approximate "natural" strength (nine seats; still a decline
from the previous Knesset total of 12), so that in the strict party sense its
campaign worked. However, viewed from the perspective of the overall
results – especially the race for prime minister – its propaganda was
disastrous (from Meretz's perspective), as it drove a significant number
of traditional (not necessarily Orthodox) Jewish voters back into the
Netanyahu camp on the basis of religious and state ("Jewish identity")
concerns, despite their political misgivings about Netanyahu's peace
process policy. Put another way, by succeeding in getting across its
religion and state platform (of secondary importance) to its supporters,
Meretz also "succeeded" in pushing enough general undecided voters
into voting for Netanyahu, thereby undermining Meretz's own position
on its primary issue.

Yossi Sarid's highly acerbic (and effective) anti-Peres performance in
Meretz's TV propaganda immediately following the Peres–Netanyahu
debate merely added to the influence of the "Netanyahu – Good for the
Jews" campaign in the last days of the election. In the final irony,
everyone was publicly talking about which of the two candidates was
better for the peace process, but the sub-text (especially in the closing
stages) was the Jewish character of the State. On this issue, obviously,
Netanyahu had the advantage (mainly because of his natural coalition
partners). The media's critique of this aspect ("Netanyahu – Good for
the Jews"), as well as Meretz's harping on the issue, boomeranged in the
end.

CONCLUSION

Israel's 1996 election campaign was more subterranean than above
ground. From several different perspectives, what one saw was not what
one got (indeed, another entirely different dimension of some
importance is the functioning of the "alternative" media[20]). The Labor
Party's formal election propaganda was quite positive in tone, while the
Likud's (perhaps of necessity) tended to be negative, but not nastily so.

However, all this was quite secondary to the real campaign which was carried out (in large part unwittingly) by the media – both as reflector of reality and, especially, as a magnifier of precisely those elements which tended to highlight the negative aspects of the Peres-Labor/Meretz government (such as terrorism and public insecurity, and not enough sensitivity to "Jewish" elements).

As argued throughout this essay, this occurred not because the media consciously wished to undermine Peres/Labor (if anything, most of the press supported the Left, as did most of the business community), but rather unconsciously and indirectly as a result of its "natural" inclination to seek out the sensational, the bizarre (by its lights), and the negative.

The most significant methodological conclusion emanating from the above analysis – and one which has important implications for future election campaign strategy – is that given an increasingly sophisticated public well versed in, or at least strongly inured to, the superficialities of the parties' formal election propaganda, the role of media coverage of the news (both campaign and non-campaign related) becomes of prime importance. The instincts of Likud and Labor strategists in 1996 were correct: the real battlefield is not the advertising spots after the television news program but rather the news itself; the best campaign strategy is not frontal advertising but behind-the-scenes public relations; the most effective tactic is not to address the public directly but rather to manipulate the public through indirection. If this continues to be the case, it will make future post-election media campaign analysis not only much more interesting, but also methodologically that much more complex and difficult. For the researcher, that would be the ultimate "negative" effect of any positively smart campaign.

NOTES

The author would like to thank the Philip Slomovitz Fund of the Center for International Communications and Policy for financially supporting the collation of the newspaper election coverage material. My thanks also to Ms. Nili Tabachnik for her highly professional and systematic work in collating, categorizing and scoring the data for this study.

1. Kathleen H. Jamieson, *Dirty Politics: Deception, Distraction and Democracy* (New York, 1992), p.41.
2. S. Lehman-Wilzig, "Israel's 1992 Media Campaign: Towards the Americanization of Israeli Elections?," in D.J. Elazar and S. Sandler, eds, *Israel at the Polls, 1992* (Lanham, 1995), pp.251–80.
3. Keren Neubach, *The Race: Elections '96* (Tel Aviv, 1996), p.271.
4. Gabi Weimann and Gadi Wolfsfeld, "Not in Anyone's Camp," *Ha-ayin Ha-shvi'it*, No.5 (September–October 1996), pp.20–22; Eli Pollack and Israel Meidar, "The Mobilized Media," ibid., No.5, pp.23–5.
5. Nachman Ben-Yehuda, *Political Assassination by Jews: A Rhetorical Device for Justice* (Albany, 1993).
6. Maxwell McCombs and Donald L. Shaw, "The Agenda-Setting Function of the Mass Media," *Public Opinion Quarterly*, Vol.36 (1972), pp.176–87.
7. Yossi Verter, "The Secret Weapon Which Wasn't Used," *Ha-ir*, May 31, 1996, pp.28–30.

8. Ibid.
9. Shanto Iyengar and Donald R. Kinder, "Psychological Accounts of Media Agenda-Setting," in S. Kraus and R. Perloff, eds, *Mass Media and Political Thought* (Beverly Hills, 1985), p.118.
10. Yossi Verter, "The Report: The Right Succeeded in Raising Doubts Whether the PLO Charter Was Canceled," *Ha-aretz*, August 2, 1996, p.A6.
11. W. Wanta, "The Effects of Dominant Photographs: An Agenda-Setting Experiment," *Journalism Quarterly*, Vol.65 (1988), pp.107–11.
12. Iyengar and Kinder "Psychological Accounts," p.119.
13. "Psychological Accounts," p.119.
14. Asher Arian, "Not Mobilizing, Not Mobilized," *Ha-ayin Ha-shvi'it*, No.4 (July–August 1996), pp.4–5.
15. Gadi Wolfsfeld, "The '96 Israeli Election Campaign on Television: Some Evidence on the Question of Influence" (unpublished manuscript, under journal consideration).
16. Guy Leshem, "Immoderate Pressure", *Ha-ayin Ha-shvi'it*, No.3. (May–June 1996), p.7.
17. Ibid.
18. Yossi Verter, "Hypothesis: The Amulet Campaign Fed Off the Unnecessary Warnings About 'The Next Bombing'," *Ha-aretz*, August 2, 1996, p.A6.
19. Idem, "Research: The Television Debate Between Peres and Netanyahu Decided the Election Results," ibid.
20. See Tamar Liebes, Yoram Peri and Zfira Grebalski, "Where Was the Real Influence Hidden? The Media and the Alternative Media in Israel's 1996 Elections," *Kesher*, No.20 (November 1996), pp.5–20.

The Great Losers:
Women in the 1996 Elections

YAEL YISHAI

Women were the victims of the 1996 elections. In the words of Alice Shalvi, the head of the Women's Network (lobbying association): "Women are the clear losers in this election, no matter which of the candidates for the premiership wins."[1] Women's representation has declined from eleven in the 13th Knesset to nine in the 14th Knesset. This decline is remarkable for two reasons: first of all, the fledgling peace process was expected to have a positive impact on the role of women in society. When the guns are silenced the female voice may be heard louder and clearer. Second, the introduction of the primaries system by the two major parties, Labor and Likud, enabled women to play a greater role in the campaign and to influence the make-up of the electoral lists. Yet, not only did the new system fail to reduce gender parities, but women actually receded from their previous attainments. Equality between the sexes, pledged in the Declaration of Independence and corroborated by a host of legislative decrees, has not materialized. This essay examines the role of women in the 1996 elections and offers some explanations for the apparent paradox – women's successful penetration into political life, on the one hand, and their downward slump in terms of Knesset representation, on the other.

I will begin by describing how women fared in the elections to the 14th Knesset compared with their attainments in previous elections. Explanations for women's vulnerability, dealt with in the latter part of this review, will be sought in institutional, behavioral, and ideological aspects of the Israeli polity and society. The main argument here is that the usual unfavorable circumstances for women's power in Israel further deteriorated in the 1996 elections. This was due to internal party processes, power constellations, the structure of the political agenda, the pattern of women's political participation, and the immutable gender-based division of roles in Israeli society.

Yael Yishai is Professor of Political Science at the University of Haifa.

THE CAMPAIGN AND ITS OUTCOME: WOMEN IN THE 1966
ELECTIONS

A woman aspiring to a legislative career in Israel has to overcome two
obstacles particular to women. First, regardless of her economic
inferiority (discussed below), she has to mobilize the resources that will
enable her to enter the race for candidacy; second, she has to be included
in a "safe" position on her party's Knesset list, overwhelmingly staffed
by men. In addition, a woman candidate faces an obstacle shared by all
candidates – the "safety" of her position has to be validated by electoral
results. The elections to the 14th Knesset revealed the incongruence
among the campaign stages, as the proportion of women declined
markedly from one stage to the other. The number of women competing
for candidacy rose considerably in comparison with previous elections;
the number of women filling presumed safe seats rose, although to a
lesser extent. However, the number of women who actually made it to
the Knesset declined, as did the number of women serving in the
government. The following shows the runners, the favorites, and the
winners.

The Election Stage

The initial stages of the 1996 campaign looked bright as a record number
of women presented themselves as candidates for Knesset lists. Three
parties held primaries open to their total membership – Labor, Likud and
Meretz. Candidates in other parties were selected by broad party organs.
The total number of women who ran for positions on party lists was 69.
Analysis by party confirms the universal finding that women fare better
in left-oriented parties. In 1996 the number of women competing in the
Labor party's primaries increased from 18 (in 1992) to 33.[2] The left-
wing Meretz and Hadash parties also showed relatively high women's
participation, with 13 women contesting in the former and two in the
latter. Women showed their presence in right-wing parties as well,
although to a lesser extent. In the united list of Likud, Gesher and
Tzomet, 18 women entered the contest, compared to only 10 in 1992.
Another woman ran in the small right-wing Moledet party. As expected,
the ultra-religious parties banned women from entering the race.
However, in the National Religious Party two women presented their
candidacy.

    Women contesting in the primaries represented a wide variety of
social sectors. Labor candidates included Arab women, previously absent
in the national electoral arena (Nadia Hilo and Suraya Nugidat); among
the women contesting in the Likud were widows and daughters of
former activists (Haya Walker, widow of Bat-Yam's mayor, and Rachel
Kremerman, Yaacov Meridor's daughter); veteran activists (Geula
Cohen), and young professionals (Mor Shamgar). Among the contestants
in all parties were ten lawyers, seven members of municipal councils, six

academics, four civil servants, three moshav members, three kibbutz members, two trade union officers, two executive members of Naamat, and two women who served as officers in the Israel Defense Forces. Seventy percent of the candidates were women with university degrees.[3]

Composing the List

Brichta and Brichta suggested that greater participation by women in the contest for nomination could significantly increase their number in the Knesset.[4] The results of the elections to the 14th Knesset run counter to this assertion as the number of women MKs actually declined, although the number of contestants increased. Despite the apparent high quality of the candidates, only 13 were selected for what were considered "realistic" positions in their respective party lists. Their selection was prompted, in most cases, by invoking the quotas principle, also termed "promotional strategies"[5] for encouraging women to enter the legislative arena.

The primaries' results reveal the distinct advantage of the veterans over the newcomers. Women who had already served at least one Knesset term, such as Dalia Itzik, Chairperson of the Knesset Committee for Education and Culture, and Yael Dayan, Chairperson of the Knesset Committee for Women's Affairs (Labor), fared better than the newcomers. Limor Livnat and Naomi Blumental (Likud) had a clear advantage over unfamiliar contestants. Newcomers, however, also won their share. Labor's list, for example, included the first Arab woman ever to be a realistic candidate (Nadia Hilo, who placed 27th on the party's list), and Ofra Friedman, Naamat Secretary General. Meretz included three women in realistic places (two of them veteran MKs), and Hadash reelected Tamar Gozansky, a Knesset member since 1981, to a safe seat. Incumbency, therefore, is a clear advantage in popular elections.

In both parties the final list for the Knesset was a product of complicated internal considerations based on territorial units (Labor) and party factions (Likud). Analysis of the Labor primaries reveals that the chances of entering the list were far higher in the regions than in the central list. Although the regions vary in size, the average support for men and women can nevertheless be calculated. In the regions, a women won an average of 2,316 votes, constituting 67.5 percent that of men; in the central list, women's average support amounted to only 45.6 percent that of men (an average of 32,098 and 70,337 votes, respectively). Yet, of the 14 women contesting in the central contest, four secured realistic positions on the Knesset list; out of the 12 women contesting in the regions, only two were regarded as winners. Both, however, failed to enter the Knesset.

The alliance of Gesher, Tzomet, and Likud had a small impact on the composition of the Likud's list. In Gesher's internal elections, three women contested for the sixth place. Two of them withdrew from the list prior to election day; the third won only 15 votes out of a total of 144.[6] The 42nd place on the list was allotted to a Tzomet woman.

The NRP's Knesset list remained womanless as the two women contestants failed to win membership support (elections took place in the 991-member party central committee). Religious women did not challenge their party's values and did not present a feminist plank. According to commentators, the reason for women's exclusion from the NRP's list lay in the fierce rivalry between them. One woman was endorsed by Emuna, the women's unit in the party, while the other ran on her own. A split of the women's votes, coupled with the reluctance of religious men to vote for a woman candidate, barred the inclusion of women in the NRP's list.[7]

Women were not prominent among the candidates in the other parties. The new Israel Ba-aliya party, representing the interests of the mass immigration from the countries of the former Soviet Union, announced the selection of four people to realistic positions on the list, with no woman included among them. Another new party, the Third Way, running on a platform favoring retention of the Golan Heights, composed its list without reference to women. Women were also excluded from the Arab list, which, adhering to traditional Islamic values, banned women from participating in public life.

Two women headed minor lists – Nava Arad, a Labor MK in the 13th Knesset who defected from her party to establish a pensioners' list; and Miriam Lapid, a mother of 12 children who lost her husband and son in a terrorist act, who joined Shaul Gutman, a defector from Moledet, to head Yemin Israel, a nationalist list.

To sum up, only one out of five women (approximately) who contested, made it to the party list. The final number, however, was unprecedented. The Labor party included six women among the first 45 candidates, the Likud had four women among the first 45 seats, and Meretz had three women on its list. Expectations were that at least 13 women would enter the 14th Knesset.

Electoral Results

The results of the 1996 elections to the 14th Knesset took Israelis by surprise. The small margin of victory of the premier, for the first time elected directly by the people, was anticipated, but three outcomes were astonishing – first, the decline of the major veteran parties; second, the dramatic success of the so-called "sectoral" parties; and third, the marked decline of women's representation. All in all, women secured only nine seats, constituting only 7.5 percent of the total.

Women's electoral attainments in Israel are low by international standards. Data gathered by the Inter-Parliamentary Union reflect the proportion of women in parliaments worldwide. The world's average was 11 percent in 1991,[8] but in most countries women's representation is on the rise. In the British Parliament, for example, the proportion of women increased from 3.4 percent in 1950 to 9.2 percent in 1992.[9] Likewise, the proportion of women in the Scandinavian countries increased dramatically during the 1980s – in Denmark from 26 to 34 percent, in Iceland from 15 to 24 percent, in Norway from 26 to 39 percent, and in Sweden from 28 to 33 percent.[10]

In Israel no linear trend of increase can be identified, but rather a cyclical pattern of growth and decline. The beginning was rather timid, with less than ten percent of MKs being women (11 women). Only once in Knesset history (between 1955 and 1959) did 12 women enter the Knesset. In three terms (7th, 9th, and 12th) the number declined to eight only. In the remaining terms the number fluctuated between nine and ten. Figure 1 shows the oscillation in women's representation in the Knesset.

FIGURE 1

WOMEN'S REPRESENTATION IN THE KNESSET 1–14 (1949–96)

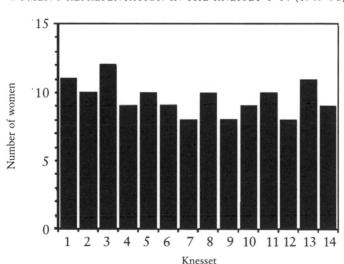

A more detailed analysis of women's representation by political affiliation reveals the preponderance of the Labor camp over the right-wing and the religious camps. Out of the total 51 women elected to the Knesset, 70.5 percent belonged to the left-wing camp (the Labor Party and its antecedents, Meretz and its historical components, Hadash and its historical components); 21.5 percent belonged to the right-wing camp (Likud and its historical components); a scant 3.9 percent were representatives of religious parties; the same proportion belonged to "other" parties including the Women's List in the 1st Knesset and Dash in the 9th Knesset (1977–81). When the number of women MKs is counted in each Knesset (see Table 1), the predominant proportion of women in the Labor camp clearly emerges. It also shows that since 1981 there has been no female MK in the religious bloc and only token representation in the right-wing camp.

TABLE 1

WOMEN MKS, BY POLITICAL BLOCS, 1949–96*

Knesset	Left	Right	Religious	Other
1949–51	9	1		1
1951–54	9	3		
1954–59	10	2		
1959–61	8	1	1	
1961–65	7	2	1	
1965–69	9	1	1	
1969–73	6	1	1	
1973–77	10	2		
1977–81	6	2	1	1
1981–84	7	2		
1984–88	8	2		
1988–92	6	2		
1992–96	9	3		
1996	6	2		1
Total	110	26	5	3
Percentage	76.4	18.1	3.4	2.1

Source: Naamat 162, April–May 1994

* The number of women MKs includes those serving part of the term.

The elections to the 14th Knesset proved the persistence of this distribution, although with fewer numbers. Only three women on Labor's list won a Knesset seat (Dalia Itzik, Sofia Landver, and Yael Dayan). The remaining three realistic candidates did not secure a legislative seat. Likewise, only two Meretz women were among the nine candidates elected to the Knesset. MK Tamar Gozansky (Hadash) won her seat without difficulty. Representation of women in the left-wing camp thus dropped to its lowest level – six. The Likud women fared worse as only two were elected. Another woman was surprisingly elected on the slate of the new immigrants' list, thus bringing the sum total of women's representation in the 14th Knesset to nine. In the United States, known for its small women's representation in Congress, the percentage of women in the House of Representatives in 1992 was 11 percent.

The following discussion will elaborate the hypothesized reasons for the decline of women's representation in the 1996 elections.

EXPLAINING THE OUTCOME

Party Process

The selection of candidates in the 1996 elections was governed by two principles relevant to women – first, the quota system, and second, the primaries. A cross-national comparison indicates considerable diffusion of "positive discrimination" measures, some of which are enacted by legislation while others are practiced by internal party rules and procedures.[11] Israel belongs to the second category, as no legislation requires parties to reserve seats for women. The quota system was first adopted by the Labor party, which was committed to reserving 20 percent of the seats in all party organs, including the Knesset faction, for women. The party, however, never lived up to its commitment, as women's legislative representation always fell short of the pledged percentage. In the 1996 campaign the Labor party responded to women's pressures by reserving six seats for women; that is, one for every ten candidates in the central list and two in the regional lists (Nos. 9, 18, 27, 37, 40, and 44). Hence, the woman winning the highest support was placed in the 9th place regardless of the size of her vote compared with male contestants.[12] The Likud also introduced measures of positive discrimination, reserving four seats for women (Nos. 13, 27 35, and 40), should they not win the support allowing them to enter the list without the quota.[13] The merger between Likud, Tzomet, and Gesher reduced the number of seats reserved for women to three – Nos. 19, 33, and 42.

Positive discrimination has apparently failed to increase women's representation. Failure may be attributed to two reasons. First, as noted by Norris,[14] approving quotas is a product of ideology; implementation, however, depends largely upon the type of party organization and personnel, evidently reluctant to live up to its pledge. Women simply did not challenge the fact that they were granted one-tenth of the realistic positions on the list rather than one-fifth.[15] In addition, gender hardly constitutes a factor even in women's electoral choice. A survey taken in 1993 revealed that an overwhelming proportion of women (79.2 percent) stated that women's equality did not have any impact whatsoever on their voting behavior.[16] This reality may have discouraged effective implementation of the quota commitment.

In Norway the quota system has worked efficiently because men were not threatened by the inclusion of women.[17] This was not the case in Israel, where the political game was based on the principle of a zero sum. Consequently, quotas were more symbolic than real. A study of the primary results in the Labor party (published by the press on March 27, 1996) revealed, furthermore, that women could have made it to the list without the crutches of the quota. Conversely, when positive discrimination was badly needed, for example, in the Likud, women actually remained outside the list and were not elected to the Knesset. The strategy of positive discrimination has thus not been very effective in the case of Israeli women.

Second, and more importantly, women were done a disservice by what was ostensibly the height of contemporary Israeli democracy: the introduction of the primaries system. Numerous studies have established the linkage between economic affluence and political power. This linkage is particularly pertinent to the primaries system. Political parties enjoy generous state funding on condition that they do not solicit contributions from members and adherents in Israel and/or abroad. This is not the case regarding the primaries, where each candidate is allowed to spend around NIS 300,000 (approximately $100,000) derived from the candidate's own resources or contributions. There is no state funding of the primary campaign; legislation does not mandate parties to fund their members' drive for inclusion on the list. No research has yet been conducted on the effectiveness of money in Israeli primaries, but lack of resources is certainly not an electoral asset. Running in the primaries is an expensive project. Celebrities running in the central list or known for their past political activity find it much easier to secure resources than women, most of whom are inexperienced in politics. Women, lacking both public visibility and financial assets, compete on the same level as their more advantaged male counterparts. Only a few women enjoy the media exposure or the financial advantages of male candidates. Women's inferior economic position may be one of the explanations for their weaker political status. The following facts and figures clearly reveal the economic disadvantage of Israeli women.

Women's Economic Vulnerability

During the last month of its incumbency (on March 12, 1996), the 13th Knesset approved a law prescribing equal payment for men and women for equal work, including all salary components such as travel funds or telephone bills. Equality was to be imposed not only on equal work but on work with equal worth, to be determined by experts nominated by the Labor Court. This legislation capped a series of laws and legal decrees ensuring Israeli women economic equality. Most prominent among these laws are the Equal Retirement Law (1987), and the Equal Employment Opportunity Law (1988). Reality, however, lags far behind the law, as women continue to suffer from clear economic differentials, placing them in a position inferior to that of men.

The image of Israeli women as pioneers participating equally in the building of the land is a comfortable myth which has never been matched by their actual status. Despite the legal pledge of equality, women continue to trail behind men in terms of economic status and possession of material resources. Two positive fundamental facts regarding women's economic status in Israel stand out prominently: employment outside the home and educational attainment. The proportion of women in the civilian labor force has dramatically risen from 26.5 percent in 1955 to 44.7 percent in 1994.[18] The massive entry of women into paid work, evident worldwide,[19] has been noted as the most fundamental change of recent decades. The educational level of women in Israel has also risen considerably. In 1970 the proportion of women with 13 or more years of schooling was only 11.8 percent; by 1994 it had grown to 27.1 percent.[20] It is not customary for an educated woman to be a housewife. In fact, educational level has been found to be the best single predictor of women's labor force participation.[21] The ratio of employed women rises linearly with education. Among those with 1–4 years of schooling, only 11.2 percent join the labor force; among those with 16 or more years of schooling, the figure is a striking 75.7 percent.

These positive developments are tarnished, however, by wide occupational segregation, defined as "the disproportionate representation of one social category in a [particular] occupation, relative to the proportion of that category in the labor force."[22] The distinction between "men's jobs" and "women's jobs" is not unique to Israel, but is a key factor in the poor position of women on the labor market worldwide. Women tend to be concentrated in a small number of large-scale, female-dominated occupations. Izraeli[23] concluded that every second woman in the country was employed in one of the "feminine" occupations such as school teaching, nursing, secretarial work, and the like.

Horizontal work segregation, between male and female occupations, is accompanied by a vertical segregation within occupations. Although a significant proportion of the female labor force is employed in academic, semi-professional and white-collar occupations, in all of them the higher the position, the smaller the proportion of women. For example, Toren has noted the dearth of women in the senior faculty positions in Israeli universities. Three-quarters of the female faculty hold lower ranks of lecturer and senior lecturer, and only a quarter hold professorial rank. Only five percent of those at the top rank of full professor are women.[24] Similarly, women are rarely members of large company boards of directors. Although legislation requiring the nomination of women to boards of public enterprises has come into effect (in legal terms: "expression be given to the representation of both sexes in government corporations" (Amendment to the Government Corporations Law, 1993), the law has not been fully implemented.

The particular pattern of women's participation in the labor force has generated significant income differentials. Although, as noted, Israeli law prescribes equal pay for equal work for men and women, women continue to earn less than men even when compared on an equal time basis. Income differentials have, in fact, increased over time. Efroni has revealed that the economic returns on educational and occupational investments are considerably lower for females than for males.[25] Data reveal that women working in services (a major female occupation) earned only 36.5 percent of males' income in 1992; women clerical workers earned 35.6 percent of their male counterparts' income. Income differentials were evident among professionals as well where women earned 44.3 percent of the males' income (the percentage is calculated on the basis of average gross income per month.[26] A recent report of the Administration of State Income revealed that on average, women's monthly income amounts to about half that of men (53 percent). Furthermore, in the upper decile, women's share is only 11.4 percent.[27]

Two factors were found to inhibit an egalitarian labor market: first, the paucity of affirmative action legislation, and the second, women's own choices. Unlike the practice in other Western societies, even career-oriented women appear to be reluctant to delay childbearing and devote themselves to pursuing demanding engagements outside their home.[28] The intrusion of family obligations into employment patterns has motivated many women to work only part-time. Comparative data on female labor force participation indicate that women, in large (and undiminishing) numbers, tend to work part-time. The proportion of women working part-time increased from 30 percent in 1970 to 42 percent in 1994. Seventy percent of part-time workers are women. The average work week is 29 hours for women and 40 hours for men. When asked to give reasons why they work part-time, women often cite their role as "a housewife" (20.9 percent) as the chief cause. None of the men mentioned domestic chores as a reason for part-time employment. To this may be added the answer "not interested in a full-time job," given by 13.7 percent of the women, as compared with 4.2 percent of the men.[29] Part-time work is thus a matter of choice, resulting from the need to balance family and work. Women choose to forego job opportunities or to avoid exacting occupations because they have to juggle their multiple roles.[30] The outcome – economic weakness – may be one of the reasons for their political vulnerability, particularly when they have to compete with men on an equal basis while enjoying only limited party protection in the form of positive discrimination.

The Power Structure

Theories on women's representation have maintained that a strong presence of women in a political institution is liable to have a positive effect on further recruitment of women. For women to be elected, they must be adequately represented in the ranks of national and local elected officials, as well as in major social organizations.[31] In Israel, as in most other countries, political institutions are dominated by men. Furthermore, the higher the political position, the lower the proportion of women. This is true for all political institutions, including the Knesset, government, local government, the bureaucracy, political parties, and interest groups. The proportion of women in the Knesset was described above. In addition, women have played a minor role on prestigious Knesset committees, including the Finance committee, and the Foreign Affairs and Security Committee. Only in four Knessets did women serve on the Finance Committee (two in the 4th Knesset, one in the 10th Knesset, one in the 11th Knesset, and two in the 13th Knesset). The number of women members of the Foreign Affairs and Security Committee is seven (one each in the 1st, 4th, 5th, 11th and 12th Knessets, and two in the 13th Knesset). In the 14th Knesset there are no women members on these two most important committees.

In the government their position was even worse. The most illustrious woman serving in the government was Golda Meir, who headed this important forum. Prior to her incumbency Meir was the first female in the government, serving in various capacities. Meir, however (once termed "the only man in the cabinet"), is the exception that proves the rule – the lack of women in the highest political institution. The next woman minister after Meir was Shulamit Aloni, serving as a minister without portfolio for six months (1974). During the Likud's term in office there was one woman minister – Sara Doron – also serving as minister without portfolio and for a relatively short period. In the late 1980s, Israel had a record-size cabinet of 26 ministers, five without portfolio, but not a single woman was numbered among them. The 1992 government, however, included two women (Shulamit Aloni and Ora Namir). Both resigned from political life before the 1996 elections.[32] Ora Namir stated: "For both of us [she and Aloni] – men have decided that we shall discontinue our political activity."[33] In the current Likud-led government there is only one woman minister, Minister of Communications Limor Livnat.

A similar distribution of power is reflected in the senior bureaucracy. Until 1996 no woman ever served as director-general of a government office, nor did a woman head an important government agency. At the time of writing (June 1996), however, two women have been appointed as directors general of two ministries – the Ministries of Environment and Justice. Despite these positive developments, data reflect the uneven share of power in the civil service. In the second tier of administration, the proportion of women is only 10.5 percent, and on the three lowest levels women employees constitute 68 percent of the total.[34]

Women's representation on the local level is also sparse. In the first local elections, held in 1959, women in the Jewish cities and local councils gained 4.2 percent of the seats. Since the late 1960s, however, their share has increased steadily, reaching 10.9 percent in 1993. Yet, on average, there are no more than two women on each local authority. Furthermore, during the state's existence only six women have served as heads of local councils, none of them in a city with a population of over 10,000. Currently there is only one woman heading a (small) local council.[35]

Data compiled by the Women's Network in 1992 revealed the paucity of women's representation in political parties as well. A distinction is made between large, popular forums, such as the party central committee, and small, elite organs, such as the secretariat or bureau, where critical decisions are taken. The Labor party has an edge over the Likud owing to the quota rule rigorously adhered to in the party arena. At the Labor party's central committee, which included 2,995 delegates, there were 613 women representatives, approximately 20 percent. Even in the bureau there was an impressive representation of 23 women out of a total of some 100 members. Note, however, that in the last census, taken in 1995, over half of the total party membership were women. The Likud fares worse than Labor, with only 13.3 percent women in its central committee, which has a total of some 3,300 members. In the party secretariat, of 30 members, the proportion of women was only 3.3 percent – that is, one woman. Women are largely absent from the interest group arena as well. None of the major economic associations are headed by a woman. Even in the Histadrut, the number of women is minuscule. Out of 45 individual trade unions, only three are headed by women. Even unions with a majority of female members, such as the Teachers Federation and the Social Workers Union, are led by men.

To sum up, comparative studies have confirmed that the presence of women in political institutions fosters their inclusion in others. This circumstance is not reflected in the Israeli polity.

The Political Agenda

The government that was formed after the 1996 elections was described as consisting of "generals and rabbis." This portrayal vividly reflects the contents of the 1996 political agenda, predominated by two major issues: first and foremost, Israel's security, and second, Israel's ethno-national identity. Content analysis of the electoral campaign reveals the total avoidance of important social issues. The obstacles to the successful implementation of the National Health Insurance Law, the persistent poverty in development towns and urban neighborhoods, the attempted reform in the educational system, congested highways, violence against women, the growing deficit in the national budget, and the problems of the deteriorating environment never appeared on the campaign agenda. The two contesting leaders, around whom the campaign evolved, reiterated the same theme, each in their own words. Peres promised the electorate a safe peace, while Netanyahu promised peace with security. Admittedly, personal safety is the number one issue on most Israelis' minds. Propaganda managers did cater to people's hopes and fears when they chose security as a major campaign theme. The problem, however, was that concentration on this particular issue was detrimental to the status of women.[36]

One of the factors inhibiting women's electoral success is their civilian background, as military service provides the most efficient ticket to success in many walks of life. Women in Israel are conscripted into the army but are not posted to combat units. Their activities in the armed forces have significantly widened, but this iron law has not been broken. Women do not fight. In a recent ground-breaking ruling the Supreme Court ruled to allow women to join pilot training programs, but so far the IDF has no women pilots, paratroopers, members of tank crews, or infantry soldiers. Most women do in the army what they do in civilian life: they work as secretaries, nurses, and teachers. Their service in the IDF is shorter than that of men. These facts inhibit women from climbing up the career ladder in the armed forces.

A military career has proven to be an effective channel for political mobility. In fact, senior officers are courted by political parties even before their demobilization. Each party takes pride in "its" generals, looked upon as a huge electoral asset. On both the Labor and Likud lists there were four retired generals among the top ten candidates. Military commanders were considered a leading electoral attraction. At least two senior commanders vacillated between Labor and Likud, opting for the higher stakes in their future political careers. One, Yitzhak Mordechai, leaped from the position of army general to Defense Minister. A former Chief of Staff, Ehud Barak, was appointed Foreign Minister without ever having run for office. Women were at a disadvantage because they never attained senior officer rank in the IDF. Furthermore, women were experts in precisely those social issues that never reached the 1996 electoral agenda.[37] A campaign specialist advised women candidates to "hunt for issues that interest the people, because women usually tend to deal with social issues, in contrast to men who deal with foreign and security affairs. I do not know a candidate participating in an electoral meeting who will not utter one or two words on the security situation."[38] Varda Pomerantz, a Labor candidate, stated explicitly that if elected she would concentrate on education. Asked why she chose to devote her efforts to this particular sphere, she answered that "children's education in Israeli families is the responsibility of women. They are more involved and more informed than men in this area."[39]

The importance of the military in political life emanates, among other things, from the salience of the security issue in the national agenda. This was particularly true in 1996 when Israel stood at a crossroads, vacillating between the option of taking further steps toward the implementation of the Oslo agreements or treating these agreements with caution and suspicion. Whether the gap between Labor and Likud was wide or not, the security issue was not only prominent but, one might say, exclusive, thus relegating women to a marginal role in the decisionmaking hierarchy.

The 1996 electoral campaign brought another issue to the forefront of the political agenda – the state's Jewish character – and the controversy was not only ideological. In fact, it was much more pragmatic than value-laden, as the outcome of the elections presumably hinged largely on the support of the religious constituency. Both contestants for premiership, Shimon Peres and Binyamin Netanyahu, attempted to court religious voters and secure their electoral support and, indeed, the outcome of the 1996 elections signified a great victory for religious parties which won an unprecedented 23 Knesset seats. This victory has short-term as well as long-term implications for women. First of all, none of the religious parties included a woman candidate, so that the rise of religious parties had an immediate effect on the distribution of power in the Knesset with regard to gender. Second, wooing the religious constituency may have affected the contents of the electoral agenda as well.

Despite some interpretations, Judaism is not anti-female. It is true that every Orthodox male Jew thanks God in his morning prayers for not having made him a woman, but the sages interpreted this prayer as an advantage for women. Women are so blessed and virtuous that God exempted them from fulfilling many commandments. Yet the religion does not treat men and women equally. A woman's honor is in her home, certainly not in public life. Even her voice is considered a mischief. Judaism believes that women are equal to men, but are different. A strict gender-based division of labor is ordained, whereby men are responsible for "external" affairs and women are in charge of domestic affairs. This balance is considered essential for both individual happiness and social survival. It is, therefore, not surprising that women were not even considered appropriate candidates in ultra-Orthodox parties (SHAS and Aguda). They were reluctantly endorsed by the NRP but, as noted earlier, did not make it to the list. It is worthy noting that the diffusion of religious ideas was not confined to the Orthodox community but was widely endorsed among secular Jews as well.

The Israeli public demonstrated a yearning for its roots, wishing that Israel would become more Jewish. In a letter to the daily *Ha-aretz*, a secular person who, according to his own statement, voted for the NRP, stated: "This is not repentance, but rather identification with our being Jewish; an awareness that without the spiritual linkage to Jewish origins there is no national resurrection and there is no foundation to our right to this land."[40] Tradition thus became an expression of deep sentiments shared by many voters. Women, according to this tradition, were not to play an important role in public life. Some Knesset members like Rabbi Avraham Ravitz (United Torah Judaism) expressed themselves quite negatively regarding the decision-making role of women.[41]

The 1996 elections also gave vent to a tacit ethnic identity. Previous attempts to establish parties based on the country of origin (*edot*) have usually failed. One exception was Tami (1981), whose political career was short-lived. However, the greatest winner of the 1996 elections was SHAS, a party representing Orthodox Moroccan Jews, which doubled its Knesset representation from five to ten MKs. Jewish communities in Arabic-speaking countries delegated activity in the public sphere to males only, and this fact, carried on to Israel, is reflected in social indicators. Studies found that Sephardi women have the lowest level of education and occupational status, and although many of them do work outside the home, they tend to be employed in highly segregated and low paid occupations.[42] SHAS did emphasize the importance of education, but it never considered the option of granting women a political voice. SHAS's campaign proved to be successful because voters could, under the new electoral system, unfold their covert ethnic identity. The defection of many voters from the big parties to SHAS is one of the reasons for the decline in women's representation in the 14th Knesset.

To sum up, the salience of the security issue, coupled with the rise of ethno-national values and forces, militated against the inclusion of more women in the Knesset.

Women's Political Mobilization

One of the reasons for women's lack of political power may be attributed to less training in political life. A survey conducted during the incumbency of the 13th Knesset,[43] looked into four aspects of political participation among both male and female respondents: political efficacy, measuring confidence in one's ability to influence public policy; political discussions held with friends and family; partisanship (ranging on a scale from unsalaried party member to salaried party member with a formal position); and voting behavior (see Table 2).

Studies of political culture have confirmed that in democratic societies the individual sense of civic competence is widespread, even among women. In Israel, though, efficacy was found to be rather low owing, among other things, to the strong reliance on the state.[44] Data collected in 1993 revealed that almost a third of Israelis had a sense of efficacy. Furthermore, data show a very small gender-based difference, and what there is favors women over men. A gender gap did emerge, however, when political interest was under scrutiny, as women tended to score lower on the indicator of political participation. Two-thirds of women respondents discussed politics with friends and family, while the comparable figure for men was 73.7 percent.

A similar finding pertained to partisanship. The predominance of parties in Israeli politics has been widely discussed in the literature. The 1993 survey, however, revealed a substantially stronger partisanship among men than among women. Among men, 17 percent reported being active, in one form or another, in party life; the comparable figure among women was merely 10.9 percent. Among the men, some three percent were active party members; among women, only a fraction of the total were, less than one percent. The gender gap is thus starkly evident when the party arena comes under review.

This is not true for voting behavior, as both men and women tend to demonstrate a high rate of voting, around 85 percent. Electoral studies keep confirming that, in contrast to the United States, there is no gender gap in Israel. Voters tend to choose a party not on the basis of their gender but on the basis of their social class, ethnic origin, and religiosity.[45] In fact, gender equality is irrelevant for making electoral choices. Over half the respondents, both men and women, were not aware of "their" party's position on gender equality. A wide majority (81.1 percent among men and 79.2 percent among women) replied that the issue regarding equality between the sexes did not have *any impact whatsoever* on their voting behavior. Furthermore, a survey conducted by the daily *Ma'ariv* revealed widespread reluctance to support women candidates. When asked, "Who is the woman most preferred by you in Likud and in Labor?" the highest percentage among the respondents (42.3 percent among men and 26.2 percent among women) answered, "There is no such woman."[46]

The gender gap, while not striking, may have contributed to the low

TABLE 2

POLITICAL PARTICIPATION, BY SEX, 1993 (PERCENT)

	Women	Men	Gender gap
Efficacy	32.2	30.0	+2.2
Discuss politics	66.9	73.7	-6.8*
Party member	10.9	17.1	-6.2**
Voted in last election	84.7	85.1	-0.4

*p<0.05; ** p<0.001

Source: Yishai, *Between the Flag and the Banner*, p. 102.

level of women's political mobilization. Women activists in political parties have failed to organize an effective lobby to advance their interests. Women's associations in Israel are quite resourceful in terms of budgets and members; they also provide services to diverse social groups. Yet, they have been unsuccessful in converting their abundant resources into political assets.[47] In 1996, there were four women's associations that could have helped women candidates to be elected to the Knesset. WIZO, basically a charity association, has traditionally refrained from partisan activity, concentrating on helping weak and vulnerable women and children. Feminist organizations, including those combatting violence against women and sexual harassment, were extremely weak in terms of resources, and their feminist message failed to be widely disseminated. Previous attempts to establish a women's party (in 1977 and 1992) proved abortive. Naamat, the largest women's association in the country, was embroiled in a deep crisis coping with financial and organizational difficulties. As a branch of the Histadrut, Naamat has suffered the loss of members and funds experienced by its parent organization. The crisis culminated in the termination of its monthly publication *Naamat*, issued uninterruptedly since 1944. Note that for the first time in Israeli history, Naamat's secretary-general was not elected to the Knesset. The only women's association active on the electoral scene, the Network, did its best to promote women's candidacy and to aid women contestants in their campaign. As an all-party association it encouraged women of all political shades to run for political office. Its limited resources, however, attenuated its efforts. Not being able to raise money and fund individual women's campaigns, the Network's efforts were of little avail.

Intra-party women's units were also ineffective in supporting women candidates. In the past, women often showed their dissatisfaction and threatened to withdraw from the party, but their warning was not taken seriously. Women were not perceived as political rebels. Considering the number of women in political parties, evidently women voters do not prefer female candidates to male.

Gendered Division of Roles

At a public gathering, President Ezer Weizman stated his opposition to women serving as pilots in the Israeli Air Force as follows: "I think there is a difference between a man and a woman. This does not mean that a woman is unpleasant. I, for myself, prefer a woman that wants to remain a woman; in the same vein, I dislike a man who wants to be a woman."[48] The president's enunciation, causing a commotion among women, reflected deep currents underpinning Israeli society. Women enjoy equality before the law, but are different from men in that they bear the major responsibility for home and family. Women are expected to remain women, and as such they are disadvantaged in political life. The responsibility for home and family has invariably been reiterated by female candidates cutting across party lines. One of the contestants in the NRP stated that "the best mother will also be the best legislator."[49] Yael Aran, a Labor candidate, described the kinds of questions she was asked: "What about your husband? Does he support you?"[50] No such questions were ever addressed to male candidates.

The centrality of the family in Israeli society, widely acknowledged by social scientists,[51] is demonstrated in demographic data and in value orientations. All Western societies (including societies in Eastern Europe) portray lower family standards than does Israel. The divorce rates in Israel (1.4 per 1000 in 1994) are similar to those in traditional and agrarian societies. Natural increase, while declining, remains high compared with Western standards. The percentage of out-of-wedlock births, although growing, was 1.1 in 1986, compared with 7.6 in Germany and 42.0 in Sweden.[52]

The importance of family is confirmed by attitudes exhibited in public opinion studies. A survey conducted in 1990 revealed that in response to a question regarding the preferred lifestyle, the overwhelming majority of respondents gave marriage priority over every other type of sexual relationship. Had they had other options and alternative lifestyles, the interviewees stated, they would have nonetheless chosen the path of marriage. Conversely, the unmarried individuals (including widowed, divorced, and single) were less satisfied with their lives. They, in fact, also preferred marriage over any alternative lifestyle.[53] These attitudes were pervasive among both sexes but particularly among women, who viewed marriage as their ultimate goal in life. A poll taken in 1984 revealed that 85 percent of men and women respondents in a national sample were of the opinion that men preferred women for whom family was a central objective.[54] According to this poll, women for whom work was central were more likely than their home-centered counterparts to be divorced. The idea, so widespread in Western society, regarding choices made by individuals about their sexual or social relationships garnered little support in Israel. Marriage is *the* choice made by well-adjusted people; celibacy could be interpreted only in terms of lack of choice.

Furthermore, marriage is extremely important, but getting married alone is not enough. A marriage without children is not considered a family and the childless couple elicits pity. As noted by Safir,[55] there are periodic news items in all the media of new breakthroughs in fertility treatments. Israel presents the highest ratio per population in the world of IVF (in-vitro fertilization) clinics. A report issued by the World Health Organization revealed that in 1992 there were 708 IVF units worldwide, 18 of which (2.5 percent) operated in Israel and were publicly funded. In an article entitled "Anything for a Baby," Alison Solomon describes the stress of being childless in Israel.[56] Families who fail to reproduce opt for adoption at almost any cost. Every once in a while a story about a couple smuggling a child from a foreign country becomes a news item.

The centrality of family in women's life has been confirmed by recent data describing the average daily time spent on various activities. A staggering diversity between men and women has been revealed. Men spend only 31 minutes on domestic work. The time spent by women on house chores is more than five times higher – 163 minutes. Men spend a meager 19 minutes a day taking care of children; women spend 62 minutes. The gender gap may be attributed to the fact that men spend 277 minutes each day on paid work while the comparable figure for women is only 105 minutes.[57] Although the gender gap narrows somewhat with increase in income, the pattern nevertheless persists. The implication of these data is that many women choose to remain home and take care of their family.

Both the importance of family and the centrality of women in family life have been sustained by deeply entrenched norms and practices. Studies showed that in the United States family life was stronger and more stable among Jews than among non-Jews.[58] This fact may be attributed to the importance of the family in Jewish history as a means of assuring individual and communal survival. The family was described as a "portable homeland."[59] For a people who, over the years, have been forced to wander and settle in foreign cultures amid different religions, the family has always been a safe haven, expected to provide the solace and security often lacking outside. Hence, Judaism was described as a religion practiced mostly within the family, a "domestic religion" linking its ethnic experience with family ritual and cultural influences.[60] Praise of the superwoman (*eshet hail*) caring for home and children, nurtured the glorification of the woman as a central figure in the family.

The centrality of the family in social life, on the one hand, and the pivotal role of women in the family, on the other, have encumbered women aspiring to political careers. Women candidates noted the conflict between a political career and family obligations. A front-runner in the elections to the Labor primaries stated that she "does not know many men sensing loss if they attend an electoral meeting instead of being home and putting the children to bed. We are asked to invest a double effort, and this is not a controversial issue."[61] Her Likud counterpart lamented the fact that when a man returns home his wife welcomes him with a hot dinner. When she gets home she goes directly to the kitchen.[62] It thus appears that one of the obstacles to women's advancement in politics is their preoccupation with chores which distance them from political life, chores not shared by male counterparts.

CONCLUSIONS

The elections to the 14th Knesset portray a decline in the political assets of women in Israel. In many Western societies there has been linear progress in women's representation. Consequently, it was postulated that gains at the national level were simply a matter of time.[63] The case of Israel does not bear out this hypothesis as the proportion of women in the Knesset fluctuates from one term to the next, not showing any fixed pattern of growth. This essay has shown, however, that the number of women aspiring to a political career has grown, and that more of them tried their luck in the primaries or in their parties' institutions. Contrary to expectations, these efforts were not successful, as the number of women MKs fell to one of its lowest levels in the country's history. The following major explanations have been offered here for this conspicuous decline in women's Knesset representation:

The organizational means taken by parties to enhance women's representation were not effective. The quota system failed to advance women, and one could argue that the main reason for the inadequacy of this measure was simply electoral results, wherein the two major parties lost seats to the smaller parties. The placement of women lower down on the lists was detrimental to their advancement. In addition, although the primaries system is perhaps more equitable and more democratic than the selection system controlled by the party's leadership, it is certainly detrimental to women, who lack the essential resources and visibility necessary for success.

Women's economic vulnerability may be a factor affecting their political power. Despite some positive developments – gainful employment and rising educational attainment – women in general fare worse than men in the economic domain. The established linkage between money and politics makes them inferior to men in the race to legislative office.

Israeli women politicians do not enjoy the backing of females already integrated into the elite. The scarcity of women in all walks of political life, from voluntary associations to the top echelons of government, serves as a disadvantage for women candidates, barred by a glass ceiling impeding their way to the top.

It has been suggested that to be elected, women candidates must address the issues that women are concerned with and women voters must be able to discern differences among candidates on these issues.[64] This condition was not met in the 1996 elections. The issues were linked with the country's security, a topic in which women do not specialize. Ethnic-national values surfaced as well, disengaging women from politics.

Women's political mobilization did not furnish women aspirants with the support required for breaking the glass ceiling. Women tend to demonstrate less activity in party politics – an area which is particularly important for electoral gains. Admittedly, parties report that half of their membership are women, but when asked individually, women clearly reveal their lesser party participation. When this disadvantage is coupled with a gender gap and reluctance among women to support women candidates, it is understandable why women find it difficult to win a legislative seat.

Finally, a woman's honor rests in her home. This dictum has been widely endorsed by both men and women. While many Israelis believe that women are equal to men, this does not mean that God has created them the same. Israeli women have widely internalized their domestic roles and have practiced them in their professional as well as their personal life. The gender-based division of roles is one of the reasons for their perpetual failure to enter the power arena.

How many of these variegated reasons were unique to the 1996 elections? One conclusion that emerges from this study is: not many. Although Israel is undergoing striking economic and political changes, the status of women remains steadfast. Their economic and political vulnerability and their preoccupation with domestic chores have remained immutable. Yet some factors were accentuated in the elections to the 14th Knesset. First, the expansion of the primaries system did not contribute to an increase in women's representation. Second, the fact that two women served as cabinet ministers during the incumbency of the 13th Knesset also failed to enhance women's electoral power. Third, the upsurge of the national-ethnic identity, evident in 1996 more than before, presumably because of the split vote between party and premier, also contributed to weakening the female political voice. Fourth, and most striking, the unprecedented peace moves had no positive affect on women's representation in the 14th Knesset. This fact underlines both the perpetuity and the profundity of the obstacles hindering women's way to the political apex.

NOTES

1. *Jerusalem Post*, May 31, 1996.
2. One woman, Dafna Sharfman, withdrew from the race before the primaries, claiming that "there is no point in running for one not supported by troops," *Koteret*, March 1, 1996.
3. *Networking*, 1996:1.
4. Avraham and Yael Brichta, "The Extent of the Impact of the Electoral System upon the Representation of Women in the Knesset," in J. Zimmerman and W. Rule, eds, *The*

Impact of the Election Systems on Minorities and Women (Westport, 1994).

5. Alice Brown and Yvonne Galligan, "Views from the Periphery: Changing the Political Agenda for Women in the Republic of Ireland and in Scotland." *Western European Politics*, Vol.16 (1993), pp.165–89.

6. Dalia Shhori, "The Chairman David." *Ha-aretz*, March 29, 1996.

7. Ibid., March 18, 1996.

8. Yael Yishai, *Between the Flag and the Banner. Women and Politics in Israel* (Albany, 1996).

9. Joni Lovenduski, "Sex, Gender and British Politics," *Parliamentary Affairs*, 49 (1996), p.7.

10. Nina Cecillie Raaum, "The Political Representation of Women: A Bird's Eye View," in L. Karvonen and P. Selle, eds, *Women in Nordic Politics. Closing the Gap* (Aldershot, 1996), p.34.

11. *Women and Political Parties*, 1992. Report No.19. Geneva: Interparliamentary Union.

12. *Ha-aretz*, March 27, 1996.

13. *Ha-aretz*, March 1, 1996.

14. Pippa Norris, "Labour Party Quotas for Women," in D. Broughton, D.M. Farrell, D. Denver, C. Rallings, eds, *British Elections and Parties Yearbook 1994* (London, 1995).

15. Yael Azmon, "Women and Politics: The Case of Israel," *Women and Politics*, Vol.10 (1990), pp.43–57.

16. Yishai, *Between the Flag and the Banner*, p.99.

17. Beryl Nicholson, "From Interest Group to (Almost) Equal Citizenship: Women's Representation in the Norwegian Parliament," *Parliamentary Affairs*, Vol.23 (1993), pp.255–63.

18. *Statistical Abstracts of Israel* (Jerusalem: Central Bureau of Statistics, 1995), p.357.

19. Victor R. Fuchs, *Women's Quest for Economic Equality* (Cambridge, 1988).

20. *Statistical Abstracts*, 1995, p.629.

21. Debora S. Bernstein, "Oriental and Ashkenazi Jewish Women in the Labor Market." In Barbara Swirski and Marilyn P. Safir, eds, *Calling the Equality Bluff. Women in Israel* (New York, 1991), p.192; Harriet Hartman, "Economic and Familial Roles of Women in Israel," in Yael Azmon and Dafna N. Izraeli, eds, *Women in Israel* (New Brunswick, 1993), p.192.

22. Dafna N. Izraeli, "The Sex Structure of Occupations. The Israeli Experience," *Sociology of Work and Occupations*, Vol.6 (1979), pp.404–29.

23. Idem, "Women and Work: From Collective to Career," in Swirski and Safir, *Calling the Equality Bluff*, p.169.

24. Nina Toren, "The Status of Women in Academia," in Azmon and Izraeli, *Women in Israel*.

25. Linda Efroni, "Promotion and Wages of Women in Israel," Unpublished Ph.D. Dissertation. Jerusalem, Hebrew University, 1980.

26. *Income of Employees 1992–1993* (Jerusalem: Central Bureau of Statistics, Pub. No.1000, 1995).

27. Administration of State Income, *Annual Report 1995*, April, 1996, p.99.

28. Izraeli, "Women and Work," p.169.

29. *Statistical Abstracts*, 1995, p.387.

30. Dafna N. Izraeli, "Women's Movement into Management," in N. Adler and Dafna Izraeli, eds, *Women in Management Worldwide* (New York, 1988).

31. Donley T. Studlar and Susan Welch, "Understanding the Iron Law of Undrarchy," *Comparative Political Studies*, Vol.20 (1987), pp.174–91; Michael X. Delli Carpini and Esther R. Fuchs, "The Year of the Woman? Candidates, Voters, and the 1992 Elections," *Political Science Quarterly*, Vol.108 (1993), pp.29–36.

32. Ora Namir (Labor), serving as Minister of Labor and Welfare in the 1992–96 government, withdrew from the list after being placed second on the list of women. She was replaced at the top by a woman of Russian origin, put there to compensate for the lack of immigrants' representation on the Labor list (*Ha-aretz*, April 4, 1996). Shulamit Aloni, the Minister for Arts and Science, resigned from her party list prior to the elections.

33. *Ma'ariv*, May 17, 1996.

34. Yael Yishai and Aaron Cohen, "(Un)representative Bureaucracy: Women in the Israeli Senior Civil Service," *Administration and Society*, Vol.28 (1997), pp.441–65.

35. Hanna Herzog, *Realistic Women: Women in Local Politics* (Jerusalem, 1994) (Hebrew).
36. Note that in electoral campaigns focusing on active wars, women's representation does not decline. This was the case in the aftermath of the Yom Kippur War, when women's representation increased from 8 in the 7th Knesset (1969) to 10 in the 8th Knesset (1973). This was also the case during the Lebanon War when the number of women MKs increased from 9 in the 10th Knesset (1981) to 10 in the 11th Knesset (1984). Interestingly, it is precisely the anticipation of peace and prosperity that has had a negative impact on women's representation. In the first election to take place after the Six-Day War (1969), the number of women in the Knesset declined from 9 to 8. This was not the case, however, after peace was inaugurated with Egypt. In the elections to the 9th Knesset (1981), women's representation increased from 8 to 9. Obviously, the insights into the possible linkage between actual war, as distinct from the prominence of the security issue, and women's electoral success are highly tentative due to the small number of cases under consideration and the slight fluctuations in women's representation.
37. Robert S. Erikson, Norman R. Luttbeg, and Kent L. Tedin, *American Public Opinion* (New York, 1988), pp.199–292.
38. Roni Rimon in Yael Chen, "Run, the Knesset is Calling You," *Ma'ariv*, March 24, 1996.
39. Amihai Alperovich, "Runners. In the Worst Case She will Administer School," *Ha-aretz*, March 11, 1996.
40. Joseph Levine, "The Seculars who Voted NRP," *Ha-aretz*, June 6, 1996.
41. *Jerusalem Post*, May 31, 1996.
42. Bernstein, "Oriental and Askenazi," pp.193–94.
43. Yishai, *Between the Flag and the Banner*.
44. Asher Arian, *The Choosing People* (Cleveland, 1973), pp.27–33; Daniel Elazar *Israel: Building a New Society* (Bloomington, 1986).
45. Asher Arian and Michal Shamir, "Two Reversals: Why 1992 was not 1977," in idem, eds, *The Elections in Israel 1992* (Albany, 1995).
46. *Ma'ariv*, February 16, 1996.
47. Yael Azmon, "Women and Politics: The Case of Israel," in Azmon and Izraeli, *Women in Israel*.
48. *Yediot Aharonot*, May 28, 1996.
49. Menachem Rahat, "There was a Happening, It was Fun. The NRP's Center Chose its Candidates," *Ma'ariv*, March 18, 1996.
50. *Israel TV*, March 21, 1996.
51. See, for example, Ruth Katz and Yohanan Peres, "The Sociology of the Family in Israel: An Outline of its Development from the 1950s," *European Sociological Review*, Vol.2 (1986), pp.148–59; Dafna N. Izraeli and Ephraim Tabory, 1988. "The Political Context of Feminist Attitudes in Israel," *Gender and Society*, Vol.II (1988), pp.463–481; Marilyn Safir, "Religion, Tradition and Public Policy Give Family First Priority," in Swirski and Safir, *Calling the Equality Bluff*.
52. *Demographic Yearbook*, 1986 (New York, 1986), pp.160, 165.
53. Varda Milbauer and Mina Tzemach, *Zug O Peret?* (Two or One?) (Tel Aviv, 1991), p.16.
54. *Naamat*, October 1984.
55. Safir, "Religion," p.58.
56. Alison Solomon, "Anything for a Baby: Reproductive Technology in Israel," in Swirski and Safir, *Calling the Equality Bluff*.
57. *Statistical Abstracts*, 1995, p.749.
58. R. Winch, "Some Observations on Extended Familism in the U.S," in R. Winch and W. Goodman, eds, *Selected Studies in Marriage and the Family*, 3rd ed. (New York, 1968).
59. Quoted by A. Baker, *The Jewish Woman in Contemporary Society. Transitions and Traditions* (London, 1993), p.124.
60. Ibid., pp.124–5.
61. Yael Aran in Chen, "Run."
62. Miki Mazar, *Israel TV*, March 21, 1996.
63. R. Darcy, Susan Welch, and Janet Clark, *Women, Elections, and Representation* (New York, 1987).
64. Carpini and Fuchs, "The Year of the Woman?"

Peace, Security and Terror in the 1996 Elections

GERALD M. STEINBERG

Analysts of Israeli politics and policy are fond of quoting Henry Kissinger's assertion that Israel has no foreign policy, only domestic policy. However, as the 1996 elections clearly demonstrated, the causal relationship is often reversed. The issues of national security and the political relations with the Palestinians and the Arab states are central to Israeli political life, and differing approaches, both in terms of policy and ideology, are determining factors in domestic politics.

In contrast to the 1988 and 1992 election campaigns, in which foreign policy issues played a limited (but still significant) role, in 1996 the evidence clearly indicates that these were the primary factors, at least in the election of the prime minister. As will be demonstrated in this essay, ideological approaches to the Arab–Israeli conflict, the Land of Israel, and the negotiation process were less significant than pragmatic concern for personal security. Although some Israeli voters remain ideological, as seen among segments of Labor and Likud voters, as well as Meretz and Moledet (and to a lesser degree, the National Religious Party, NRP), the size of these groups is diminishing, the importance of ideology continues to decline. (The support for the non-ideological Third Way party, and for Yisrael Ba'Aliyah also underlines this trend.)

Rather, the continuing terrorism and the dissatisfaction of Jewish swing voters with the negotiation process as conducted by the incumbent government were deciding determinants in this election campaign. These concerns even overwhelmed the negative impacts of the assassination of Prime Minister Yitzhak Rabin on Binyamin Netanyahu and the Israeli Right, Netanyahu's perceived inexperience and the questions regarding his personal life, the disunity in the Likud-Gesher-Tsomet "alliance," and the economic successes of the Labor government.

After Rabin's assassination, public opinion polls showed that Shimon

Gerald M. Steinberg is Associate Professor in Political Studies at Bar-Ilan University.

Peres held a lead of between 25 and 30 percent, and over the next two months, the head of the Labor Party maintained a 10 to 15 percent lead over Netanyahu. Although the differences were less dramatic, the same trends were seen in polls regarding party preferences, with the Labor-Meretz coalition holding a substantial advantage over the right-wing parties.

However, this situation changed dramatically after four brutal terrorist bombings at the end of February and the beginning of March 1996. Immediately after, polls showed that Netanyahu and the Likud had closed the gap, and in some cases, were marginally ahead. As will be seen below, this wave of terrorism led to intense public criticism of the Oslo Accords, of Arafat's continued anti-Israeli rhetoric and his failure to take action against the Islamic extremists, such as HAMAS, and of the ineffectiveness of the government's responses. At the same time, Netanyahu's actions and statements during this period were designed to present the image of a responsible statesman, and the head of the Likud emerged as a credible national leader.

Between early March, following the suicide bombing at the Dizengoff Center in Tel-Aviv, and the elections on May 29, the polls did not change significantly. Netanyahu and Peres continued to be essentially even (the differences in the polls were within sampling errors). Peres attempted to regain his earlier lead by emphasizing security issues. He delayed the Israeli redeployment from Hebron until after the elections and, in late April, launched a major military campaign (*Grapes of Wrath*) in response to rocket attacks on Northern Israel. However, these actions appeared to be a case of "too little, too late," and had no apparent impact on the elections. The same is true for the ambiguity of the Palestinian National Authority, with respect to changing the Palestinian Charter and the increasingly visible support for Peres from President Bill Clinton and the U.S. government. In the debate between the two major candidates for prime minister two days before the polling, Netanyahu emphasized the theme of security, and this exchange solidified Netanyahu's small overall lead (and the 11 percent margin among Jewish voters).

Other factors, such as the Haredi vote, which went overwhelmingly to Netanyahu, balancing the Arab vote for Peres, and the support Netanyahu received from immigrant groups (65 percent) and from Jews from Arab states, clearly influenced the outcome. However, polls indicate that structural factors would not have been enough to elect Netanyahu before the wave of terrorist bombings, even allowing for significant inaccuracy in the polling data and voter responses.

The campaign was also affected by other aspects of the Middle East negotiations, including the lack of visible progress in discussions with Syria, and the Egyptian government's growing hostility to cooperation with Israel, despite the 1979 Peace Treaty. In contrast, closer relations with Jordan, Oman, Qatar, Morocco and Tunisia served to offset these negative developments, at least in part. The differing scenarios for the next four years, particularly with respect to Syria, were of importance in voter perceptions. Widespread concerns over evidence that Peres and the Labor Party were preparing for a major agreement with Damascus, which would have included Israeli withdrawal from the Golan Heights, played a role in the elections. In response to these concerns, Peres extended Rabin's previous commitment to a national referendum on any agreement with Syria.

For his part, Netanyahu was confronted with the need to appeal to the non-ideological centrist swing voters who had supported Rabin in 1992, but were dissatisfied with the results and concerned about the security implications. Polls showed that the majority of Israelis were in favor of maintaining the negotiation process and opposed to reversing the results of the Oslo agreements. To appeal to them, Netanyahu sought to reduce the role of ideology in his campaign speeches and appearances, and to emphasize pragmatism and a commitment to a continuation of the negotiations. Despite the ideological opposition of some members, the Likud platform accepted the Oslo agreements, and the party slogan was "peace with security'. The Likud leadership did not call for a return of the Israeli military to Gaza or to the large Palestinian cities that had been incorporated in the second (interim) agreement. Netanyahu also met with King Hussein and Crown Prince Hassan of Jordan, and pledged to meet with Palestinian officials (despite his very harsh criticism of Rabin and Peres for meeting with Arafat in 1993). In the very close race that developed after the suicide bombings, the two candidates for prime minister sought to obtain the support of the swing or undecided voters in the center of the Israeli political spectrum, whose view of the negotiation process was largely determined by the impact of this process on perceptions of personal security.

PRELUDE: THE NEGOTIATION PROCESS AND ISRAELI POLITICS, 1992–96

The period between 1992 and 1996 was marked by fundamental changes in the political structure of the Middle East. The series of agreements between Israel and the Palestinians, beginning with the 1993 Declaration of Principles, (the Oslo accord, DOP), as well as the 1994 Israel–Jordan Peace Treaty, and the establishment of trade and low-level diplomatic relations with a number of North African and Gulf States, all were at the center of these changes. The formula of "land for peace" was the agreed basis for developing what Shimon Peres envisioned as "The New Middle East."[1] This process began with Israel's military withdrawal from Gaza and Jericho in 1994, and a number of other cities in the Judea and Samaria regions of the West Bank (under the interim agreement of September 1995), and transfer of control to a Palestinian National Authority headed by PLO leader Yasser Arafat. In addition, negotiations with Syria had begun, with the goal of reaching an agreement which would involve Israeli withdrawal from the Golan Heights and some degree of "normalization" in relations between Jerusalem and Damascus.

In the 1992 elections, the future of relations between Israel and its neighbors (the Palestinians and the Arab states) was the subject of intense debate and a significant (but not deciding) factor. The narrow majority that allowed the Labor Party and Meretz to form a government under the leadership of Yitzhak Rabin was, in part, a reflection of the perceived failures of the Shamir government to take advantage of the openings presented by the 1991 Gulf War and the negotiations that began after the Madrid Conference. The lack of movement in these negotiations, and the continued conflict with the U.S. government over what was seen by the Bush administration as Israeli intransigence with respect to both the Palestinians (which were represented in the Jordanian delegation), and the Syrians, led some centrist voters in Israel to support the Labor party in 1992. Rabin, who had defeated Peres in the leadership contest in the Labor Party, presented himself as a pragmatic security oriented leader ('bitchonist') who would be willing to take prudent risks, but not to the degree that endangered Israeli security.[2] Although favoring autonomy for the Palestinians, Rabin did not discuss negotiations with the PLO and Arafat.

After the elections, Rabin pledged a breakthrough in negotiations within one year. His first approach was towards the Syrians, which he viewed as the primary threat to Israeli security, following the 1979 Israeli–Egyptian peace treaty, and therefore as the key to regional stability. This assessment was shared by a number of Israeli decisionmakers, including IDF Chief of Staff, Ehud Barak. However, despite significant changes in the Israeli negotiating team and the positions that were presented in the talks in Washington, the Syrian government failed to respond.[3]

The focus then shifted to the Palestinian track. In contrast to the Shamir government, Rabin and Foreign Minister Peres, agreed to separate Palestinian and Jordanian delegations in the bilateral talks. However, progress was slow in these formal meetings as well, and it appeared that the year would pass without significant change in positions. In contrast to the policies under the previous government, which classified Arafat and the PLO as terrorists with whom any discussions were illegal, the new government authorized and encouraged contact and meetings.

During the spring and early summer of 1993, one of the many informal or track-two channels that had been used for off-the-record exchanges between Palestinian and Israeli academics and leaders assumed greater importance. Talks taking place in Oslo and sponsored by the Norwegian government intensified, and Palestinian and Israeli leaders became closely involved. By August 1993, a preliminary agreement had been drafted, consisting of mutual recognition and a Declaration of Principles, which included the outline for a three stage process leading to a permanent status agreement within five years.

This marked a fundamental change in relations between Israel and the Palestinians. In September, Rabin and Arafat participated in a signing ceremony on the White House lawn, that was climaxed by a handshake between the two leaders, (albeit, with clear discomfort on the part of Rabin). In May 1994, after nine months of further negotiations and periodic crises, agreement on the first stage of the process was reached, and in June 1994, Israel withdrew from most of Gaza as well as Jericho. Shortly thereafter, Arafat returned triumphantly to Gaza, and the Palestinian National Authority began to function. Negotiations also began on the second, or interim stage, and in September 1995, after another series of crises and reconciliations, agreement was reached on the extension of Israeli withdrawal and autonomy for Palestinian cities. The agreement also specified details for elections under the PNA, and the creation of a legislative body. The election, held in January 1996, formally confirmed Yasser Arafat as head of the PNA.

Within Israel, this period was marked by increasing political support for the negotiation process and the agreements. This support continued steadily, despite periodic crises, waves of terrorist attacks, and occasional statements by Arafat and other PLO leaders calling for a *jihad* to establish Jerusalem as the capital of a Palestinian state, or the "liberation" of all Palestinian or Arab lands. The peace treaty with Jordan, signed along the border in October 1994, and witnessed by President Clinton and other leaders, enhanced the standing and credibility of the process among Israeli voters.

These events created a sense that the long siege, that began even prior to 1948 was over, and Israel was no longer "a small isolated state surrounded by enemies." However, public opinion polls still showed a high degree of skepticism. In January 1996, over 60 percent of Israelis agreed with the statement that "most Palestinians have not come to terms with the existence of Israel and would destroy it if they could." Full approval of the autonomy process increased from 6 percent to close to between 20 and 30 percent, but was still short of a majority.[4]

In response, the opposition parties, led by the Likud and Netanyahu, were divided and had difficulty responding to these major diplomatic successes. They argued on both ideological and pragmatic lines, predicting that the agreements would create a major security threat to Israel. They also accused Rabin of violating his 1992 campaign pledges. The initial reports of efforts to reach an agreement with Syria, and discussion of withdrawal from the Golan Heights led to public movements designed to block this process. The internal conflict was fueled by highly visible speculation and leaks in the press regarding the first settlements in the Golan that would be transferred to Syria. Large numbers of Israelis placed banners on their houses and stickers on their cars declaring opposition to withdrawal from the Golan. As a result of these pressures (which also came from some members of his own coalition), Rabin was pressed to pledge to hold a referendum on any agreement with Syria.

Terrorism continued, with periodic drive-by attacks against Israelis in Judea and Samaria, and in Gaza. In February 1994, Baruch Goldstein entered the Cave of the Patriarchs in Hebron and killed 29 Palestinians in February 1994. In the summer of 1994, a series of suicide bombings in Afula and Hadera, which killed 70 Israelis and injured many more, increased the focus on terrorism. In October, the kidnapping and death of Nahshon Wachsman, who was killed when an IDF rescue attempt failed, had a traumatic impact in Israel (over 50,000 people took part in a prayer vigil at the Western Wall) and forced Rabin to warn Arafat that the peace process was in danger.[5] A few days later, a suicide bombing in a Tel-Aviv bus took a heavy toll.

These attacks, the speeches by Arafat and other Palestinian leaders indicating support for terror and refering to the Islamic fundamentalist suicide bombers affiliated with HAMAS as "martyrs," and the absence of visible action by the Palestinian authority, eroded domestic support in Israel for the negotiation process. Opposition leaders such as Netanyahu, Binyamin Begin, Ariel Sharon, and David Levy claimed that instead of receiving peace in exchange for land, this process was leading to increased terror. They pointed to terrorist cells operating in Gaza, in the area under Palestinian control, and the failure to end their operation. The opposition demanded that the release of Palestinian prisoners (terrorists and members of the supporting network) be halted, and charged the government with turning responsibility for Israeli security over to the PLO.

In addition, Netanyahu and other critics called attention to what they termed the government's passivity in the face of the Palestinian Authority's violations of the 1994 agreement, including the lack of response to Israeli requests to extradite terrorists who participated in recent attacks against Israel. Continued attacks against Israeli forces and civilians from Southern Lebanon, conducted by Hizbullah, which, like HAMAS, is a fundamentalist organization, were linked by Likud leaders to the continued Palestinian terrorism.

On January 22 1995, a HAMAS suicide bombing at the Beit Leid junction killed 21 Israelis. This marked a major turning point in public perceptions of the peace process. President Weizman called for suspending the talks with the Palestinians, stating "we signed an agreement with Yasser Arafat as the leader of the Palestinians, now we should suspend the talks, not stop them, and tell Arafat to make more of an effort.[6] Large demonstrations opposing government policy took place in Tel-Aviv and Jerusalem, and Netanyahu declared "The government's present so-called peace policy has reached a disastrous dead end."[7] The Rabin government responded by closing access to Israel for Palestinians, (approximately 100,000 Palestinian workers were employed in Israel, and this was the primary source of income for residents of Gaza, Judea and Samaria), suspending the release of prisoners, and halting preparations for the opening of the Gaza–Jericho transportation corridor through Israel. In a somber address to the nation, Rabin also acknowledged the possibility of a more permanent separation, in response to increased public support for such policies.[8] Peres reportedly told Arafat that Israel is getting close to its "limit of patience" and demanded that Arafat take action against HAMAS.[9]

Although a period of relative calm stopped this erosion in public support, in August 1995, a bus bombing in Jerusalem that killed 5 and wounded 100 led to another round of demonstrations and response by the government, including closure and renewed discussion of separation. However, the negotiations for the second interim stage of the Oslo process resumed after a few days, and on September 28, this agreement was finally signed. Once again, there was an elaborate signing ceremony in Washington, with the participation of Rabin, Arafat, and numerous heads of state. A few days later, another very large demonstration took place in Jerusalem in opposition to the policies of the Rabin government. Likud leaders addressed the rally, calling for the reversal of these policies. Netanyahu declared that "The Zionist public in Israel has not approved Oslo 2." (However, when the crowd chanted "Rabin is a traitor," Netanyahu signaled disapproval.)[10]

These large rallies opposing government policy were an indication of a change in public opinion. In January 1995, following the Beit Leid attack, polls showed Rabin trailing Netanyahu by a narrow margin.[11] Continued terrorism, including the August attack in Jerusalem reinforced this trend. However, in the aftermath of Rabin's assassination on November 4, Netanyahu's standing plunged. In February, when Peres decided to hold early elections, the Prime Minister maintained a substantial lead over Netanyahu.

In a campaign speech delivered on February 12, Peres boasted of the government's achievements, declaring "No other government has a [comparable] record in four years, except for that of the early years of the state." He described the peace with the Palestinians as "flourishing, unlike those in Ireland and Bosnia."[12] Within two weeks, his vision of a New Middle East had been torn apart by another and more deadly series of suicide bombings. On February 25, two terrorist blasts took place; one in a bus in Jerusalem, killing 25 and wounding 50, and another at the Ashkelon junction in which two were killed and 34 wounded. One week later, another Jerusalem bus bombing killed 18, and the next day, a similar bombing in Tel Aviv took a similar toll.

As a result of these bombings (which had been planned to take place on a single day) support for the peace process was dramatically reversed. Polls showed that before the bombings, a substantial majority of Israelis felt that personal security had been enhanced by the process, but after these events, only 16.5 percent thought security had improved, while over 51 percent felt less secure. 63 percent supported suspension of negotiations with the Palestinians.[13] This was translated into electoral terms, and Peres lost his substantial lead (10 to 15 percent) over

Netanyahu in Israeli polls.[14] In a series of public addresses to the nation, Peres was shaken and had difficulty responding to reporters' questions and in providing responses. The government imposed a closure on Judea, Samaria, and Gaza, and around Jerusalem, and demanded that Arafat "take decisive steps in order to block the activities of the HAMAS and Islamic Jihad."[15] Peres also announced a postponement of the IDF redeployment (withdrawal) from Hebron, scheduled for March 28.[16]

This wave of bombings and Arafat's failure to prevent it placed the Prime Minister and the Labor Party on the defensive. In interviews, Peres was asked repeatedly to justify his policies in the wake of the suicide bombings. As both Prime Minister and Defense Minister, but without Rabin's military record to justify maintaining both portfolios, he was particularly vulnerable to criticism in the area of security failures. Issues of Peres' age and allegations of depression were also published.[17] (Polls did not show a significant decrease in the support for the Labor Party, which maintained a steady level of the equivalent of 40 to 43 seats, reflecting the fact that the primary impact was on support for Peres and Netanyahu).

Although Arafat and the PNA began to take action against HAMAS and terrorist groups,[18] the Palestinian leader also continued to undermine Peres, repeating claims that the wave of terror was caused by an unholy conspiracy of Israeli "fanatics" who were allegedly members of a shadowy group of ex-IDF people, called "OAS," and Muslim extremists were behind the suicide bombings. The newly elected Palestinian Council members condemned the closure imposed by Israel without condemning the bombings which provoked it.[19] Arafat failed to order the capture of "the engineer" (Yahya Ayash), who had planned many of the bus bombings in 1994 and 1995, and was living openly in Gaza. When Ayash was finally killed in an operation generally attributed to Israeli security, Arafat praised the HAMAS terrorist as "a holy shahid "(martyr) and praised Dalal al-Moghrabi, who was responsible for a series of terrorist attacks in the 1970s. Arafat also referred to an earlier terrorist as "the commander, the star, who established the first Palestinian republic in a bus."[20]

In the wake of the national emergency triggered by this wave of terrorism, Netanyahu's image changed radically, from fiery opposition leader to statesman and potential leader. He told Likud activists to refrain from holding demonstrations for the two days of national mourning. After the first double bombing, Netanyahu called for unity and said "We won't enter into a political battle on a day like today. This is a day for uniting the ranks and that's how we will act."[21]

Netanyahu also addressed a special session of the Knesset, which was broadcast live on radio and television. In this speech, he spelled out the central themes of his campaign:

> In recent years we hoped and wished that perhaps the hatred of our enemies against us had reached an end. ... We are all partners in this hope for peace. And so we also hoped that our generosity and open

arms would silence, and not by a little, the lust for murder of those from among our neighbors who seek our lives. But to my sorrow it becomes clear to us again and again, and each time in a more painful way, that our generosity is interpreted as weakness and our open arms are seen as surrender. And instead of reducing the terror, the terror increases; and instead of bringing us closer to peace and tranquillity, we don't have peace and we don't have tranquillity.[22]

In their reports, journalists gave prominence to the Likud's "restrained response"[23] (In contrast, Tsomet leader Rafael Eitan said the attacks "proved that Prime Minister Shimon Peres does not know how to fight this murderous terror and is leading the country to an impossible and false peace with terrorists, with encouragement from Meretz."[24])

Another step in Netanyahu's transformation from a radical opposition leader to responsible statesman and potential prime minister took place when Netanyahu and Peres were briefed together by the heads of the Israeli security system on March 3. He also released a five-point program, including a halt to all talks with the Palestinians until it acts concretely to eliminate the terrorist infrastructure, a complete closure until this infrastructure is eliminated, complete freedom of action for the IDF and the security forces, and "the eradication of all centers of activity" of the PLO and HAMAS in Jerusalem and its environs.

Peres and the Labor Party also lost credibility during this crucial period as a result of what was seen as an effort to manipulate the state-owned media for partisan purposes. After the Dizengoff bombing, the Palestinian police arrested Muhammad Abu Warda, who was charged with recruiting some of the bombers for HAMAS. He was held in Jericho and from there, was interviewed by Israeli state television. Abu Warda claimed that HAMAS had conducted this wave of attacks in order to help the Likud gain power in order to block the peace process. On the evening news, Peres was shown listening to the interview and nodding. He then said he wasn't surprised. "I had known this all along, but I did not want to fan the flames ... now the picture is complete." This appeared to be the result of collusion between Arafat and Peres. MK Benny Begin came to the television studio during the broadcast and denounced the episode as a cynical attempt to manipulate the Israeli public and place the blame for terrorism on the Likud. Other Likud leaders called Abu Warda's statement a "counterfeit confession" made under torture and threats.

In contrast, Netanyahu took the high ground, saying he is "willing to overlook and forgive Peres." In attempting to draw a contrast with his own actions, Netanyahu suggested that "In these days of flared tempers, Peres should have exercised leadership and sought to calm the storm. I hope he will take his words back and not repeat this failure in the future, though I am sure that Arafat will repeat his attempts to interfere crudely in our political process."[25]

Thus, the combination of terrorism, the perceived weakness of the government's responses, the increased criticism of the peace process and the failure of Arafat to act to end terror, Netanyahu's "statesmanlike" policies and public appearances, and the Abu Warda affair served to change the relationship between the main candidates for prime minister. These events led to the disappearance of Peres' 15-point lead in the polls, and this lead never returned.

A Dahaf Poll published in *Yediot Aharonot* on February 26, 1996, predicted that if elections were held the same day, Shimon Peres would win 48 percent of the votes, compared with Netanyahu's 46 percent (with 6 percent decided).[26]

TABLE 1

IMPACT OF TERRORISM ON POLL RESULTS: PRIME MINISTER (%)

If elections were held today for personal election of the prime minister, and Shimon Peres and Binyamin Netanyahu were the candidates, who would you vote for?

	1995 Nov 7/8	Dec 5/6	1996 Jan 2/3	Jan 30/31	Feb 7/8	Feb 13/14	Feb 20/21	Feb 27/28*	Mar 5/6
Peres	54	46	50	46	51	50	50	48	46
Netanyahu	23	28	29	30	36	37	36	48	49
Undecided	12	16	12	11	5	7	8	4	5
Won't vote	10	1	9	13	8	6	6	+	+

+ Included in "Undecided"
* After Jerusalem bus bombing.

TABLE 2

POLL DATA ON PARTY PREFERENCE

If there were elections for the Knesset today, which party would you vote for? (number of mandates).

	13th Knesset	1995 Nov 7/8	Dec 5/6	1996 Jan 2/3	Jan 30/31	Feb 6/7	Feb 20/21	Feb 27/28	Mar 5/6
Labor	44	46	44	44	44	45	45	40	43
Likud	32	30	31	31–32	29	36	35	40	43
Tzomet	8	6	5–6	6	5	*	*	*	*
Meretz	12	8	8–9	7–8	7	8	7	7	5
Moledet	3	2	3	2	–	1–2	1–2	2	2
NRP	6	6	6	6	7	6–7	6	6	5
Torah Party	4	4	4	4	4	4	4	4	4
SHAS	6	5	4	4	4	4	4	4	4
Arabs/ Communists	5	6	6	6	7	7++	7	7	7
Gesher	–	2	2	3	4	3	2–3	3	**
Third Way	–	3	4	3	4	2	4	4	3
Israel Ba'Aliya	–	2	3	3	3	3	4	3	4
Shulamit Aloni	–	–	–	2	–	–	–	–	–

* Survey presented "Likud Tzomet Bloc" – results appear in Likud figure.
** Levy Party added to Likud
++ Includes Ahmed Tibi

While the wave of terrorism triggered a basic change in public perceptions and had a major role in determining the results of the elections, other issues related to the negotiation process between Israel and the Palestinians were also of importance. These issues included the final status issues, such as Jerusalem, Jewish settlements, boundaries, the prospects of a Palestinian state, and the question of the Palestinian Covenant.

JERUSALEM

The Likud's official election campaign opened on February 18 (before the wave of suicide bombings) with a publicity barrage focused on Jerusalem. A series of advertisements in the major media charged that if they were reelected, the Labor/Meretz coalition and Peres would "divide and give away Jerusalem." Although Peres and other Labor party officials denied the charge, they were immediately placed on the defensive, and the charge was credible enough to require a response, and an official cabinet statement.[27] (Labor Party Secretary-General Nissim Zvilli proposed a signed agreement to keep the Jerusalem issue out of the election campaign, and Netanyahu and Jerusalem Mayor and Likud MK Olmert dismissed the idea as "ridiculous."[28]) The status of Jerusalem is a major issue for a majority of Israelis, which oppose any division or transfer of sovereignty from Israeli hands.

In the 1993 DOP, Israel and the Palestinians agreed to postpone discussion of this divisive issue until the permanent status talks. After the signing ceremony in Washington, however, Arafat spoke continuously about the goal of establishing a Palestinian state, with Jerusalem as its capital. In numerous public appearances, he pledged to create such a state with Jerusalem as its capital, to which Peres responded by saying that Arafat is entitled to his dream.[29]

The Palestinians also established a number of institutions in East Jerusalem, including a quasi-Foreign Ministry operating out of the Orient House. Palestinian security forces were also active in Jerusalem. The Israeli Right saw these activities as violations of the Oslo Accords, and while government officials such as Police Minister Moshe Shahal agreed, they did not take action, and the Likud charged that Labor's policies tacitly encouraged the Palestinian presence in Jerusalem.

Peres, like Rabin before him, pledged to keep Jerusalem undivided and under Israeli sovereignty, and denied reports that secret talks were already being held on this issue. In campaign speeches, he declared "Like a solid rock, we will stand firm on a united Jerusalem as the capital of Israel."[30] Similarly, Barak stated that in the final status talks, "our position will be that greater Jerusalem should remain undivided under our sovereignty, the eternal capital of Israel."[31]

However, Rafael Eitan charged that secret negotiations on the "division of Jerusalem" were being held, and this "shows lack of honesty and demonstrates deceit, just as the Labor Party decided that the consensus on the Golan Heights issue in the last elections meant the subject could be taken off the agenda, only to later agree to give the Golan Heights to Syria with nothing in return."[32] Although vigorously denied by Peres and Labor, reports of secret "track two" negotiations between Israeli and Palestinian representatives on the final status issues, including Jerusalem, were published a few days later. These talks involved Yossi Beilin and Abu Mazen, as well as Yair Hirschfeld and Ron Pundak, who were centrally involved in the initial Oslo agreements. (Jordan also claimed the major role in East Jerusalem, and the link to the city was part of the Hashemite claim to legitimacy. These talks disturbed the Jordanian government, which remained formally neutral during the campaign. Informally, King Hussein and Crown Prince Hassan provided some assistance for Netanyahu, meeting with him and his advisors during the campaign, thereby providing the Likud candidate with a basis for claiming to have good relations among Arab states.)[33]

As Likud strategists recognized, Israeli public opinion strongly opposed any change in the status of Jerusalem. The systematic pillaging and deliberate destruction of the Jewish Quarter that took place during the Jordanian/Palestinian occupation between 1948–67 remained a major factor in public opposition to compromises on Jerusalem. Polls showed that 68 percent of Israelis supported moves to close official Palestinian offices, including the Orient House, operating in Jerusalem.[34]

Although the impact of the Jerusalem issue in the campaign is difficult to measure, the centrality of this issue hurt Peres and Labor, and the revelations over the secret talks further damaged their credibility. In addition, this exchange was indicative of the public disquiet regarding the final status issues, such as borders, a Palestinian state, and future boundaries, and the difficulties and controversies with respect to relations with the PNA and with Arafat.

RELATIONS WITH ARAFAT AND THE PNA

The handshake on the White House lawn between Rabin and Arafat, and continuing meetings were condemned by opposition leaders, and early in the campaign, Netanyahu declared that he would "not meet or deal with Arafat."[35] MK Moshe Katsav proclaimed that the Likud has "no intention of recognizing the Oslo Accords, and will at any price prevent the establishment of a Palestinian state." He declared that "The Likud continues to see the agreements as a historic mistake liable to endanger the existence of the state."[36] (The head of research in military intelligence, Brigadier-General Yaakov Amidror told a Knesset committee that "Arafat is not assimilating in Palestinian society the concept of peace, nor is he inculcating the understanding that the most that the Palestinians can strive for is the 1967 borders. This policy leaves within the public consciousness the principle of stages."[37])

TABLE 3

THE PRESENT AND FUTURE IN THE TERRITORIES:
PREFERRED AND LIKELY SOLUTIONS (%)

Respondents were asked what solution for the territories they preferred; the results were:

Annexation and transfer	9
Annexation, no transfer, no full rights	11
Annexation, no transfer, full rights for Arabs	4
Autonomy	28
Return most of the territories to Jordan in peace agreement	4
Jordanian–Palestinian confederation	22
Palestinian state in territories as part of peace treaty	22

Source: Asher Arian, *Israeli Security Opinion*, Jaffee Center for Strategic Studies, Tel-Aviv University, February 1996, p.16; based on polls conducted in January, February and March 1996.

TABLE 4

TERRITORIES TO BE RETURNED IN THE PERMANENT AGREEMENT (%)

	Western Samaria	Jordan Valley	Etzion Bloc	East Jerusalem
1994	30	18	14	18
1995	30	19	18	9
1995	38	20	20	12

Source: Asher Arian, *Israeli Security Opinion*, Jaffee Center for Strategic Studies, Tel-Aviv University, February 1996, p. 21.

TABLE 5

SUPPORT FOR DISCUSSING...IN TALKS WITH PALESTINIANS (%)

	1990	1993	1994	1995	1996
Independent Palestinian State	26	30	41	44	48
Palestinian state in some of the area with acceptable security arrangements for Israel	—	45	51	50	53
Jordanian–Palestinian confederation	34	48	57	58	66
Removing Jewish settlements	32	43	50	45	49
East Jerusalem	13	17	14	15	17
Right of Return	9	12	14	12	11

Source: Asher Arian, *Israeli Security Opinion*, Jaffee Center for Strategic Studies, Tel-Aviv University, February 1996, pg. 21

222   *Israel at the Polls, 1996*

As the election drew closer and the gap between the candidates remained very small, Netanyahu changed his position, declaring that his government would hold talks with the Palestinian Authority "but only if it fulfills all of its undertakings, something which it is not doing now." These requirements included "the handing over to Israel of terrorist murderers, the ending of anti-Israel incitement, the destruction of terror bases and terror infrastructure and the amendment of the Palestinian Covenant which continues to call for Israel's annihilation."[38]

In the move towards the center, Netanyahu declared that he "will continue the peace process, but this with the utmost care and caution." Israel, he stated, "must pursue a peace that will be borne of might and which will safeguard Israel's security and most vital interests."[39] He also shifted his stance on the Oslo agreements, noting that "We are inheriting a reality which none of us wanted, but with which we shall have to cope. We are like the businessman who takes over a business with debts and entanglements. ... We strenuously and justly oppose the Oslo accords, but they created a situation which we will have to face to prevent it from getting worse."[40] Netanyahu claimed to have links with moderate Arab leaders, and his spokesman claimed that the pen used to sign the new agreement with Rafael Eitan of Tsomet "would be the same pen that he uses to sign future treaties with Arab states."[41]

Peres firmly rejected the criticism and referred to Arafat as a partner in the peace process. However, Arafat's statements and actions (or inaction, as noted above), did not provide much support to the Labor Party's campaign. Other Labor leaders were more blunt, with Housing Minister Ben-Eliezer declaring that "Those who put all their trust in Arafat and thought that he could guaranty our security were mistaken."[42]

The question of the PLO Covenant also became a major campaign issue. The 1995 Interim agreement ("Oslo 2") included a Palestinian commitment to formally repeal those sections of the charter (or covenant) calling for Israel's destruction, within two months of elections for the Palestinian National Council. These elections took place in late January, and for many weeks, Arafat made no move to convene the PNC or change the covenant. This inaction was seen as an effort to "pressure Israel and to extort more concessions."[43] Rabin declared that amendment of the covenant was a requirement for continued Israeli withdrawal, and Peres repeated this pledge shortly after Rabin's assassination.[44] As the weeks passed without action, Labor Party leaders warned that if Labor comes to the elections without action on this issue, "We are liable to pay a high price in the elections. ... The public will be astonished, and rightly so, that the covenant wasn't canceled."[45] Similarly, Barak declared that Arafat "has to live up to his commitment, to forcefully combat terror and nullify the Palestinian covenant in a straightforward manner. If the Palestinian Authority fails to deliver on these promises, then I see no way to proceed with the permanent status negotiations as planned. There are no compromises here. No 'ifs,' 'ands' or 'buts'."[46]

In April, the PNC finally met and took action on the covenant, but its meaning was ambiguous. While Labor leaders such as Peres and Barak hailed what they called the decision to delete the sections of the covenant that call for the destruction of Israel, opposition leaders argued that the PNC had only created a committee to study the issues, and that in the absence of specific language deleting the individual paragraphs of the covenant, nothing had really changed. Professor Yehoshua Porat, considered an authority on Palestinian society and politics, and a member of the Meretz leadership, publicly supported the latter interpretation, and severely criticized the Labor and Meretz leadership for claiming that the covenant had been changed. This incident did not increase the credibility of Labor's policies. (As of May 1997, this committee had not met.)

In debating their respective platforms, there were divisions in both major parties regarding relations with the Palestinians. In the latter stages of the campaign, Netanyahu and most other Likud leaders favored a practical or pragmatic approach, and acceptance of the need to negotiate with the PNA.[47] (Some Likud leaders, such as Roni Milo and Ehud Olmert had taken this position much earlier.) This position was also endorsed, if somewhat reluctantly, by the NRP.[48] However, there was also significant opposition, particularly from MK Benny Begin and Ariel Sharon.[49] In response to the changing positions in the Likud, Sharon wrote that "If the Likud accepts the Oslo pact, it no longer has a right to exist."[50]

The Labor Party was divided on the issue of a Palestinian State and the future of Jewish settlements in the final status negotiations. In its 1992 platform, Labor included a statement opposing the establishment of a Palestinian state, and both Peres and Barak favored maintaining this position. In campaign appearances, Peres clearly stated his preference for a "Jordanian–Palestinian solution," and declared that the Jordan River is Israel's security border. "We want peace without unnecessary risks, and no foreign army will cross the Jordan River."[51] Barak stated that "We will not go back to the 1967 borders, most Israeli settlements will remain under Israeli control and no army other than the IDF will be deployed between the Mediterranean and the Jordan River."[52] In contrast, others Labor leaders, such as Zvilli and Beilin sought to delete this provision from the platform.[53] (Meretz explicitly called for the creation of a Palestinian state in its platform.)

The issue of settlements created a similar conflict. Barak favored an explicit statement pledging the retention of the vast majority of Israeli settlements, including in the Jordan Valley north of Jericho. Beilin supported a policy in which most of the settlers remain under Israeli sovereignty, and in which Israel would not act to dismantle those settlements under Palestinian control in the final status arrangements.[54] In the end, the Labor party platform did not change significantly with respect to these issues, but the debate and the public differences provided the public with indications of the divisions within both parties on these final status issues.

SYRIA, LEBANON, AND TERRORISM

In the 1992 election campaign, Rabin had declared that the Golan Heights were vital to Israeli security and would not be subject to negotiations, at least in the period of this government. However, shortly after the elections, his views changed, and an agreement with Syria was seen as the key to Israeli security and the avoidance of war. (Barak, who was the IDF Chief of Staff, shared this assessment.) This change led to the charges that the government and Rabin lacked a mandate for withdrawal, and triggered a large-scale public relations campaign. Public opinion polls also showed general opposition to a full withdrawal from the Golan. Support for full withdrawal ranged from 24 percent to 32 percent, at the highest (after the assassination of Rabin and the beginning of the Wye Plantation talks), with opponents ranging from 45 percent to 55 percent (from 35 percent to 42 percent were opposed to any withdrawal.)[55] As a result of demands from his coalition partners, particularly SHAS, Rabin pledged to hold a referendum if an agreement was reached with Syria involving territorial withdrawal from the Golan.

TABLE 6

POLL DATA ON THE GOLAN AND SYRIA (%)

Support for withdrawal from the Golan	December 95	January 96
Support full withdrawal	23.9	18.3
Partial withdrawal	41.2	37.7
Oppose any withdrawal	30.0	41.7

Note: The survey of 505 adult Israeli Jews was performed by "Modiin Ezrachi" on behalf on the Steinmetz Center for Peace Studies at Tel-Aviv University at the end of December and January. The error is +/- 4% (*Ha-aretz*, 5 February, 1996).

Throughout the campaign, relations with Syria, the future of the Golan, security arrangements, normalization, and the continued low-level warfare in Southern Lebanon were important political issues. In 1995, Israeli and Syrian military delegations met for the first time, but little progress was reported. In a number of public appearances, Assad did not indicate any interest in normalization with Israel, and these appearances had the effect of increasing public opposition to an agreement with Syria, and to the sense that Assad was not prepared to make peace, even in return for complete Israeli withdrawal from the Golan. Rabin and Peres indicated that they would be willing to withdraw to the international border, and Assad demanded a return to the June 4 1967 lines (including the territory that Syria had captured in 1948), as well as access to the Kinneret.[56] (According to some reports, Rabin had told Clinton that Israel would be willing to withdraw from the entire Golan, but that this position was kept hidden from everyone else in the Israeli government, including Foreign Minister Peres. Peres reportedly discovered this after Rabin was assassinated.)[57]

After Rabin's assassination, Peres increased the emphasis on the Syrian track, and direct negotiations at the Wye Plantation in the U.S. began. According to the available evidence, Peres sought and expected some dramatic shift in the Syrian position, and perhaps a meeting with Assad, before the elections, then scheduled for October. Military plans for separation of forces and demilitarization were presented to the Syrians.[58] Peres spoke of his vision of a link between peace with Syria and Israeli security, declaring that 10 hotels on the Golan will provide more security than 10 bunkers. (In a rare public clash between the military and political leadership, Peres' view was rejected by the head of Army Intelligence Research, Brigadier-General Amidror, who stated, "I don't accept this. A hotel is important as long as there is no war, but when the other side decides to go to war, the bunkers will decide more than the hotels..."[59])

In late January, after the second round of Wye Plantation talks, Peres reportedly hoped for a breakthrough and a meeting with Assad, which Peres and Labor concluded would give them an overwhelming victory in the elections.[60] However, after Christopher visited the region, including Damascus, in February, and failed to bring word of a change in the Syrian position, hopes for a meeting between Peres and Assad, and for rapid progress, vanished. Peres then decided to advance the elections from October to May.

At this stage, Peres and the Labor leadership recognized that in the absence of a dramatic breakthrough before the elections, a significant portion of the Israeli public would be wary of providing him and Labor an ambiguous mandate to negotiate an agreement with Syria after the elections. Party Secretary Zvilli stated that "If we don't separate the Golan Heights from the elections we will lose the support also of our traditional voters, who support us on everything else but the Golan question."[61] Thus, in the effort to reduce this vulnerability, and following Rabin's example, Peres also pledged to hold a referendum on any agreement with Syria after the elections.[62]

Syria was also perceived as closely linked to events in Lebanon, and the continuing attacks on Northern Israel and on the Israeli outposts in Southern Lebanon. In 1995, these attacks had increased by over 50 percent,[63] and the situation there was a source of tension and conflict. After a series of Hizbullah attacks on Israeli soldiers in the security zone, the IDF began to counterattack against Hizbullah positions in villages in the zone, which led the organization to launch Katyusha rocket attacks against civilian targets in northern Israel, in violation of the oral agreement reached between Israel, Syria and the U.S. at the end of Operation Accountability in 1994.

At this stage, Peres ordered a large-scale counterattack against Hizbullah forces and bases. Military sources claimed that the planning for the operation (dubbed *Grapes of Wrath*) had been completed many months earlier, but for political reasons had not been implemented. It is possible that this operation would have taken place earlier in the absence of the election campaign, but it is also possible that the campaign had an impact on the timing. Under attack for failing to respond to HAMAS terror, Peres and his government would have lost even more credibility had they failed to act after Katyushas were fired at Israeli towns and settlements. However, this operation was ended abruptly after an Israeli unit responded to a Hizbullah rocket attack launched near a UN position at Kafr Kanna. In this counterattack, over 100 refugees taking shelter in the camp were killed, leading to international pressure on Israel to end its operation. A hurried verbal agreement (similar to the one in 1994, but with the creation of a monitoring group) ended the fighting, and allowed Peres to leave for a trip to Washington. This rapid end to the operation did not increase support for Peres or Labor in the polls, and, if anything, reinforced the image of Peres as militarily indecisive and unable to maintain security for Israeli civilians.

RELATIONS WITH EGYPT

Under the Labor-led government, the peace process was consistently linked to the promise that it would lead to the end of Israel's international and regional isolation. Rabin and Peres invested a great deal of time and effort in establishing relations with Arab states, from North Africa to the Gulf. In the 1992 elections, the Labor leadership claimed that the peace process would end Israel's exclusion and the hostility of neighboring states.[64]

They made considerable progress towards this goal, but links were still fragile. Jordan was the only other Arab state to establish full diplomatic relations (after Egypt had done so in 1979). While a few other states opened small interests sections and trade bureaus, they avoided more formal ties. However, this did not prevent Peres from declaring that if he was elected, "Israel would achieve a comprehensive peace with all Arab countries in the next four years. ... We will make real peace with all the Arab countries in the coming four years."[65]

At the same time, in the context of relations with Syria and the Palestinians, and public support for the peace process, the deterioration of relations with Egypt undermined the campaign of Peres and the left. Despite expectations after the 1979 Peace Treaty, Egyptian policy towards Israel remained quite cold. In the 1992 election campaign, Rabin and Peres blamed the policies of the Likud, and the absence of progress in the peace process for this "Cold Peace." They declared that with a Labor government committed to agreements with the Palestinians, and developing agreements with other Arab states, relations with Egypt would warm considerably.

However, this did not occur, and there was little visible change in relations with Egypt. Despite numerous visits by Rabin to Egypt, and a visit by President Ezer Weizman in December 1994, President Husni Mubarak did not pay a return visit to Israel. The Egyptian government continued to place bureaucratic obstacles in the way of visits by Egyptian citizens to Israel, and the government controlled press maintained its campaign of hostility, blaming Israel for everything from AIDS to poison candy and chewing gum, as well as earthquakes, and other natural disasters. The Egyptian leadership made no move to change this atmosphere of hostility towards Israel.

In 1994, Egypt began to block agreements, particularly regarding confidence building measures, in the multilateral talks, and increased policy coordination with Syria. Cairo vetoed proposals to establish regional organizations, and in the Casablanca and Amman economic summits, sought to prevent commercial cooperation between Israeli and Arab firms. Mubarak and his Foreign Minister, Amre Mousa, embarked on an international campaign designed to isolate Israel on the nuclear issue, and to press for the dismantling of the ambiguous nuclear deterrent capability. Israeli Foreign Ministry assessments included reference to the possibility of renewed warfare with Egypt, albeit not in the near future, and the Egyptian press responded in kind. Such policies and statements led Ze'ev Schiff, widely regarded as Israel's leading military affairs analyst, to write that Egypt "has come to the conclusion that it must do everything it can to weaken Israel's military strength; to make Israel's entrance into the Middle East contingent on its agreeing to give up various elements of its strength there."[66] Egypt also used the nuclear issue as a means of returning to the center of the negotiation process, which was dominated by the other Arab parties and Israel.

The Cold Peace with Egypt reduced the credibility of Peres' and the Labor Party's efforts to present the peace process as triumphant, and provided support for the opposition's assertion that the process was being pursued without sufficient regard for Israeli interests. While perhaps not a major factor in determining the outcome of the elections, the continued hostility in relations with the first Arab state to sign a peace agreement with Israel did not increase public confidence in this process.

THE U.S. ROLE

In the 1992 election campaign, the Bush administration (which had a relatively cold and conflictual relationship with the Shamir government), visibly supported Rabin and Peres.[67] Following the elections, the links between the Rabin and Clinton governments were very close – perhaps the most cooperative in the history of relations between Washington and Jerusalem. The level of coordination regarding the peace process was high, and while there may have been differences on tactics, the U.S. could not have hoped for a better relationship. This relationship extended to the personal level, and President Clinton came to Israel and delivered moving speeches to the Knesset in 1994, on the occasion of the signing of the Jordan–Israel Peace Treaty, and led the foreign leaders at the funeral for Prime Minister Rabin in November 1995.

In contrast to Rabin, who had a strong affinity for the US, Peres was more European oriented and the closeness of both personal and political relations between the two governments was reduced to some degree. Journalists reported American "impatience" with the unrealistic visions and emphasis Peres placed on intangibles, such as transportation links between Israel and Syria, in contrast to Rabin's more concrete security-oriented approach.[68]

However, in the election campaign, the U.S. government conveyed the impression that it favored Peres and the Labor-led coalition over Netanyahu and the Likud. Peres came to Washington twice in this six month period; the first time one month after the assassination, where he was welcomed in the White House and addressed the Congress, and then in May, a few weeks before the elections. The photo-opportunities in the White House and with American leaders highlighted American support for Peres.

Following the HAMAS terror campaign in February and March, the U.S. quickly organized the summit meeting in Sharm el-Sheikh, which took place on March 13. President Clinton also paid another emotional visit to Israel. This was seen by many Israeli analysts as a blatant attempt to assist Peres (Clinton had a very short and perfunctory meeting with Netanyahu), but in the absence of any impact, and the failure to implement the decision to create a special coordination body, including Egypt and other Arab states, the political role of the summit was minimal. Indeed, some critics in Israel argued that the international extravaganza was worse than nothing, because it allowed the leaders to create the impression of fighting terror, without substantive responses.[69] Netanyahu, however, maintained his statesman-like posture, and after the short meeting the Clinton, called the summit "a boost for Israel and as an effort in the war against terrorism."

THE AFTERMATH

Foreign policy, the negotiation process, and, in particular, the expectations that were not fulfilled, have had an increasing impact on the campaign and outcome of the elections. This was the case in 1992, when the failure of the Shamir government to demonstrate progress in this process contributed to its defeat, as well as in 1996, when the failure of Arafat to prevent terrorism contributed to the defeat of Labor and Peres.

After the elections, the campaign and its results determine Israeli policies and the course of regional relations. Rabin's victory in 1992 led to a major change in Israeli policy, and the Oslo process would have been unthinkable if Shamir and the Likud had formed the next government.

Similarly, the 1996 elections brought about an immediate change in Israeli policy. The negotiators of the Oslo agreements and the group that conducted the discussions with Syria were suddenly replaced by decision-makers that are collectively more skeptical and less enthusiastic about this process.

Netanyahu's move towards the center was a combination of electoral tactics and overall political philosophy. Tactically, the pragmatic approach to the peace process was necessary to win the election. Philosophically, Netanyahu appears to be ideologically more flexible than many of his colleagues in the Likud and the Israeli right.[70] As a result of this division, the new government lacked unity on central issues. Immediately after the elections, Netanyahu and his foreign policy advisors indicated that they favored a relatively pragmatic approach and sought to maintain the frameworks developed with the Palestinians and Jordan, and to continue discussions with Syria. At the same time, many members of the Likud leadership, including ministers Binyamin Begin and Ariel Sharon, and MK Uzi Landau, the head of the Defense Committee on Foreign Affairs and Defense, held more ideological positions. (Foreign Minister David Levy is primarily motivated by personal political interests, and it is difficult to discern a consistent approach to foreign policy. However, during and after the elections, Levy was politically aligned with Sharon.)

The clash between these positions manifested itself very quickly. The ideological wing called for suspension of IDF redeployment in Hebron (delayed by Peres after the suicide bombings), opposed further withdrawals from villages in Area B, as called for in the 1995 Interim Agreement, supported increased settlement activity, and objected to any contacts with Arafat and the PNA. In the first seven months after the elections, there was no clear majority in the cabinet for proceeding with redeployment in Hebron.

However, Netanyahu recognized that his election victory, and ability to govern and be reelected depended on maintaining a pragmatic middle ground. After three months of consultations, and discussions between Abu Mazen and Dr. Dore Gold, Netanyahu's foreign affairs advisor, Netanyahu met with Arafat, and the links between Israel and the PNA resumed. (Levy and Defense Minister Yitzhak Mordechai also met with Arafat). During this period, Arafat and the PNA controlled HAMAS and blocked most efforts to conduct terrorist attacks, and Netanyahu emphasized the link between the continuation of this policy and cooperation with the PNA. The right wing of the Likud attacked the meeting between Netanyahu and Arafat, accusing the Prime Minister of betraying the Likud ideology. However, no minister resigned.

In late September, following a decision by the government to open the exit to an ancient tunnel in the Old City of Jerusalem,[71] relations with the PNA exploded in violent attacks on Israeli military checkpoints and positions in which 15 Israeli soldiers were killed by Palestinian police gunfire, and many more wounded. Although the conflict over Jerusalem provided the "match" that ignited the protests, this violence was seen as the result of the perceived lack of movement in Hebron and in the overall framework of the Oslo process. As a result, Netanyahu and Arafat met in Washington, and, under the direction of the Clinton administration, intense negotiations over security arrangements in Hebron began. However, the negotiations dragged on for many months, and tension continued.

This incident heightened the conflict within the Likud. Begin and Landau argued that the involvement of the Palestinian paramilitary forces in the violence provided incontrovertible proof that the Middle East peace process, as defined in the Oslo framework, would not provide Israel with security. At the same time, Netanyahu sought to avoid a clash with the U.S. and agreed to proceed with redeployment in Hebron, albeit with stronger security measures than had been envisioned.

Nevertheless, the internal divisions with the government and the party threaten to create an impasse in decisionmaking. If Netanyahu is unable to resist demands and pressures to greatly expand and accelerate Jewish settlement activity, particularly in the smaller settlements close to areas under PNA control, this could also lead to clashes within Israel and with the U.S. government.

Shortly after the elections, Netanyahu met with Egyptian President Mubarak and King Hussein of Jordan, thereby creating the appearance of continuity. However, Egypt hosted a summit meeting of Arab League members, in which many participants called for a slowdown in creating diplomatic and commercial links with Israel. Relations with Egypt, which had been strained under the previous government, grew worse, with threats of conflict and reports that Egypt would provide Syria with a "safety net" in the event of war with Israel. In November, the Egyptian government arrested an Israeli citizen on espionage charges.

The new government in Israel and the Hashemite regime shared interests in containing the extent of Palestinian autonomy and blocking a Palestinian state, and Palestinian control over sections of Jerusalem. During the campaign, King Hussein carefully avoided indicating any support for Peres, and Jordanian officials met with Netanyahu on a number of occasions. However, after the elections, the Jordanians did not want to be seen as cooperating too closely with Netanyahu, while on the Syrian front, Netanyahu rejected Syrian demands that negotiations resume at the point that they had been suspended under the previous government. Netanyahu refused to recognize a non-binding "non-paper" presented by the previous government, which reportedly included conditions under which Israel would withdraw from the entire Golan Heights. He also called for negotiations on Lebanon first, prior to discussions of the future of the Golan. Syria rejected these policies, and began to move some military forces from the Beirut area to the Golan sector, in what was interpreted as a threat to attack the Golan if the

Syrian demands were rejected.

Perhaps most importantly, in his first months in office, Netanyahu sought to create close links with the U.S. government. He went to Washington twice in a period of ten weeks, meeting with the President, Secretary of State, Congressional leaders, and Jewish groups. Although relations appeared to be quite cordial, differences over the Hebron agreement, the implementation of the interim agreement with the Palestinians concerning further Israeli redeployment, and Jewish settlements threatened to create friction between Israel and the U.S. This government, like all others, will be judged by its achievements and failures during its entire term in office. If Palestinian terrorism resumes, if conflicts with Egypt and Syria lead to military clashes that weaken Israel, or diplomatic conflict resumes between Jerusalem and Washington, the middle-ground or swing voters who supported Netanyahu and the Likud in 1996 are like to swing back to Labor and the left in the next election. Security and foreign policy issues, the decisions of the Israeli government in this area, and the actions and responses from the Arab world (and, to a lesser degree, the U.S.) will continue to play a major role in determining the outcome of Israeli elections.

In a broader sense, it is increasingly apparent that over the past decade, the role of foreign policy in Israeli domestic politics and as a determining factor in elections has increased steadily. A detailed analysis of this trend and the factors that explain it is beyond the scope of this chapter. However, a preliminary analysis suggests a number of factors. For the first time in many years, and some might argue, for the first time since 1948, there are choices between fundamentally different options with respect to war and peace. This process began in the late 1980s, with the secret meetings between Peres and King Hussein, and the proposal to convene an international conference. This proposal was rejected by Shamir, and the debate over this issue had an impact, albeit limited, in the 1988 elections.[72]

The development of options and choices, and the public debate over these options increased between 1988 an 1992, with the changes brought by the Gulf War and the Madrid Conference. Thus, the 1992 elections provided a stronger contrast between two opposing perspectives.[73] Between 1992 and 1996, the Labor Party had the opportunity to implement its policies, and the 1996 elections provided a referendum on its successes and failures.

This theory suggests that the role of foreign policy and the critical questions of war and peace will continue to dominate Israeli domestic politics as long as choices continue to exist. In contrast, a sudden change in the policies of the Arab states, and the end to the perception among at least some significant portion of the Israeli public that progress and peace is possible, will relegate the debate and the role of this issue in domestic politics to a secondary or tertiary factor, as was the case during most of the period from 1948 to 1988.

NOTES

1. Shimon Peres, *The New Middle East* (New York, 1993).
2. Gerald M Steinberg, "A Nation That Dwells Alone? Foreign Policy in the 1992 Elections," in Daniel Elazar and Shmuel Sandler, eds, *Israel at the Polls: 1992* (Lanham, 1995).
3. David Makovsky, *Making Peace with the PLO: The Rabin Government's Road to the Oslo Accord* (Boulder, 1996).
4. Survey performed by "Modiin Ezrachi" on behalf on the Steinmetz Center for Peace Studies at Tel-Aviv University at the end of December and January, and reported in *Ha-aretz*, February 5, 1996.
5. *Jerusalem Post*, October 14, 1994.
6. *Israeline* January 23, 1995, (Internet service provided by the Israel Information Service, Ministry of Foreign Affairs, Jerusalem).
7. Sarah Honig, "Thousands Attend Opposition Rally," *Jerusalem Post*, February 2, 1995, p.2
8. Israeline, January 24, 1995.
9. *Davar*, January 24, 1995.
10. Herb Keinon and Liat Collins, "Zion Square Flooded with Oslo 2 Protestors," *Jerusalem Post*, October 6, 1995, p.1.
11. *Israeline*, January 6, 1995.
12. Liat Collins, "Peres: We've Never Had It So Good," *Jerusalem Post*, February 13, 1996.
13. Survey of 500 adult Israeli Jews which was carried out by "Modiin Ezrachi" for the Steinmetz Center for Peace Studies at Tel-Aviv University on February 28, *Ha-aretz*, March 7, 1996.
14. Sarah Honig, "Netanyahu, Sharon Prepare Proposal for Gesher," *Jerusalem Post*, February 29, 1996, citing Teleseker poll (Channel 2), Smith poll (Channel 1); idem, "Polls Give Netanyahu Slight Lead," ibid., March 8, 1996.
15. Prime Minister Peres' remarks on Bus Bombings (Communicated by Prime Minister's Media Advisor), provided via internet by the Israel Information Service, March 4, 1995.
16 Later, Peres claimed that Arafat had requested the delay in Israeli redeployment in Hebron, in order to prevent HAMAS from taking power in the city. Nitzan Horowitz, "Peres: Arafat Asked Me to Delay the Withdrawal from Hebron, to Prevent It from Falling into the Hands of HAMAS," *Ha-aretz*, October 6, 1996, p.5A (citing Jean Daniel, *Novel Observator*, Paris).
17. Yerach Tal, "Peres: I See No Reason to Apologize for My Policies," *Ha-aretz*, March 5, 1996.
18. Jon Immanuel, "Arafat Bans Armed Groups, Promises 'Serious Steps'," *Jerusalem Post*, March 4, 1996.
19. David Makovsky, "Arafat: Israeli 'Fanatics' Provided Bombs in Sunday's Attacks," ibid., February 27, 1996.
20. Benny Begin, *Ha-aretz* March 7, 1996.
21. Liat Collins, "Netanyahu: Not a Time For Politics," *Jerusalem Post*, February 26, 1996.
22. Remarks of MK Binjamin Netanyahu before the Knesset February 26, 1996.
23. *Ma'ariv*, February 25, 1996.
24. Liat Coliins, "Netanyahu: Not a Time for Politics," *Jerusalem Post*, February 26, 1996.
25. Sarah Honig, "Likud Fuming Over Peres's Reaction to Abu Warda," ibid., March 8, 1996.
26. The survey was carried out on Tuesday and Wednesday (November 7–8, 1995) within days of the assassination of Prime Minister Rabin, and covered 501 interviewees; on Tuesday and Wednesday December 5–6; 512 interviewees on Tuesday and Wednesday January 2–3 1996; 515 on Tuesday and Wednesday January 30–31, 1996; 517 on Tuesday and Wednesday February 6–7, 1996, when details of the Likud/Tzomet bloc were not yet finalized; 508 on February 13–14; 505 on February 20–21; 508 on February 27–28; 501 on March 5–6, and 504 from a representative sample of the adult population in the country. The standard error is +/- 4 percentage points. (Published in *Yediot Aharonot* on November 10 and December 8, 1995 and January 5, February 2, February 9, February 16, and February 23, March 1 and March 8, 1996).
27. Sarah Honig, "Labor: Keep Jerusalem Out of Elections," *Jerusalem Post*, February 19,

1996; *Ma'ariv* (editorial), February 19, 1996.

28. *Jerusalem Post*, February 18, 1996.

29. *Ma'ariv*, February 4, 1996.

30. Liat Collins, "Peres: We've Never Had It So Good," *Jerusalem Post*, February 13, 1996.

31. Address by Foreign Minister Ehud Barak, to the annual Plenary Session of the National Jewish Community Relations Advisory Council, February 11, 1996.

32. Sarah Honig, "Labor: Keep Jerusalem Out of Elections," *Jerusalem Post*, February 18, 1996.

33. Peres' claims that he did not authorize these talks and agreements were undercut by the events surrounding an exchange of letters on Jerusalem in the context of the 1993 DOP. Initially, the government denied Arafat's claims that he had received side letters on Jerusalem, but later, the government acknowledged that Peres had written a letter recognizing the important role of Palestinian institutions and of the holy places for Moslems and Christians in "East" Jerusalem. The use of this term, alledgedly acknowledging the division of the city, was also atttacked by the opposition. Zeev Schiff, *Ha-aretz*, February 22, 1996; David Makovsky, "Peres Ended Beilin-Abbas Talks Last Fall," *Jerusalem Post*, February 23, 1996. The agreement reportedly included the creation of a Palestinian state and handing over the Jordan Valley to the Palestinians in the year 2007. Israel would hold onto the large Jewish settlements contiguous to the area under Israeli control prior to 1967, and the Palestinians would have an extraterritorial corridor connection Gaza and the rest of the areas under their control. With respect to Jerusalem, the central formula would have given the Palestinians control of the Temple Mount in the form of "extraterritorial" status, as well as full control over Abu Dis and Eizariya, in the eastern part of the city.

34. Gallup poll carried out on behalf of *IMRA (Independent Media Review & Analysis)*, February 15, 1995.

35. Sarah Honig, "Netanyahu: I Will Not Meet or Deal with Arafat," *Jerusalem Post*, February 6, 1996.

36. Herb Keinon, "Katsav: Likud Will Never Recognize Oslo Accords," ibid., February 7, 1996.

37. *Ha-aretz*, January 29, 1996.

38. Sarah Honig, "Netanyahu: PA Must Fulfill Its Undertakings," *Jerusaelm Post*, February 29, 1996.

39 Ibid.

40. Sarah Honig, "Netanyahu: I Will Not Meet or Deal with Arafat," ibid., February 6, 1996.

41. *Ma'ariv*, February 9, 1996.

42. *Ha-aretz*, March 4, 1996.

43. *Jerusalem Post*, February 13, 1996.

44. Ibid., February 2, 1996.

45. Deputy FM Eli Dayan, quoted in *Jerusalem Post*, February 4, 1996.

46. Address by Foreign Minister Ehud Barak, to the Annual Plenary Session of the National Jewish community Relations Advisory Council, February 11, 1996.

47. *Yediot Aharonot*, January 30, 1996.

48. *Ha-tzofeh*, February 1, 1996.

49. Liat Collins, "Likud Nearing 'Practical' Approach to PA," *Jerusalem Post*, January 30, 1996.

50. Ariel Sharon, "Questions of Principle," February 11, 1996.

51. David Rudge, "Peres: No Settlements Will be Sacrificed for Peace," *Jerusalem Post*, February 23, 1996.

52. Address by foreign Minister Ehud Barak to the Annual Plenary Session of the National Jewish Community Relations Advisory Council, February 11, 1996.

53. *Davar Rishon*, February 9, 1996

54. Ibid., February 15, 1996.

55. "Back to Square One..." (Peace Index: January 1996), *Ha-aretz* February 5, 1996 (Tami Steinmetz Center for Peace Studies at Tel-Aviv University); Asher Arian, *Israeli Security Opinion, February 1996*, JCSS Memorandum 46, University of Tel-Aviv, March 1996, p.19.

56. Ibrahim Hamidi, "al-Hayat," quoted in *Davar Rishon*, February 9, 1996.

57. Orli Azulai-Katz, *The Man Who Did Not Know How to Win: Shimon Peres in the*

Sysiphus Trap (Tel-Aviv, 1996) (Hebrew).
58. Davar Rishon, February 11, 1996.
59. Ha-aretz, January 29, 1996.
60. Jerusalem Post Staff, "Savir, Rabinovich: Syrian Agreement Possible in '96," Jerusalem Post, February 2, 1996.
61. Davar Rishon, February 9, 1996.
62. Douglas Davis and Sarah Honig, "PM: Referendum Even If We Win Elections," Jerusalem Post, February 2, 1996.
63. Yediot Aharonot, 24 Hour Section, December 24, 1995, p.9.
64. Steinberg, "A Nation That Dwells Alone?"
65. David Rudge, "Peres: No Settlements Will Be Sacrificed for Peace," Jerusalem Post, February 23, 1996.
66. Ze'ev Schiff, Ha-aretz, February 9, 1996.
67. Steinberg, "A Nation That Dwells Alone?" See also James A. Baker III (with Thomas M. DeFrank), The Politics of Diplomacy: Revolution, War and Peace, 1989–1992 (New York, 1995).
68. Steve Rodan, "Washington Growing Impatient with Peres," Jerusalem Post, February 5, 1996.
69. Elyakim Ha-etzni, "Peres's Extravaganza," ibid., March 11, 1996.
70. For the most comprehensive view of Netanyahu's political philosophy and ideology priror to the election, see Benjamin Netanyahu, A Place Among the Nations: Israel and the World (New York, 1993).
71. Both the Shamir and Peres governments had considered opening the back-end of the 2000 year-old tunnel, which reached into the Muslim Quarter of Jerusalem, but decided against it for fear of provoking violent Palestinian reactions. Netanyahu's decision to proceed with the tunnel opening may be seen as an expression of ideology, but the government was clearly unprepared for the impact and extent of opposition. Thus, although the motivation may have been, in part, ideological, and part political (responding to pressures from Jerusalem Mayor Ehud Olmert and other constituencies in the government), it is doubtful that Netanyahu would have taken this decision had the result been correctly assessed.
72. Gerald M. Steinberg, "Israel Among the Nations: Foreign Policy in the 1988 Election Campaign," in Daniel Elazar and Shmuel Sandler, eds, Who's the Boss: Israel at the Polls 1988–89 (Detroit, 1992), pp.172–92.
73. Steinberg, "A Nation That Dwells Alone?"

THE NEW POLITICS

The Direct Election of the Prime Minister: A Balance Sheet

BERNARD SUSSER

The direct election of the prime minister in the May 1996 elections represented the culmination of more than a decade of public debate and controversy.* From the mid-1980s until early 1992 when *Basic Law: The Government* was passed, the idea of directly electing the prime minister as a remedy for the ills that afflicted the Israeli political system was the subject of a great deal of academic analysis, legal dissection and ideological wrangling. Moreover, in the roughly four years that elapsed between the law's passage and its actual use, there were many attempts to subvert it or at least to postpone its implementation. Although it was massively supported by the public and received a substantial majority when voted upon in 1992, the idea of direct election was opposed by the majority of Israel's political scientists as well as by many leading political figures.

For those who hoped that the actual implementation of the law would set this often acrimonious debate to rest, the results are a disappointment. It is unlikely that this, the first direct election of the prime minister, will be clearly decisive in assessing the qualities of the law. On the contrary, those who supported the bill in the past continue to be convinced that it fulfilled its promise, just as those who opposed it are certain that it failed. Nevertheless, the strident and speculative debate that preceded the election must now change character: claims need to be squared with empirical data and speculations checked against actual

---

* This paper was written roughly two months after the election and relates exclusively to the events and trends visible at that time. In the subsequent year and a half a great deal of information and a far broader perspective have been gained – information and perspective that support a more complex and many-sided interpretation. To deal with this, however, would require a separate study.

Bernard Susser is Professor and Chair of the Political Science Department, Bar-Ilan University. He was one of the academics responsible for conceiving and drafting *Basic Law: The Government*.

results. Even if interpretation turns out to be unavoidable, henceforth it will be disciplined by the constraints of evidence and proof.

Doubtless, as with all significant electoral-constitutional reforms, it will take a number of implementations to assess the full potential of direct election. After its first use, therefore, no more is possible than an initial appraisal that must await further implementations to be fleshed out and corroborated. Inevitable as well is the confounding of the specific, substantive results with the performance of direct election itself. Critics are far more likely to be found on the losing side. (And since the large parties were both hurt in the elections, this criticism is, not surprisingly, quite widespread.) The object of this essay is then to make a very preliminary analysis of direct election in its first trial, one that focuses on the dynamics of the law itself rather than on (the very different question) of who won and who lost.

QUESTIONS TO BE DEALT WITH:

I propose to analyze direct election from a number of complementary perspectives:

1. What were the objectives of the law as formulated by its authors, and were they actually achieved?
2. What did the critics claim would occur were the prime minister elected directly? Were these predictions borne out by the facts on the ground?
3. How are we to assess direct election in the light of the general normative criteria by which electoral/constitutional arrangements are usually judged by political scientists?
4. How does what actually happened compare to what would have happened had the same results (at least in the party vote) been obtained in the old system?

Question 1

There can be little doubt about the objectives the law's drafters and defenders hoped to achieve.[1] First of all, they wished for it to be clear, as soon as the election results were tabulated, who would be prime minister and form the government. Or, to put this same idea negatively, they wanted to eliminate the confusing interregnum between the elections and the formation of the government. During this period of uncertainty – a period that regularly lasted for many weeks – there was a dangerous vacuum of power, a window of vulnerability and of national confusion in which it was entirely unclear who would be fashioning the government and what its policies would be. Direct election was meant to put an end to this interim period of uncertainty and there can be little doubt that, on this score at least, it accomplished its purposes fully. From the moment the electoral results were clear, Binyamin Netanyahu's position as prime minister was unassailable – even though his majority was razor thin.

The law's formulators had an even weightier reason for wanting the prime minister directly elected. They wished to avoid the demoralizing spectacle of coalition-making parties abjectly prostrating themselves before their potential junior coalition partners – that is, making deals that were as hateful to themselves as they were to the vast majority of the electorate. It was argued that these deals, odious though they were, would prove to be unavoidable as long as the leaders of the large parties needed to operate within the logic of the old system. These leaders knew that the opposition party might well accede to what they had refused to grant a potential coalition partner – in which case the party that stuck to its principles would be doubly damned: the opposition would be in power and the hateful practice they sought to resist would, nevertheless, be in effect.

Electoral results, the law's drafters emphasized, are often compatible with many different coalition governments. Even the President's entrusting a particular party with the responsibility for forming a coalition, is hardly the last word. With two competing parties seeking to form coalitions with the same smaller parties as necessary partners, a logic of capitulation is set into motion. Playing one large party off against the other, the small parties are in a position to constantly up the ante by transforming the promises made by one side into baseline demands for negotiating with the other. In this way, the smaller parties – at times even individual members of Knesset – extracted staggering political prices from their larger counterparts. The byzantine intrigues and nasty machinations that accompanied these negotiations created, so the law's defenders warned, a dangerous threat to the democratic consensus, a growing loss of faith in the fundamental fairness of the system.

In recent years, these small parties have been largely religious ones. This rendered political payoffs both easier for the large parties to make and, at the same time, more galling for popular sensibilities to accept. Easier to make, because religious issues were clearly secondary to the central struggle between hawks and doves that divides Israeli society. Large parties could, therefore, pay in a lesser currency in order to achieve success in the cardinal field of battle. Religious issues, it was often said in justification, will await their day in the era of peace. Since religious concessions are reversible while territorial concessions are not, it is wise to be accommodating now. It is fair to say that for as long as the smaller party's demands would have continued to avoid direct confrontation with the larger parties' central territorial and security policies, the logic and practice of the old system would have perpetuated itself.

Despite the political wisdom in acceding to religious demands, public abhorrence for the ritual of capitulation created an immense reservoir of mutual ill-will that renders the religion–state issue in Israel second to no other Western country in animosity and intensity. Religious issues are not what the great majority of the Israeli electorate vote about; hence, when they find themselves compelled to acquiesce to religious demands in order to form a workable government, there is a sense of having been party to a corrupt, demeaning bargain. That these issues relate to highly charged and sensitive matters of conscience, only aggravates the sense of repugnance.

Nevertheless, it needs to be stressed that neither the large parties that accede, nor the religious parties that demand, are to be blamed for their behavior. The large parties need to make rational calculations in regard to their interests and these lead inevitably to coalitions with the religious parties – with their inevitable price. As to the smaller parties, any party so favorably placed in the bargaining process as to be able to extract serious concessions, could be expected to do much the same. Indeed, were such a small party to desist from bringing home to its supporters all it could, it would be betraying its constituency's trust. What is amiss here, the bill's defenders claim, is not the calculations of the parties, but the very context that makes these calculations imperative.

Direct election of the prime minister, it was claimed, would alter the basic context in which coalitional negotiations take place. Since it is immediately clear who will be forming the government, the entire logic of capitulation would be avoided. Prime ministers would negotiate with their potential coalitional partners from a position of strength and exclusivity because there would be no other alternative open to the small parties. The dynamic of spiraling demands would be neutralized at the outset.

Moreover, even in the bargaining process as it takes place between the smaller parties and the elected prime minister, a major transformation will have taken place. Because there would be no alternative to the elected prime minister, the small party's options would be reduced to just two: either they join the government or they do not. With only these stark alternatives available, there is an overwhelming logic that militates toward entering the coalition. Joining the coalition means influence, budgets, patronage, ministries; staying out means impotence, privation, and irrelevance. It is difficult to see parties with even serious ideological differences with the prime minister and his party, not being tempted to do what is necessary to avoid the political wasteland.

Strengthening this logic immeasurably is the very formidable price that small parties would need to pay were they nevertheless to oppose the prime minister. The linchpin of the new system is the provision that if the prime minister does not receive a majority when he presents his government (or, for that matter, in any vote of confidence thereafter), elections follow for both the prime minister *and* the Knesset. For a party to vote for the prime minister's fall means relinquishing the parliamentary seats it has just won and, besides, facing elections against the background of having defied a prime minister elected by more than 50 percent of the vote. Moreover, would newly elected Members of Knesset, having just survived a "primary" battle, be likely to support a vote of no-confidence if this would mean a renewed struggle for a place on the party's parliamentary list? Not a likely prospect.

We might profitably compare the difference between the old and new system, it has been argued, to the difference between a seller's and a buyer's market respectively. In the old system, the small parties aim to sell their coalitional services to larger parties when there are two buyers, each of which has no alternative but to purchase just these goods being sold by the smaller parties. Not surprisingly the price skyrockets. The new system, by leaving no alternative but the elected prime minister, alters the political market's dynamic fundamentally. The smaller parties are drawn into the coalition by the promise of power and payoffs; they are deterred from resisting the prime minister because that would involve jeopardizing the parliamentary seats they have just gained. Lacking political leverage, the coalitional price the smaller parties are able to exact drops dramatically. Indeed, their power is rendered proportional to their size.

This at least is the theory. Has it been borne out by the facts? One obvious way of proceeding is to compare what the smaller parties – especially the religious parties – achieved in coalitional negotiations in 1996 to what they attained in the past.[2] This comparison should be especially instructive because the small parties grew substantially in numbers and we would expect a concomitant rise in payoffs rather than the decrease foretold by the law's supporters. In terms of payments related to the principled issues of policy and legislation, the results are striking. Only two concessions were made to the religious parties by Netanyahu and both of them are distinctly secondary – dramatically so if we judge them against previous coalitional payoffs.[3] They are: first, only Orthodox conversions will be recognized, and second, non-Orthodox members are not to be included in local religious councils. When these coalitional payments are placed alongside the initial demands of the religious parties immediately after the election results were in,[4] they appear paltry indeed. These concessions are surely not extravagant (whatever one's political views as to their "legitimacy") given their 23 seats in the Knesset – more than a third of coalition's total strength.

Neither did their ministerial representation in the new government grow in proportion to their numerical growth.[5] Where matters are not as clear is in regard to budgeting for religious institutions and the apportionment of Knesset committee chairmanships. Although unlikely, we cannot discount the possibility that the religious leadership has deliberately retreated with regard to legislative achievements, only to advance with regard to financial ones. When this government's budget is tabled, we will be in a better position to tell. The religious party's representation in Knesset Committee chairs has grown somewhat. Here too it is difficult to tell if this constitutes a bending to religious party pressures, or, as has been suggested (in camera even by religious party leaders), that Netanyahu's inexperience and his haste to form a coalition in two weeks time drove him into unnecessary payments to his coalitional partners.

One further example of enhanced prime ministerial authority will suffice. The Derekh Shlishit (Third Way) party campaigned on a platform of no concessions on the Golan Heights. (It was, in fact, on this very issue that its leadership broke away from the Labor Party.) The Likud's platform was also categorically opposed to any territorial compromise on the Golan. After the elections however, Netanyahu, wanting to leave himself as much room for manoeuvre as possible, refused to have the principle of no territorial concession explicitly incorporated in the coalitional agreement. And he got his way even on this, an issue that is so fundamental to Likud policy.

All told, the authors' intentions were largely realized: Netanyahu formed his government quickly and easily; there was no doubt from the start but that his coalition would be successfully formed; he made few concessions of major significance to his coalition partners; the initiative remained clearly with him rather than with his partners throughout the negotiations.[6]

Question 2

For their part, critics of direct election lodged a number of serious grievances. The law, they claimed, would have the following deleterious effects:

A. It would grant the prime minister dictatorial powers that would undermine Israeli democracy.

B. It might well create an oppositional Knesset, that is, a Knesset dominated by one party confronting a prime minister from the other. This would cause political gridlock.

C. The Knesset would be disabled by the power of the prime minister.

D. Negotiations between the coalition-maker and its potential electoral partners would be even more intense and unprincipled than before. Whereas in the old system negotiations took place after the elections, in direct election the negotiations would take place both before the elections, after the elections, and between the first and second rounds of the elections. This would increase rather than diminish the power of the smaller parties.

E. Direct election would lead to fragmentation. Because of the vote-splitting that the new system allowed, smaller parties would gain significantly while the larger ones would lose proportionately. Increased numbers would lead to greater rather than reduced political influence of the smaller parties.

A. Perhaps the most oft-heard reproach levelled at direct election was that the increased power of the prime minister was dangerous because it could create a one-person government able to sweep aside all opposition and criticism. Israeli democracy, with its crisis-ridden character, it was said, could ill-afford a system that was focused on a single individual. It is, of course, impossible only a few months after the election to make definitive assessments as to the future. Nevertheless, insofar as the elections and their aftermath are an indicator of things to come, there is every reason to set this criticism aside as unfounded. Although the prime minister acted swiftly and with relative ease in establishing his government, he was shown to be deeply beholden to and constrained by a variety of political actors and groups. Whatever his own clear predilections, he could not resist pressure from within his own party to appoint Dan Meridor Minister of Treasury. Nor could he, as he wished, remove the *Agaf Hataktzivim* (budget management) from the Treasury and move it into the prime minister's office. Neither could he separate *Minhal Mekarke'ey* (the Israeli Land Administration) from Deputy Minister Porush's Ministry of Housing.

Most dramatically, his desire to freeze Ariel Sharon out of his government was stymied by a combination of individuals and groups that refused to see Sharon snubbed so blatantly by Netanyahu. In the end, the rather undignified retreat that Netanyahu was compelled to beat, demonstrates both the power *and* the limitations on power imposed by the new system. On the one side, Netanyahu's power was clearly displayed in his ability to rearrange and redistribute the power of various ministries so as to create for Sharon a new Ministry for National Infrastructures. On the other, his being forced to run the gauntlet of the ministries, taking one sector from here and another from there in order to satisfy the demand that Sharon's ministry be suitably substantial, sets to rest the fear that the logic of direct election clearly leads to a prime minister so powerful as to be immune from the daily pressures of his own party, his coalition partners, the Knesset and sundry interest groups.

B. The fear of an "oppositional Knesset" figured significantly in the deliberations of the law's drafters, both academic and political. In syncretizing elements of the Parliamentary and Presidential systems ('parliadential' is an ugly but expressive term), it was recognized that the imperfect fit between the two systems was most clearly visible in the possibility of an "oppositional Knesset". Many of the law's provisions are, in fact, attempts to meet the challenge of debilitating gridlock caused by a prime minister facing a hostile Knesset. Despite these efforts, the law's detractors argued that an oppositional Knesset was a real possibility and that it posed the prospect of real disaster.

It is, of course, impossible to infer from a single election in which an oppositional Knesset did not arise, that it will continue to be so in the future. Nevertheless, the actual implementation of the system made certain of its essential characteristics more readily manifest. It became obvious that the prospect of an oppositional Knesset, although surely not impossible, was, nevertheless, quite remote. It was possible because, theoretically at least, an elected prime minister could face a Knesset in which the opposition controlled at least a *gush chosem* – a majority oppositional bloc. This might have happened only in the very unlikely eventuality that Netanyahu won the popular vote for prime minister while the Labor party's *gush chosem* of the previous Knesset was reestablished. Were this to have occurred, it is likely that a "national unity government" would have been formed – which renders the new system of direct election no different than conventional parliamentary arrangements in which national unity governments (of which Israel had its share in the last decade and a half) are the favored solution to insurmountable coalitional difficulties.[7]

Those who argued that an oppositional Knesset was a real and alarming prospect did so because they appear to have assumed that the Israeli Knesset is divided into sharply split and hermetically sealed right and left camps. Were this the case, were all of the smaller parties irrevocably committed to one or the other of the large parties, that is, unable to join the other large party in forming a coalition, their fears of an oppositional Knesset would have been justified. It would have been entirely possible that in a close race between the two camps, the results of the elections for prime minister and for the Knesset would not have been congruous.

But this is not and never has been the reality of Israeli politics. There have always been parties that could have gone either way, parties that we might call "AC/DC parties." The right and left camps typically control 40–45 percent of Knesset representation each,[8] while those parties that remain committed to neither side populate the ambidextrous center of the political map. There are, first of all, those parties that are truly uncommitted and have little difficulty in joining with either of the large parties: Yisrael Ba'Aliya (the party representing ex-Soviet immigrants) with seven seats and the Derekh Shlishit (Third Way) with four seats. And there are also those parties with tendencies in one direction that can, nevertheless, make the necessary accommodations and join with the other side as well: SHAS (the Sephardic ultra-Orthodox party) with ten seats is a clear example, and some would claim that the Mafdal (the National Religious Party) with nine seats is another.

As long as an "AC/DC" center exists in Israeli politics, the prospect of an oppositional Knesset remains quite implausible. Whichever of the candidates for prime minister wins and will form the government, these centrist parties are virtually his/her "prisoners," that is, they lack insurmountable ideological differences that would keep them out of the prime minister's government. They aspire to power, ministerial posts and budgets that are only available in the government, and they have no other alternative. Barring the total polarization of Israeli politics and the complete disappearance of parties that are ideologically barred from joining a coalition with either of the large parties – an unlikely prospect – the probabilities of an oppositional Knesset are slim indeed.

C. Some complained that with his/her augmented power, the prime minster would ride roughshod over the Knesset, that the legislative responsibility for restraining and disciplining a wayward chief executive would be seriously impaired. As of this writing some two months after the election, it is still difficult to assess this critique fully. Only the perspective of years will afford the distance and experience necessary to make a satisfactory judgement. Nevertheless, there are a number of early indications that the Knesset can still hold its own against prime ministerial *dictats*. First of all, we should note the new powers that the law itself grants the Knesset to compensate for the enhanced power of the prime minister. Among them are:

* The responsibility for secondary legislation, which had heretofore been located in the executive branch's staff, will be transferred to the Knesset.

* The Knesset can now summon any minister to appear before a Knesset committee – whereas in the past, the minister had to agree to accept such an invitation.

* An increase in the Knesset's role in regard to Declarations of a "State of Emergency".

* The Knesset can now vote no confidence in a single minister without bringing down the government.

Beyond these legal provisions, the prime minister, in practice, continued to act as any prime minister in a conventional parliamentary system would. Most notably, he did not for a moment believe that he could rule without the support of a variegated, broad-based parliamentary coalition. Despite his direct election, it was perfectly clear that he was no president in the American style. His need to capitulate to the power of his own and other parties has been already touched upon obliquely in our earlier examination of Netanyahu's travails in creating the government he seems to have envisioned. There can be little doubt that pressures from the Knesset were among the most formidable obstacles that prevented him from having his way.

Moreover, the power of the Knesset to block prime ministerial initiatives has already been attested to in at least one concrete instance. Netanyahu, in order to provide more seats for party stalwarts who had failed to enter the Knesset, attempted to pass what is known as the "Norwegian Law" – a law stipulating that ministers relinquish their Knesset seats upon assuming ministerial responsibility. As of this writing he has failed to do so despite vigorous efforts because of significant Knesset opposition – including a substantial number of opponents from his own party. Nor was his case helped by the fact that the "Norwegian" arrangement was expressly included in his coalitional agreements.

D. Critics alleged that the new system would exacerbate rather than ameliorate the problem of undue small party influence because demands for political concessions would be made not only after the elections – as in the old system – but at three different points in the electoral process: prior to the elections, between the first and second rounds of the prime ministerial contests, and after it was already clear who would be prime minister. They argued that in order to attain the more than a 50 percent majority required to elect a prime minister, the large parties would be compelled to seek small party support and to make all manner of promises in order to secure it.

We have already discussed the post-election dominance of the prime minister; what remains is the pre- and inter-election stages. During the pre-election period, a great deal of political "courting" undoubtedly took place. Apart from the *de rigeur* appearances at ultra-Orthodox assemblies, both candidates canvassed the Arab sector,[9] and made appearances at very many local and sectorial meetings of ex-Soviet immigrants, slums, and development towns. This is only natural and legitimate. Did they, however, make any hard promises, any definitive deals with other parties or groups? The answer here must be a simple "no".

There were no such agreements made because the new law mandates that all such agreements must be immediately publicized. (Informal understandings are also problematic if for no other reason than that they are entirely unenforceable.) Both the Likud and Labor were hesitant to make such deals because they feared losing voters to other parties were it known, for example, that they had made substantial concessions to the ultra-Orthodox parties. Moreover, the motivation of the larger parties to make such concessions prior to the elections is quite limited because the smaller parties cannot, in the nature of things, effectively guarantee the deliverance of certain quantities of votes. (If they can, it is because their voters are naturally disposed to vote for one of the two candidates in any case. And if that is the case, there is little need for concessions in the first instance.) Much the same is true in reverse: the desire of the smaller parties to enter into such deals with the larger ones is also quite unenthusiastic because such agreements are notoriously difficult, if not actually impossible, to enforce legally. What is more, being uncertain of which of the two candidates will win the prime ministerial election, many small parties will fear betting on the "wrong horse" and hence prefer avoiding early entangling alliances.

The real test of inordinate small party pressure did not arise in these elections because it was a two candidate race without a run-off second round. Some of the limitations on deal-making noted above would probably no longer be quite as decisive in second round voting. Fewer reservations would exist in regard to publishing agreements, for example, because voters are less likely to switch their basic loyalties whatever their camp's standard bearer has promised. (Nevertheless, with four percent of the voters having cast invalid and white ballots – that is, ballots not counted in the final tabulation – it is difficult to be certain.) In a word, the ability of the smaller parties to extract exorbitant prices for their inter-election support must remain a moot question until such time as a second round contest does in fact take place.

E. Critics charged that direct election would aggravate political fragmentation by strengthening the smaller parties at the expense of the larger ones. They argued that direct election would turn out to be counter-productive with regard to the central objective it had set for itself: the quick and easy formation of stable coalitions. Although the defenders of the law conceded that the vote-splitting possibilities inherent in the law would strengthen smaller parties somewhat, they rejected the argument that this would lead to fragmentation and increased political uncertainty. They contended that the prime ministerial election would naturally focus the vote on the two large parties. The "coattails" effect, they claimed, would more than offset the vote-splitting possibilities.[10]

Here the critics were clearly in the right – at least in regard to the factual prediction that the new system would encourage larger small parties and smaller large parties. In the event, a full 45 percent of the voters split their vote, that is, voted for a party different from the party of their preferred prime ministerial candidate. The two large parties together lost roughly 20 percent of their seats (by comparison with the outgoing Knesset) while new and smaller parties advanced by the same margin. Although Meretz fell by three seats and Moledet and Agudat Yisrael were unchanged in their parliamentary strength, SHAS, Mafdal (National Religious Party), Yisrael Ba'Aliya, Derekh Shlishit (Third Way Party) and the two Arab paries all made impressive showings.

This change can be attributed, of course, to the direct effects of the law itself. But in that case it is difficult to account for the weakness of Meretz, Moledet and Agudah all of whom should have gained as well. (If it is argued that they might have lost more were it not for the law, we are already introducing factors outside the law to account for the results.) One can also ascribe the prevalence of vote-splitting to the brilliant PR stroke (of Derekh Shlishit) that compared voting for the same party in both the prime ministerial and party vote to "putting bread in pita." Both these explanations may well be important but they do not tell the full story. Accounting for this quite dramatic shift in voting patterns requires a broader, more inclusive political perspective.

Although the two large parties early understood the unprecedented logic of direct election – to wit, victory in the prime ministerial vote is considerably more important than the results of the party vote – they seem to have exaggerated this priority into a thoroughly lopsided division of energies. They acted on the assumption that the Knesset election's outcome would be of no great import so long as their candidate for prime minister prevailed. All the party's resources were focused on victory in prime ministerial contest, while virtually nothing was invested in convincing voters that a good party showing was an integral part of electoral success. Both parties had large staffs working for the individual candidates and virtually no staff working on the party vote. Neither of the large parties used any of their TV time to counter the argument for a split vote made so effectively by the smaller parties. Indeed, they did not even attempt to distinguish themselves from their potential coalitional partners, to say nothing about directly attacking them as was the common practice in previous elections. Instead, both large parties, with their eyes on only the prime ministerial race, set up joint electioneering organizations with their likely coalition partners, culminating, on election day, with the actual merging of their staffs in a common effort to get out the vote.

This mistake will not be repeated in the next elections. The large parties will surely do all they can to emphasize the importance of the party vote, to differentiate themselves from their ideological neighbors, and to separate their electoral organizations from each other.[11] Besides, the voters themselves, having realized the effect of ticket-splitting on the larger parties may well moderate their own tendencies to abandon Labor and the Likud for the allegedly greener pastures of the smaller parties. All of this is only to say that it remains unclear whether the very high levels of ticket-spitting in this election will be a permanent feature of direct election.

There are also a number of specific explanations not related to direct election that account (at least partially) for the growth of the smaller parties. In regard to the two Arab parties, there can be no question but that the impact of the ill-considered and damaging military action in Lebanon *Invay Za'am* (Grapes of Wrath) was keenly felt. The argument put forward by the Arab parties was very cogent indeed: even left-wing Jewish parties (including Meretz, that approved the campaign) are insensitive to Arab suffering. Only a vote for Arab parties will express your outrage at the deaths and dislocation of so many Arabs. The result is clear: although about 95 percent of Arab voters cast their ballot for Peres, there was a substantial migration from the dovish Zionist to Arab parties in the party vote.

The rise of an immigrant party, Yisrael Ba'Aliya, represents quite a novelty in Israeli politics. Sensing that their interests were not a high priority for either of the large parties, ex-Soviet immigrants organized themselves politically and, in a remarkable *tour de force*, broke onto the political stage with seven Knesset seats. In a profound sense, the ability of a recently arrived, disempowered group, that felt itself marginalized by establishment politics, to take matters into their own hands and enter the political stage with such force is a badge of honor for Israeli public life. It will henceforth be difficult to ignore their remonstrations and, consequently, will likely serve to bring them closer to the Israeli mainstream, to moderate rather than exacerbate the fractionalizing tendencies of an alienated and angry minority.

Doubtless, a substantial part of this vote would have gone to the immigrant party regardless of the voting procedures employed. Their central concerns were not so much with Peres or Netanyahu (although they preferred the latter by a substantial margin after having supported Labor in the 1992 elections) but with their own travails in a new and perplexing reality. Hence, it is simplistic and unconvincing to attribute their spectacular rise simply to the peculiarities of the new system. Moreover, their forsaking the large parties was not an unforeseeable eventuality; they had long complained about the condescension and neglect with which they were treated by mainstream Israeli politics.

The large parties, for their part, invested little in "on the ground" work in the immigrant communities. They appear to have operated on the assumption – one that was not directed, as we shall see, only toward the Olim – that the sporadic budget, the coopting of a leader or two, the valedictory rhetoric of "ingathering the exiles" – would be sufficient to secure the loyalty of these voters. (The fact that the Labor Party lost control of the Histadrut, both reflects and actively perpetuates this estrangement from the day to day political work in neighborhoods and places of work). We may conclude then that the very extensive vote-splitting among the Olim was perhaps facilitated by a two vote arrangement but it was surely not generated or driven by the logic of the new system.

In any event, an immigrant party will not be a permanent feature of Israeli politics. In the not too distant future, their votes will return to the parties preferred by veteran Israelis. Although some of the more visible and talented leaders may well find their way into other parties, the life-expectancy of an immigrant party is limited, ironically, by its own successes in redressing its constituency's grievances.

The dramatic growth of SHAS (from six to ten Knesset seats) was also facilitated but not caused by, the two-vote system. SHAS supporters are convinced that they have been short-changed in the market place of Israeli life. Their response has been to organize locally (with remarkable energies) in a great many areas: education, social services, welfare, and religious counselling. Like the Olim, only preceding them by a decade or so, they combined systematic "groundwork" with political organization. And they too have succeeded in raising the visibility and legitimacy of Sephardi, socio-economic and religious concerns – with a concomitant rise in self-esteem, confidence and sense of full membership in Israeli society. This too is not the stuff of which "fragmentation" is made.

Indeed, they have been so successful in their efforts that they are displacing the Likud as the voice of the "second" Israel. Having long ago ceased to be a palpable presence on the ground, it is no wonder that the Likud is progressively losing its dominance to SHAS. The Likud has centered its concerns on the needs of its central party organization and (much like Mapai in its heyday) has attempted to secure the periphery via patronage, budgetary largesse, cooptation, and warmed-over rhetoric. It has become what might be called a "superstructure" as opposed to an "infrastructure" party. Much as with the Labor party's loss of the Histadrut, the Likud's gradual displacement by SHAS both reflects and perpetuates their estrangement from the street and the work place. (It must be noted, if only parenthetically, that for many Sephardi voters deserting the Likud was a gesture of anger and disappointment over the perceived "betrayal" of Sephardi causes by David Levy in the pre-election period.)

The gradual decline of the Likud and the rise of SHAS did not begin with, nor is it attributable to, direct election. It seems fair to speculate that at least some, if not most of the shift from the Likud to SHAS would have taken place under the old system as well. Our conclusion should be, therefore, that the success of "communitarian" parties like Yisrael Ba'Aliya and SHAS reflect both their superior groundwork[12] and the failing "remote control" strategies of the large parties – at least as much as the dynamics of two-ballot voting. Far from representing a disintegration of Israeli public life into clannish fiefdoms as has been charged, the strong showing of these "communitarian" parties portends a growing "stake in society" for otherwise marginalized and potentially disruptive groups, a political enfranchisement leading to full membership in Israel public life.

One last autonomous factor accounting for the weakness of the larger parties relates to the growing impasse that divides them from Israel's religious community. In the past, the Labor Party displayed considerably more pluralist latitude than it does today. Apart from satellite Arab parties, it had a not-insignificant religious cohort organized as the *Oved Hadati* (religious worker). In the 1992–96 term especially, this catch-all pluralism gave way to an image of monochromatic Ashkenazi secularism and cosmopolitanism. Labor became associated – especially in the religious community – with a well-heeled, Western, professional class living in very specific genteel, up-market neighborhoods, whose objective it was to create a consumerist, permissive, high-tech, non-traditional Israel in a "new Middle East". Labor's frequent clashes with religious settlers and their supporters during their term in office, as well as the cozy partnership with the combatively secular Meretz only sharpened this image. Meretz's election campaign, which included TV images of great masses of Haredim above which the logo "stop them" appeared, made a Labor vote unthinkable for the bulk of religious Jews. Add to this the growing consolidation of the overwhelming majority of the religious community around religious-right-wing precepts, and the impasse becomes quite unbridgeable.

The Likud too made a clear step in the secular direction when it included Tzomet into its ranks. Tzomet, which in many ways constitutes the right-wing analogue to Meretz, is no favorite of the religious community. Even if Tzomet effectively ceased existing after the merger with the Likud, the idea of voting for a party that called itself Likud/Tzomet/Gesher must have given religious Likud voters a great deal of pause and, in the end, driven many of them into more congenial expressions of their position via the National Religious Party or SHAS. In a word, religious voters who might otherwise have supported one of the large parties were effectively deterred from doing so by the secularizing tendencies that had, ostensibly, overtaken both parties. The result was a drop in support for the large parties and a swelling of support for the religious parties – even before considering the effect of the newly adopted two-ballot system.[13]

All of this, however, is prefatory to the central issue raised by the critics. The new system, they argue, by favoring the smaller parties, diminishes rather than augments the ability of governments to repulse sectarian demands and to rule effectively. Evaluating this critique brings us directly to the third general objective we set for ourself at the outset: examining direct election in the light of the general normative criteria by which electoral/constitutional arrangements are commonly appraised. We can best judge the soundness of the critic's charge in the context of this discussion.

Question 3

Two general criteria for electoral arrangements are regularly applied. The first is: does the system in question provide an equitable, expressive, and democratic framework within which the voters can satisfactorily signify their choice? To this the answer must be a definite "yes". The two-ballot arrangement is a major improvement in that it affords voters considerably more control over the expression of their preferences than was available in the simple choice between parties. Voters operating within the two-ballot system can fine-tune their choices, balance their votes against each other and, in general, make far more sophisticated calculations than were ever possible before. It is, in fact, just this finer control over the implications of one's vote that accurately revealed (rather than created) the cleavages marking the terrain of Israel's electoral topography, cleavages that had been occluded by the old system's undiscriminatingly simple choice of a party. This much is obvious.

The second criteria, which brings us back to the critics' allegations, asks whether the system provides for effectiveness, stability and governability. Balancing the expressive capacities of a system with its contribution to effective government is mandatory lest overly expressive electoral arrangements create turmoil and confusion. Does the new system provide such effectiveness?

Earlier on, we examined the initial coalition-making period and noted that Netanyahu created his government swiftly, easily and with few substantive concessions to his smaller partners. The recognition on part of the smaller parties that there was no choice but to accept the prime minister's offer or to face reelection, transformed them into reasonably docile negotiators. Which is only another way of saying that the augmented numerical strength of the smaller parties was more than balanced by the authority and decisiveness that direct election affords the prime minister.

Although the new system allows previously un- or under-represented groups to enter the political mainstream, it effectively limits their ability to extort hateful concessions from a needy government. In the past, small parties were able to make extravagant demands and have these demands met because the threat of leaving the coalition and forming a new government with the opposition parties was a "doomsday" scenario for the large party in power. Rather than see their rivals make the repugnant concessions while they were relegated to the opposition, they were willing to make whatever deals were necessary to placate their smaller partners. It is critical to keep in mind that these weighty concession were granted *although* the large parties were larger and the small parties were smaller than they are at present. Despite the appearance of a patron–client relationship between the coalition-maker and its partners, in the old system the numerical superiority of the large parties did not translate into superior power because it was fatally undermined by the "logic of capitulation" we described above.

This "logic of capitulation" is effectively nullified by direct election. First of all, governments cannot be brought down by obstreperous coalition partners. The most smaller parties can do, and this only in the event that they are willing to vote themselves out of office, is to have the contentious issue decided in new elections for both Knesset and prime minister. It hardly needs to be explained why under these rules, sectarian demands lose their sting. Second, given a multi-party system operating within the logic of a "buyer's market," the departure of one party from the coalition may well be offset by the eager entrance of another. (The withdrawing smaller party may also leave the coalition without actually voting no-confidence, in which case the government continues to function even if it does not command a parliamentary majority). Only when there are no alternatives to the departing party, and when this party is willing to put its future on the line by voting "no confidence" and facing general elections, can a sitting government be changed – and then only by popular mandate. The stability-enhancing qualities of this design are manifest. It should be added, that issues critical enough for a coalition partner to stake its future on, legitimately deserve to be submitted to popular vote for resolution.

There is another ironic stabilizing quality to direct election that ought to be mentioned. To the degree that parties joining the coalition have been successful in the popular elections, to that very degree will they be unwilling to challenge the coalition-maker – for fear that their successes will not be repeated in new elections. In the recent elections, for example, at least SHAS, Mafdal (National Religious Party) and Yisrael Ba'Aliya (the ex-Soviet immigrant party), find themselves in this curious position. Having made what are very possibly one-time gains, they are effectively locked into Netanyahu's government. Ironically, their impressive showing limits their room for manoeuvre. If we add to this that the lion's share of their constituents voted for Netanyahu, we begin to understand why disruptive behavior on their part would be quite counter-productive in terms of their own welfare.

Beyond its stability-enhancing qualities, direct election also works against the alarming rise of political extremism in Israel. In the recent elections, both candidates, responding to the inherent logic of direct election, did all they could to pitch their arguments to the political center. So much so that complaints arouse on all sides that the campaign messages of Netanyahu and Peres were basically indistinguishable – either security with peace or peace with security. Because ideological purism is punished by majoritarian systems, the campaign, despite the momentous issues at stake, was reasonably tame and civil. In a word, direct election fosters the rise of moderate, centrist political leaders. (Indeed, it is arguable that it was his position as a directly elected prime minister that provided Netanyahu with the requisite control and authority to freeze the extreme right-wing party, Moledet, out of his coalition).

We conclude then that the direct election of the prime minister is first, highly equitable in that it facilitates the rise of otherwise neglected sectors of the population and second, stability-enhancing in that it limits the ability of coalition partners to pressure the government unfairly. Direct election brings together two normally antagonistic qualities: greater expressiveness *as well as* greater governability. The key to this unusual balance lies in the position of the prime minister who, owing his position to popular election rather than to a parliamentary majority, can effectively rebuff the immoderate demands of coalition partners. There is then a piquant paradox to our conclusions: in the old system, when numerically large coalition-forming parties faced numerically small coalition partners, this did not translate automatically into stable, effective government; in the new system, when smaller coalition-makers face larger coalition-partners, stability and effectiveness are nevertheless achieved through the agency of a directly elected prime minister.

It is easy to understand why first blush reactions to the results led to fallacious and short-sighted conclusions, why the report of small party growth and large party decline created the optical illusion that the system had failed. More circumspect examination gives the lie to these impressions. Many of the critics' judgements of failure rested on the unstated, partisan premise that the large parties properly ought to receive a more generous share of Knesset representation – in the range of, say, 40 seats.[14] Their decline to lower levels was taken to be *ipso facto* proof of failure. There is, of course, no reason to make such an assumption. Even if all our analyses demonstrating that there were specific, powerful, autonomous forces leading to large party decline and small party growth – reasons that will not necessarily be operative in future elections – should prove to be unfounded, there is no judicious reason for the conclusion that the system has failed. If direct election can provide a sensitive barometer of popular sentiment while, at the same time, guarantee effective and stable government, it should have our warm support.[16]

Question 4

This conclusion is only reinforced when we consider what would have happened in the 1996 elections had roughly similar results been obtained under the old system. Without entering into grisly detail, the rising *deja vu* images of patently corrupt deals, of political "clearance sales," of extravagant prices paid for coalitional services rendered, of the few dominating the many, are enough to induce shudders. Given his party's greater support among the Knesset fractions, Netanyahu, in all likelihood, would have been called upon to form the government, and it probably would have been one very similar to the one that today rules the State of Israel. The differences would have been (1) in the time it took to create, (2) in the spectacular price the smaller parties exacted, (3) in the popular revulsion at the spectacle, and (4) in the vulnerability of the government to political extortion even after it had been sworn in.

For it must be understood that past spectacles would have returned – with a vengeance. Israeli politics has become increasing divided and ideologically fraught, to the point of tragic political assassinations. The fault line running between a territorial-traditional and a non-territorial-cosmopolitan perspective deepens apace, and, what is more, cleaves the country into two virtually equal camps. Both sides perceive the issues in contention as life and death matters, as determining the very character of the Jewish State. Both are determined to create irreversible "facts on the ground," whether via negotiated mutual concessions with Arab leaders or via settlements. It should cause no wonder that in such a charged and pivotal moment, each of the large parties would be willing to pay virtually any price to have *its* vision of a future Israel triumph over that of its rival. Nor should it occasion surprise that given the momentous stakes involved, religious gurus, sectarian politicians and unscrupulous adventurers, by brokering their critical coalitional leverage, would determine the outcome of this most basic of struggles while feathering their own nest in the process. The "logic of capitulation" would be irresistible.

There is, I believe, a final and very weighty reason to support direct election, one that relates to what has just been said. Over the course of the roughly three decades since the Six Day War, Israel has moved from being a country marked by (what Political Scientists call) "cross-cutting cleavages" to one that is increasingly characterized by "overlapping cleavages." (Although this subject surely requires a separate, comprehensive study, what is important for us here are the general conclusions rather than the detailed analysis.) In the middle 1960s, the degree of correlation between the major Israeli socio-demographic categories such as religiosity, ethnic origin, income, education on the one hand, and one's political views on the other, were relatively weak. Religiosity, for example, was entirely compatible with dovish views. The Haredi world, to take one concrete illustration, was not notably aligned with either dovish or hawkish positions. In varying degrees, much the same holds for the other enumerated categories.

This is the world of "cross cutting cleavages" in which knowledge of one's socio-demographic profile does not entail – at least not with high degrees of probability – one's political views, any more than knowledge of one's political views provides a reliable indicator of one's socio-demographic attributes. "Complex identities," in which assorted attributes correlate with diverse political views, are abundantly present. So that if one is unhappy about policy in area A, satisfaction in area B will moderate the degree of anti-government animus. Because cleavages do not "aggregate," that is, because specific political views are not held by groups with recurrent and predictable sets of characteristics, political contention tends to be moderate, more in the consensual than the conflictual style.

Overlapping cleavages, by contrast, tend to generate contentious, conflict-ridden societies. Here, cleavages aggregate: resentments are piled one upon another, disaffection in one area tends to inflame and amplify bitterness in others. Predictable sets of characteristics go together with predictable political positions so that the perception of a "us" ranged against a "them" comes to predominate.

It is toward this unenviable position that Israel has been moving. The correlation between political views and "attribute packages" has reached high levels of statistical "significance". Religiosity, Sephardic ethnic origin, lower income, and moderate to low educational attainments each correlate with hawkish, right-wing views. When they are "aggregated," the degree of predictive power becomes quite formidable. By contrast, liberal/secular views, Ashkenazic ethnic origin, middle and higher income and higher educational attainments correlate with dovish, left-wing views. Similarly, when they are "aggregated," prediction enjoys a high degree of accuracy. To be sure, there are religious, Sephardic, lower income and simply educated supporters of the "left," and secular, Ashkenazic, higher income and well educated individuals who support the "right," but they are becoming a relatively small minority within their respective camps.

Pitted against each other and roughly equal in numbers, the acrimonious and ideologically over-heated political style necessarily intensifies. Because the Knesset is elected proportionately, it mirrors this rancorous divide with great faithfulness – threatening to undermine the common basis of Israeli politics. As such, its ability to provide focused and steady leadership is seriously impaired. It is the arena of struggle and division, not the focus of resolute direction and stability. A political system resting on the slim, inconstant,[15] often volatile majorities in the Knesset is, therefore, in danger of losing both its balance and its legitimacy.

Since so many will owe so much to so few in the formation of coalitions, the threat of political extortion, recurrent crises and popular demoralization looms large. As parliamentary divisions deepen, the more necessary it becomes to provide for a decisive, extra-parliamentary voice of authority. A directly elected prime minister, resting on a popular vote of confidence, goes far toward providing such a voice of leadership. Secure in office, reasonably immune from sectarian pressures although unable to dismiss parliamentary and party interests out of hand, a directly elected prime minister promises the steadying hand that is mandatory in an increasingly stormy political sea.

NOTES

1. They are documented in many places. One systematic presentation can be found in *Direct Election of the Prime Minister* (September, 1990) jointly published by the Jerusalem Center for Public Affairs and Constitution for Israel. It contains explanations of the bill's objectives and speeches of the four Knesset members (David Libai, Uriel Lynn, Amnon Rubenstein and Yoash Tsiddon) who sponsored it. See also the well documented accounts of Gidon Alon in *Bechira Yeshira Chukah Le'Yisrael* (Direct Election) (Tel-Aviv, 1995) and Guy Bechor in *Chukah Le'Yisrael* (A Constitution for Israel) (Jerusalem, 1996).
2. This, of course, does not apply to the two new parties: Israel Be-aliya and The Third Way.
3. For a more detailed codmparison see Giora Goldberg, *Ha'aretz,* July 4, 1996, B3.
4. See, for example, *Ha'aretz*, May 30, 31, June 1, 2, 1996.
5. See Goldberg, op.cit.. Although the Likud's Knesset fraction (32 seats) was smaller than the combined representation of its coalition partners (34 seats), the Likud still maintained a majority in the government.
6. We should add to the law's accomplishments its successfully limiting the government's size to 18 members. Otherwise, the government would surely have reverted to more than 25 members which was standard in past years.
7. Had Peres won the prime ministerial race, an oppositional Knesset would have been virtually impossible because the parties of the left – Labor, Meretz and the Arab parties – are ideologically barred from joining a right-wing government, while some of the parties on the right – SHAS (and perhaps Mafdal) as well as Olim and Derekh Shlishit in the center – are able to join a left-wing government.
8. There is here a sharp and important asymmetry between the right and the left-wing camps. A left-wing coalition is very difficult for a right-wing prime minister to penetrate. With the exception of a "national unity government," Labor, Meretz and the Arab parties are unavailable for a Likud-formed coalition. On the other hand, the single small party that is "unavailable" to a Labor-led coalition is Moledet. The religious parties, although they are "natural allies" for the Likud, cannot be ruled out as coalition partners for a Labor government. The 40-45 percent figures relate to these camps of natural allies.
9. One of the more interesting effects of the new law was Netanyahu's electioneering in the Arab sector. Realizing that their votes could be decisive, he promised to make for true equality between Arabs and Jews in budgets, in educational grants, etc.

10. Although the defenders were wrong on this count, the focussing effect of direct election was, nevertheless, powerfully felt in the pre-election period. It militated toward reducing the field of candidates to only two. Indeed, Netanyahu was willing to decimate the Likud by transferring a third of Knesset representation to Tzomet and Gesher so as to enhance his chances in the prime ministerial race.

11. There are, nevertheless, built-in limits to the degree of differentiation and criticism possible in a two-ballot system. The large parties dare not attack their satellites too intensely, lest they deter the smaller party's supporters from voting for their prime ministerial candidate, or, alternatively, drive them into casting a white ballot. The smaller parties are constrained in their attacks on the larger ones by the same logic: if the critiques are overly caustic, their own supporters will hesitate to vote for the prime ministerial candidate favored by the small party.

12. Although the National Religious Party's growth is probably more directly related to the change in system than that of any other party, let it only be noted that it too is a party with a substantial infra-structure – Bnei Akiva, schools, Yeshivot, settlements, etc.

13. It is difficult to speculate about the fate of The Third Way party had the old system still been in effect. That there was considerable dissatisfaction with the choice between the two large parties and their candidates – which would have favored a vote for Derekh Shlishit – is dramatically evidenced in the nearly 150,000 invalid and white ballots, many of which, it may be conjectured, were cast by Third Way supporters. If this turns out to be the case after closer inspection of the vote, The Third Way would have done well even under the old system.

14. This is not the first time that large parties have fallen to these levels. In 1977, for example, Labor received only 32 seats.

15. It is not likely that the law will be substantially changed in the foreseeable future. All the smaller parties oppose change, Netanyahu would prevent its alteration on the Likud's side, and the two front-runners to inherit the Labor Party's leadership, Barak and Ramon, both are firm supporters of the bill.

Elections 1996:
The Candidates and the
"New Politics"

MICHAEL KEREN

In their first direct elections for prime minister on May 29, 1996, Israelis have voted for the unknown. The young, witty, good-looking Binyamin Netanyahu, who seemed to have landed in his country's TV boxes from nowhere just a decade earlier, had won the elections over the exhausted Shimon Peres, who seemed to have been there forever.

Political commentators have understandably focused on the differences between the two candidates: their ages, their respective characters, their media skills, their economic orientations, and their approach to the peace process. In a two-candidate race, it is natural to point out the differences between the contenders. Here, however, I focus on the similarities between the two candidates which, I argue, outweigh the differences to an extent which allows us to describe the 1996 elections as an important phase of the "new politics" in Israel.

In what follows, I describe the main features of the "new politics" and the ways in which both candidates – Netanyahu and Peres – had been immersed in them. I then discuss the implications of the "new politics," as exhibited in the 1996 elections, for Israel's future.

THE "NEW POLITICS"

The notion of "new politics" has been proposed by political scientists in the 1970s in reference to Western Europe where political agendas, formerly dominated by class conflicts, began to reflect new political concerns, such as arms control, ecology, or minority rights, and new political movements devoted to these concerns began to emerge.[1] Observers noted that the old European party structure, based on class cleavages, was giving way to new forms of political action. This observation was reinforced by studies identifying value shifts in modern

Michael Keren is Associate Professor of Political Science, Tel-Aviv University.

industrial societies, and subsequent changes in political participation, mobilization and leadership.

Foremost among these were Ronald Inglehart's studies conducted at the University of Michigan.[2] Inglehart had shown that value priorities of Western publics were changing from the materialist emphasis on physical sustenance and safety to a "post-materialist" emphasis on belonging, self-expression and the quality of life. He traced this change to the high level of economic and physical security in the postwar era and associated it mainly with the student generation of the 1960s. As the students grew older, Inglehart claimed, post-materialist norms were introduced by them into the professions, the civil service and politics:

> "Post-Materialism" has moved out of the student ghetto. By 1980, a post-materialist outlook had become more common than a materialist one among young technocrats, professionals and politicians of Western countries. As experts, congressional staffers and members of ministerial cabinets, post-materialist had direct access to the command posts of the sociopolitical system.[3]

While critics disapproved of Inglehart's insistence upon a linear value shift,[4] his findings contributed to an understanding of changes occurring in modern industrial societies, both on the level of mass mobilization and of elite politics. The emergence of political movements, notably the "Greens," whose range of concerns and forms of action differed substantially from those of traditional European parties, was attributed to post-material priorities. Russell Dalton, for example, has shown a decline in the importance of political parties for mass political behavior and a shift toward "cognitive mobilization," that is, the mobilization of sophisticated individuals who lack party ties.[5] The growing tendency in Europe and the Commonwealth to personalize political power in party leaders, turning elections into American-like contests between personalities, was attributed to the weakening of the electoral significance of class, accompanied by the growth of electronic media.[6]

New forms of political action were identified in modern industrial societies, notably a strong link between knowledge and policy. Knowledge was seen as playing an increasing role in mediating policy decisions. Professional experts were described as intermediaries between elite decision makers and the groups toward which specific policies were aimed, and their growing influence in shaping the discussion of policy alternatives, if not the specific outcome, had been acknowledged.[7] The rising importance of knowledge was related to the declining importance of class. Sociologists drew the model of a "new class" – a stratum of highly-educated young technocrats who defied traditional class-based norms in their respective societies and took an adversary stance toward them.[8]

On the level of political leadership, "new realities" were identified. Peter Drucker wrote that old issues and programs were nullified so as to force political leaders to become bland, eschew issues and commit themselves as little as possible: "The press, the intellectuals, the political commentators want traditional politics, with their excitement, their sharp clashes, their clear-cut choices. The politicians know better – and they get elected."[9]

"NEW POLITICS" APPLIED

The press, the intellectuals and political commentators on Israel have hardly acknowledged the "new politics." Considering Israel a unique case, operating by different rules than those by which modern, industrial societies operate, analysts insisted that the Israeli party system, originating in the social and ideological diversity of the pre-state era, was congruent with class, religious and ethnic cleavages.[10] More than reflecting on the unique features of the Israeli case, such contentions stemmed from the difficulty of abandoning classical analyses of European party politics and acknowledging Israel's new realities.

Israel that went to polls in 1996 had an annual income per capita of $16,000, high-tech enterprises, a strong middle class, a flourishing business sector, a wide professional stratum applying expertise to problem solving in spheres such as security, immigrant absorption, and social welfare, a free press bringing to public attention universal concerns such as ecology, globalization and feminism, a diffused electronic media, lively political discourse, and many other indicators of a modern, industrial state.

Under these conditions, election analyses based on mapping of cleavages is as misdirected as the tendency to place the 1996 candidates on opposite poles. By presenting Peres as candidate of the rich, secular, Ashkenazi cluster and Netanyahu as candidate of the poor, religious, Sephardi one, as had commonly been done, lots of information is missed. For one thing, this portrayal does not explain the tame nature of the election campaign, in spite of the assassination of a prime minister just a few months earlier, the large floating vote, the need sensed by the parties to professionalize their campaigns, the similarity in messages conveyed by both sides, and the surprise inflicted on the pollsters by the election results.

The surprises inflicted on pollsters time and again,[11] can be attributed to the fact that their projections are largely based on traditional class considerations rather than on the "new politics." The "new politics" does not imply that old cleavages disappear but that they can no longer be taken as prime determinants of electoral behavior, definitely not in the case of direct elections for prime minister. Clusters of norms that are not necessarily related to fundamental social divisions over class, religion or ethnicity must be accounted for, and techniques of "cognitive mobilization" may be as influential in determining the election outcome as socio-political affiliations. The "new politics" also implies that the traditional fear of government changes in Israel (better known as "upheavals") must give way to the realization that elections do not necessarily entail a significant change in political course.

In applying the notion of "new politics" to the 1996 elections in Israel, three attributes of the candidates stand out: their post-material norms, their reliance on cognitive rather than partisan mobilization, and their pragmatic approach to problem-solving.

Post-Material Norms

A generation apart, the two contenders nevertheless propounded in their speeches and writings a similar image of the good society. That image is not identical with the post-material model but shares many of its facets. To both, the good society was the modern, industrial, democratic state resembling the United States. Peres, the former socialist, was more concerned with social engineering and Netanyahu, the MIT graduate, with the free-market. Both, however, faced the same enemy – fundamentalism – which challenged their vision of the modern, technological Israel.

Much of Peres' adult life was spent in technocratic roles. Born in 1923, he was active since an early age in the *Ha-no'ar Ha-oved* youth movement affiliated with the workers' party – MAPAI. During the War of Independence, he was recruited by Prime Minister David Ben-Gurion to fulfil tasks concerning weapons acquisition and manpower policy. After the war, Peres served in the ministry of defense for many years. In 1953, at the age of 29, he was nominated its director general, and from 1959, when he became Knesset member, served as deputy minister of defense, a position he held until 1965.

In 1965, with Ben-Gurion's secession from MAPAI, Peres joined him in forming the small RAFI Party, which advocated an updated socialism relying more on science and technology than on the individual labourer. As RAFI's Secretary-General, he led the move towards its reunification with MAPAI and other parties to form the Labor party in 1969. Between 1969 and 1977, Peres held various cabinet positions in Labor governments, such as minister of communication and transportation. Between 1977 and 1984, he headed the Labor opposition in the Knesset, from 1984 to 1990 served as prime minister and in several ministerial posts in the national unity governments of the 1980s. In 1992 he was nominated foreign minister in Yitzhak Rabin's government and in November 1995, after Rabin's assassination, replaced him as prime minister.

In all these roles, Peres served as an advocate of the modern, industrial state. Under his leadership, the defense ministry took over the armaments industry, expanded the aviation industry, established electronic industries, and constructed the nuclear reactor in Dimona. Peres' speeches and writings always called for industrialization, modernization, economic productivity, national planning, the encouragement of higher education, and the extended use of science and technology. At a time in which leftist ideologies still cherished agrarian values, Peres stressed the importance of industrial development, claiming that it was mainly industry, not agriculture, which demanded an individual's ingenuity, resourcefulness, and vision.[12] Peres was often criticized for his technocratic zeal, especially when, as minister of communication, he demanded that Israel join the cybernetic revolution.

It is possible to identify the same cluster of preferences in Peres' expressions of the 1990s. A close look at his eulogies of Rabin, for instance, reveals how overwhelmed they were by the vision of the modern, industrial state. The late prime minister was portrayed, rather inaccurately, as concerned with education, science, economics and other technocratic values:

> In this room, I found great plans for the future. They are waiting to be realized. We have never been closer to becoming a state of science and technology than we have in the past few years. Israel has experienced the most impressive rate of growth in the Western hemisphere. Yitzhak understood that political strength translates itself into economic strength.[13]

Not only was Rabin's memory "coopted," the young mourners of the late prime minister were also expected "to alight in the next century, able to compete with other young people from around the world, proudly carrying the torch of the new Israel. Ultimately, Yitzhak Rabin's leadership concentrated on this great change."[14] The great change was one toward the modern era in which Israel would reach the level of national income comparable to that of the United States and Europe. What better place to present that vision (as Netanyahu would a year later) than the U.S. Congress:

> As the end of the 20th century is nearing, it can verily be described as the American century, the century of America. America now charts a way of life that has made competitive creativeness the engine of economic development in practically every corner of the world.[15]

Netanyahu's speech before Congress in July, 1996 sounded strikingly similar:

> In the 19th century, citizens of all free states viewed France as the great guardian of liberty. In the 20th century, every free person looks to America as the champion of freedom.[16]

Although Likud's Netanyahu catered more to the congressional conservatives than did Labor's Peres, the conception of the United States as the role model for Israel was the same:

> We have a common vision of how societies should be governed, of how civilization should be advanced. We both believe in eternal values, we both believe in the Almighty. We both follow traditions

hallowed by time and experience. We admire America not only for its dynamism, and for its power, and for its wealth. We admire America for its moral force.[17]

This normative stance can be largely explained by Netanyahu's biography. Born in 1949, he was drafted in 1967 into the army where he served for five years in an elite commando unit, earning the rank of captain. After his military service he studied architecture and business administration at the Massachusetts Institute of Technology from which he graduated in 1975. He was employed as marketing director for a big furniture company. From 1982 to 1984 he served in the Israeli embassy in Washington and from 1984 to 1988 as Israel's ambassador to the United Nations. He was elected to the Knesset in 1988, served as deputy foreign minister and deputy minister in Prime Minister Yitzhak Shamir's office. In 1993, in a meteoric move, he won the nomination as leader of the Likud Party.

In all the above roles, Netanyahu was strongly indulged on expertise. Following a tradition evolving among young contenders to political office in Western democracies, his political claim was largely based on his self-portrayal as an expert on terrorism, about which he wrote and edited several books.[18] His polished media appearances may also be attributed to his professional approach to public relations. While Netanyahu, catering to a large Jewish-fundamentalist constituency, did not articulate the role of expertise in modern democracies as frequently as Peres, an analysis of his speeches reveals the norms and preferences of the modern industrial state. He said in his victory speech:

> I am committed to the values of freedom and democracy, just as I am committed to the eternal values of the Jewish people, and there is no contradiction between the two...On the basis of these values we intend to make social and economic changes in the country.[19]

Though addressing a loud, impassioned crowd of cheering right wingers, the changes Netanyahu proposed in that speech were more in line with his upbringing than with their own:

> We believe that every citizen is entitled to equal opportunity to realize his full potential. We will finally introduce a truly free market in Israel. An economy which is not controlled by bureaucrats, an economy that does not stunt initiative... Every child in Israel will receive the means to develop his or her abilities so he can be part of the world of tomorrow and succeed in it.[20]

A week later, in his presentation of the new government to the Knesset, Netanyahu revealed his blueprint for success in the "world of tomorrow." It differed somewhat from Peres' vision of social transformation dependent upon the achievements of science and technology. As a right-winger, he objected to all forms of social engineering, putting his faith in the forces of the free market. However, the American-like good society waiting at the end of the road was remarkably similar:

> Members of the House, there is a solution. We can reduce the hardships; we can give a real future to people without hope. But first, we must solve the basic problems of the Israeli economy: unbridled spending, national debt at record levels, inflation ... We must tackle these problems. As a prime minister, I see addressing economic problems as a central task. We shall shape a policy that will stabilize the market and bring real growth and prosperity. This requires wide-range privatization, dismantling monopolies, encouraging initiatives and creating a competitive climate.[21]

Cognitive Mobilization

Both candidates had risen to the highest leadership posts in their respective parties while remaining, in some ways, outsiders. Although skilful in playing the political game and winning nominations, neither of them was ever competing as the candidate preferred by the party apparatus or embraced by its grass-roots. It is hard to tell whether their outsider's status stemmed from the candidates' adherence to post-material norms or whether these norms were developed as a response to their outsider's status. Be that as it may, Peres and Netanyahu were both employing unconventional means to mobilize political support.

Peres' political career began under the patronage of Ben-Gurion, the legendary prime minister and head of MAPAI. This, however, was also the source of great political difficulty. The MAPAI apparatus, operating in the name of a socialist ideology, feared the young technocrats surrounding Ben-Gurion and waited for an opportunity to take its toll. The opportunity came when Ben-Gurion was weakened in the early 1960s, as a result of a partisan struggle known as the "Lavon Affair." That affair was a struggle over Ben-Gurion's inheritance between his protegees, notably Shimon Peres and Moshe Dayan, and the party machine. The latter's victory in that struggle resulted in Ben-Gurion's resignation from MAPAI and his formation of the RAFI party.

In 1969, RAFI under Peres' leadership joined forces with MAPAI in forming the Labor Party, but MAPAI's elders had never accepted Peres as part and parcel of the Labor movement. Prime Minister Golda Meir, who headed the Labor Party after reunification, was particularly resentful, but so was the entire party elite. After the 1973 Yom Kipur War, when Meir was forced to resign as prime minister, every effort was made to prevent Peres from rising to the top – war hero Yitzhak Rabin was brought in 1974 from his ambassadorial post in Washington to serve as prime minister. It was only after the latter's resignation in 1977 that Peres could manipulate his way to the top and become party chairman shortly before Labor lost the elections to the Likud.

As a populist party, the Likud never had a strong party apparatus resembling that of Labor. The party was dominated for years by the towering personality of Menachem Begin who, upon his retirement in 1983, nominated his successor – Yitzhak Shamir. After Begin's retirement, the party center became a major arena for the party's political struggles, with personal patronage constituting the main source of power. Netanyahu, a relatively unknown figure living in the U.S., developed in the early 1980s a close relationship there with Moshe Arens, Israel's ambassador to Washington, who was one of Shamir's closest confidants and later served as minister of defense in his government. Under Arens' and Shamir's joint patronage, Netanyahu was nominated to his diplomatic and political posts in the U.S. and in Israel. Although the posts of ambassador to the U.N. or deputy foreign minister had never before been considered levers for higher political office, Netanyahu, equipped with exceptional public relations skills, made himself highly visible in these roles.

In 1993, when he competed for the nomination as party leader, it seemed that these skills would not suffice, as all of the other contenders had far deeper roots in the socio-political structure of the Likud. Benny Begin carried the halo of his charismatic father, David Levy and Moshe Katzav were "authentic" leaders of Sephardic origin who rose from the grass-roots of local community politics. The other candidates could relate more easily to traditional, religious values while Netanyahu, after two divorces, a well-publicized extra-marital affair and a "yappy" life-style seemed to lag behind. But this was the era of the "new politics," in which media manipulation could be counted on no less than grass roots-politics, and Netanyahu had won the nomination.

The outsider's status of leaders vis-a-vis party structures demands of them a greater effort at cognitive mobilization of support. As they cannot rely on the grass-roots, they must develop new coalitions by catering to issues which exceed mainstream party politics. Peres' most important base of support were the country's technocrats – scientists and professionals who shared his interest in technological development, and his belief in knowledge as a means to overcome external and internal fundamentalist forces posing a danger to Israel. Technocrats, who were often critical of the country's socialist policies, could easily be mobilized by the vision of a modern industrial state, which included an important role for them. For example, in 1984, when Peres became prime minister of a national unity government, while lacking the power to act (partly because of rivalries in his own party), the technocrats – economists, legal professionals, strategic experts – were mobilized.[22] The professionalization of the Peres government sparked even more grievance for the party machine but strengthened Peres' ties with the country's technocrats who, as I had shown elsewhere, constituted one of his main bases of support for his moves in the peace process.[23]

Netanyahu's campaign rhetoric was more in line with his party's political platform, with its emphasis upon the right of the Jewish people to the entire land of Israel, the need to nurture Jewish settlements in the occupied territories, the obligation to maintain the unity and integrity of Jerusalem, the precedence given to security over peace, the bashing of the Palestinians, and the call for a free market economy. However, an observation of the guidelines set by Netanyahu for his government[24] reveals an interesting deviation form the traditional party line. The guidelines begin with a mention of all the above points. As the document proceeds, however, a set of concerns can be identified which is not only worlds apart from traditional Likud voters, but from the issues which prevailed in any partisan discourse in Israel in the past.

The document states that social welfare is consistent with the encouragement of private enterprise, and calls for investment in physical and human infrastructures in such spheres as transportation, energy, communication, education, and research and development, with the explicit aim of creating in Israel "the environment necessary for the Israeli economy to join those of the developed countries of the world."[25] It further pledges the development of databases and national information infrastructures, and proposes a variety of projects which could have been derived directly from the platform of the "Greens":

> The government of Israel will raise environmental issues to the top of the national agenda, and act to enhance public consciousness regarding the preservation of the environment as an integral part of the struggle to preserve the country and out of a desire to build in it a prosperous society of values.[26]

The "society of values" emerging from the document is a post-material society. It is managed by a government which not only preserves natural resources – water, air, soil, flora and fauna, it gives high priority to waste recycling projects and to the establishment of waste-water purification plants, and operates with strict adherence to a policy of preserving green areas as much as possible. It is a society aiming at the full and equal integration of Israeli women into all areas of life, taking care of single-parent families in need, treats with special gravity all forms of violence against women, and even pays attention to such neglected matters in Israel as its citizens' right to information or to "fair, efficient and polite service"[27] by government agencies and employees.

Pragmatism

The pragmatic approach to problem solving, shared by both candidates, is demonstrated in two books in which their updated visions were presented: Peres' *The New Middle East* (1993), and Netanyahu's *Fighting Terrorism* (1995). Both books belong to the genre of leaders' election-pamphlets which requires special caution in their analysis. Also, both are too embarrassing – the first in its far-fetched fantasy, the second in its shallow demagoguery – to allow serious substantive treatment. It is possible, however, to show that while both leaders identify huge problems on the national and international agenda, the solutions are taken from the sphere of the possible rather than the desirable. This is the essence of pragmatism. The pragmatist operates by the constraints of reality rather than by the imperatives of ideology. The transformation from the ideologue to the pragmatist – a main attribute of the "new politics" in modern, industrial states – has not by-passed the Israeli state or, for that matter, its leaders.

Both books refer to a common enemy – fundamentalism – which endangers regional stability and world peace. To Peres, fundamentalism poses a challenge to a world marked by scientific progress, higher education, artificial intelligence, and advanced technology. To Netanyahu, militant Islam has replaced Soviet Communism as champion of world terrorism. Both call for determined action to meet the fundamentalist challenge.

Peres calls for the construction of a "systematized regional structure that will introduce a new framework for the region and that will provide the potential for economic and social growth, extinguishing the fire of religious extremism and cooling the hot winds of revolution."[28] His model of the new regional structure includes a three-tiered pyramidal program of cooperation resembling the European project in the post World War II era. The first stage consists of binational or multinational projects, such as a joint research institute for desert management or cooperative desalination plants. The second stage involves international consortiums carrying out projects which require large capital investments such a Red Sea–Dead Sea canal with development of free trade and tourism along its length, a joint Israeli–Jordanian–Saudi Arabian port, development of hydroelectric power for electricity and desalination, and well planned, rapid development of Red Sea industries. The third stage includes regional community policies accompanied by the gradual development of official institutions.

This model seems quite remote from present conditions in the Middle East, but it is also pragmatic in two ways. First, in the precedence given to economics over politics. Peres attempts to encourage a new reality in the region in which business precedes politics and hence allows cooperation between people set apart by political difference. Second, in the pursuit of regional partnerships that can be instituted before borders are drawn and peace treaties signed. Peres, highly aware of the obstacles to a comprehensive peace in the Middle East, attempts to propose a different path. Impressed by the European and Asiatic experiences, where economic cooperation had been reached despite national differences, he aspires to tame the Middle East conflict in a similar way. His book thus marks a shift from problem solving to problem management, which had also been his motto in designing the Oslo Accords. While not solving the differences between Arabs and Jews on the cognitive level, the accords allowed both sides to engage in economic cooperation, with the hope that it would subsequently entail political cooperation.

Netanyahu's call – addressed mainly at the U.S. – to defeat domestic and international terrorism is no less ambitious in its overall aims. Providing a shuddering survey of domestic terrorism in the U.S., describing the rise of international terrorism in Europe and elsewhere, warning of the rise of militant Islam in America and the rest of the world, discussing the specter of nuclear terrorism, and connecting all of the above to Yasser Arafat's "enclave" in Gaza, Netanyahu voices the need to act firmly:

> Today's tragedies can either be the harbingers of much greater calamities yet to come or the turning point in which free societies once again mobilize their resources, their ingenuity, and their will to wipe out this evil from our midst. Fighting terrorism is not a 'policy option'; it is a necessity for the survival of our democratic society and our freedoms.[29]

In his proposals how to win the battle, Netanyahu displays clear pragmatism. To him, the task at hand requires that ideological beliefs be subordinated to the demands of reality:

> The ideal of an absolute civil liberty – whether a 'leftist' liberty such as absolute free speech or a 'rightist' liberty such as the absolute right to bear arms – should be tempered by political realities, and the attempt to apply it in its pristine form has grave consequences ... Advocates of absolute civil liberties forget that legally protected freedoms are not *ends* in and of themselves; they are *means* to ensuring the health and well-being of citizens.[30]

One is tempted to learn more about Netanyahu's willingness to exchange ends for means, but his writings provide no further clues. What can be said, however, is that *Fighting Terrorism* exhibits an extraordinary adherence to existing, available means in the fight against terrorism. The anti-terrorist measures offered by Netanyahu to modern democracies could have been easily derived from the annual report of any anti-terrorism agency: Impose sanctions on suppliers of nuclear technology to terrorist states, impose diplomatic, economic, and military sanctions on the terrorist states themselves, neutralize terrorist enclaves, freeze financial assets in the West of terrorist regimes and organizations, share intelligence, revise legislation to enable greater surveillance and action against organizations inciting to violence, subject to periodic renewal, actively pursue terrorists, do not release jailed terrorists, train special forces to fight terrorism, and educate the public.

CONCLUSION

Netanyahu's election as prime minister has raised concern throughout the world. The concern stemmed from uncertainty about the man whose campaign tactics consisted of hiding rather than revealing his political preferences. However, in positioning Netanyahu within the category of the "new politics," several conclusions may be drawn. One conclusion is that in the new political era in Israel, elections may no longer entail a significant structural or ideological change. Peres and Netanyahu had certainly represented two opposite camps, especially in their approach to the peace process, and yet, the policies of their respective governments may be similar in many respects. The main reason for this expectation is that both cater to a similar stratum: the "new class." Netanyahu, it may be argued, is no less dependent on economic and political elites whose interests and preferences are no longer congruent with the traditional polarization in Israeli society.

This may entail important implications for the peace process in the Middle East. That process has never been the outgrowth of attitude changes among peoples but the making of ruling elites in the region. When Yitzhak Rabin and Shimon Peres came to power in 1992, they carried a long tradition of mistrust of the PLO, and a scepticism – proven to be justified – over its capacity to restrain Palestinian terrorism against Israel. And yet, they developed a strategic alliance with the PLO when it became clear that such alliance is the key to a new Middle East, in which Israel could emerge from its regional isolation. This strategic decision was not easy to accept; it cost Rabin his life. But the Israel–Palestinian alliance took hold due to the support granted it by elites on both sides conceiving its enormous benefits.

The Oslo Accords of 1993, and all subsequent agreements between Israel and the Palestinians, were rather consistent with the norms of technocrats, industrialists, businessmen, managers, public administrators, professionals, and other incumbents of the "new class." As in other modern industrial societies, Israel in recent years has seen an enormous rise in the influence of these groups in every sphere of activity – especially in the sphere of security where no serious decision can be made without their input. Their norms and interests are clearly reflected in the assumption underlying the Oslo accords that the conflict may be *managed* but not *solved,* and in the stress upon economic cooperation as a means to overcome political differences.

The peace process has never satisfied those seeking maximalist solutions in the Middle East. It has, however, received wide support from those who detected the opportunities opened by peace in the region. Nothing indicates it better than the rise in the Israeli stock market after the announcement of the Oslo accords. One can imagine that Netanyahu, the advocate of the free market, is paying close attention to messages conveyed by the stock market. As a politician determined to win an election, he oriented his 1996 campaign at those forces in Israeli society that felt threatened by the peace process. Large segments of the population could be counted on to vote for the energetic right winger promising an end to terrorism and a return to the good old traditions imperiled by his opponent's vision of a "New Middle East."

The support given to Netanyahu by the ultra-orthodox Chabbad movement, for instance, (under the slogan: "Netanyahu is good for the Jews") may be interpreted as the outgrowth of that movement's fundamental fear of a modern Israel abandoning its religious and nationalist exclusion as a result of the peace process.

And yet, the fundamentalist forces which helped Netanyahu get elected by a close margin must still win the war against the "new politics" in order to make a strategic difference. In fact, they may be afflicted twice. First, they were hit by Labor's peace adventures which were perceived to challenge their way of life. After beating Labor in the elections, however, they may find out that Netanyahu is a product of modern, technological Westernized Israel no less than his predecessors. While his election campaign made use of blessings by fundamentalist community leaders, in his major decisions concerning security, the economy, and foreign relations he could not be expected to operate in the same manner. Steering a modern, industrial state, he is largely constrained by the industrial and business sectors, the Supreme Court, the military, the press, and other bodies and institutions by which modern states are ruled. And one would like to believe that the elites composing these bodies and institutions have too strong an interest in peace, in spite of its obstacles, to give it up.

NOTES

1. Thomas Poguntke, *Alternative Politics: The German Green Party*, Edinburgh, 1993; Ferdinand Muller-Rommel and Thomas Poguntke, eds, *New Politics*, Aldershot, 1995.
2. Ronald Inglehart, "Post-Materialism in an Environment of Insecurity," *American Political Science Review*, 75 (1981), pp.880–900; idem, "Value Change in Industrial Societies," *American Political Science Review*, 81 (1987), pp.1289–303.
3. Inglehart, "Post-Materialism," p.894.
4. Scott C. Flanagan, "Value Change in Industrial Societies," *American Political Science Review*, 81 (1987), pp.1303–19.
5. Russell J. Dalton, "Cognitive Mobilization and Partisan Dealignment in Advanced Industrial Democracies," *Journal of Politics*, 46 (1984), pp.264–84.
6. Brian Graetz, and Ian McAllister, "Popular Evaluations of Party Leaders in the Anglo-American Democracies," in Harold D. Clarke and Moshe M. Czudnowski, eds *Political Elites in Anglo-American Democracies: Changes in Stable Regimes*, DeKalb, 1987.
7. Frank Fischer, *Technocracy and the Politics of Expertise*, Newbury Park, CA, 1990.
8. Alvin W. Gouldner, *The Future of Intellectuals and the Rise of the New Class*, New York, 1979.
9. Peter F. Drucker, *The New Realities*, New York, 1989, p.108.
10. See, for example, Peter Y. Medding, *The Founding of Israeli Democracy 1948–1967*, New York, 1990.
11. Michael Keren, "The Pollsters' Race: 1984," in Asher Arian and Michal Shamir, eds *The Elections in Israel*, Tel-Aviv, 1986, pp.251–263.
12. Shimon Peres, *David's Sling*, London, 1970.
13. Idem, "Remarks at Special Knesset Session in Memory of Rabin," November 13, 1995, Information Division, Israel Foreign Ministry, Jerusalem (http:/www.israel-info.gov.il).
14. Ibid.
15. Idem, "Address to the Joint Session of the U.S. Congress, December 12, 1995, Information Division, Israel Foreign Ministry, Jerusalem (http:/www.israel-info.gov.il).
16. "Netanyahu's Address to Joint Session of Congress," July 10, 1996, Information

Division, Israel Foreign Ministry, Jerusalem (http:/www.israel-info.gov.il).

17. Ibid.
18. Benjamin Netanyahu, *Terrorism: How the West Can Win*, New York, 1986; *International Terrorism: Challenge and Response*, New York, 1991; *Fighting Terrorism: How Democracies Can Defeat Domestic and International Terrorists*, New York, 1995.
19. Idem, "Victory Speech," Jerusalem, June 2, 1996 (Likud home-page).
20. Ibid.
21. Idem, "Inaugural Speech," Jerusalem, June 18, 1996 (Likud home-page).
22. Michael Keren, *Professionals against Populism: The Peres Government and Democracy*, Albany, 1995.
23. Idem, "Israeli Professionals and the Peace Process," *Israel Affairs*, Vol.1, No.1 (Autumn 1994), pp.149–163.
24. "Guidelines of the Government of Israel," July 1996 (Likud home-page).
25. Ibid., p.5.
26. Ibid., p.6.
27. Ibid., p.7.
28. Peres, *The New Middle East*, p.62.
29. Netanyahu, *Fighting Terrorism*, p.6.
30. Ibid., pp.42–3.

Index